THE RASP OF WAR

THE RASP OF WAR

*The Letters of H. A. Gwynne
to The Countess Bathurst
1914–1918*

selected and edited by
KEITH WILSON

Foreword by William Deedes

SIDGWICK & JACKSON
LONDON

First published in Great Britain in 1988 by Sidgwick & Jackson Limited

Copyright © 1988 by K. M. Wilson
Foreword copyright © 1988 by William Deedes
Maps by Neil Hyslop

ISBN 0-283-99655-2

Typeset by Rowland Phototypesetting Limited
Bury St Edmunds, Suffolk
Printed in Hong Kong
for Sidgwick & Jackson Limited
1 Tavistock Chambers, Bloomsbury Way
London WC1A 2SG

for Sally Scott

Contents

Acknowledgements

My largest debt in connection with this volume is to The Earl Bathurst, who in the first instance kindly allowed me to see his grandmother's papers at Cirencester Park and who then offered to deposit them on loan at the University of Leeds, where they now reside under the title of the Glenesk–Bathurst MSS. I am pleased to acknowledge permission to utilise material copyright in which is held by the following: The Earl Bathurst, Admiral Sir Ian Hogg, Viscount Long, H. D. Miller Esq., the Earl Balfour, the Marquess of Lansdowne, the Warden and Fellows of New College Oxford, Lord Bonham Carter, Mrs Maxse, the Duke of Northumberland, the Trustees of the Imperial War Museum, Professor A. K. S. Lambton, Lord Robertson of Oakridge, Mrs D. Boyes, Andrew Rawlinson, the Earl of Derby, Lord Esher, Mr A. J. P. Taylor and the Trustees of the Beaverbrook Foundation, and the *Spectator*; material in the custody of the House of Lords Record Office is reproduced by permission of the Clerk of the Records; material from the Royal Archives is reproduced by gracious permission of Her Majesty the Queen. Should I have inadvertently failed to consult any copyright holder I do apologise most profusely.

I would like to express my thanks to the staffs of the following libraries and archives for their assistance in the course of this project: the Brotherton Library, and in particular the Librarian, Mr D. Cox, who before he retired took receipt of the Glenesk–Bathurst MSS; the Bodleian Library; the Liddell Hart Centre for Military Archives, King's College London; the Public Record Office, Kew; the Public Record Office of Northern Ireland; the Scottish Record Office; the National Library of Scotland; the Imperial War Museum; the British Library; the India Office Library and Records; the House of Lords Record Office; the Institute of Commonwealth Studies, the University of London; the Library of the University of Sussex; Churchill College Cambridge; Berkshire Record Office; Devon Record Office; West Sussex Record Office; Wiltshire County Record Office; Liverpool City Libraries.

I am grateful to Michael Brock, for reading and making suggestions upon a very early version of the typescript; others who have answered queries of a greater or lesser degree of urgency include Dr G. Boyce, Dr I. Beckett, Dr P. Buckland, Dr E. M. Spiers, and Dr E. D. Steele. Some of the research and writing was done during a most welcome spell of study leave from the School of History at the University of Leeds in 1985; a grant from the Wolfson Foundation under its scheme for Grants for Scholars in the fields of History and Classics was of the utmost assistance in the later stages of the work.

Editor's Note

Forms of greeting and of signature have been dispensed with. So have the addresses from which these letters were sent. Those of Gwynne were on the whole despatched either from the *Morning Post* offices or from his London address, 9 Collingham Gardens, SW5. One or two were sent from one of his clubs, the Bath Club, on club notepaper, and from his cottage in Little Easton, Essex. Whether they were typed or handwritten is not indicated here. The device (. . .) indicates that a passage has been omitted. This has sometimes been necessary in order to reduce the bulk of the volume, to avoid undue repetition, and such things as personal remarks about health. Normal conventions of italicising titles of newspapers and names of ships have been followed, but all other italics in the text represent underlinings by the writers of the letters. Obvious mistakes in spelling or punctuation have been corrected. Less obvious ones have been retained: e.g. Bosch [*sic*]. Even when producing his letters and memoranda for Asquith and other political figures Gwynne wrote, dictated and typed at great speed. The resultant presentational inconsistencies and idiosyncrasies have been ironed out so far as is consistent with retaining the flavour of the originals; where the same individual is given a marginally different diminutive or nickname, these variations have been retained: hence Fisher is both Jacky and Jackie, Robertson both Wully and Wullie.

K.M.W.

Foreword

H. A. Gwynne had a long span – from 1911 until 1937 – as editor of the *Morning Post*, long enough to have enjoyed Lady Bathurst as his proprietor at the start, and to have suffered me as a member of his editorial staff at the end. She had departed, and the *Morning Post* had fallen on hard times, when I turned up for my first day's work in the summer of 1931. The proud building in Aldwych, Glenesk House, named after Lady Bathurst's father – and still standing exactly as it always did – belonged to our past. Our two premises in Tudor Street, 15 and 27, were meagre, and I believe rented from our printers, the Argus Press. Sir Percy Bates, also chairman of Cunard, headed a small syndicate of businessmen which had taken over from Lady Bathurst. The cold economic wind which had blown across the world since 1929 made the newspaper's position precarious. Within six months of my arrival there were swingeing economies.

At no time in my six years with the *Morning Post* before it was bought and closed by the first Lord Camrose in 1939 did I feel I knew Gwynne as well as I do now after reading his correspondence with Lady Bathurst. He gave me a small, generous talk before sending me to the Abyssinian war in 1935. 'Go to a good outfitter,' he said (the last thing they could afford), 'and bear in mind that a little whisky in a water bottle is a great safeguard.' Gwynne had been a distinguished war correspondent in South Africa.

My only other direct link with him was before the Abdication of King Edward VIII. I had been collecting overseas material for him on the subject, and he wanted to show it to the Prime Minister, Stanley Baldwin. Gwynne expressed sympathy with the plea that some of us made for an editorial in the *Morning Post* on the King's position; but he turned it down at the Prime Minister's urging some time before the Bishop of Bradford broke the long silence.

Part of my time was spent gathering material and writing stories designed to embarrass Baldwin's Government on its declared course of self-government for India. The *Morning Post* was strongly opposed to the idea. Churchill was our man because he led the parliamentary opposition to it. Gwynne must have sharply changed his mind about Churchill since writing some of the passages about him which appear in this book. At certain points in the war, Gwynne makes clear, he considered Churchill to be off his head.

The fact is that Gwynne was much more interested in shaping national politics than he was in editing the *Morning Post*. That emerges beyond argument from this correspondence and it did not escape his boss, Lady Bathurst. She wrote to him sharply, we find, in July 1918: 'I should be very much obliged if you would edit the paper more carefully, and devote less of your time to seeing politicians and to all sorts of cabals and intrigues. . . .' It is a wounding but apposite summing up of what Gwynne indeed spent much of his time doing.

Several pages of this book are taken up by Gwynne's wartime memoranda to members of the Cabinet, and by his letters to Asquith *et al* on the conduct of the war. He felt in his heart that his experience would be of value to the men in charge and help them to avoid blunders – a very favourite *Morning Post* word. In fairness, Gwynne displays at one point a strong desire to thrust it all away from him, put on uniform and go to the front. There are poignant passages in his letters to Lady Bathurst of 11 January and 29 April 1915. The lady must have thought it a bad idea.

Confined to London, he had to direct his war effort towards advising senior ministers on how to do better. He seems to have visualized himself and the *Morning Post* as active partners in the business of prosecuting a successful war.

Of course it was expected of editors in those days, and even in my early days, that they should be on intimate terms with the great and the good. London at the social top was a different capital from the one we know today. Many of the great houses remained open during the war; countless dinners were arranged in them, and editors were expected to suspend their office duties for a couple of hours and join the company round the table.

Editors were not expected to render cutlet for cutlet, but the long letter to Lord Bathurst of 2 November 1918, in which Gwynne explains how his expenses are incurred, is instructive. It follows his rather painful plea to Lady Bathurst in July 1918 for a rise in salary. In 1914 he had been on £2600 a year – his income tax £60–70! By 1918 he reckoned that his income had fallen in value to £1400. Lady Bathurst concedes another £400 from her privy purse. I have always understood that, when Gwynne retired in 1937 with a CH recommended by Baldwin, Lord Camrose gave him a generous pension of £5000. In those days £1000 was a decent salary, so he finished up all right.

The difficult question to resolve is how far Gwynne's enthusiasm for politics and desire to have a hand in public affairs interfered with his functions – and judgements – as editor of the *Morning Post*. My reckoning is that under any editor the *Morning Post* would have had a hard struggle to survive in the later 1930s, and in the world of Beaverbrook, Rothermere and Camrose. The post-war years had turned against it, socially, politically and economically.

There is a significant passage in Gwynne's letter to Lady Bathurst of 9 March 1917. He is defending his Fashion Column – which was not about dress but tittle-tattle. Why? Because, he says, 'the solid basis on which we build up our revenue is the servants' advertisements, and the servants' advertisements depend, in my opinion, very largely upon the reputation for being a fashionable paper. . .'. In truth, the *Morning Post* revenues had depended heavily before the war on what we might term the Upstairs, Downstairs connection, of which it had a monopoly. The stately homes of West London called for an immense number of servants. When I fi st came to London as a child my grandmother and her daughters, living modestly in Chesham Street, employed five in the house. If a duke required a butler, he advertised his need in the *Morning Post*. A footman seeking a fresh master read the *Morning Post*. The newspaper had a unique *cachet*, and derived a large income from this department of classified advertising.

Just as this correspondence ends in 1918, many of London's great houses were putting up their shutters for the last time. The war had changed it all. Men and women were returning to a land fit for heroes (*sic*), not to jobs in pantries and sculleries. Income tax had soared. So an invaluable source of revenue for the *Morning Post* slowly dried up; and the newspaper, with its too narrow political and social base, was not poised to raise revenue elsewhere.

The name of Ian Colvin, chief leader writer on the *Morning Post*, appears in these letters. He was still there in my day, and he calls for special mention because he was the main instrument of Gwynne's editorial policy. His son of the same name was an exact contemporary of mine on the staff of the *Morning Post*, and later was to provide from Berlin invaluable intelligence – of which we made scant use – about Hitler's intentions. Churchill refers to him at the start of his history of the Second World War.

The prose style of Ian Colvin senior was widely admired, and to young men like myself a model at which to aim. Writing of the *Morning Post*'s financial difficulties brings to my mind a sample of Colvin's style. The *Daily Mail*, in circumstances I have forgotten, published a rough passage addressed to their advertisers, boasting that their columns drew far more business than those of the pitiful *Morning Post*. Colvin raised his pen in protest. His leader concluded with these words: 'A cigar merchant is not galled when he learns that his neighbour has sold more of Woodbine cigarettes in a year than he has sold of Corona Coronas in a lifetime.' Gwynne seldom wrote leaders himself. With Colvin at his elbow, there was no call for him to do so.

So what we have here is a penultimate chapter in the life of a very old newspaper, as well as some startling passages about the conduct of the First World War. I have in my possession a copy of the Maurice letter which hung for many years in the *Morning Post* office. It is unlikely to be the original, but it gives a taste of those times. I also have in a frame a letter from Lady Bathurst to Gwynne which is not, I think, included here. It runs:

October 16, 1915

Dear Mr Gwynne,

I was greatly impressed by all I saw at the *Morning Post* yesterday. October 13 happens to be my birthday and the Huns nearly succeeded by accident in celebrating it in the way which would most appeal to them. But thank God none of the staff of the *Morning Post* was injured.

Will you tell the staff from me that I am thankful for their merciful escape; that I glory in the fact that the *Morning Post* Building has received its baptism of fire; and that I think they all behaved like soldiers when, with true British pluck, they brought out the paper earlier than usual, in spite of damage to the Linotype machines.

That short letter tells us a lot about Lilias Bathurst. No wonder Gwynne apologises whenever he addresses a letter to her which is not handwritten but typewritten.

A postscript is called for. The *Morning Post* under Gwynne was in my experience in every way an honourable newspaper. He refers in some of his letters to his attitude towards censorship and war secrets. His sentiments do him honour, but would not be echoed by many of the world's editors today. The *Morning Post*'s young men were seldom reproached for missing news, but if they falsified it in any particular they were in hot water. Gwynne believed above all in 'playing the game', to use a phrase far behind us. It was not, even in those days, the high road to a successful newspaper. Perhaps the belief lay in his own nature; perhaps it was attributable to Rudyard Kipling, who was always close to the *Morning Post*; perhaps Gwynne caught the habit from Lilias. Even after reading these letters, we shall never be quite sure.

William Deedes

Notes on Correspondents

Asquith, Henry Herbert: Prime Minister, April 1908–December 1916; Leader of the Liberal Party; created Earl of Oxford and Asquith, 1925.

Asquith, Margot: née Tennant; married H. H. Asquith, 1892.

Balfour, Arthur James: Prime Minister, 1902–December 1905; Leader of the Conservative Party until October 1911; First Lord of the Admiralty, May 1915–December 1916; member of the War Committee from November 1915; Foreign Secretary, December 1916–October 1919; created Earl Balfour, 1922.

Buckmaster, Sir Stanley: Solicitor-General, October 1913–May 1915; Chief Press Censor from September 1914; Lord Chancellor, May 1915–December 1916.

Callwell, Major-General Sir Charles E.: Director of Military Operations, August 1914–December 1915.

Carson, Sir Edward: Leader of Ulster Unionists from 1910; Attorney-General, May 1915–October 1915; Chairman, Unionist War Committee from January 1916; First Lord of the Admiralty, December 1916–July 1917.

Cecil, Lord Robert: Conservative MP for Hitchin; Parliamentary Under-Secretary for Foreign Affairs, May 1915; Minister for the Blockade, February 1916–July 1918.

Colvin, Ian: journalist and author; leader writer on the *Morning Post*.

Davies, J. T.: Private Secretary to Lloyd George, 1912–22; knighted, 1922.

Derby, Lord: Chairman, West Lancashire Territorial Association; Director-General of Recruiting, October 1915–July 1916; Under-Secretary of State for War, July–December 1916; Secretary of State for War, December 1916–April 1918; Ambassador to France, 1918–20.

Esher, Viscount: member of the Committee of Imperial Defence from 1904; head of British Intelligence organization in France until spring 1918.

Fitzgerald, Lieutenant-Colonel O. A. E.: Military Secretary to Kitchener.

French, Field-Marshal Sir John: Chief of the Imperial General Staff, 1912–April 1914; Commander in Chief British Expeditionary Force France and Flanders, August 1914–December 1915; created Viscount, January 1916 and Earl of Ypres, 1922.

Gough, Lieutenant-General Sir H. de la P.: Commander 3rd Cavalry Brigade, 1914; Commander 2nd Cavalry Division and 7th Division, 1915; Commander 1st Army Corps, 1916 and 5th Army, 1916–April 1918.

Haig, General Sir Douglas: Commander 1st Army, 1914–15; Commander in Chief British Expeditionary Force France and Flanders, 1915–19; created Earl Haig 1919.

Irvine, J. D.: journalist on the *Morning Post*.

Kitchener, 1st Earl of Khartoum: Commander in Chief, India, 1902–9; British Agent and Consul-General, Egypt, 1911–14; Secretary of State for War, August 1914–June 1916.

Lansdowne, Lord: Foreign Secretary, 1901–December 1905; Minister without Portfolio, May 1915–December 1916.

Law, Andrew Bonar: Leader of the Conservative Party from October 1911; Colonial Secretary, May 1915–December 1916; Chancellor of the Exchequer and Leader of the House of Commons from December 1916; Prime Minister, 1922–3.

Lloyd George, David: Chancellor of the Exchequer, 1908–May 1915; Minister of Munitions, May 1915–July 1916; Secretary of State for War, July–December 1916; Prime Minister, December 1916–October 1922.

Long, Walter: Conservative MP for Strand; President of Local Government Board, 1900–5; Chief Secretary for Ireland, 1905; Minister of Health and Local Government, May 1915–December 1916.

Marsden, Victor Emile: journalist; St Petersburg correspondent of the *Morning Post*.

Masterman, C. F. G.: Chancellor of the Duchy of Lancaster, 1914–May 1915; head of the British propaganda organization at Wellington House from September 1914.

Maurice, Major-General Sir Frederick: Director of Military Operations, December 1915–April 1918; knighted, 1918.

Maxse, Leo J.: journalist; editor of the *National Review*.

Milner, Lord (Alfred): Governor of Transvaal and Orange River Colony and High Commissioner for South Africa, 1897–1905; Chairman of Food Production Committee from June 1915; Chairman, General Council of National Service League from July 1915; member of War Cabinet, December 1916–April 1918; Secretary of State for War, April 1918–December 1919.

Percy, Earl: 8th Duke of Northumberland, 1918; ADC to King George V, 1902–20.

Rawlinson, General Sir Henry: Commander 4th Corps, 1914–15; Commander 1st Army, 1916–18; British Military Representative on the Supreme War Council from February 1918.

Robertson, Field-Marshal Sir William: Chief of General Staff British Expeditionary Force, 1915; Chief of the Imperial General Staff, December 1915–February 1918; Commander in Chief Eastern Command, 1918.

Sandars, J. S.: Private Secretary to A. J. Balfour, 1892–1915.

Sassoon, Sir Philip: Conservative MP for Hythe; Private Secretary to Haig.

Saunderson, Major Somerset: landowner, Co. Cavan; member of Ulster Unionist Council.

Simon, Sir John: Attorney-General, 1913–May 1915; Home Secretary, May 1915–June 1916.

Stamfordham, Lord: Private Secretary to King George V.

Strachey, John St L.: journalist; editor of the *Spectator*.

Tyrrell, Sir William: Private Secretary to Sir Edward Grey 1907–15; Assistant Under-Secretary of State for Foreign Affairs from October 1918.

Wilson, General Sir Henry: Director of Military Operations, 1910–14; Assistant Chief of General Staff, August 1914; Chief Liaison Officer with the French Armies from February 1915; Commander 4th Corps, January 1916; British Military Representative at Versailles, 1917; Chief of the Imperial General Staff, February 1918–February 1922.

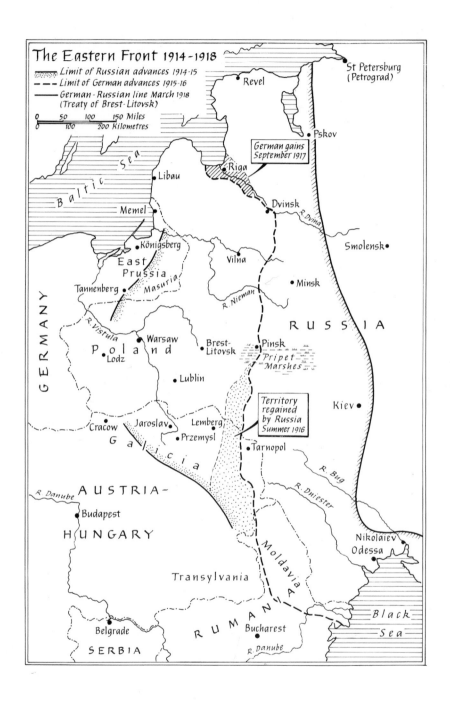

The Eastern Front 1914-1918

Limit of Russian advances 1914-15
Limit of German advances 1915-16
German-Russian line March 1918
(Treaty of Brest-Litovsk)

0   50   100   150 Miles
0   100   200 Kilometres

St Petersburg
(Petrograd)

Revel

Pskov

German gains
September 1917

Riga

Libau

Baltic Sea

Dvinsk

R. Dvina

Memel

Smolensk

Königsberg

East
Prussia

Vilna

Minsk

Tannenberg

Masuria

R. Nieman

R U S S I A

GERMANY

R. Vistula

Warsaw

Brest-
Litovsk

Pinsk

Lodz

P o l a n d

Pripet
Marshes

Lublin

Kiev

Cracow

Jaroslav

Lemberg

Territory
regained
by Russia
Summer 1916

G a l i c i a

Przemysl

Tarnopol

R. Bug

R. Dniester

R. Danube

AUSTRIA-

Budapest

Nikolaiev
Odessa

H U N G A R Y

Moldavia

Transylvania

Black
Sea

Belgrade

R U M A N I A

Bucharest

SERBIA

R. Danube

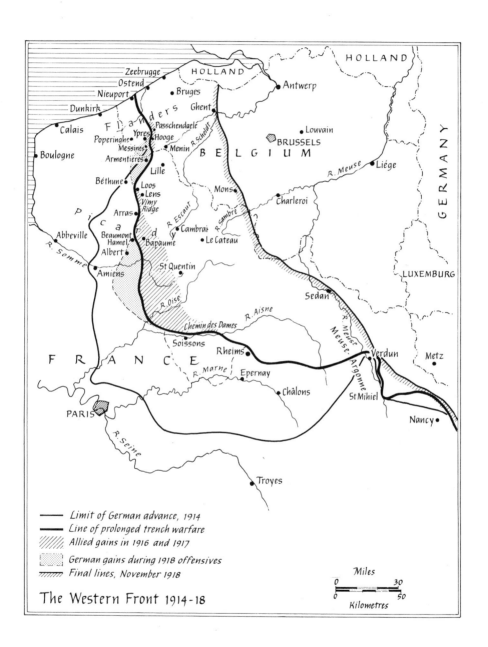

The Western Front 1914-18

Legend:
—— Limit of German advance, 1914
▬▬ Line of prolonged trench warfare
▨ Allied gains in 1916 and 1917
▨ German gains during 1918 offensives
▨ Final lines, November 1918

Miles
0   30
0   50
Kilometres

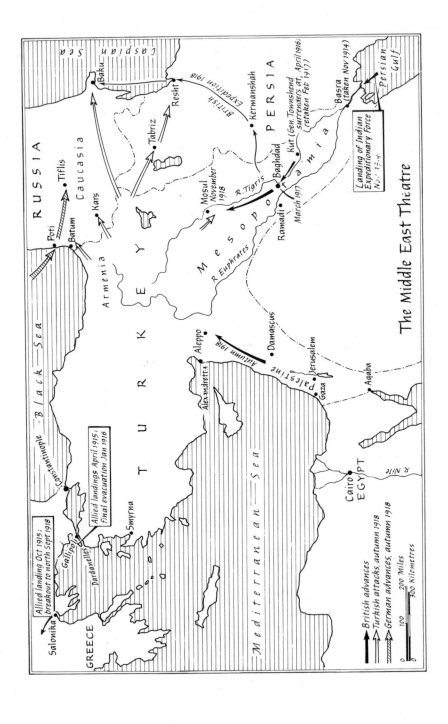

The Middle East Theatre

Caspian Sea

Baku

Resht

British Expedition 1918

Kermanshah

PERSIA

Kut (Gen. Townshend surrenders at, April 1916; retaken Feb 1917))

Basra (taken Nov 1914)

Persian Gulf

Landing of Indian Expeditionary Force Nov. 1914

Tabriz

RUSSIA

Tiflis

Caucasia

Kars

Mesopotamia

Baghdad

March 1917

R. Tigris

Mosul November 1918

Ramadi

Poti

Batum

Armenia

R. Euphrates

Black Sea

TURKEY

Autumn 1918

Aleppo

Damascus

Alexandretta

Palestine

Jerusalem

Gaza

Aqaba

Constantinople

Gallipoli

Dardanelles

Smyrna

Allied landings April 1915; final evacuation Jan 1916

Salonika

Allied landing Oct 1915; breakout to north Sept 1918

GREECE

Mediterranean Sea

Cairo

EGYPT

R. Nile

British advances

Turkish attacks, autumn 1918

German advances, autumn 1918

0   100   200 Miles
0   300 Kilometres

INTRODUCTION:

Editor and Proprietor – H. A. Gwynne, The Countess Bathurst and the Morning Post before the War

Towards the beginning of the second of the world wars of the twentieth century the Thurber Woman, who was of course an American lady newspaper-reader, was made to ask her cartoon husband, 'Who is this Hitler and what does he want?' Towards the end of July 1914 The Countess Bathurst asked a similar question of H. A. Gwynne, the editor of her newspaper, the *Morning Post*, and a man who might be expected to know the answer. She received the beautifully matter-of-fact reply: 'Servians are inhabitants of Servia. Serbs are of Servian nationality but not inhabiting Servia.'

For the next four and a half years the correspondence of Gwynne with Lady Bathurst was dominated by the subject of the Great War – how to fight it, how to win it, how to use it in such a way as to advance the causes they both espoused, how in the course of it to make the *Morning Post*, one of the most important of the London daily papers in addition to being the oldest, into 'the premier paper of England'.

The *Morning Post* had been founded in 1772. In the mid-nineteenth century it had been acquired by Lady Bathurst's grandfather, Peter Borthwick. It was further developed and expanded by his son and her father, Algernon Borthwick, who received from Lord Salisbury a baronetcy in 1887 and a peerage and the title of Lord Glenesk in 1895, partly for services to the Conservative Party.[1] Lady Bathurst's younger brother, Oliver Borthwick, was expected to take over the *Morning Post* on the death of their father, and prepared to do so in the years before his own death, in 1905, at the age of twenty-two. On the death of Lord Glenesk in November 1908 his daughter, who had married Seymour Henry, 7th Earl Bathurst in 1893, inherited her father's holding in the company he had formed on Oliver's death for

1

the carrying on of the newspaper. Filial duty combined with her love for her younger brother, whose loss she felt acutely, and with her own passion for politics, to cause her to accept the new responsibility. She wrote to one of the members of the board of directors, Ivor Maxse, on 30 November 1908: 'I have thought much about the *Morning Post* and I am anxious as far as I am able to devote as much time to the work as possible. You know that politics have always been absorbingly interesting for me even when I had no personal cause to be interested. Now of course such interest is a duty.' She was thirty-six years of age and the only woman ever to own and run a major national daily newspaper.

Between the deaths of her brother and her father she had begun to play an active part in the affairs of the *Morning Post*. Indeed she had been involved in championing the cause of the editor appointed in April 1905, Fabian Ware, who was engaged in what turned out to be a long and bitter struggle with the chief leader writer, Spenser Wilkinson, who had acted as editor himself before Ware's appointment, and who tended to seek, and receive, the support of Lord Glenesk.[2] As the new proprietor, she was able to give her favourite a freer hand with his schemes for streamlining the paper and for pushing the causes of Tariff Reform, Imperial Federation, Conscription, Naval Building and even a pre-emptive strike against Germany. However, she herself was ultimately responsible, as her father had been in his time, for setting the tone of the *Morning Post*.

Some idea of her achievement between 1908 and 1924, when she finally relinquished control, may be gathered from the trouble taken by Lord Northcliffe, owner of both *The Times* and the *Daily Mail*, to insult her in 1914 and to flatter her in 1922. On the earlier occasion, the *Daily Mail* described the *Morning Post* as having, unknown to the public, 'the unique distinction of daily voicing the views of a very gifted lady', and retailed as 'an amusing and delightfully feminine incident' the *Morning Post*'s initial acceptance of a full-page advertisement for *The Times* at its new price of one penny 'and the equally characteristically feminine refusal to print it when the *Morning Post* found out the gigantic demand that is being made for *The Times*'. In his book *Newspapers and their Millionaires*, published in 1922, Northcliffe described her as 'the most powerful woman in England without exception – other than Royalty'.[3]

Some idea of the tone and policy lines that she gave to the *Morning Post* may be derived from one of her letters to her editor and from some of her own contributions to issues of the paper. In July 1911, for instance, she wrote to Gwynne, who had just taken over from Ware, complaining about a recent leading article and stressing the policies which she wished the *Morning Post* to promote during the constitutional struggle between the Liberal-dominated House of Commons and the Tory-dominated House of Lords:

> The things I want the *Morning Post* to say and to say clearly and emphatically are these – The peers were prepared and anxious to throw out the Veto Bill on the 2nd reading. Lord Lansdowne cajoled and tricked them in passing it. They meant to throw it out on the 3rd reading, again they were tricked by the solemn assurance that Lord Lansdowne would stick to his own amendments. Now, Lord Lansdowne, Mr Balfour, Lord Curzon and the rest of our miserable leaders want to trick the peers into abject submission to Mr Asquith without one hostile vote being recorded. I want to say boldly, we have done with such leaders. They have been the bane and ruin of the Unionist party for 10 years. All the good men and true are on our side – why should we fear to openly proclaim that we follow the Chamberlains, Lord Halsbury, Lord Selborne, Lord Milner, Lord Roberts, Sir E. Carson etc. etc. Those are our leaders, and the best of the Unionist party will have to boldly ask for Balfour's resignation. He has said he would stand or fall with Lord L[ansdowne], well, let them fall together. They are utterly discredited in the country and no amount of brilliant speeches will atone for cowardice indecision and utter lack of principle.
>
> I am really amazed that, after all our talks, you should have allowed such a leader to pass, positively urging peace where there is no peace 'As Mr Balfour well says' etc. 'All sections must, we feel sure, respond to the Leader's appeal for agreement.' Good Heavens what a sentence, from us who preach no surrender. I am sure that this leader was passed under some misapprehension but I feel perfectly helpless to make you understand my ideas. The policy of the *M.P.* is to give Balfour his due when, by accident he is prodded into doing the right thing but when his true self appears, the Freetrader and intriguing compromiser, the man who doesn't want office and doesn't want any other to take his place, Balfour who would give votes to women, Balfour who refuses to pledge himself to National Service, the true Balfour in fact, then the *Morning Post* must go for him, calmly and dispassionately, but, there can be no question of following such a leader. . . .[4]

In the aftermath of the rebellion which took place in Ireland at Easter 1916 Lady Bathurst wrote an article called 'Ireland and the Irish – some wholesome home truths', in which she delivered herself of the Irish problem and of her own solution to it. The problem was that

> The Irish race is, when undiluted with Anglo-Saxon blood, a weak, ignorant, lazy, emotional race, quite incapable of loyalty even to its own chiefs or leaders, and it has been so for centuries . . . for many years their priests and political leaders have carefully kept them

3

ignorant, have fostered racial animosity, and have extorted money out of them by playing alternately on their superstition, their hatred of England, and on the best trait in their character, the love of their land.

Part of this problem was the spoiling of 'disloyal Ireland' as opposed to 'loyal Ulster' by the pandering of English governments to Nationalist demands:

Did they [the Nationalists] object to paying rent or to the natural consequences of not doing so, being evicted? The Government upheld them. Did they require land to spoil by farming it in a primitive Irish way? Land was forcibly taken from its lawful owners and handed to the ignorant to misuse. Did the Irish wish for more facilities for getting drunk, all right – though in England stringent laws exist on the subject of the number of public houses in town or village and the licences to sell beer or spirits, all this was set aside for Ireland. . . . Finally, and this is the greatest crime of all, Ireland . . . is exempt from compulsory service. . . .

The solution was obvious to her:

Mix the races, import Irish into England and vice versa. In the meantime even the pure Irish can be vastly improved by a course of Army training. . . . The fusion of races and military service, for all – that, in my humble opinion, is the only solution of the Irish question.

This being so, the question then became one of steeling 'the Dare-nots of the Coalition' to find the moral courage to implement the solution:

Let them be plucky for once and dare to ask Irishmen to fight for their country in the true and loyal sense. Treat the Irish as you would one of their own fine hunters. If the horse is high-spirited and difficult to manage you don't shut it up and stuff it with corn and employ grooms who are afraid to go near it, but you give it a good gallop across country, and it enjoys itself and learns to behave and obey its master. The Irish must be reminded of a little fact they have forgotten. They are subjects of his Majesty King George V, heirs of the privileges and duties of the British race, and they must take their stand with their brothers-in-arms, English, Scotch, Welsh, Canadians, Anzacs, and South Africans, and share in their fight against wrong and in their deathless glory.

That article was published in the *Morning Post* on 29 May 1916. On 28 July Lord and Lady Bathurst, as Vice-Presidents of the British Empire Union, which had been founded in the previous year and whose head offices were at the same address as the *Morning Post* (346 Strand), subscribed to a full-page advertisement in the *Morning Post*, appealing for funds for that organization, the objectives of which were listed as follows:

1. To consolidate the British Empire and to develop Trade and Commerce within the Empire and with our Allies.

2. To alter our existing naturalisation laws to render it impossible for aliens seeking naturalisation to become British citizens so long as they remain subjects of other countries. This to apply to existing cases.

3. To pursue an Educational propaganda throughout the country in furtherance of the policies that have been expounded by Mr W. M. Hughes [Prime Minister of Australia]; to establish branches in every constituency and county, and to support candidates pledged to these policies both in the country and in the House of Commons; to urge the importance of the measures proposed to assist the more vigorous prosecution of the war, and to bring about its speedy and satisfactory termination, and to controvert the false economic doctrine so aptly described as 'Laissez-faire'.

On 19 August of the same year Lady Bathurst published a letter to the editor of the *Morning Post*, on the subject of Women and the Vote. Writing from France, where she was acting as a nurse, she deplored the fact that Prime Minister Asquith had become a supporter of the Women's Suffrage Movement:

I trust that all who, like myself, are strenuous opposers of Women's Suffrage, will do their utmost to resist this final act of betrayal on the part of Mr Asquith and his Coalition. . . . I have seen much of women during the war, and . . . I have seen nothing to make me alter my opinion that as a sex they are inferior to men, and are totally unfitted to take part in the government of the country. What we want is not government by women, nor government by a set of weather-cocks, who veer to every quarter in search of the breeze of popularity, but government by real virile, strong men, such as Mr Hughes and Sir Edward Carson. . . .

I should like every soldier and sailor who has fought in the Great War to have a vote for his lifetime, and later on to see the vote given only to males who have passed some test of education and usefulness to their country.

When the new franchise proposals were passed into law, in 1918, Lady Bathurst drafted another letter on the subject:

Now that the great betrayal is accomplished and that votes are to be given to women of 30 and over I trust that the Government will lose no time in passing another measure, namely the Compulsory Service Act for women. If women are to have equal rights with men, they must also share men's liabilities, therefore all women between the ages of 30 and 50 should be called up, paid 1/- a day, sent, if fit, anywhere abroad and if unfit to make roads or do odd jobs in camps in England. They must have no voice in the matter of their work but just as a farmer's son is sent to handle guns or a hairdresser to drive motor ploughs, so the women should take their chance of congenial or uncongenial work. . . . Unless such a measure is passed the female sex is likely to be given the most enormous advantages over the male and admitting that we are decadent enough to be ruled by women, there are surely limits to unfairness.[5]

Interviewed by *The Gentlewoman* magazine for an article on Gentle-women and the Terms of Peace, which appeared in the issue of 3 February 1917, Lady Bathurst was quoted as saying:

I am not one of those who dissociate the German people from the so-called military caste. Every nation has the Government it deserves, and on the whole I think the German system is far better than ours. . . . But while I admire the German system which gives power to those fit to use it and does not ask the most ignorant section of the community to govern, just because they are more numerous, I hate and abominate the German character which, from highest to lowest is false, overbearing, occasionally foolishly sentimental, and usually cruel. With the German system and the English character we should be a really great people, and that is the combination I hope for when peace comes. By the German system I mean all that is good in it – loyalty to the Crown, recognition that it is every man's duty to serve his country and every woman's duty to begin with her husband and children and home; that respect should be shown to learned men, and patriotism taught in the schools; that law and order should be enforced and work properly carried out. The German system of government was all right, only their horrible character, their materialism, paganism and total incapacity to understand principles of honour and chivalry make it desirable that they should never have power to harm the world again.

Howell Arthur Gwynne was seven years older than Lady Bathurst. He was born at Kilvey, near Swansea, in 1865 and was educated at Swansea Grammar School. He left school for a career in journalism. After a spell as a correspondent for *The Times* in the Balkans, he joined Reuter's News Agency in 1893. He worked for Reuter's in Roumania in 1893, in Ashanti in 1895, in the Sudan, on Kitchener's Dongola expedition, in 1896, in Greece (for the Greek-Turkish war) in 1897 and in Peking in 1898. Having been Reuter's chief war correspondent since 1896, he organized their coverage of the Boer War and remained in South Africa for the duration of that conflict, getting to know and to admire Lords Roberts, Kitchener and Milner, and Joseph Chamberlain. In 1904 he was appointed Foreign Director of Reuter's, but left almost immediately to become editor of the *Standard*, a London evening paper of a rightist persuasion. It was thus as an editor that Gwynne first set foot in a newspaper office. As he later told the man to whom he turned for assistance and advice: 'I knew as much about it as the office cat.'[6] That man was R. D. Blumenfeld, editor of the *Daily Express*. In the end, in terms of twentieth-century British journalism, only Blumenfeld and J. L. Garvin of the weekly *Observer* were to exceed in length of tenure as editor of a single newspaper Gwynne's time at the *Morning Post*, which lasted from 1911 to the absorption of the *Morning Post* by the *Daily Telegraph* in 1937. Throughout that time Gwynne enjoyed arguably one of the best views in London: through the curved window of his office in the *Morning Post* building on the corner of the Strand and Aldwych he looked due south across Waterloo Bridge.

Gwynne's decision to sever his connection with the *Standard* coincided with the fall from grace of Fabian Ware, whose failure to draw up certain contracts tightly enough had cost Lady Bathurst and the *Morning Post* a good deal of money. It was Rudyard Kipling, who had a long-standing connection with the *Morning Post*, and who had also become a good friend of Gwynne's during the Boer War, who drew the attention of Lady Bathurst to this coincidence. He wrote to her on 15 June 1911: 'Have you ever thought of Gwynne as a successor to Ware? I ask because I am keenly anxious that the one really independent paper we have on our side should be captained by the best man I know . . . Gwynne is good – good all through. I've seen him serene and adequate under fire in the war where it was difficult to edit and be shot at at the same time.' When Lady Bathurst replied that she did not wish to replace Ware with a man from one of the other London papers, Kipling stressed that Gwynne was by no means typical of London journalists: '. . . as Reuter's chief he gathered a direct and first-hand knowledge of men and things and politics all over the world. He either possessed naturally or developed under this training the gift which is a very special one, of handling men.' As Kipling saw it, 'his seven years on the *Standard* has simply given him further knowledge in addition to these things but it has in no way blunted him nor weakened his convictions; and as you know he is a good fighter'.[7] Lady Bathurst interviewed Gwynne on 7 July and on the following day offered him the editorship of the *Morning Post* at a salary of £2000 per annum.

On 26 June 1911 the business manager of the *Morning Post*, Peacock, reported to Lord Bathurst, who had become a director and had

7

assumed considerable responsibility for the paper's financial affairs, that the previous week's circulation of 537,800 (a daily average of nearly 90,000, and about double that of *The Times*) was a record in the history of the newspaper. It had risen to this level from a daily average of 74,874 in December 1910. In December 1912, after seventeen months as editor and with daily sales averaging over 80,000, Gwynne announced to Lady Bathurst his 'deliberate opinion . . . that we should aim at becoming *the* London paper'. He did not regard this proposal as in any way extravagant:

> *The Times* is doing badly. I am told that Lord Northcliffe is losing, roughly, about £20,000 a year on it. I am also informed that he does not regret this inasmuch as this indebtedness to him gives him more power and will ultimately give him an absolutely free hand, and may result in his becoming sole Proprietor. The *Daily Telegraph*, chiefly owing to the fact . . . that it has gone in for papers of enormous size, and also, I think, to the fact that it has neglected too much affairs of importance and has dissipated a good deal of its energy on lighter matters, is also doing rather badly. The *Standard* is in a very bad state indeed, and although it is making desperate efforts to keep up its circulation . . . it is only by means of free distribution of copies and by dint of other methods which give a false idea of its condition. . . . Of all three papers at a penny, the *Morning Post* is the only one that can be said to be making steady progress.[8]

Gwynne wanted to raise the circulation of the *Morning Post* to 100,000. At that figure, with the increase in advertising revenue that would accrue, Gwynne believed the future of the paper would be secure, and that it could then go on to achieve a circulation of 150,000. The next moves in this particular war were, however, made by *The Times*, which reduced its price from threepence to twopence and then, in March 1914, to one penny. Gwynne took this opportunity to make public in the *Morning Post* something which he believed was not generally known, namely the connection of Lord Northcliffe with *The Times*. As he told Lady Bathurst, 'If the staid and respectable readers of that staid and respectable paper were told that the proprietor of *The Times* was at the same time the proprietor of *Comic Cuts*, the paper would die.' Northcliffe was indeed sensitive on this score (in 1918 he was to issue an instruction that no mention of his name was to be made in the *Daily Mail* without his permission).[9] He responded in kind to Gwynne's revelations, and produced the back-handed compliment to Lady Bathurst already mentioned. His reaction only reinforced Gwynne's optimism. He wrote to Lady Bathurst on 14 March 1914, temporarily forgetting that the subject of his letter was no longer a commoner:

Harmsworth's brother Harold (now Lord something or other [Rother-mere]) said yesterday that his brother wouldn't have a paper left in five years. He sees red whenever he is *froissé* and in these 'brain storms' he does the most impossible things. I have our victory over *The Times* on the very simple reasoning: *The Times* is now in the hands of a halfpenny paper man who believes that the right role of *The Times* should be that of a rather better and fuller *Daily Mail*. We on the other hand are the *Morning Post* with all its fine traditions unchanged.

Gwynne maintained that Northcliffe's making the *Morning Post* his chief enemy betrayed the fact that he was most afraid of it; this was because the *Morning Post* was 'gradually ousting *The Times* since it has taken the attitude of dignity and straightforwardness which *The Times* once possessed'. Gwynne wanted to step in quickly and annex all the old reserve and dignity abdicated by *The Times*' entry into the arena of mud-slinging. He believed Northcliffe had personally written the *Daily Mail*'s words about Lady Bathurst, but regarded them as 'a first-class advertisement' for the *Morning Post*: 'The public will be charmed to think that their favourite daily paper is directed daily by "the young and beautiful Countess".'[10]

The new price of *The Times* had been regarded at the *Morning Post* as a desperate move – as 'the last throw of the die' on Northcliffe's part. In fact it trebled the circulation of *The Times* to 150,000 and produced a drop of about 6500 in that of the *Morning Post*. Neither Gwynne nor Peacock was alarmed at this. Peacock, who on the basis of the *Morning Post*'s profits on the quarter to June 1914 was projecting a profit for the year of £21,000, believed that on *The Times* the loss was enormous – 'anything, say, from £50,000 to £100,000 a year'. He was also sceptical of the sales figures which *The Times* had begun to publish. These, he thought, were designed to produce a bandwagon effect: advertised success would bring real success. He was aware that the number of copies of *The Times* sent back unsold by the major retailing outlets of W. H. Smith's, Marshall's and Wyman's was, as he put it, 'staggering'.[11]

For the *Morning Post* there was also, at this time, a morale-boosting revelation from the *Daily Telegraph* that its circulation was only 182,000 in the month of May 1914. Though the *Telegraph* had trumped *The Times* it had, in Peacock's view, inflicted a serious blow on itself:

The figures it disclosed were larger than people who knew anticipated, but to the great mass of the public and even to many journalists and people in the trade they came as a great surprise. The general idea was that the *Telegraph*'s circulation was about a quarter of a million daily and the disclosure of their actual figures has shattered this valuable illusion.[12]

Nevertheless, from Gwynne's point of view *The Times* was the paper to displace, and in this regard he placed much faith in the personality of the proprietor of the *Morning Post*'s rival. Northcliffe, he was told, was losing his head:

> He has furnished some rooms at *The Times* and sleeps there, appearing at odd moments in the night in a most gaudily-coloured dressing gown. Our game is to go on giving the best paper we can but sticking to our own tone and style. It is going to win I know and I am very confident that in a year's time we shall occupy permanently the position of pre-eminence in English journalism which has been so conveniently vacated for us by *The Times*.[13]

In his letter recommending Gwynne to Lady Bathurst Kipling had described the *Morning Post* as 'the one really independent paper we have on our side'. This apparent contradiction in terms was actually a fair statement of the position. The *Morning Post* was independent in the sense that it was Lady Bathurst's property and was running at a healthy profit. It was entirely appropriate however that Gwynne, who when he was about to sever his connection with the *Standard* wrote to A. J. Balfour, the Leader of the Conservative Party, that he was looking for 'a paper in which I might do useful work for the party and the Empire',[14] should be selected to edit the *Morning Post*. Nor was it unexpected that Unionist Central Office should ask him, as they did in December 1914, to try to persuade Lady Bathurst to purchase the *Evening Standard* with a view to keeping it in the hands of Balfour's successor Bonar Law. All this was of a piece with the wish of the owner of the *Daily Express*, in January 1915, to invite Gwynne, and Garvin of the *Observer*, to join in protesting against the conduct of Central Office towards Unionist newspapers and newspaper editors.[15]

Kipling had also referred to Gwynne's 'direct and first-hand knowledge of men and things and politics all over the world'. He was indeed probably as well connected as Lady Bathurst was, in her complementary sphere. He was particularly well connected with Unionist politicians, such as Sir Edward Carson and Walter Long. He was on intimate terms with serving officers in the Service Departments, and especially with the higher echelons of the War Office. Late in 1911 he had deployed Lord Roberts to investigate and encourage a rumoured disposition on the part of Lloyd George, then Chancellor of the Exchequer in Asquith's Government, to come out of the closet and advocate conscription.[16] In the spring of 1914 he had been instrumental in stiffening the resolve of Field-Marshal Sir John French to resign as Chief of the Imperial General Staff over the handling by the Government of the indisposition of certain units of the British Army in Ulster to put down by force of arms the 'loyalist' cause.[17] Successive Directors of Military Operations – General (later Field-Marshal) Sir Henry Wilson, General Sir Charles E. Callwell and General Sir Frederick Maurice – supplied him with figures, information and assistance. So did other military men, from the heir to the Dukedom of Northumberland, Earl Percy, through General McDonagh, the Director of Military Intelligence, to Field-Marshal Sir William Robertson, CIGS for the greater part of the war. Until the two men were lost when the cruiser *Hampshire* hit a mine in June 1916 Gwynne had access to the Secretary of State for War, Lord Kitchener, through the latter's Secretary, Colonel Fitzgerald. He was on close terms with Sir William Tyrrell, Private Secretary to the Foreign Secretary, Sir Edward Grey, a part of whose duties was to brief the press, both as to what to say and what not to say. He was also, later, in touch with Sir Basil Thomson, head of Special Branch of the Criminal Investigation Department at Scotland Yard and responsible for internal security matters. Gwynne's brother, who became Deputy Chaplain General of the Forces in France, and the *Morning Post*'s own war and foreign correspondents, were additional sources of information.

Gwynne's contacts, especially those with the War Office, were obviously of more significance in time of war than in time of peace. Together with the status, standards and reputation of the *Morning Post* they do much to account for two developments early in the war: the initial exemption of the paper from the censorship restrictions imposed on other newspapers, and Asquith's request that Gwynne write him letters for the benefit of the Cabinet. Clearly the *Morning Post* was regarded as a voice which might be raised more highly and more frequently against the Government's handling of the war if its editor were not encouraged to speak his mind privately.

From the very beginning of his association with the *Morning Post* Gwynne had written regularly and frequently to Lady Bathurst. This was necessary because Lady Bathurst required to be kept informed, and because she refused to install a telephone at her residence in Cirencester, Gloucestershire, and did not often go up to London. Though the war gave Gwynne more freedom from proprietorial interference than he would otherwise have enjoyed, his letters to Lady Bathurst continued, interrupted only by the nursing duties that she undertook, by the visits he made to the front in France and by the occasional illness. To his distant and demanding proprietor Gwynne, who was forty-nine when the war began, transmitted under the headings 'secret' and 'private and confidential', much of the information that came his way – much of which was, in turn, so secret and sensitive that it could not always, or easily, be given out in the columns of the *Morning Post*. This correspondence, one side of which has survived almost in its entirety, is redolent with the values held at that time by the classes to which the *Morning Post* appealed, and constitutes the bulk of this volume. It is supplemented, where appropriate, with other material indicating the range and scope of the activities, opinions and concerns of the editor of arguably the most important journalistic organ on the right of British politics.

The themes of the correspondence in the volume as a whole may briefly be described as follows:

1. The making of the *Morning Post* into 'the premier paper of England', with the sub-themes of rivalry with *The Times* in particular, and the upholding of certain standards of journalistic conduct during wartime and its consequent restrictions.

2. The fighting of the war 'all out', with the sub-themes of the campaign for the adoption of conscription, and then the application of it to Ireland.

3. The search for 'a man' to lead the country to victory, with the sub-themes of the ousting by Carson, or Derby, or Lloyd George, of Asquith and the more radical or laissez-faire element such as McKenna and Runciman from Asquith's Cabinet, of the honeymoon period at the beginning of Lloyd George's premiership, of the setting up of the National Party in 1917, and of the attempted conspiracies with Robertson, Repington and Maurice, at least one of which envisaged the CIGS as head of the government.

4. The freedom of the Army and Navy from civilian control, on the assumption that in wartime they came into their own, with the sub-theme of the sustained antagonism to Winston Churchill which was exacerbated by his role in the fiascos of the Antwerp and Dardanelles operations of 1914 and 1915 respectively.

5. The maintenance of good relations between editor and proprietor, on the basis of Lady Bathurst's being informed about, and approving of, those activities of H. A. Gwynne which in many cases went far beyond the call of his duties as editor of the *Morning Post*.

Notes

1. Salisbury to Iddesleigh, 23 December 1885; Salisbury to A. Borthwick, 20 June 1887; A. Borthwick to Salisbury, 21 June 1887. (Glenesk–Bathurst MSS).
2. See K. M. Wilson, 'Spenser Wilkinson at Bay: Calling the Tune at the *Morning Post* 1908–9', pp. 33–52.
3. *Daily Mail*, 12, 13 March 1914; Lord Northcliffe, *Newspapers and their Millionaires*, London, 1922, p. 17.
4. Lady Bathurst to H. A. Gwynne, 26 July 1911 (Glenesk–Bathurst MSS).

5. Note by Lady Bathurst, n.d. but 1918 (Glenesk–Bathurst MSS). Published as a letter in the *Morning Post*, 14 January 1918.
6. R. D. Blumenfeld, 'What is a Journalist', *Journalism by Some Masters of the Craft*, London, 1932, p. 65.
7. Kipling to Lady Bathurst, 20 June 1911 (Glenesk–Bathurst MSS).
8. Memorandum on the *Morning Post*, enclosed in Gwynne to Lady Bathurst, 4 December 1912 (Glenesk–Bathurst MSS). According to N. Blewett, *The Peers, the Parties and the People*, London, 1972, p. 301, the *Daily Telegraph* was averaging 230,000 and the *Standard* 80,000 during the two general elections of 1910.
9. R. Pound and G. Harmsworth, *Northcliffe*, pp. 618–19.
10. Gwynne to Lady Bathurst, 14, 16, 17 March 1914 (Glenesk–Bathurst MSS).
11. Peacock to Lord Bathurst, 24 March, 3, 9 June 1914 (Glenesk–Bathurst MSS).
12. Peacock to Lord Bathurst, 9 June 1914 (Glenesk–Bathurst MSS). The figures given in J. M. McEwen 'The National Press during the First World War: Ownership and Circulation', p. 467, should be revised accordingly.
13. Gwynne to Lady Bathurst, 2 June 1914 (Glenesk–Bathurst MSS).
14. Gwynne to Balfour, 6 May 1911 (Balfour MSS BL Add. MSS 49797).
15. Steel-Maitland to Bonar Law 18, 23 December 1914, 27 January 1915 (B. Law MSS 35/5/48, /54, 36/2/44).
16. Gwynne to Lady Bathurst, 30 October 1911 (Glenesk–Bathurst MSS).
17. See K. M. Wilson, 'Sir John French's Resignation over the Curragh Affair: the Role of the Editor of the *Morning Post*', pp. 807–12.

PART I

July 1914–May 1915

On 28 June 1914 the Archduke Franz Ferdinand, heir to the throne of the Dual Monarchy of Austria–Hungary, was assassinated in the course of a visit to the capital of the province of Bosnia, Sarajevo. Only in the allied capitals of Vienna and Berlin were there those who regarded this assassination as sufficient excuse for a war. And even in those capital cities the war as originally conceived only amounted to a localized conflict such as would give Austria–Hungary the opportunity to reassert her influence in the Balkans at the expense of her neighbour Serbia, which had doubled in size (largely at the expense of the Ottoman Empire) as a result of the First Balkan War of October–November 1912.

As recently as 18 May 1914, in a letter to the British Ambassador in St Petersburg, the Permanent Under-Secretary at the Foreign Office, Sir Arthur Nicolson, had stated: 'I do not myself believe there is any likelihood of an open conflict between Russia and Germany. There is no real reason why their relations should be strained. . .'. The assassination of Archduke Franz Ferdinand did not deflect him from this stance, and as a result he delivered himself of what can only be regarded, and then only in retrospect, as worthy of a listing under the heading of 'famous last words'. For to the same Ambassador he wrote, on 30 June: 'Sarajevo will not, I hope, lead to any further complications . . .' – a sentiment which he compounded by adhering to it in letters of 6 and 20 July to the British Ambassador in Vienna. The main focus of Nicolson's attention was elsewhere. It was on the increasingly menacing policy of Russia in Persia and Central Asia, which threatened to end what had been regarded as the cornerstone of British foreign policy since 1907, the Anglo-Russian Entente; it was also on the row between the governing Liberal Party and the opposition Conservative and Unionist Party over Home Rule for Ireland. The state of the latter problem was such as to cause

Nicolson to write, on 30 June 1914, that 'in this country the situation is becoming more and more anxious and disquieting day by day'.

The delivery therefore on 23 July of an ultimatum from Austria–Hungary to Serbia which was far more wide-ranging than anyone outside of Vienna and Berlin could reasonably have expected, had about it the quality of a bolt from the blue. Austria–Hungary's precipitate declaration of war on Serbia on 28 July further reduced the amount of time with which those who were interested in the maintenance of peace had to work. Even so, as M. and E. Brock's edition of Prime Minister Asquith's letters to his confidante Venetia Stanley demonstrates, solutions of what was the main domestic difficulty, the Irish Question (the eighty Irish Nationalist MPs under John Redmond held the balance between the parties in the House of Commons), remained very much on the agenda of the Cabinet and the minds of ministers up to and including 30 July, with the solution preferred by Churchill, the First Lord of the Admiralty, being the somewhat drastic one of British involvement in a great continental war. Churchill was to get what he professed to only half-desire. Germany declared war on Russia on 1 August, despite being fully aware that Russia's mobilization, which had already commenced, did *not* in itself mean war. On 2 August Germany concluded an alliance with Turkey which was to induce the latter to declare war on Britain and Russia early in November. Germany declared war on France on 3 August. Great Britain, as a result of the threats to resign and split the Liberal Party made by the Foreign Secretary and the Prime Minister (the result of which would have been the disappearance of the Liberals into the political wilderness for the foreseeable future) unless France and Russia were offered British support, declared war on Germany on 4 August. On the same day Germany and Belgium declared war on each other. Austria–Hungary declared war on Russia on 6 August, as did Serbia on Germany. Finally, Britain and France declared war on Austria–Hungary on 12 August. Italy, the peacetime ally of Germany and Austria–Hungary, though heavily compromised in this relationship by an agreement made with France in 1902, had already declared a neutrality that was to last until the early summer of the following year. In September 1914 France, Russia and Britain constituted themselves allies, agreeing not to enter into negotiations for, nor to conclude a separate peace with, either of the Central Powers, Austria–Hungary and Germany.

The possibility of a great war in Europe first entered Gwynne's correspondence with Lady Bathurst at the beginning of the last week of July 1914. Having, before the British decision for war was taken,

16

attempted to bring pressure to bear on the Foreign Secretary to ensure that the decision taken was one *for* British participation in the war, Gwynne went on almost immediately to produce what might well be the first unofficial programme of British war aims. He does not appear to have been a victim of what has been called 'the short-war illusion', although when he wrote on 1 September that 'we are in for a long and desperate war' he did not realize just how long, and just how desperate, it was going to be. By then he was convinced that his private views were being placed directly before the Cabinet. This conviction did not prevent him from commencing to try to influence Lord Kitchener, the Secretary of State for War, on the basis of material supplied from inside the War Office, towards policies and arrangements which the suppliers of this material wished to see implemented. Having achieved something of a coup in regard to the relaxation of the censorship regulations for the *Morning Post*, Gwynne then incurred the wrath not only of the Chief Censor but of a portion of the Cabinet: Churchill's expedition to Antwerp provided him with material for what was to be a long-running campaign, not only against Churchill personally but against any form of civilian control in or over the Service Departments. By the end of November 1914 Gwynne was confident that he had placed the *Morning Post* on such a footing that it might meet the demands of a war which he had thought from the beginning 'would make us or mar us'. In the New Year of 1915 he found his enthusiasm to go to the front the more easily curbed by an invitation to lay his ideas on the war before the Cabinet, an invitation which was to lead to a number of substantial letters to the Prime Minister, H. H. Asquith. By no means losing sight of matters of direct concern to Unionists, and determined that the leadership of the Opposition should not lose sight of them either, in March 1915 he tried to warn the Leader of the Conservative Party, Bonar Law, against making the very kind of coalition that was put together in May, which continued to be dominated by the Liberals and in which Asquith retained the premiership.

1

H. A. Gwynne to Lady Bathurst, 24 July 1914

. . . Servians are inhabitants of Servia. Serbs are of Servian nationality but not inhabiting Servia.

The outlook in Europe is most grave. It looks to me as if Germany thinks her time has come to challenge France and Russia. We shall soon see the need for a strong fleet and a ready army.

We are going on very well over the train business.[1] If we bring it off, I'll give *The Times* a year to be beaten by us. If we don't, I'll give them two years. . . .

1. Peacock, the business manager of the *Morning Post*, had initiated a consortium of all the fifteen London daily newspapers (with the deliberate exception of *The Times*) to bring pressure to bear upon the railway companies to run their newspaper trains rather earlier, so as to improve the distribution of the consortium's papers. (See Peacock to Lord Bathurst, 22, 27 July 1914 (Glenesk–Bathurst MSS).)

2
H. A. Gwynne to Sir William Tyrrell, 1 August 1914

My impression yesterday of our policy was that we were willing to announce to Germany that if they gave guarantees that they would respect Belgian neutrality we should stand out. But I also understood that this policy was agreeable to France, if not suggested by her, the idea being that if we could prevent Germany's attack on her from the north in this way, we should be doing just as effective a service as if we sent our divisions across.

But it is quite evident from Paris messages that this has come as a shock to France. If we are taking this step *against her wishes* then I think we are doing a hideous wrong to her and, at the same time, are doing a great injury to ourselves. In 1911 we stopped war by telling Germany that if she entered into the game we would take a hand.[1] In 1911 Germany was ready and willing to fight, Austria was without a Balkan entanglement and Italy was free to put forth her strength and would have if Libya had been offered to her or the Trentino. Today, Germany is fighting as you say with a corpse round her neck for Austria is in difficulties and may have a check in Serbia and Italy is stone cold.

If we do not act in full accord with France and if we show Germany that we are lukewarm and inclined to take an independent line war will be inevitable and though we may secure comfort by neutrality we shall regain the old name of Perfide Albion.

Besides, even if France may not have been assured formally of our military help, she has always counted on our fleet. Are we going to let our fleet lie idle while France's coast is threatened by German warships and transports. One more thing – we have been led by the F.O. under your chief's guidance to be prepared for this co-operation. We have worked hard to prepare public opinion for it and now when we get to the jump, as it were, we are refusing it.

Of course if France says to us 'We are quite happy if you can prevent an invasion from the north' well and good. But I fear we are disappointing France and leaving her in the lurch at this great crisis. If so, all the arguments that the F.O. used to use about the folly of standing out come back to one with greater force.

Let Sir Edward [Grey] remember that he holds the *honour* of England in his hands, that 80% are behind him and that he has enormous personal power if he likes to use it with which he could force his views on the Cabinet and the country.

We want a lead, a strong manly lead. We have always expected to get it from Sir Edward. Surely now we are not to be disappointed?

1. This is Gwynne's interpretation of the speech delivered by Lloyd George, then Chancellor of the Exchequer, on 21 July 1911 at the Mansion House, during the Franco-German crisis over Morocco. The reality was more complex. (See K. M. Wilson, *Empire and Continent*, pp. 89–109.)

Editor's postscript: The leading article in the *Morning Post* of 1 August was called 'The Need for Guidance'. It began:

A prompt and whole-hearted decision on the part of His Majesty's Government might yet preserve the peace, and, if that is impossible, may determine the issue of the war. Englishmen are all agreed that this country must stand by France, which means, in the existing situation, standing by Russia also. The decision required is to announce plainly that such is British policy, and that a mobilization of Germany will be instantly followed by the mobilization of the British Navy, the Expeditionary Force, and the Territorial Force.

It continued: 'The French people in the hour of their trial are looking across the Channel for the encouragement to be derived from the palpable determination of England to make good her professions of friendship.'

Whilst preparing this the previous evening, Gwynne had been interrupted by a telephone call from L. S. Amery, one Conservative politician who was engaged in mobilizing the leadership of the Opposition into putting pressure on the Government to stand by France and Russia. Amery had urged Gwynne to write 'as strongly as he could' (J. Barnes and D. Nicholson (eds), *The Leo Amery Diaries*, p. 103). It is of interest that Gwynne's article did not mention any of the content of the first paragraph of his letter to Tyrrell. That letter was delivered by hand to the Foreign Office. Late that same Saturday, relaxing with his Parliamentary Private Secretary over a game of billiards at his club, Grey announced that he had decided upon a 'tussle' with the Cabinet at the meeting it was due to have the following morning. As it was only in the course of that 'tussle' that a letter from the Opposition leadership of Bonar Law and Lord Lansdowne, promising Conservative Party co-operation for measures in support of France and Russia, arrived, it might be argued (on the not unreasonable assumption that Tyrrell passed on to Grey his letter from Gwynne) that the letter from the editor of the *Morning Post*, with its careful reference to what Grey's colleagues would have regarded as his duplicity, was the more important of the two letters in steeling the Foreign Secretary to escalate matters to the extent of threatening his colleagues with his resignation and the consequences it would have for the Liberal Government. (See K. M. Wilson, *The Policy of the Entente 1904–1914*, pp. 135–47.) Gwynne followed up with a leader on 'Our Clear Duty' on 3 August, and welcomed the Foreign Secretary's speech on that day as 'A Straight Lead at Last' (*Morning Post*, 4 August 1914).

3
H. A. Gwynne to Lady Bathurst, 5 August 1914

. . . The secrecy is tremendous and quite right. . . .

The Fleet will not have a big action. The Germans won't come out. But we are playing the game splendidly.

Italy, I think, may join us actively. There are indications that way. We are going to bring Germany to her knees and, please God, we'll make her pay for all this.

4
H. A. Gwynne to Sir William Tyrrell, 6 August 1914
(MS Gwynne 24)

I expect you are getting a vast amount of amateur advice, most of which doubtless you are consigning to your wastepaper basket; and I should not be a bit offended if you do the same with this letter.

Diplomacy, it seems to me has yet a very great part to play, and I would like to put before you a few ideas that have occurred to me, which may perhaps be worthy of your consideration. I am optimistic enough to believe that in this war we are going to bring Germany to her knees absolutely; but it sometimes happens that a victorious war so far as allies are concerned is almost as dangerous as a defeat, for there is often a quarrel about the division of the spoils. If on the other hand my optimism is not justified and Germany and Austria bring the rest of Europe to its knees, then they will dictate the terms and we would have nothing to say.

Let us presume for a moment that we are going to win. Do you not think that we ought to lose very little time in initiating negotiations with our Allies, France, Russia and Belgium, as to what each is going to ask as its share of victory? We have had a most appalling example of nations squabbling over the spoil in the late Balkan war,[1] and I am very strongly of opinion that we should do everything we can to avoid a repetition of this on a larger scale. It should be our business, it seems to me, to get this agreement with our Allies as soon as possible. It sounds rather like selling the skin, but as I said before, if we lose, it is Germany and Austria who will dictate the terms and not ourselves.

What do you think that Russia will ask as her price? and what Belgium? and what France? Presumably Russia, apart from all questions of monetary compensation, which I put out of the question, may ask for a strip of territory on the Baltic, or may try to take her spoils from a disintegrated Austria. I do not know what her desires are, but I think they certainly should be formulated. Belgium perhaps may be content with a renewal of guarantees for her integrity and France if she gets back Alsace-Lorraine. We I suppose will get Kaiser Wilhelm's Land, Walfisch Bay, and German West Africa, or German East Africa, and the Islands of the South Pacific, leaving to France the Cameroons. In this way France would be satisfied and so should we. But if we want to complete the downfall of Germany and do it quickly it seems to me we should try to increase the number of Allies who are fighting against her.

Italy has declared her neutrality, but she might perhaps be induced to throw in her lot with us if we and Russia and France would promise her compensations in the Adriatic. We might, of course, give her the Trentino; but that she would expect, and we might go further and let her come down south on the east coast of the Adriatic as far as Fiume. This might be a great inducement to her to throw in her lot with us. But more should be done if we are to increase the number of our Allies. Bulgaria is sullen and uncertain because she has been kept out of what she considers the rights she acquired by her arms in the war against Turkey. It should not, however, be beyond the power of diplomatists to offer her something which might persuade her to join with Servia and Roumania. We should have to allow Montenegro Scutari, but if we could compensate Servia by letting her have everything south of the Save as far as Fiume, practically Bosnia Hercegovina, she might be willing to give Bulgaria an outlet in the Adriatic in Albania, provided, of course, that Italy raised no objections; and for the life of me I cannot see what objections Italy could raise because her port of Taranto practically closes the Adriatic, and the enormous accession of territory she would get and the great economic advantages she would obtain by the possession of Trieste and Fiume would more than make up for any fears she might have of a hostile Bulgaria or Servia opposite her.

As I said before, probably this letter will be put into the waste-paper basket; but I put these suggestions forward just as a reminder how often wars are caused by the differences arising out of the division of spoils.

1. The Second Balkan War, of July 1913, was fought between the states which, as allies, had defeated Turkey in the First Balkan War, of November 1912.

5
Lord Milner to H. A. Gwynne, 16 August 1914
(HAG/21 no. 23, IWM)

. . . I take a very grave view of the outlook. I believe that Germany's attack on France will probably fail. On the other hand Russia's attack on Germany is by no means certain to succeed! Germany at bay is a very formidable proposition, especially if the line spreads, and Turkey, as seems very likely, comes in on the German side.[1] If we have trouble in Egypt and India, our resources in fighting men (always our great difficulty, as we have been preaching for years) will easily be exhausted.

However. It is no use taking too bleak a view. But I am grateful to you & others, who, without being croakers, are inclined to call a halt to the excessive optimism of the moment, which is a real danger.

1. Turkey commenced operations against Russia on 27 October and officially declared war on Russia, France and Britain on 11 November 1914.

6
H. A. Gwynne to Lady Bathurst, 21 August 1914

. . . I am sure you must be furiously busy and I will not therefore intrude very much; but I am sure it will comfort you to know that our Military people are delighted that the Germans have entered Brussels. It was part of our scheme to entice them there and they have walked into the trap. You will now see in a very short time a very vigorous French offensive and I shall be much surprised if it does not result in a devastating blow to Germany.

7
Lord Milner to H. A. Gwynne, 21 August 1914
(HAG/21 no. 24, IWM)

. . . I still think people are unaccountably, and most unfortunately, far from being alive to what we are in for. As you know, I am no alarmist. I am far less put out by the occupation of Brussels than the people who let themselves be taken in by the intolerable shouting and boasting and jeering of the Yellow Press over the first checks encountered by the Germans. I do not think there is any need to be frightened, but there is need, steadily, continuously, and day after day to impress upon the public, how gigantic an effort is required to bring this thing to a satisfactory conclusion.

The practical point is that any premature feeling of relief *stops enlistment*, and unless enlistment is maintained at full swing, it is impossible to say how we are to keep up pouring those fresh forces on to the Continent, which will certainly be required before this business is over. 100,000 men a month is rather a tall order, but we shall have to keep up something like that, if we are to have an effective – not to say a decisive – influence upon the land war at all. I believe they could be got if – but only if – people were kept every day, from now to the end, face to face with the gravity of the crisis, and not allowed to slide off, as we only too readily do – not having our houses burnt over our heads like the Belgians – into our various avocations and interests.

There are just 2 delusions, or rather one dubious hypothesis & one certain delusion, which are doing an immense amount of harm and encouraging that fatal false optimism, which is as far removed as possible from quiet resolution and endurance, & the maximum effort to help ourselves.

One is the excessive reliance upon Russia. I do not under-value the enormous importance of this factor *in the long run*, and of course I hope it may make itself felt sooner than I expect. But there is no evidence, no certainty that one can base oneself upon, that Russian pressure on the East will *soon* begin to affect the really vital struggle on the Franco-Belgian frontier.

The second and worse delusion, because it is certainly false, is the idea that the Germans, as a nation, are dejected, disunited, and in face of a severe reverse will go to pieces, that socialism would become formidable, the Poles would rise, etc., etc., etc. This is not only contrary to what we know of the character of the people, but it is *directly contrary* to *the quite recent testimony* of *experienced and impartial eyewitnesses*. They tell me that Germany is making a most colossal effort; that the nation is calm and united and confident – the very reverse of the reluctant, dis-spirited, and tyrant-driven crowd which fills the paragraphs of the halfpenny evening papers.

All this rubbish fritters away the seriousness, the resolution, and the real patriotism which, at bottom, exists in the nation, and was so strongly exhibited at the outset.

I am not alone in feeling this. I have heard the same ideas strongly expressed by men whom I greatly respect, and who are working like demons, especially in getting up the new army.

I am sure that in a general way you quite agree with it, and that you won't mind my pointing out one or two aspects of the case which have come very much under my own observation.

8

H. A. Gwynne to Lady Bathurst, 24 August 1914

. . . The latest news shows that the Germans have collected rather more men than was thought possible in Belgium; but on the other hand the neutrality of Italy has allowed the French to supplement their army corps, which they did not expect, so that, roughly speaking, the forces in Belgium are very nearly equal, the Germans having a slight preponderance over the Allies. My difficulty is that I do not know whether the Allies are holding the line from Mezières, Givet, Maubeuge, Valenciennes and Lille, or the line from Lille, Givet, Namur and Charleroi. The latter means, as you will see in the map, a somewhat acute angle projecting into the enemy's country, and this is always a dangerous position because you are liable to be attacked on both flanks at the same time. Personally I hope that the French are keeping their original line of Mezières, Givet, Maubeuge, for this must be very strongly prepared with field works now. In such a case, we may hear of Charleroi being taken and the Sambre being crossed, and public opinion will get concerned here; but it would really be the best thing that could happen, for it would mean that the French are sticking to their original idea and are holding lines that are very strongly prepared. What will then happen, I think, is that the French will allow the Germans to hurl themselves upon them, and if they repel them, then they will make the offensive movement forward which, if successful, should be a decisive point in the whole war. I have got a letter from Lord Percy[1] and he is a little bit uncomfortable. I enclose it. I do not agree with all he says, but I do agree with what he says about our not sending the third Army. What on earth it can do here I cannot understand. . . .

I am afraid you must be overwhelmed with work now with all the committees you have joined. I wish there was some great organisation at the head of it all, so that people would know that their work was being made use of.

The reason why the Russians are advancing in north-east Prussia is due to the formation of the land. You will see from the map that eastern Prussia goes up into a triangle on the north and makes a great arc on the east opposite Posen. If the Russians marched in the direction of Posen without first securing eastern Prussia, they would run a terrible risk of having their communications with Warsaw cut off. That they will move on Posen I have no doubt. Indeed I think their direct objective is Berlin, but they have got to secure their flanks before they can do this. This will take some time, and although I think the Russians have made their pressure felt much earlier than I ever anticipated, and much earlier than the French anticipated, yet their advance will be very slow, because the difficulty of feeding the enormous force will be increasingly great; though the Russian soldier can be fed on less than any other soldier.

. . . I hear that they may take the best of the Yeomanry[2] abroad.

1. With his regiment at this time.
2. The Yeomanry was an auxiliary, mounted force, largely though not uniformly recruited from the farming communities of the shires.

9
H. A. Gwynne to Lady Bathurst, 26 August 1914

. . . This question of recruiting is not easy and it is not going too well, unfortunately; but I have got an idea which I think will be very effective, namely, to send Lord Charles Beresford[1] throughout the country. I have got a letter from him in which he promises he will do it, provided the suggestion comes from outside and not from himself. I am going to suggest it in a leading article tomorrow.

I think Lord Bathurst deserves enormous credit for getting 35 recruits. From what I hear from men who have been trying the same thing, I can assure you that his was a very big success. Men who have worked for days and days have had to be content with 5's and 10's and to them a dozen is a huge number. It is not that the men will not serve, but you cannot bring it home to them that we are fighting for our existence. They will persist in thinking it is a Continental war and not one in which England is most intimately involved. I am so glad to get your accounts of the spirit of the people. That after all is the chief thing and if they will still make sacrifices I have no doubt whatever about the future of the war.

Things are much better to-day than they were when I wrote last. The Germans have not followed up their undoubted success in Belgium, which shows that they were very severely handled in the misguided offensive which the French took on Saturday and Sunday. You will be glad to hear that our people behaved remarkably well. They took up an offensive position at Mons, in accordance with the orders of the Generalissimo of the French Army. They hastily prepared some field works and then the Germans came on at them. They seem to have made a dead set at our people, but our fellows remained quite cool and calm, and simply mowed the Germans down. They calculate that in these actions of Saturday and Sunday as many as 10,000 Germans were killed and wounded. Our men were very anxious, seeing the effect they had produced on the Germans, to go forward; and indeed they would have gone forward but for the fact that the French on their right were driven back, which necessitated the retirement of the British Force also. The result was that they lost a good deal in the retirement. In the 24 hours' battle before the retirement I am told that their casualties were practically nothing, no more than 200.

1. Admiral Sir Charles William de la Poer Beresford, former Commander in Chief Mediterranean Fleet, 1905–7, Channel Fleet, 1907–9; retired from the Navy, 1911; Conservative MP, 1910–16; created Baron, 1916.

10
H. A. Gwynne to Lady Bathurst, 1 September 1914

I have done everything I could about the casualties, but although, through a friend of mine in the Cabinet, I got the question mentioned at a Cabinet meeting, and I got two members to urge very strongly that the list should be omitted altogether; yet I am afraid my effort was useless, and tonight I think a portion of the casualty list will be issued. I hear that most of them are missing. There are really very few killed and wounded that they know of. Of course, a vast number of missing probably are dead and wounded, but the majority of them are no doubt prisoners. It was a desperate encounter and we were very nearly surrounded. You notice that I have not spared *The Times* yesterday and today, and I shall have another go at them in tomorrow's paper. The Editor of *The Times* has just sent me a message and asked me to meet him on neutral ground and I am doing so at 6.45. I expect to be overwhelmed with dire threats of all kinds, but I do not mean, provided you have no objection, to move in the slightest degree from the position I have taken up. *The Times* I consider behaved abominably in publishing the message.[1] It is no excuse for them that the censor passed it.[2] Every Editor must be his own censor in these days when there is no law, and in the case of the *Morning Post* I have exercised a censorship from July 27, i.e., long before the war broke out not a single movement of troops or ships was published in the *M.P.*

There is not a word of truth in the story about the Russian troops, though I wish there were.[3] The only foundation for it is that some officers of the Russian Headquarter Staff came round from Archangel to join the English Headquarter Staff with their horses, servants, and clerks, which helped to fill quite a good sized train. Things are going fairly well for us. The German Army is pounding away, and the Allies are pounding back. The Germans are losing more than we are of course, because they are on the offensive and we are on the defensive; but I think they will succeed in driving us and the French south of Paris. That, however, must not discourage us. It must be remembered that as long as the French Army is intact, so long is victory within our grasp. What would be a disaster, and one which we in England would have to repair, would be if a large portion of the French Army was surrounded and taken; and of this there seems to be no fear at present. The morale of our men and of the French is very good. The only thing I do not like is that there is a certain amount of quarrelling between our Headquarter officers and the French.

The factors in our favour are very many. Russia is moving steadily on; Austria will not be able to show a firm front very much longer because of the various elements which go to compose her. These must split up sooner or later. Gallant little Servia is on her way to Sarajevo. There is undoubted uneasiness in Berlin over the Russian advance. Meanwhile you will be glad to know that we are building ships day and night so that if the Germans think they will in time bring a more formidable fleet against us, they will find themselves very much mistaken, for we can build three times as fast as they can, and we have a greater number of trained men to fall back on, although I wish we had more. No, the truth is we are in for a long and desperate war, and we must make up our minds that as in the big wars of the last century, England will have to come in at the end with her Army. Would to God she had been ready now; but it is no use crying over spilt milk. We have got to put our shoulder to the wheel and produce the best Army we can in as short a time as we can. We shall have, I think, 150,000 trained troops of the regular Army extra in the field by the end of this month, and another 150,000 very efficient troops at the end of next month. After that they will come in greater numbers, and on our shoulders will fall the big burden, unless, of course, Russia moves quicker than we expect. So far she has done remarkably well. There is nothing either in the telegrams or in the private information I get, which gives me any reason to doubt that they are going on splendidly. Meanwhile we must keep our hearts up and the *Morning Post* will do its best to keep up the hearts of the rest of the people.

The Times have done themselves an enormous injury over their Sunday telegrams, and today we are inundated with letters telling us that the writers will no longer take that paper. I do not like, in a crisis like the present, to carry on a newspaper controversy, but the very existence of Northcliffe in a time like this is to my mind a great national danger, and from that point of view I shall fight it, if you have no objection. I have not forgotten what he said about you.[4]

1. The message, from a correspondent at Amiens, described the rout and desperate plight of the British Expeditionary Force. It was published in a special Sunday edition of *The Times*. Gwynne immediately wrote to the Prime Minister protesting against the conduct of *The Times*. (See M. and E. Brock (eds), *The Letters of H. H. Asquith to Venetia Stanley*, p. 209.)

2. A Press Bureau had been hastily improvised on 8 August 1914. F. E. Smith, the Conservative politician chosen to head it, had not only passed the offending telegrams but made matters worse by adding to them sentences designed to increase recruitment: 'We want reinforcements and we want them now.' Late in September 1914 he was replaced as Chief Censor by Sir Stanley Buckmaster, who devised new and more stringent procedures (see letter 16).

3. The rumour was that Russian troops were passing through Britain to the Western Front. (See A. Ponsonby, *Falsehood in War-Time*, pp. 63–6.)

4. In the *Daily Mail* in March 1914. (See Introduction, p. 2.)

11
H. A. Gwynne to A. Bonar Law, 3 September 1914 (Law MSS 34/5/14)

I have got the following telegram privately from our Washington correspondent:

'Incredible harm would be done British cause here were Irish question again to be made active political issue.'

I thought I would let you know this. Low (our Correspondent) is a very sensible fellow and I think he is speaking the truth.

12
Lord Milner to H. A. Gwynne, 3 September 1914 (HAG/21 no. 25, IWM)

I am glad to see you publish the German 'wireless' messages. No doubt it is wise to take these *cum grano*. They no doubt exaggerate successes & minimise defeats, but a judicious study of them may give any fairly well informed person an idea of what is happening. And in view of the determination of our own Government to treat this singularly patient & reasonable people like an infant school & to keep them in the dark about events that vitally affect our national existence, we must do our best to pick up by roundabout means what in the past has always been fairly & squarely communicated to us.

The worst of it is that the concealment of material facts, like the childish & withal extremely cruel juggling with the casualty lists, entirely defeats its own object. The intention no doubt is to prevent discouragement & panic. But the British are not a panicky people. They are prepared to take hard knocks, & these will only stiffen their resolution to see the thing through. What does discourage, & may end by completely demoralising them is the feeling that they are kept in the dark – the obvious inference being that actions which cannot even be referred to, though everyone knows them to have taken place, were so bad, that those in authority are afraid of their becoming known.

There is no object in being reticent, or attempting to deceive, about military operations, which are entirely finished. Why should we not know all about Mons & Le Cateau, St Quentin & Compiègne? This is a very different thing from revealing facts, which it may still be possible, & no doubt, if possible is desirable to conceal, about the present position & strength of our forces.

In one lucid interval, on Monday morning last, the War Office gave us a succinct & to all appearance perfectly candid & businesslike statement of the series of operations, which had concluded some 3 days before. I doubt whether that statement would ever have appeared, had not the lurid exaggerations of the previous day, which spread panic far & wide throughout the country, absolutely forced the Government to depart from their policy of concealment. They have now once more relapsed into it. Must we wait till we are again deluged with the bloodcurdling tales of enterprising but unauthorised 'correspondents' before those in authority once more consent to lift a corner of the veil, behind which the most momentous events in the history of this nation for nearly a century are taking place.

Editor's postscript: This letter was printed in the *Morning Post* on 5 September, without attribution; a second letter from Milner, advocating Government-appointed war correspondents, was also printed, over Milner's name.

13
H. A. Gwynne to Lady Bathurst, 3 September 1914

. . . I was very glad indeed to get your letter and I am sorry that they have published a list of casualties. I am, however, urging them to stop publication altogether, of course letting the relatives know. Our losses have been very heavy indeed. I do not think myself that we shall get out under 15,000, and it is not any use harrowing people's feelings by printing lists as long as your arm in every paper in England.

The military situation continues satisfactory, i.e., while there is certainly no cause for jubilation, there is not any cause for great depression. The allied armies are fulfilling the task they allotted themselves after their unsuccessful offensive in Lorraine, which is to retire stubbornly, making the enemy suffer heavily for every yard of territory they acquire. The losses of the Germans must be something appalling. I have spoken now to two officers who were in the retreat from Mons, and they tell me that they did not think it possible that any troops could stand the punishment they had been receiving. One officer told me of a case where he saw a regiment one thousand strong practically wiped out. Of course, a lot of the men fell down, pretending to be dead, and to say that the regiment was wiped out is perhaps an exaggeration; but for all soldiering purposes it was wiped out and I defy that regiment to come on again for three months. What the Germans are doing is to sacrifice a regiment or battalion in that way and let another battalion come on and by sheer force of numbers press back the allies.

There has been a good deal of friction between General French and Joffre,[1] but it has now been put all right. I can tell you now, quite confidentially, that Kitchener went over the day before yesterday, and came back yesterday, in order to put matters straight. Of course, you will keep this to yourself. We have finished with *The Times* and they have had a nasty blow. Everybody is indignant with them and I think that they will suffer very considerably. I am sorry that Milner is not an agricultural expert. I know that he is always supposed to be coached by Prothero,[2] who is more or less of an expert. Fox[3] is in Antwerp at the present moment, though we date his telegrams from Terneuzen. He is doing extremely good work, and was the first to give a good account of the burning of Louvain.

I think the nation is playing up well. A lot of men are leaving us at the office for the army, and everywhere I hear the same story; but of course we cannot create an army good enough to equal the regular army of France, though I think we can in a comparatively short space of time get together an army quite good enough to meet the second line German, as that line consists of somewhat old men. The German artillery is so numerous that we shall have to devise some method of making up for it. I am in the happy position of being able to write directly to a Cabinet Minister and I am told by him that most of my letters are read to the Cabinet. This affords me opportunities of putting forward some suggestions based on my practical knowledge of tactics, which I think may be useful. I will send you a copy of a letter which I hope to write to-day. It may come by the second post. . . .

P.S. I am almost beginning to believe in the story of Russians passing through England. I hear it corroborated from so many sources, although officially it is denied.

1. General J. J. C. Joffre, Commander in Chief French Armies of north and north-east, 1914, and of all French Armies in the west, December 1915–December 1916.

2. R. E. Prothero, President of Board of Agriculture and Fisheries, December 1916–August 1919.

3. War correspondent on the *Morning Post*.

14

H. A. Gwynne to Lord Kitchener, 24 September 1914

I have been studying very closely all that has been written and said regarding the armed forces which we are preparing to put in the field on the Continent, and I can easily realise that the enormous burden of improvising, where we should have prepared long ago, will fall upon you and your colleagues at the War Office. I know of the shortage in equipment and material generally in which we are caught, and the lack of officers and non-commissioned officers which are necessary to train the new Army. Indeed so great is this latter want that I am beginning to have grave doubts whether it is possible to put into the field the armies that we are creating in the units in which they are being formed, and I put before you an alternative plan which I hope you may find worthy of consideration.

The principle on which I base my suggestion is that it is better to have a comparatively speaking small force in the field of absolute Efficients than it is to have a large force composed of a great number of Inefficients. I go further and say that the primary task with which we as a nation are faced is that of filling up the wastage in the ranks of Efficients as quickly and as amply as we can.

Going on the present plan of putting an enormous number of men into the field, I presume that perhaps in eight or nine months we may really be able, as Mr. Churchill[1] said the other day, to put a million men in the field; but what we have to consider in this respect is whether these million men in the field, trained hurriedly and of necessity somewhat imperfectly, would be able to carry out the tasks that will be allotted to them. They will have to meet – we hope on German soil – a veteran army determined to fight to the last, and whose policy is that the real defensive lies in the offensive. They will have to manoeuvre quickly, to meet sharp and sudden attacks which would try their discipline to the utmost, and above all, they will have to meet an Artillery fire which will be greater in comparison than the present Artillery fire which the Germans can at present bring to bear; for as the Germans contract so will they be able to mass their Artillery.

The national needs require an army of veterans superior in efficiency to the Germans, capable of meeting the Germans at any move, and with an accompaniment of Artillery which will equal, if not out-number, that of the enemy.

I would therefore suggest that you and the British Government should decide on a definite number of men to be kept in the field, and that this number should be maintained throughout the whole course of the war at its full establishment and in a state of absolute efficiency. The following is my calculation of the numbers we ought within a comparatively short time to be able to put in the field:–

300,000 Regulars, including Indian troops
150,000 Best Territorials
 60,000 Oversea Contingents
 60,000 Services, including A.S.C., R.A.M.C., &c.

This will give us a grand total of 570,000. Later on as we advance into Germany we would want at least 50,000 men for lines of communication and these might be composed of the second best Territorial Divisions. We would then have a grand total of 620,000 men, of which probably 500,000 would represent sabres, rifles, and guns.

It seems to me that if we kept 620,000 men in the field, always up to that strength, perfectly equipped, considerably over-gunned, sending in the shape of drafts the very best that we have at home, we should more effectively carry out our task than if we put a million imperfectly trained men in the field.

We are forming new Army Corps, new Divisions, and new Battalions, and the general impression is that these are to go to the front as units. I am sure you will agree that in view of the lack of officers to train them it will be at least a year before these troops will be fit to go into the firing line as Army Corps, Divisions, and Battalions. The best of our officers are either engaged in the huge and important administrative work of the War Office or are at the front, or are doing depot work – also most important work – at the various depots; and for the new Army it is necessary to fall back on officers who have long retired and non-commissioned officers who have been out of touch with their battalions for a great number of years; and I am convinced that both owing to their inexperience and their scarcity the task of bringing recruits up to such a state of efficiency as would justify their being put in the firing line is one which cannot be accomplished in time to be effective in the decisive moments of this war.

I would therefore suggest that we should fix on a number, say 620,000 men, as the number of troops that are always going to represent Great Britain in the firing line throughout this war, and that all other forces being raised will be used only as feeders to this force, so that whatever happens there will be an army of 620,000 men, composed of the most efficient soldiers in the world, always in front of the Germans. I am sure the effect of this would be greater than if in six or nine months time we put an enormous number of imperfectly trained men into the field, and for this reason: if you take a battalion that has already been shot over and has been fighting for some time its efficiency is enormously increased. If it loses 25% of its men, the new drafts sent to repair this wastage become efficient certainly ten times as quickly as they would if they went out as a separate unit. One of the advantages of the plan would be that we should know exactly what we are going to do. We would have a definite object at which to aim and I claim that 620,000 efficient men constantly kept up to strength would be more effective than new armies turned on to the field. But there are other advantages which I think will appeal to you.

This war is a war of Artillery. In all that I have read and heard of this war, it is quite obvious that the enemy's artillery is superior both in calibre and in numbers to ours, i.e., their Howitzers are much more powerful than our guns, and they have heavy artillery which they will use constantly now in retreat on to their prepared positions which is more powerful than anything we can bring forward. With a comparatively small but efficient army of 620,000 men, we can concentrate on to that force all the Artillery that is available in England so that it probably would be over-gunned. I understand from letters from the front that this is exactly what our men desire. I know the great difficulty that we have both in producing guns and training the gunners, but it seems to me that as soon as we have a battery and have trained the men, its place should be at the front rather than manoeuvring here at home with one of the Divisions now in process of formation. The consequence would be that the British force, always efficient, always up to strength, always over-gunned, would impress itself upon the Germans to a greater extent than would a larger but less efficient force.

If this plan were adopted the process that would then follow in regard to the new armies would be that they would be trained as drafts for definite battalions and in this way the men who showed the greatest degree of efficiency and aptitude could get to the front quicker than would those who were less competent, and a fine spirit of emulation would undoubtedly arise in the new force.

Take the opposite case. A battalion is formed that is going out on active service. The efficiency of that battalion would be represented by the average efficiency of all the men composing it, and it would take a much longer time to attain this general efficiency than it would to make proficient the number of men that would be required as drafts.

It seems to me that something should be done in this matter pretty quickly. I see that there is a Welsh Army Corps being formed and no doubt Scotland will try to follow suit. If this scheme of recruiting is persisted in we shall have the new armies clamouring to be divided into more or less local Army Corps, probably a northern, a Midland, a southern, a south-eastern and a south-western. This method of forming the new armies would tie your hands to such an extent that if at any future time you wished to alter your scheme, you would find yourself faced by these national and semi-national forces which you would not be able to break up without arousing a considerable amount of local feeling which might reach the Government and result in Government pressure being brought to bear on you. While if it were announced that the men composing the new armies would get to the front in drafts as soon as they were efficient and would have the honour of serving with regular regiments who had distinguished themselves, the emulation that would be aroused would form a very valuable stimulant to those armies.

In this connection it seems to me that something has got to be done with the Yeomanry, who are at present neither fish, nor flesh, nor fowl, nor good red herring. They are not cavalry, and in the opinion of men whose judgment I follow, they are not yet efficient mounted infantry. The question to be decided by the Military authorities is whether they will not encourage in the Yeomanry the teaching of shock tactics, so that they should form not units of their own, but be a sort of special reserve to the Regular cavalry regiments at the front. Of course there would be a tremendous howl about this, but when I was talking the other day to an old soldier who commands one of the Yeomanry regiments, he expressed hearty approval of the idea.

The question of Home defence, which it is impossible altogether to ignore, may make it necessary to retain for purposes of rapid movement and effective use against an invader, the units as they are at present, so that if Germany did attempt to invade us we should have an army to oppose her troops. Of course you are in the best position to appreciate at its true value the danger of invasion; but it seems to me that as long as we press the Germans on the Continent, they cannot spare the men even if they could get the transport for anything more than a very small raid. The real way to make invasion impossible is by constant pressure upon the German armies in the field in France and, let us hope soon, in Germany.

1. Winston S. Churchill, First Lord of the Admiralty, October 1911–May 1915.

15

H. A. Gwynne to J. S. Sandars, 25 September 1914 (Balfour MSS 49797)

. . . I think the best thing I can do is to send you the letter I wrote to K[itchener] yesterday. I have approached Churchill and I hope to see him today. I am told he really has some influence with K. I have been to the W[ar] O[ffice] this morning and have seen all the big pots. Every one of them to whom I showed my letter cordially agrees with it.

As a matter of fact they say it would have come to that anyhow, but they are very keen that a definite decision on these lines should be taken lest the country should be educated up on the wrong lines for too long a time. If it is not done pretty quickly there will be a great disappointment among those who are working hard to get up separate units. I wonder what the Welsh A[rmy] C[orps] people will say when they find it is impossible to send them out as Army Corps?

10 p.m.   I have seen Winston Churchill and he is wedded to his one million men in the field – damn him. I was most terribly disappointed with him. He really knows nothing of military things. I enclose Callwell's comments on K's letter. He is the best brain at home now among the soldiers.

16

H. A. Gwynne to Sir Stanley Buckmaster, 27 September 1914 (MS Gwynne 3)

I am in receipt of the notice issued by the Press Bureau on Friday the 25th inst. at 7.45 p.m., in which newspapers are notified that all maps, sketches, and diagrams which purport to illustrate the dispositions and operations of the Allies, and all articles written by Military critics or experts must be submitted to the Press Bureau before publication. I have throughout this war been a steadfast believer in a strict censorship and even before the Press Bureau was established I myself kept a most vigilant eye on everything that went into the *Morning Post*. I think you will find on inquiry at the Press Bureau that the *Morning Post* has not sinned in any way in respect of giving information which might be of use to the enemy. My Military correspondent has made a practice of dealing with the operations of the enemy and leaves out all surmise as to the possible or probable movements of the Allies. From the beginning we came to the conclusion, after consultation, that this was the only way to second the work of the Censors and to ensure the achievement of their wishes as far as the *Morning Post* was concerned.

These being the circumstances, I sincerely hope you will take into consideration our good behaviour in this respect and that you will not treat both the innocent and the guilty in exactly the same way. I do think that those papers which have throughout this war conducted themselves with a due regard for national interests deserve more considerate treatment than those who have flouted the desires and wishes of the authorities and have, in their insensate desire to obtain 'copy', given away information which might have been of the utmost value to the enemy. If such a discrimination were shown, it would be a great encouragement to those papers who have sinned in the past to discover that it pays better in the long run to play the game honestly and properly than it does to try to outflank, as it were, the Press censorship.

I am led to make this request because the restrictions that are put on us by this last order are really very severe and render it almost impossible for our Military correspondent to write his explanatory comments, since there would be no time for us to submit to the Press Bureau his manuscripts or proofs of his articles if he is to deal with the latest news. Indeed next to the leading articles and the very latest telegrams, his is the latest 'copy' to go to press. I am, of course, submitting tonight's article as directed, but I sincerely hope that in return for our assurance that nothing prejudicial to the Allies and nothing which might indicate their possible or probable movements shall appear in the *Morning Post*, you may see your way to trust to our discretion in those cases where it would be extremely difficult and, indeed, impossible for us to submit the 'copy' to the Press Bureau. I would gladly give such an undertaking and in that case my censorship would probably be even stricter than your own. I may say that I have frequently censored telegrams here in the office which appeared to me to have passed the eyes of the cable and telegram censors, and in every case I have tried my best to comply not only with the letter but with the spirit of the regulations of the censorship.

17
Sir Stanley Buckmaster to H. A. Gwynne,
28 September 1914 (MS Gwynne 3)

Private and Confidential

I quite appreciate the difficulty to which you refer and at the same time I am glad to say that there is no difference of opinion here as to the loyal and effective way in which you have guarded publication in your paper. There is a very real difficulty and a very real danger against which we are bound to protect our force and that is the publication of any matter that gives information as to the action or position of units of the forces or anything from which it would be possible to ascertain the disposition of the various elements that make up the Allied Forces. I feel sure that you both understand and realise the importance of this matter and I think therefore that I can relieve you from the necessity of submitting your descriptive articles, remembering as I do how careful you have been, and relying as I am sure I can on the same, or if possible increased, vigilance in the future. Let me repeat it is only real and urgent necessity that has made it needful for us to impose a general restriction, in order that we might deprive people who are not so careful as you are of any excuse for careless details in their press.

P.S.   In the event of a mistake occurring in your office you will I am sure understand that this letter will not acquit you of responsibility.

18
H. A. Gwynne to Lady Bathurst, 2 October 1914

I am sure you will be pleased and proud to know that the *Morning Post* has been exempted from Censorship. Of course all telegrams and cables are censored in the ordinary way but we alone of all the papers in England, have not to submit our articles and descriptive accounts before publication.

19
H. A. Gwynne to Lady Bathurst, 6 October 1914

I am so glad you are pleased with the fact that the *M.P.* is exempted from Censorship. That is a great tribute to all connected with the paper. It is, of course, confidential for if it was made public the Chief Censor's life would not be worth living.

I wish you would give your impressions of the visit to the German prisoners for publication. The Home Office who are in charge of them would gladly give me an order to visit them but, if he did, he would have to give it to other papers and the trouble is they cannot be trusted? I don't think I ever felt so ashamed of my profession as I have during this war. They never seemed to have given a thought to the fact that we were at war. Joffre telegraphed two weeks ago to the

W[ar] Office here 'Thanks to your *Times* we nearly had a disaster in the East.' I think I should shoot myself if that was said of the *M.P.*[1]

Things are bad at Antwerp. The Belgians wanted to give in but we've stiffened them with English troops and hope that they'll stick it out now.

The Germans are trying to outflank and are doing it with Cavalry but they have left their Centre weak. This may be their undoing.

1. It was, ten days later, by Buckmaster, who berated Gwynne for having been less ambiguous than *The Times*, and who told him that several members of the Cabinet regarded his article 'as one of the most deplorable things that has happened during the War'. 'Had it been published', Buckmaster continued, 'by a paper whose integrity and principle I had less reason to respect than yours, I should have felt myself compelled at once to take the necessary steps to have had the Editor tried by Court Martial.' (Buckmaster to Gwynne, 16, 17 October 1914 (MS Gwynne 3).) There was a certain informality about the Censorship at this stage in the war. In time, it took a stronger grip on the *Morning Post*, and in February 1918 Gwynne was to complain to the head of the Press Bureau that 'Some of your excisions seem to be verging on the political'. As the excisions in question had been made by Lloyd George, there was truth in this. (Gwynne to Swettenham, 28 February 1918 (MS Gwynne 3).)

20
H. A. Gwynne to Lady Bathurst, 8 October 1914

. . . *The Times* incident is characteristic of that beastly paper. When Joffre made up his mind to try a big turning movement on the German right, he withdrew from the East the famous 20th Corps under Castelnau. It was a somewhat dangerous proceeding as the Germans would take advantage of the withdrawal to attack the attenuated right. However, every precaution was taken. The troops were withdrawn at night so that the aviators could not see and the coup was in every way so well arranged that Joffre really hoped and had a right to hope for a big success. Before Castelnau could strike, *The Times* published the fact that he was at Amiens. This announcement was made on a Wednesday. On Friday the Germans attacked the Camp de Roumaine and St Mihiel on the Verdun–Toul line and nearly succeeded in breaking the line. For some time it was touch and go. But not only that, the Germans apprised of Castelnau's presence at Amiens moved troops to meet him – thus defeated the aims of Joffre. No wonder he sent the telegram.[1]

I am trying to make our Government make up its mind about Contraband. See tomorrow morning's Naval Note. Not only are the Government undecided about Contraband but in the instructions to officers, they lay it down that if officers make a mistake they are liable to be sued.

I frankly don't understand this long continued line of fight. The Germans have not enough men to do a really effective turning movement. The only explanation is that they are trying to prevent the French sending a force to help Antwerp.

1. See letter 19.

21
H. A. Gwynne to Lady Bathurst, 13 October 1914

I am terribly in your debt over letters, but I hope you will forgive me as I have been busier than usual. I have been trying to get at the bottom of the story of Winston Churchill. I am sure you would like to know what was the meaning of the article we published this morning,[1] and I intended to have written to you last night, but was too busy getting full particulars to find the time. I am afraid our casualties in this little adventure of Mr. Churchill at Antwerp cannot be much under 8,000. Fox, our man at Antwerp, puts them at 9,000, and he is a very careful man. The whole adventure was one which in my opinion deserves the severest condemnation inasmuch as it was, as far as I can make out, wholly a Churchill affair and does not seem to have been considered or thought over, or consented to, by the Cabinet.[2] I enclose you a confidential account written by Fox, which will give you some idea of the state of affairs; but I could add a good many things which make it worse. This man Churchill gathered from all the ends of England a force which he called the Naval Reserve Volunteer Force. It consisted of old men and youths, men who had not fired a rifle in their lives, officers who had not been trained and had just come from the Officers' Training Corps. The consequence was that they were led to perfect slaughter.[3] Do you know that the first night, my information is, that 800 Marines were killed dead by German shells. The whole thing was a horrible blunder which deserves not only the severest condemnation but which ought to bring about the resignation of Churchill. Imagine our Fleet being commanded by a man of this calibre. A man who gets an idea into his head and without waiting to consider or think, shoots off motor cars and motor 'buses and transport and very nearly involves us in a quite new expedition; and this at a time when every man we have to spare is wanted at the front.

I must now answer the questions in your letter. I am much interested in what Mr. Wallingford said about the officers getting

39

soft-nosed bullets for their revolvers. I wonder whether he is confusing the lead bullet of the Webley revolver with the soft-nosed bullet? Of course the lead bullet is a pretty big thing and gives a nasty wound, but it is not against the rules of civilised warfare. I wonder whether you could get him to give me quite confidentially a few more particulars, so that I can approach my friend at the War Office in regard to it, because if it is as he states it requires careful investigation.

I am glad you approve of what we did in the matter of the Speyer family. Of course one has to be very careful and it is a very delicate question to touch, but this great Sir Edgar Speyer,[4] whose brother the other day said that England was the only obstacle to peace, is a friend of Mr. and Mrs. Asquith, constantly lunching and dining there, and his country house at Overstrand, near Cromer, is where Mrs. Churchill was lately brought to bed.[5]

Prince Louis of Battenberg is still carrying on the duties of First Sea Lord. It is curious what an enormous number of rumours there are about his loyalty. Personally I am inclined to think he is quite loyal, but the view that I take is this: if the Navy thinks he is disloyal, even if they think so without cause, still that in itself weakens the Navy to a certain extent. And beside that, I do not think he was ever a great Naval genius. That truth is that he is, I think, bearing a good deal of the blame which ought to be apportioned to Churchill, for I am told that the latter interferes every day with the detailed working of the Admiralty, with which he ought really to have nothing to do.

I had a short leader about the Disabled Soldiers, but I have enlisted the sympathies of Bonar Law and I think if he speaks at the Guildhall he will bring it up and that will give me another opportunity. I do agree so much with you that while we are paying enormous sums to keep fat merchants going, we are neglecting the men who are willing to sacrifice their lives. . . .

1. This was called 'The Antwerp Blunder', as was a letter from the Opposition frontbencher Walter Long, published on 14 October.

2. On 3 October Churchill had in fact secured the assent of Grey and Kitchener to his transferring the Marines from Dunkirk to Antwerp, and to his taking what Asquith called the '8000 Winstons' of the two Royal Naval Divisions. (See M. and E. Brock (eds), *The Letters of H. H. Asquith to Venetia Stanley*, no. 174.)

3. 'Like sending sheep to the shambles' was Asquith's phrase for this. (See M. and E. Brock (eds), no. 182.)

4. Banker, industrialist and Privy Councillor.

5. Sarah Churchill was in fact born at Admiralty House, on 7 October.

22

H. A. Gwynne to Sir Stanley Buckmaster, 14 October 1914
(MS Gwynne 3)

I am much obliged to you for your letter of yesterday's date, the spirit of which I quite understand and appreciate. I take it that you do not object to the publication of yesterday's leading article inasmuch as it essentially and exclusively referred to the policy of the Government in sending to Antwerp. Thus far, I take it, the Chief Press Censor is speaking. The latter part of your letter, in which you administer to me a mild rebuke, is I assume your private opinion, and as such I need scarcely tell you that it has as much weight with me as your official opinion. You see an objection in an article which attacks a Minister who cannot reply without disclosing to the public things which it is his duty to conceal. That of course is a point of view I appreciate very much, but it does not altogether meet the difficulties of the case.

I feel I ought to speak to you quite plainly because, first of all, I have always believed in plain speaking, and secondly because I am sure you will not misunderstand or misinterpret what I say; and, I may add, that I speak to you as Sir Stanley Buckmaster and not as Chief Press Censor. The expedition to Antwerp was, in my opinion, a very grave military blunder; but it was worse. Whoever was responsible for it sent men without any training to fight a skilled and powerful enemy. Will you believe it when I tell you that some of the men who were placed in the trenches had not fired a rifle before and were seen in the trenches putting their cartridges in the wrong way? There were officers in those same trenches who had never commanded men before in their lives and had only seen their present command a few days before. My 'biting' criticism was directed against a gentleman who holds the position of First Lord of the Admiralty and who therefore is responsible for the safety of these Islands. This gentleman hurriedly, and I cannot help thinking, without due thought, organised this expedition to Antwerp. Within the last month he has left his work at the Admiralty to pay visits to the Army Headquarters in France, to Dunkirk, and to Antwerp. He was under shell fire at Antwerp. He took part in the details of the expedition and so, in my opinion, must have neglected the high office which he holds.

We are living in times when we cannot afford to beat about the bush if we see grave faults being committed which may involve the nation in destruction; and I cannot promise now or at any other time to withhold what I believe to be perfectly legitimate and absolutely necessary criticism. You may rest assured that there will never appear in the *Morning Post* as long as I am Editor of it, anything which can give the slightest information, aid, or comfort to the enemy; but I put it to you, what course is a newspaper editor to take when he sees things going absolutely wrong? I do not ask for any ruling on this question, but I do want you to understand that in this or in any other criticism which I may from time to time publish, I shall be guided only by what I consider to be the needs of the nation. Of course, there may be two opinions as to the necessity of this, but I think in this present case I could prove to you conclusively not only that I am quite justified in the criticism I have made about this Antwerp affair, but that as an Editor, with a sense of responsibility which is sometimes overpowering, it was my bounden duty to make it. . . .

23
H. A. Gwynne to Lady Bathurst, 16 October 1914

. . . You will be glad to hear that we are doing extraordinarily well in France and I hope to have very good news soon. I am afraid the casualties are a bit heavy and poor Hubert Hamilton, a very old friend of mine, has been killed by a stray shell. I do not know whether you knew him. The sinking of the *Hawke*[1] will only increase a certain amount of anxiety in the Navy regarding the way in which secrets are kept at the Admiralty. There is a good deal of dissatisfaction throughout the whole of the Fleet and I may have to take up the matter. Even if this dissatisfaction is not based on fact, still its very existence is a detriment to the efficiency of the Fleet. I hear that the Cabinet are quite upset by our disclosures.[2] Kitchener has given Winston Churchill a dressing down; but we want to have the man out and have a man like Custance[3] in. I am working at it steadily,[4] and I hope to have on Monday a full account of the whole thing, and then I am going to ask the Government what they intend to do.

I am still sticking to the question of contraband and the non-arrest of belligerents on neutral ships, which I really cannot understand except on the assumption that there is some treason; and that I do not like to believe. . . .

1. British cruiser, sunk 15 October by a submarine.
2. See footnote 1, letter 19.
3. Admiral Sir R. Custance (retired).
4. On this same day Gwynne sent a letter to a number of Cabinet ministers – Asquith, Lloyd George, Grey, McKenna, Pease, Masterman – with a note condemning the Antwerp Expedition and describing Churchill as 'unfitted for

the office he holds'. At this stage he intended to publish this in the *Morning Post* with comments calling for the removal of Churchill and his replacement with a serving officer. On 20 October he informed the Prime Minister that he had decided against publication. Later he was to regret this. He wrote to the Director of Military Operations at the War Office, Callwell, on 7 April 1915: 'I wish I had persisted in my original intention of getting Winston out of the Cabinet. I believe I could have done it at one time, but K[itchener] over-persuaded me.' (Gwynne MS 14, 17.)

24
H. A. Gwynne to Lady Bathurst, 19 October 1914

I hope again you will forgive a typewriter, but this Churchill business has brought on a correspondence which is almost more than I can cope with. In the first place, I think things are going very well indeed, and I am optimistic enough to believe that the Germans will be forced to fall back on the line formed by the Meuse in Belgium and as far in France as to bring them along the line to Metz. That would practically send them out of French territory, though not quite. You will be glad to hear that they have already left the Aisne position and are moving back. It was a bold move of French's, but it apparently succeeded. He moved away from the Soissons position secretly and is now very much reinforced and in very good fettle, well in the centre of their right. If he succeeds Ostend will have to be evacuated and I am not sure that the Germans will not be obliged to leave Antwerp. I think the Germans have now evacuated Lille without much of a fight and it is probably their intention slowly to retire on to the Meuse.

About the *Hawke* I do not like it at all because it was so far north, and we have a theory that submarines cannot go up so far north as that, and return. As a matter of fact Winston [Churchill] had nothing to do with the *Hawke*. He only has to do with operations at Harwich and south of that place, so Jellicoe[1] was himself responsible for her movements. I am told that they searched Speyer's house but of course they would find nothing. Personally I do not believe that he is a spy at all, because the Jews always divide their firms into three parts so that one belongs to one country and one to another. Each of them does his work quite independently and is quite loyal to the country in which he lives; but one does not like the idea of a German Jew who has been very generous to the Government, being made a Privy Councillor and more or less in their secrets.

We could not unfortunately cut off our Wireless as all the movements of troops would be stopped in consequence. I will let you know if I see the King. I have already written for an appointment and hope to get it in a day or so. I had a long talk with Kitchener on Saturday. I was with him over an hour. He told me enough to show that this Government ought to be hanged, drawn, and quartered for entering into a war in such a state of unpreparedness; but he is making things good, and doing it very well, and really in the circumstances, very quickly. Of course, there will be a good many grumbles, but I have seen a little into his organisation and I must confess I am very pleased with it. He thinks that the German Army has lost its sting now, and we have to do with scraps and second-raters who will not be able to put up the same fight as they did in the earlier part of the war. All this is, of course, very good hearing. I will let you know any further news I get.

Winston is now cowed I am told, and Kitchener has given him such a dressing down that I do not think he will forget it. I am still in hopes that I may persuade the Government that the best thing they can do is to have a sailor at the head of the Admiralty, as we have a soldier at the head of the War Office.

1. Sir John Jellicoe, Commander in Chief of the Grand Fleet.

25
H. A. Gwynne to Lady Bathurst, 20 October 1914

. . . I think my optimism is justified though the news I have heard tonight about Russia is not quite so good. Apparently they are not making so much way in Galicia as they had hoped. Still I have no fear whatever as to the ultimate results. You have always to bear in mind that at the present moment – I speak now with absolute knowledge of the facts – if we held up our little finger Germany would be quite ready to make peace on the terms of the *status quo*, which of course we refuse. But that is not the point. The point is really that this means that the Germans have given up hopes of winning the war, which is a great thing. In France it is really worth while being optimistic, because although I do not think we shall smash up von Kluck,[1] as the papers say we shall, still we are on the offensive and they are on the defensive, and at any time their line may break, while ours seems to be quite safe.

1. General Alexander von Kluck, commander of the German 1st Army.

26
H. A. Gwynne to Lady Bathurst, 22 October 1914

. . . I saw Lord Stamfordham yesterday and told him all the facts of the case.

What has happened is that Winston Churchill has practically taken command of the Board of Admiralty and the *Navy is being run by a civilian instead of by naval experts*. That was the burden of my song and I put it to him and through him to H[is] M[ajesty] that if this is allowed to continue we shall have disasters. The whole point is put most clearly in tonight's leading article which you will read before you get this. That contains practically the whole of my argument. At the end of the conversation Lord S. gave me to understand that he knew the King was of my opinion.

In consequence of our outspoken articles the Cabinet is really moving and I am told that on the lines of my leader today we shall be successful with the Government. It is a very difficult and delicate matter as one has to keep one's eye cocked on the enemy – while criticising the authorities we must not give comfort and aid to the enemy. The aim and object of our articles is this. W[inston] C[hurchill] likes a weak Admiralty because with a strong Admiralty he would have to go. I want a strong Admiralty because I want him to go.

I will take the very greatest care about my enquiries on the subject of soft-nosed bullets.

I am afraid we are allowing a good deal of stuff to go into Germany. Sir E. Grey is in such a funk of neutrals.

The *M.P.* seems to be doing very well. Everybody talks very well of us. If we are going to achieve a success I would like you to know that it is all owing to you. I could have done nothing here without your backing and your support and I feel that there is nothing I cannot do with it. You have no idea what a tremendous help it is to me to know that you will stand by me provided I play the game for the nation. You see I have no hesitation or doubt about your approval when I take up a strong attitude for I know that I shall get it as long as the attitude is prompted by national motives. You may not perhaps quite realise, being down in your little county town, that it is you who are really the motive power of this great machine which with God's help, I hope to make *the* power in England.

27
H. A. Gwynne to Lady Bathurst, 28 October 1914

. . . My mouth has been closed for a long time about the French plan of campaign, but you will be glad to hear that today the whole of the French Army from the east to the west has started a forward move, and I imagine that France is putting in nearly the whole of her strength. Joffre has been very wonderful in his plans. You will hardly credit it when I tell you that he has not used even the whole of his first line, and people have often wondered why it is that Germany, inferior in numbers to the French first line, and grossly inferior in number to the whole of the French Army, should still be in France. Joffre's idea, to which he has been consistent all along except for two small modifications, has been that it was his duty to hold the French Army intact. Let the Germans beat their heads against the stone wall of their entrenchments and then when he thought they had had enough punishment, to move forward with a great *élan*. This forward move has been made today and I do not know the result yet, but I think and hope and pray that it will be successful.

28
H. A. Gwynne to C. F. G. Masterman, 28 October 1914
(MS Gwynne 20)

. . . I have been optimistic from the moment I knew that Russia had taken precautions to mobilise the outlying parts long before official mobilisation took place. That gave them a good fortnight's start. . . . I want our people here to realise that we are up against something very big indeed, and not to go to bed with the idea that everything is for the best in the best of worlds. . . .

29
H. A. Gwynne to L. J. Maxse, 30 October 1914
(Maxse MSS 469)

Many thanks for your letter and congratulations, but all my pleasure is rather dashed by the fact that Fisher[1] is going to be First Sea Lord,[2] and the worst of it is that I cannot see I can say anything at present. Keep the Antwerp correspondence a little bit longer in order to work up an article for the *N[ational] R[eview]*, but as a matter of fact I am committing a breach of journalistic etiquette in letting you see the letters at all, so do not quote any words or expressions from them which might give away the source of information. Otherwise I shall get into very hot water indeed from the writers.

The larger movement that Churchill mentioned had some foundation in fact.[3] I know the whole business now as it was told me by K[itchener], but there has been no explanation why with a couple of hundred thousand really fine Territorials here, he should have been allowed to use the raw Marine levies. The real reason is that he simply wanted to gratify his inordinate vanity.

1. Lord Fisher, First Sea Lord, 1904–10. During those years Gwynne, then editor of the *Standard*, had supported Admiral Lord Charles Beresford's campaign against all aspects of Fisher's regime at the Admiralty. (See A. J. Marder, *From the Dreadnought to Scapa Flow*, vol. i; R. F. MacKay, *Fisher of Kilverstone*; and R. Williams, 'Arthur James Balfour, Sir John Fisher and the Politics of Naval Reform, 1904–10', pp. 80–99.)

2. The King had agreed to this appointment on 29 October.

3. This refers to the initial German military operations of the war, which Churchill likened on one occasion to a 'long, straining, encircling arm'.

30
H. A. Gwynne to L. J. Maxse, 2 November 1914 (Maxse MSS 469)

I am rather like a man I once met in South Africa, who prayed for rain and had his house washed away. I wanted the change from a weak to a strong Admiralty in the hopes that it might ultimately end at least in curbing Winston's activities and restoring some confidence to the Fleet. Now Jackie Fisher's advent has made me thoroughly miserable, especially as I do not see how I can make any further attack. I have said my say about him and it was hardly eulogistic. All I can do is to trust and pray that he may be a better man than I ever thought he was. My Naval friends who mistrust him very much, advise me that this is the best policy to adopt, for if I continue attacking Jackie they are perfectly sure that I shall not succeed in getting him out, and the only result would be that I should create a profound mistrust in the Navy for their leaders, which, of course, would be a very bad thing indeed, especially in the present state of jumpiness. So there I am, tongue-tied and very unhappy.

31

H. A. Gwynne to Lady Bathurst, 11 November 1914

. . . I think it is a good idea to have a kind of County census of the proportion of people who have enlisted or are serving. It would have the added advantage of showing up the [Irish] Nationalists. . . .

Things are going fairly well on the whole, but the trouble we are in is that the Government are obsessed with this idea of invasion and in consequence will not send troops abroad. The line is very thin indeed there, and our casualties have been enormous. I should say that it would be no exaggeration to state that since the beginning of the war we have certainly lost nearer 60,000 than 50,000. This out of our small Army is pretty heavy, and what the civilian here does not understand is that the finest regiment in the world cannot stand being battered about without losing its sting. French, referring to this the other day, is stated to have said that there may be one or two British regiments which have lost their sting, but the whole German Army has lost its sting; and this I think is true; but they do pour out men most recklessly.

As regards the Navy, things are in *status quo*. I firmly believe the Germans are meditating something, but what it is I am unable to say. The presence of the squadron off the coast of Yarmouth the other day was a particularly bold thing and showed that they had very excellent information. On the other hand, the loss of the *Audacious*,[1] which is now nearly a fortnight old, is still apparently unknown to the Germans, or at any rate they do not officially announce it; and this makes me doubt whether their information is quite as good in this sort of way as we were led to expect. I am convinced that that squadron did not come over here except with some object, and what that object is we have yet to find out. Personally I think it means that they were looking for the possibilities of a bigger raid having success.

This is very secret, but Sir John French has sent for me very urgently to go over and see him. I imagine he wants me to help him here over his Army, for I know that he has been feeling the strain and has been begging for officers and men, and especially officers. The mistake, I think, that K[itchener] has been making is using too many officers here for staff billets whereas they would be much more useful at the front. The whole mistake is, I think, the idea that the best thing we can do is to place K's Army in the field as units. It is possible to do this with Territorials, at least with the best of them, but with K's Army what I should particularly like it to be is a feeder to the forces at the front, which I would like to see kept at a full strength of half a million. With such a force we should be able to impose our own tactics and our own strategy. It would be a point of steel to the French Army, which would never be below strength and always be superb, for it has to be remembered that we have made only a small draft on the youth of our country. As regards recruiting, I am not a bit pessimistic. I believe we can get as many recruits as we like the moment we are in a position to equip and train them. What has been happening is that there are now men who joined in the first burst about the end of August, who are still without rifles, clothes, and equipment generally. All this is the fault of a Government that has been living on its stores for the last five years, who never would believe in war and looked upon it as the most unlikely thing in the world. I have been trying to bring all this home to our people in the *M.P.* and I hope they will see it in time. I have told Colvin that if ever that arch-humbug Haldane[2] gets up and speaks again, we shall just confront him with some of his old speeches and tell him to hold his tongue ever more during this war.

1. *Audacious* was one of the most modern dreadnoughts. It was sunk by a mine on 27 October, off the northern coast of Ireland, where Jellicoe had taken the Grand Fleet for a rest and for gunnery practice. The sinking was announced by the Admiralty only on 13 November 1918, despite a letter in *The Times* on 4 December 1914 signed 'Audax' berating the Admiralty for not publishing the loss. (See E. Cook, *The Press in War-Time*, pp. 148–9.)

2. Lord Haldane was Lord Chancellor in the Liberal Government which lasted until May 1915. From December 1905 to June 1912 he was Secretary of State for War. In the early days of August 1914 Gwynne and the *Morning Post* had inveighed against his return to the War Office, which Asquith had contemplated. (See J. M. McEwen, '"Brass-Hats" and the British Press during the First World War', p. 45.)

32
H. A. Gwynne to Lady Bathurst, 25 November 1914

. . . In the first place, let me express to you my entire sympathy with you in your anxiety about the paper. For all of us who are devoted in its service, there is less responsibility than falls to your lot, to whom it is everything both spiritually and materially. But this very anxiety, if I may be permitted to say so, may cause you to see matters from a less broad and impersonal point of view.

It is essential that you should look at the *M.P.*'s history especially in recent years in order to understand thoroughly where we stand. For years as you know, the bugbear of the paper was the reduction of *The Times* to a penny. Some of the most acute journalists thought the *M.P.* could never weather that rock, others thought that it would reduce our circulation by half and all thought it would have a very serious effect on us. But the prophecies have all been falsified and we have today a bigger circulation than we ever had.[1]

We have achieved that great result by the very judicious outlay of money but also to a very great extent owing to the splendid devotion of the staff. I was, in my innermost heart of hearts, dreadfully nervous about the war which would, I knew, either make us or mar us. It was so easy to be panicked into gross expenditure but I refused to follow the examples of the other papers. *The Times* had 12 special men out, the *Telegraph* about the same. The *Chronicle* more but we never had more than 4 and they were members of the staff or working on a small weekly salary. I think I can reduce that number by two. But you will see that we were really more economical than any other paper. It is true that our telegraphic expenses have been great but this was essential though it has to be borne in mind that we used our own staff at the various capitals and did not increase our staff by a single man.

Now, I can reduce expenditure in a week or ten days' time by 25, 50 or 75% (I mean, of course, extra war expenditure) and I can make various economies in other directions which will enable us not only to avoid losing but make a profit but it would only last for a month or so and the paper would be ruined.

Now let us look at the paper from a purely business point of view, not putting any sort of sentiment into the question at all. You have got a property worth £x. If the circulation is increased say by 5000, your property is worth £x + 5000. Equally if circulation falls 5000, your property is worth £x − 5000. Now by altering, as drastically as you desire, the whole make up of the paper, you will lose circulation and lose value.

I look upon myself as your trustee in this matter and I should consider myself as a man failing in his trust if I did not put before you the danger of such drastic alterations as would result in deterioration of the paper and its value to you.

The war is hitting everybody very hard but I honestly think that we are feeling the rub as little if not less than any other paper. Numbers of them will die as a result of the war but I want the *M.P.* to emerge triumphant. Never have its prospects looked better and never have I felt so confident about it. The question before us is whether we are to risk it all now.

... I believe that a most rigid economy should at once be instituted but I should be doing you an ill service if I led you to believe that any economy is possible which would obviate the raising of a loan. Personally I think that our advertisements will go on gradually increasing and that a large loan will be unnecessary. But of one thing I am convinced and that is that if we go on as we are doing now, we shall be able to pay off in a very few years, without affecting our ordinary revenue, the advance which may be necessary for carrying on the paper.

Of course I am an optimist and you will say, and rightly so, that you cannot risk your fortune on anybody's optimism. But my optimism about the *M.P.* is shared by every newspaper man in London. We cannot help but win out on top now and when we do and the war is over I firmly believe the *M.P.* will be the finest property (commercially speaking) in the newspaper market.

The war, of course, may be a long one but that the critical part of the war will be long delayed I do not believe possible. If and when the Germans retire, there will be almost at once a great renewal of trade from which we should not fail to benefit. As things are now, I think the tendency of advertisements to increase is undeniable. . . .

1. For the week ending 24 November 1914 the average daily circulation figure was 84,919.

33
Lady Bathurst to H. A. Gwynne, 27 November 1914

. . . I must however point out a matter in which I am quite sure we might save space and therefore paper without detriment to the public. Take the Russian victory in today's *Morning Post*. First there is a leader in which it is discussed and Lord K's words quoted, then a column on Progress of the War, Statement by Lord Kitchener, then we have it all over again in The Military Situation, fourthly we have German Rout in Poland, official communiqués, fifthly we have The Russian Campaign by our special correspondent (2 columns). I am glad to find that we didn't report Lord K's speech all over again in 'Imperial Parliaments' but still that makes 5 different descriptions of the same thing. You often say that you test public opinion through me in some measure, well I must confess that 5 descriptions of the same thing bores me – that I like my news in one or at the most two paragraphs and I like those paragraphs full and salient and all items of interest on one subject, *together* in one place and not scattered about the paper, so that it is possible to miss them, especially if, by repetition of certain portions you think you have read the whole before.

Now as to your letter, I may alter my opinion, after I have seen Lancy,[1] but I think not. The choice I have to make is between a gamble, i.e. carrying on as we are doing now by means of a large loan, which may or may not be repaid. You may be perfectly right and we may reap a huge profit, on the other hand we may lose everything. I am no Gambler, moreover I hold the *Morning Post* in Trust for my children and I have no right to play blindly with their inheritance. The other alternative is reduction all round and especially of paper – & though we shall not make a profit we shall not also risk a loss. I unhesitatingly choose the second alternative & moreover I do not believe that we shall lose in prestige as much as you think. Will you pardon me for saying that I think you imagine the public read their papers much more carefully than they really do. If you knew how seldom they read anything but one page, how often they miss really good things even when headed by the largest of headlines & how little they know or care whether the paper is 16 or 10 pages I do not believe you would attach so much importance to the reductions I ask for. If it makes you happier we will call a meeting of directors & discuss the whole question. . . . I am sorry that there should be the slightest disagreement between us in practice, there is certainly none in policy or principle & I know that it is only your zeal for the paper & all that it stands for which inclines you to take greater risks than I am prepared to face.

1. Lancelot Bathurst, Lady Bathurst's brother-in-law, also a director of the *Morning Post*.

34
H. A. Gwynne to Lady Bathurst, 29 November 1914

I have read with great interest your letter of the 27th.

Please do not think me obstinate or unreasonable but in all these matters I think of nothing else but the good of the paper and its future. And remember that whatever you decide, I will carry out not only without a single grumble but with all the energy and power I am capable of. Even if your decision should prove wrong (which Heaven forbid) I'll carry on with the same spirit as though you had adopted my suggestions.

I only pointed out considerations which I think should weigh with you but I quite see and thoroughly appreciate *your* position, which is much more difficult than mine or the manager's. But I should be doing something very less than my duty to you if I did not urge with all the force I can my point of view. And I realise that as yours is the heavy responsibility your decision must be final.

I will not go over the ground I have already covered but will you look at the *M.P.* from the point of view of ten years hence? Then I want you to be able to say that through the greatest war of all times, when papers were hit right and left, the *M.P.* came out with only a small debt on it which is now repaid.

And I want to be quite frank and open with you. All your dealings with me have been so utterly frank that I should be a scoundrel if I did not reciprocate it fully. Therefore I must advise you in considering the questions, to bear in mind that I am frightfully ambitious for the paper. You see I have made it my career and have determined to devote the rest of my life to it. Naturally I may exaggerate and you must, in your calculation, allow for an ambition for the paper which may go beyond your own desires. But, at the same time, I always start with the principle that the success of a daily paper is to be measured by its revenue. If its circulation increases and its revenue decreases then it is not a success for circulation and revenue should increase together.

What you say about the reductions is partly true but when we have got rid of S[penser] W[ilkinson][1] this will to a great extent disappear. You see he can only write about the war or foreign affairs. About anything else he is as dangerous as a bull in a china shop.

I know you must be feeling all this as well as the war, so I hope this letter will at any rate prove that your Editor, with all his faults of ambition for the paper, would prefer serving you with a single broadsheet than run another man's fifty-page paper.

1. Spenser Wilkinson had been chief leader writer on international and military and naval affairs on the *Morning Post* since the 1890s. For a brief period he had edited the paper. In 1909 he accepted the appointment of Professor of Military History at the University of Oxford. He continued to contribute leaders to the *Morning Post*, though on a reduced scale. His employment there was terminated at the end of 1914, and he joined the staff of the *Daily Mail*.

35
H. A. Gwynne to Victor Marsden, 1 December 1914
(MS Gwynne 24)

I have lately conducted nearly all my correspondence with you by telegraph because one is never certain how long it takes a letter to reach you. You must therefore not take the absence of correspondence to indicate a lack of interest in you and your work. I can only reiterate what I have said before, that we very highly appreciate all that you have done for us and we congratulate you and the *Morning Post* on the ability with which you have put forward the Russian news of the war and the Russian points of view. I received your telegram of the 26th in which you asked to have your name put at the head of your correspondence, and I replied as follows: 'Your request opens up serious question am writing.' The truth is that *The Times*, having abdicated its position as the premier journal of England, the *Morning Post* is now quite visibly taking its place, and some time before I received your telegram I came to the conclusion that as we were gradually taking up the position of the old *Times* I would revert to those features in the old *Times* which made it the best paper in England. One of the first decisions at which I arrived was that in future no permanent member of the staff should have his name put to anything he wrote for the paper, for I want the *Morning Post* to imitate the old *Times* in its anonymity, which had this great advantage: that everybody worked for the paper and looked upon the paper as a soldier looks upon his regiment. Therefore about six weeks ago I issued a circular to the staff saying I had come to this decision and expressing the hope that everybody would loyally accept it. I received only one protest and that came from a member of the staff who is only on the paper temporarily and for whose claims something could be said, since he has perhaps a right to some degree of publicity owing to the temporary nature of his engagement. But as long as he is in receipt of a salary from the paper he will be anonymous. I am sure you will agree with this decision. The *Morning Post* is on the upward tendency. It is taking the place which *The Times* only in its rosiest days took, and I shall use every endeavour to enhance its position. I know how loyal you are to whatever paper you may be serving and I am sure you will accept the ruling I have made with the same loyalty as other members of the staff. As a matter of fact, as you doubtless know, it does not militate against you really in any way, since everybody in Fleet Street and all the newspapers throughout the country know the name, and by this time no doubt the history of the Petrograd correspondent of the *Morning Post*.

I have read today your telegram about Russia and Constantinople, and I think this is a good opportunity for letting you know what I think of the whole question of Russia and ourselves. There is a section of English public opinion which has been, as I once wrote you before, pro-Zulu, pro-Arabi, pro-Boer, pro-Everything else except their own country. This section is noisy, but it has just about as much influence on public opinion as *Titbits*. They are the people who go about and talk with dread of the settling up after the war, and give their hearers to understand that once Germany is finished there opens up a vista of a new war with Russia. But you must not pay the slightest attention to this kind of talk, for it has no real basis in any sort of public opinion here. The pro-Everything else except their own people never had any power, but they always had a voice and a very strident one at that. Foreign observers have often mistaken this noise for public opinion, and they have invariably been mistaken. I think I can interpret to you pretty accurately what English public opinion is like now in regard to Russia. Let me begin by saying that one of our most prominent public men, a man whose influence is very great, said to me when he heard of the Turkish bombardment of the Russian Black Sea forts, 'Thank God, that settles the Constantinople question';[1] and that I think you will find is the opinion of the vast majority of Englishmen. Remember this: that there is a feeling of enormous gratitude towards Russia for her chivalrous intervention in east Prussia in the early days of the war when she was not altogether ready and when she suffered in order to help us in the west. We realise that now she has to fight on two fronts against Germany and Turkey, and we realise equally that this confounded Turkish question is not going to be settled by us but by Russia, and in our heart of hearts we are thankful. We hope that the days of enmity between Russia and ourselves are over for good and all, and I will tell you what is mainly the reason for it. There is no comparison to be made between the Russian temperament and the Prussian temperament. We feel, and have felt, that in the Prussian we have to deal with a cruel, ambitious, calculating, utterly unscrupulous foe, who wants to dominate the world. In the Russian we feel that we have to do with a nation that has all the instincts of generosity, a temperament very much like the French, full of enthusiasm, seeking for the light, and really anxious to forward the aims of civilisation. With Prussia we feel, and have felt, that she would like to put back the hands of the clock of civilisation. We also realise that this great war is the fire that is going to try nations, and those nations who cannot stand it must go under. Turkey might have saved herself, but I think you will find that the majority of people in England are very glad that Turkey has intervened, for it will give Russia an opportunity of once for all settling that eternal and infernal question. Of course, as regards Asia Minor there may be some points of difference, but I am perfectly sure that if the three Allies will at once set about taking in hand the settlement of these questions, there will be no difficulty whatever. There is not only good will, but actual rampant enthusiasm for Russia. You have to bear in mind one thing: this war is not a 'Mafficking' war.[2] We all feel it too deeply and too strongly. They do not even cheer the troops as they march through the streets. They do not shout or yell. No bells are rung for a victory. There is no outward sign of rejoicing or grieving; but it is England at its very best, silent, undemonstrative, but absolutely determined. You will therefore not get throughout this war any cheering or shouting or yelling either for Russia or against Russia; but that public opinion is solidly and overwhelmingly enthusiastic regarding Russia's splendid part in this war and absolutely determined that she shall reap the rewards of this war there can be no manner of doubt.

One word more, and that about yourself. Do not be too optimistic in your accounts. We can stand hard blows here. We know and appreciate all the difficulties of the Russians and we do not expect a victory every other day. We have been rather taken aback by the prognostications that a great part of the German Army has been surrounded and on the point of surrender, and in consequence the more sober communiqués and telegrams that are coming in have rather given the British public the idea that things are not as favourable as they really are. I would therefore suggest to you that you should err on the side of underestimating than over-estimating Russia's successes, unless, of course, they are undoubted. . . .

1. i.e. the future of Constantinople.
2. i.e. the Boer War.

36
H. A. Gwynne to Lady Bathurst, 7 December 1914

It is a pity the French have more or less whitewashed the Churchill adventure in Antwerp. But we must have patience to bide our time and tell the damning truth.

. . . It is the most difficult thing in the world at this time of national crisis to do the right thing. I am really nervous about the Navy because I think W. Churchill has no sort of capacity for the job of First Lord. Indeed I would prefer Fisher as First Lord (if he had a first class 1st Sea Lord) rather than the present state of things. What do you think his latest is? He has dismissed Admiral Savory who was Director of Naval Transports and the man who did the whole of the conveyance of the Expeditionary Force to France, and put in his stead a civilian. And why? Because Admiral Savory refused to take Lady Sarah Wilson's hospital without War Office suggestion. . . .[1]

1. Gwynne's informant was Savory's son-in-law, Captain D. A. Lynch, then on the War Office staff. According to Lynch, on 13 November Churchill had told Savory, whose appointment was due to expire on 1 December, that he would be replaced by Mr Graeme Thompson; on Savory's insistence, the War Office had been consulted about the sending of Lady Sarah Wilson (a daughter of the 7th Duke of Marlborough) and her private hospital to France, and Kitchener had refused permission. (See HAG/38 no. 2, IWM.)

37

H. A. Gwynne to Lady Bathurst, 9 December 1914

I think I have cured the French Government of any further attempts to favour *The Times*. I have had a long talk at the French Embassy and they are in full sympathy with us. I saw some of the despatches sent by the Embassy to their Government and I can assure you that there was nothing left out that I could have wished to be in.

Your theory that the murder of Franz Ferdinand and his wife was arranged is so novel as to take away one's breath. But the obvious preparations which the German Emperor made for war this year quite a long time ago tempts one to believe anything. . . .

I propose going next Wed. or Thursday.[1]

1. Going out again to France.

38

H. A. Gwynne to Lady Bathurst, 10 December 1914

The question of Admiral Savory was indeed an amazing case and before I took up the matter I heard what I considered both sides of the affair, i.e., I heard the Savory side through a son-in-law and the other side from a man in the Admiralty whom I know. They both agreed that it was a bad business. Last night, however, I met Captain Hall, who is Director of Naval Intelligence at the Admiralty,[1] and he said that Savory was no good at his job and that the whole of the admirable work that had been done in the transport of troops was accomplished by Mr. Graeme Thom[p]son. I am afraid, therefore, I shall have to let the matter drop.

As regards our Petrograd correspondent and his prognostications, I have written to him to-day to say that he must not be too optimistic and in fact I have advised him not to prophesy at all, as prophecy in journalism never pays. If one is wrong, people gird at you, and if one is right, it is forgotten. I do not think there is any danger of his giving away the Grand Duke's[2] plans, as all he sends is passed by the Russian Censor, and it is possible that some sentences in his telegrams are intended to deceive the Germans.

I hope my fellow Welshmen will turn out better than you expect.[3] They are very amenable to reason, though rather wild, like all Welshmen, when they are excited. . . .

1. Reginald William, later Admiral, Hall, DNI from October 1914.
2. The Grand Duke Nicholas, supreme commander of the Russian Armies.
3. A reference to recruiting and a Welsh Army Corps.

39

H.A. Gwynne to A. Bonar Law, 28 December 1914
(B. Law MSS 35/5/59)

I enclose you the private notes of Mr J. D. Irvine a member of my staff who has been in Ireland recently in the belief that you may find them of interest.

Enclosure in letter 39

Confidential

NOTES ON IRELAND AND THE WAR   19 December 1914
The object of these notes is to supplement five articles which appeared in the *Morning Post* on the respective dates, December 8, 9, 11, 15, and 17. They cover points and incidents which, having regard to the political truce and the progress of the war, it would be undesirable, and also, having regard to the Censorship, in many instances impossible to print.

I have endeavoured as far as possible to verify statements made to me, particularly in regard to German spies in Ireland, but direct proof is unattainable. At the same time the state of things I observed for myself convinced me that there has been reprehensible laxity in dealing with alien enemies – a state of things which still exists to some extent.

Position of the Nationalists
Leading Nationalists themselves admit that the appeal of Mr Redmond[1] and his colleagues for recruits to Lord Kitchener's Army has been 'in the nature of a disappointment'. The fallacy and inaccuracy of the figures of recruiting used by Mr Redmond in his speech at Tuam on the 6th of December have been publicly demonstrated, notably by the Nationalist organ, the *Irish Daily Independent*, which has the largest circulation in Ireland. Roughly, at the end of November 28,000 recruits had enlisted since the war began in the Province of Ulster and only 11,000 in the three Provinces of Leinster, Munster, and Connaught. Apart from the Sinn Fein movement, which has exercised a pernicious influence by its open pro-German and furious anti-British propaganda, widespread apathy and indifference prevail among the Nationalists of military age. Apologists account for this by pleading that Ireland is a poor country, that already she has sent to the Army nearly all the men who can be spared from Leinster, Munster, and Connaught; that in the rural districts especially the 'few young men remaining' are needed to till

the land and assist in the support of aged parents. The absurdity of these and other pleas is apparent. There are thousands of young men loafing about the country who, with the necessary training, would make excellent soldiers.

In the small towns and the rural areas young men who might otherwise join the Army are terrorised and threatened by the extremists, or, in the absence of threats, are jeered at as 'England's liverymen'. Parents who have been nurtured in the tradition of hatred for England tell their sons that 'England's war' is no affair of theirs, and in many cases the priests are either indifferent or openly hostile. They preach the doctrine that the first duty of Irishmen is to remain in Ireland and look after their own homes. I have talked with Nationalists who assured me that Mr Redmond and his party had no authority to pledge Irishmen to go abroad and fight in this war; and while the Nationalist Parliamentary Party has succeeded in capturing the machinery of the 'National Volunteers', there remains in most districts a hostile minority (in some instances a majority) which agitates against recruitment except for the purpose of establishing 'a National Army for service in Ireland'.

Since the meeting at the Dublin Mansion House addressed by the Prime Minister and Mr Redmond took place I have discovered no record of any gathering of Nationalists at which a resolution was passed directly urging men to join Lord Kitchener's Army. At the Tuam meeting Mr Redmond spoke to a resolution which congratulated him on the passing of the Home Rule Bill and calling on the Government to make further provision for breaking-up the grasslands in the West. It contained no reference whatever to recruiting.

A sinister feature of the situation is the appeals which are now made for funds to arm and equip the National Volunteers. Mr Redmond himself presided at a meeting in the Dublin Mansion House on December 15 called for the purpose of inaugurating a Fund 'to efficiently arm and equip the National Volunteers of Dublin City'. Subscriptions amounting to £642 were raised on the spot. No reference was made at this meeting to the War. At all Nationalist gatherings the Volunteers are described as existing for purely national purposes in Ireland, and it is notorious that an infinitesimal proportion of them have offered their services to the Imperial Government. In Dublin the response has been most meagre. In Belfast about one thousand have joined the Army on the urgent representations of Mr Devlin[2] as in some respects a set-off against the enlistment of 16,000 Ulster Volunteers in the Ulster Division. The Mansion House meeting was held after the Government Proclamation forbidding the sale of rifles and ammunition had been issued.

All appeals to Nationalists to enlist take the form of a reminder that the present Government has granted Home Rule to Ireland and that Irishmen must now show that they are united in Imperial sentiment with the British democracy. They are appeals not to patriotism but to political self-interest. The political truce is broken habitually by the Nationalist newspapers, the *Belfast News* distinguishing itself by its virulent diatribes and jeers at the Ulster Unionists and 'Carson's Army'. Great perturbation prevailed throughout Nationalist Ireland on a rumour that the Government were about to resort to some form of conscription. The Nationalist M.P.s were bombarded with indignant letters and telegrams, and in the South and West young men of military age made preparations to emigrate to the United States. A few had actually left before the reassuring news reached them that no compulsion was intended.

Mr Redmond's Authority Weakened

Mr Redmond's own friends speak of the famous speech delivered in the House of Commons on August 3, in which he pledged whole-heartedly Nationalist Ireland to the support of the war on the side of Great Britain, as in the nature of a 'bold experiment'. It was a distinct 'lead', and though the bulk of the supporters of the Nationalists in the country profess to have accepted it, action following on this pledge has been lamentably inadequate. Mr Redmond possesses nothing like the power that was wielded by Parnell[3] in the early Eighties. He has many active enemies, whom he calls wreckers of the principles of Nationalism, and his grip on the Nationalist organisation is relaxing. Mr Devlin, operating through the Ancient Order of Hibernians, is more powerful, but even he was unable to avert the open rupture which occurred at the Tullamore by-election, when Graham, an unofficial Nationalist, was elected in preference to Adams, the nominee of the official Convention. Adams had working on his side the whole party machinery, including the services of half a score of M.P.s. The following letter written by an elector and forwarded to me is of interest:

King's County, 12th December 1914

There is no revolt against Redmondism here, the successful candidate at the recent election being a life-long Nationalist and follower of Redmond, but there is a revolt against the choosing of members of Parliament by a Convention.

My butcher said to me: 'We might as well not have the franchise for all the use it has been to us for the last 30 years, this time we are determined to have a say in the matter.'

Mr Graham, the new member, is an elderly man, while Mr Adams, the chosen of the Convention, is young and hot-headed; so many preferred the man of experience.

Adams led a very violent cattle-drive[4] at Geashill on 15th November, with a view to increasing his popularity amongst the labouring class, but as they were unsuccessful and he and 45 of his followers were arrested, there was a great revulsion of feeling, those who formerly approved now blaming him bitterly for getting so many men into trouble. He and six others were sentenced at the Assizes yesterday. One man who struck the police with an iron bar getting 12 months and Paddy Adams and the other five getting six months each, all with hard labour.

These two circumstances – a desire to upset the Convention system – and the disinclination to be represented in Parliament by a cattle-driver, account for the election, for in politics there was not a pin of difference between the candidates. They are both local men, but Graham was the more popular of the two.

That is all the light I can throw on the matter. One feature of the election amused us greatly, which was that the priests in the constituency were fairly equally divided, and a considerable amount of vituperation they contributed to the proceedings. One informed an M.P. sent by Redmond to work for Adams, that only for the Irish Party they would have had Home Rule long ago. 'You and your party', said he, 'cheering the Boers in the House of Commons kept us back for years.'

The writer, I think, does not make sufficient allowance for the spirit of revolt, which, of course, is not against Redmondism as a synonym for Nationalism, but represents undoubtedly an intolerance of authority and a flouting of Mr Redmond personally which I know has aroused considerable concern in the minds of the Parliamentary party. The Sinn Feiners, of course, claim the result of the election as vindicating their condemnation of Mr Redmond's pro-English attitude. It will at least encourage other constituencies to reject the authority of Conventions, and the payment of £400 a year to members of Parliament will be a not unimportant factor in bringing into the field rival Nationalists who will insist on attempting to win this prize by going to the poll.

Sinn Feiners and the Spy System

At a Sinn Fein meeting which I attended in Dublin hints were given of money coming from America to aid 'the cause'. Despite the heavy blow dealt to Larkinism by the long Dublin strike and its ignominious collapse the extremists do not lack funds. I have already stated (*Morning Post*, December 8 and 9) that Larkin has bought in his own name within the past few months 'Liberty Hall' and the property surrounding it for a sum of £5500, of which £3500 was paid in cash at the time of the transfer. He is now pursuing a 'mission' in the United States.[5] There is very strong presumptive evidence that the money remitted from America really is German money, and that Sinn Feiners have been supplied with funds from that source for a long time past. It is a well-known fact that men who have 'no visible means of support' have been, during the past few months, 'flush of cash' and spending it freely. This applies in particular to one or two individuals in the county of Sligo. A prominent resident in that county informed me that mysterious strangers had been seen on several occasions, particularly during the month of October, on the shores of Sligo Bay, and while it is impossible to obtain any direct evidence, it is believed that mines were conveyed on board trawlers which subsequently proceeded north. The mines are said to have been packed in sections, placed inside boxes, and conveyed on board the boats, where the sections were screwed together and the mines thus made ready to be launched. These may have been the mines which caused a disaster off the northern coast of Ireland at the end of October.[6] It is believed, however, that mine-laying was carried on by vessels approaching from the east as well as from the west. A Swedish steamer, timber-laden, was detained in Belfast and the crew placed under arrest. A trawler from an English port also was strongly suspected, and she was seized and searched. In neither of these cases is the result known. One of the leading citizens in Belfast – a prominent Unionist – told me that he obtained information on the subject of mine-laying of a character so valuable and circumstantial that he proceeded at once to London and placed it before the Admiralty. He was personally thanked by the First Lord and Lord Fisher for his prompt patriotic action.

There were many spies of German nationality in the north and west of Ireland prior to the outbreak of the war. Not all of them have left the country or been interned. The proprietor of a certain well-known hotel is stated to be a German and to be assisted by two German waiters. The police say they have all Germans 'under observation' but there is a strong feeling in the community that more drastic measures are urgently called for. It is not enough to keep an eye on alien suspects. There are extremists in Ireland who, if they mean what they say, would not hesitate to help the enemy. Their Press has been suppressed, and their sayings and doings are ignored in the Irish papers. This has exasperated them and made them more vehemently seditious in their speeches as well as boastful on the subject of 'reprisals'.

1. John Redmond, Leader of the Irish Nationalisst Party at Westminster.
2. Joseph Devlin, Irish Nationalist, MP for Belfast 1900–18.
3. Charles Stewart Parnell, 1846–91, Irish Nationalist politician.
4. This expression was sometimes used to describe a form of electioneering.
5. James Larkin, Irish Nationalist, raiser of a civilian army with the motto:

'Neither King nor Kaiser, but Ireland'; purchaser of several buildings opposite Eden Quay in Dublin.

6. The loss of HMS *Audacious*. (See footnote 1, letter 31.)

40
H. A. Gwynne to Lady Bathurst, 31 December 1914

I have had a talk with Sir Alexander Henderson[1] who will most probably come in to control of the *Standard* tomorrow, owing to default in the payment of the debentures.

He suggested that I should put before you the following suggestion. (He was careful that it should be called a suggestion and not a proposal.) That the *Morning Standard* should be allowed to die but that the *Evening Standard* which is a first class paying property should be taken over by you and run by you as an evening paper.

The question of buying it could be arranged without your putting down any money i.e. he should have debentures in it – as long as the interest were paid the liability would be only his and not yours.

His chief reason for wanting you to take it was that he was afraid it might fall to Harmsworth.

I saw Bonar Law this morning and he said that I might tell you that he thought the idea worth considering and that he would be glad to talk it over with you or Lord Bathurst.[2]

This is the merest sketch of the scheme and I put it forward without comment regarding myself merely as a telephone wire.

I shall, of course, be very glad to give you my opinion for what it is worth, if you wish.

1. Unionist MP for St George's, Hanover Square, later Lord Faringdon; member of the council of the Anti-Socialist Union and a channel for the distribution of Unionist Party monies (see A. J. P. Taylor, *Beaverbrook*, p. 95; and K. D. Brown, 'The Anti-Socialist Union 1908–49', p. 250.)
2. That Law should see Gwynne had been suggested by the Unionist Party Chief Whip, A. Steel-Maitland, on 23 December, with the political objective of keeping the *Evening Standard* in the hands of the Unionists. (Steel-Maitland to Law, 18, 23 December 1914 (B. Law MSS 35/5/48, /54).)

41
H. A. Gwynne to Lady Bathurst, 4 January 1915

Now that you have decided[1] I can tell you what I thought of the proposal and that is that it is not a feasible one. As far as the money is concerned I don't believe you would have to risk a shilling but I think so strongly with you that we can and shall make the *M.P.* a success but only by giving all our thoughts and minds and energies to it. Any diversion of force would be very dangerous. But I felt that would be a case where you must make a decision off your own bat without any suggestion from me.

Don't be anxious about the future of the *M.P.* I may be a terrible optimist but if I have any sort of prescience whatever, it will be the foremost paper in England in 12 months and *the most prosperous*.

1. Against Sir Alexander Henderson's proposal.

42
H. A. Gwynne to Lady Bathurst, 11 January 1915

. . . I was sorry I was not in last night but I came in but was called out by the arrival of the Sub Chief of the General Staff,[1] who is now in England and wanted to see me about all sorts of complications that are cropping up.

About Haldane. It is true that the *Westminster*[2] has tried to defend him and has done it very cleverly. What is true is this. Haldane abolished about 30 battalions but created about 150 new Territorial so-called battalions. That is to say he took the old guns of the army, superseded by the new arms and handed them over to the Territorials. It was a swindle and a farce but he can, as a matter of pure arithmetic, claim to have a balance of 120 battalions. I am waiting for a favourable opportunity to go for him.

I am afraid you are too busy to read the *M.P.* very carefully or you would have seen that we have, in an article, attributed the real difficulty with freights to the shortage of labour at the docks. That is why in our leader on the Belgian Relief Commission we advocated the absorption of Belgian labour, which would not disturb the labour market in the slightest.

About the size of the paper I must write to you tomorrow at greater length. . . .

I feel, sometimes, that it is very hard on you that you should be worried to death with all the burden of a paper in time of war. I have had it frequently in my mind to make a suggestion to you. I am a heavy expense to the paper and I have felt that, now that it is running so well, I might without disadvantage leave it for a time. Suppose I go out to the front. I have horrible mental struggles with myself as to my clear duty to my country just now and at times I have felt that my experience and knowledge of war could be better utilised at the front. Indeed I am tired of saying to other men 'go! go!' while I remain in my armchair. After all one's life is but a small sacrifice to make. If we are beaten I really don't think I would want to live, and I feel sometimes that I could, in my small way, give a helping hand to victory. What do you think?

1. General Sir Henry Wilson. The 'complications' had to do with differences of opinion between Sir John French and Kitchener concerning the role of the New Armies. Gwynne went to see French on the 13th, and reported to Wilson afterwards. (See C. E. Callwell, *Field-Marshal Sir Henry Wilson*, vol. i, pp. 200–1.)

2. *Westminster Gazette*, edited by J. A. Spender.

43

H. A. Gwynne to Lady Bathurst, 13 January 1915

. . . Frankly what I feel is this. I know I am doing a little for the country in the *M.P.* but I am *not* risking my life. When the time comes to go forward, my little influence with the Commander in Chief may persuade him that to move forward it is necessary to sacrifice many many lives. Now, it is utterly distasteful to me to urge the bold and costly stroke, sitting upon an armchair and knowing that I have nothing more to fear than an apocryphal and utterly improbable Zeppelin raid. May I be allowed to go out when the advance takes place, if I can get permission?

As regards the size of the papers, do believe that I am not extravagant. The aim of all my endeavours on the *M.P.* is to produce the very best paper I can consistent with the very strictest economy. But I confess to an overweening desire to make the *M.P. the* paper of England now while the war is on. A war is such an opportunity. I do believe (without optimism) that we are all making the *M.P.* the foremost paper. . . .

44

H. A. Gwynne to Lady Bathurst, 15 January 1915

Your letter received today has quite convinced me where my duty lies and that is *here*. But you will I hope not misunderstand what I have been going through. Here I am, fit sound and able to walk men of 20 off their legs. I sit in an office and tell the public rich and poor that their duty lies at the front. 'At the front' means death or disablement or at any rate danger. And what danger do I run? It seems cowardly to me and yet I know you are right. But it is hard to sit still while other people are dying. Yet I *know* you are right and this is the last you'll hear of it all.

Your letter made me feel a perfect beast. Here have I been worrying you when my chief job is to save you from worry. Perhaps it is all due to influenza or indigestion and after the weekend's rest I shall see things quite in their right light. . . .

45

H. A. Gwynne to Lady Bathurst, 20 January 1915

. . . I dread the idea of a strike and they threaten one if Belgian labour is employed. Besides Belgian labour is so small that it would be of very little avail. The only course I can see is for the Government to decide that the matter is one of national urgency and unload the ships with the aid of the military. Our staff is like yourself, afraid of nobody but, believe me, one has to walk warily in this question or we'd get organised labour on its hind legs. Personally I hope it will, for the nation is in no mood to stand nonsense but I want the offence to come from them.

I am rewarded by my decision to get out of my mind all thoughts of going to the front by an invitation to lay my ideas on the war before the Cabinet. I will send you a copy of what I have said tomorrow.

46

Memorandum to the Cabinet by H. A. Gwynne,
22 January 1915[1]

In a few days six months will have elapsed since the beginning of the war and both in point of time and in point of the actual posture of affairs, it is worth while to review the situation both as it has been, how it is now, and in what direction it may undergo a change. A brief but accurate account of what has taken place is that Germany, after six months attempt, has failed in her original plan of campaign owing to the speed with which Russia has mobilised. Instead of crushing France first while containing the Russians, she has been able to do neither of these things. The German army holds practically the whole of Belgium and a fair slice of the north east of France. She is put on the defensive by the Russians in Poland and in East Prussia, and it looks as if the only mobile operation possible must lie in the direction of the Hungarian Plain, where Russia can strike on the weak spot in the Germanic combination and make a change much to the advantage of the Allies. Germany's original plans have failed and we have no means of knowing what plan she is substituting for the original failure. By attempting to put oneself into the position of the German General Staff, we may perhaps be able to see what plans they think might have a probability of success.

The State of Germany

Admitting the first failure, the German General Staff can with justice boast that if the Allies are holding them, they are making no great progress. The position in Russia is rapidly coming to resemble the position in Flanders and France: i.e. it approaches nearer a deadlock than anything we have yet seen in war. The German Headquarters have to realise another thing: that the longer the deadlock lasts, the worse it is for them, for every day Germany is being subjected to an economic pressure which in the long run must tell. I do not for one moment endorse the opinions of those who think that the economic pressure has already made itself felt to a great extent. In some respects undoubtedly it has, but in no vital point. Once the financial world realises what we all hope to be the fact, that Germany not only cannot win but must lose, then immediately economic pressure becomes the dominant factor; for it seems to me to be incontrovertible that Germany is now living entirely on her credit, not merely her financial credit, but her credit as a victorious Power, or, at any rate, a nation that can hold its own. For this reason Germany has not taken the sound strategic step of retiring to the Rhine and holding it with a small force, and dealing blows at her enemies on the East and her potential enemies on the South East. Such a course it seems to me is the one that would bring Germany nearer to a 'Stale-mate Peace' which, I imagine, is now the most she hopes for. But unfortunately for her she has not prepared her people for such a move and she knows that economic pressure will really begin to be felt as soon as she moves back either at the point of the Allies' bayonets or in obedience to sound strategy.

The Pressure of Policy on Military Operations

We must bear in mind that the German General Staff is now, owing to faults of its own government, unable to work on purely military lines. Its moves and operations have to be governed by political and economic motives. Limited as it is, therefore, by other than purely military considerations, having the knowledge that a move back would be probably her end, and knowing that the utmost she can expect out of the war now is a 'Stale-mate Peace', let us look at her probable action. She is enormously strong in a military sense. Her military resources are untouched, for Germany has not been invaded. It is true she suffers from a scarcity of some metals, such as copper, but I daresay that this lacking is not altogether vital. She therefore is faced with a problem, partly military, partly political, and partly economic, and it seems to me that the only solution of the various phases of this problem can be found by sticking to what she has: by making her field fortifications so strong as to render any operations of the Allies more in the nature of an investment of a town than of mobile military operations. With such a plan she can hope that at some time or other the Allies will attempt to break through this barrier, and will lose so heavily that a counter-attack may be possible with some chances of success.

Great Britain's Part in the War

We would do well, therefore, to make up our minds that the future operations of war are going to be in the nature of a siege; but we can, at the same time, with justice believe that if we can break through their lines either in Poland and Galicia, or in Flanders and France, and force them back to their second line, the end of the war is very nearly in sight. Great Britain's part in this war lies in the western area, and we have to consider how best we are to help break through the line, or, if that is impossible, how best we can use our troops for the destruction of the enemy. In this respect the issues narrow themselves down to two: Can we help our French Allies to break through the line, without incurring such excessive losses as would render a counter-attack by the Germans a possible, and, perhaps, profitable operation? Or, if we cannot, should we not try to use our Army elsewhere? I will deal with the first of these two problems: Is it possible to break through the German line without such excessive losses as would render us liable to a dangerous counter-attack?

Breaking through the Line

One of our foremost soldiers now with the British army in France told me that he calculated that an attempt in present circumstances to break through the line would cost us, roughly, a man a yard. As the German lines in front of us are five miles wide, it is easy to calculate what our losses would be, even on a narrow front; and certainly with the forces and the implements of war now at our disposal out there, this would be an operation of war where success would be bought so dearly that it would not be sound tactics or strategy to attempt it.

A War of Wits

How are we then to achieve this object? It seems to me that in these siege operations, which are quite new to us, though in a way not quite unexpected by the Germans, and certainly more or less familiar to the Russians, we shall have, if we are to break through, to blow our way through: i.e. by means of high explosive, heavy guns, every sort of mechanical, chemical, and other scientific device, render it impossible for human beings to live in an area five miles by ten; for if we are to break through we must be on a broad front of ten miles. That, if I may say so, is not so much a military problem as a scientific problem, and it seems to me that we are going about it in quite the wrong way. To relegate this task to the ordinary machinery of the War Office is to restrict the powers of the country enormously. The Ordnance people at the War Office are admirable, but naturally they are tied by years of tradition, and it is perhaps unfair to demand of them work which is outside the range of their duties. For my part I would not neglect a single man of chemical or any other scientific experience, and I would harness to our great war machine the whole of the scientific thought of the country. It should be organised as well as we would organise a military unit. Money should be spent upon experiments so as to encourage these men to put their brains at the service of the Government. I would give them that problem of breaking through a line ten miles by five and rendering human life impossible in that area. If they cannot solve it, so much the worse for us; but at least they should be given the opportunity. At present our scientific genius is dissipated because it is not organised, and I would lay it down that the organisation of the scientific men of this country should be undertaken at once.

A Change of Venue
This method of blowing a way through the German line is not, of course, the only method. We may find it expedient to sacrifice 30,000 or 40,000 men and break through with the help of such ordnance and such appliances as we now possess. If that fails, we are no worse off than before, but the Germans would have the advantage of repelling our attack, which no doubt would be to them a matter of considerable importance inasmuch as it would strengthen their *morale*. If the Government in its military consultations, come to the conclusion that the British army can do little or nothing except hold a part of the French line and that it might with advantage be employed elsewhere, there are of course several alternatives. But before any step is taken in this direction, it would be wise for those who direct our military policy to bear in mind that the withdrawal of the British troops from the line, even for service elsewhere, would have a very injurious effect upon Belgian opinion, and indeed it might create complications which it would be difficult to compensate. Another point is that the withdrawal of the British force from that line would be an open acknowledgement of the fact that England considered it impossible to break through the German fortifications; and that

again would be an advantage to the enemy. All projects for moving the British force from one part of the French line to another seem to me to be based on altogether wrong conceptions. The German works are no stronger in front of us than they are in the Argonne or at the Yser, or in Alsace. The dislocation and waste and effort involved in the changes of bases that would have to follow a change in our position in the line do not seem to give any advantages that would outweigh the disadvantages and the trouble and loss that would ensue. This, however, would not affect a project to take over the French lines lying between us and the Belgians, since it would save a great deal of cross-transport behind the line. At the same time, it has to be borne in mind that if such a movement should be a prelude to an attempt to bend back the extreme German right, it would have many disadvantages. Such a mistake was made by the German General Staff. If instead of trying to outflank us at Ypres and along the Yser they had broken through the lines somewhere about Arras, all the French and Belgian forces to the north of them would have had to retreat to the sea or surrender.

Other Possible Projects

If the military operations continue to be in the nature of a stalemate, and we have failed to break through their line, then I certainly think that the Government should discuss the advisability of withdrawing our force and using it elsewhere, not necessarily in France or Belgium. In such a case, of course, several places present themselves as likely spots. We could imitate the Russians and bring pressure to bear upon the weakest spot in the Germano-Austrian combination, which is Hungary; but I have yet to know how it would be possible to transport troops until Pola, or Fiume, or Trieste is taken. That operation would not be an easy one. Besides which, if Romania comes in, the Romanian army, acting in conjunction with the Russian force moving from Bukovina, would exercise a pressure which ought to be sufficient. Denmark has always appeared to me to be the ideal place to land troops, and I presume that Denmark would come in with us if we could guarantee that we would land half a million troops there. If we could ensure, which we ought to do quite easily, that the Kattegat would be immune from hostile raids, by shutting up the Great Belt and the Little Belt, as well as the Sound – none of them difficult naval operations – we could secure a footing in Denmark and in the islands which would force the Germans to reduce their troops either on the Polish and Austrian line or in Flanders and France. We could also by means of submarines and small craft generally so threaten the Kiel entrance that the Russian fleet would be able to operate with some degree of safety along the northern coast of Germany. In fact a glance at the map will show that by means of mines we could keep the German fleet locked up in Kiel Bay and so gain the great strategical advantage of knowing that they could only come out on one side.

The Question of Hungary

Meanwhile I think we might with profit to ourselves take some notice of the Independent Party in Hungary. I do not for a moment pretend to imagine that they are able to stand up against Tisza[2] and the Government; and probably a good many of their pretensions are grossly exaggerated; but rightly handled, the Independent Party in Hungary could be a direct menace to Austria and might help to bring about the debacle which I am sure will first show itself in Austria–Hungary.

1. A copy of this was sent separately to Balfour, who had been invited to attend meetings of the War Council in November 1914, to the distress of some Unionists. (See Long to Law, 25 November 1914 (Long MSS 62404).)
2. Prime Minister of Hungary.

47

H. A. Gwynne to General Sir Henry Wilson, 7 February 1915 (HAG/35 no. 4, IWM)

It was more than good of you to take the trouble to read and comment on the stuff I sent you. I don't think I shall publish it after reading your opinions.

My news is scanty and rather gossipy for all real news is with you over there. The country is settling down into its stride and the Government can, I feel sure, make many more demands on its patriotism without fear of disappointment. There are various peace sections showing their heads now and again. They are only interesting inasfar as they show the possibilities of a real split in the Radical ranks when the time comes to get down to details. I think I told you that Lloyd George's idea was to give Germany Asia Minor!

There is a plot on (how far it is likely to be successful I don't know) to shift Haldane, put the Jew Isaacs[1] on the Woolsack and put a fellow countryman of my own (Sam Evans)[2] into the job of L[ord] C[hief] J[ustice], filling his place with Ellis Griffith. The blasted Radical leopard can't change his dirty spots even in war time.

The military pundits continue to discuss the Servian adventure. It is well to bear in mind that the proposal is really a scheme to cover Grey's incompetent handling of Bulgaria. He has flattered and cajoled instead of speaking plainly. There is only one thing to say to Bulgaria and that is that her neutrality is insufficient and that if she wants anything she must fight for it. I really do not see why she should be impressed by a British Army Corps or soon by two. Besides that Salonika–Nish railway is a very dicky thing to trust to and there's not a damn loaf of bread or pound of meat in the country. I don't want to see a second Walcheren expedition.[3] And, besides all this, where are we to get the guns, gunners & ammunition for another two Corps?

Our friend J. F[rench] seems to be getting himself into bad odour over here with some of the people who have authority. His mad and unnecessary hatred for K[itchener], so often & so openly expressed, does him harm. Besides being injudicious, it is positively dangerous because if it comes to a cat and dog fight K. will win. I told him that when he was over here. There are too a lot of uncomfortable rumours about his American friend.[4] People have no confidence in him and they do not like the idea of having an alien so friendly with the Commander in Chief.

I hear that Winston has been out again. I wonder what treason he has been concocting.[5] He it is, I imagine, who fans and encourages F.'s animosity against K. It is such a pity. All of us who really like and admire F. are depressed about him. His line of country is comparatively speaking so easy – go ahead with his job & think of nothing else.

B[onar] L[aw] returns tomorrow. I hope you have seen him out there. He is desperately keen to do something for you. We all feel *most keenly* that political influence has been brought to bear against your military career.[6] It's damnable & we all feel like swearing. But we might do more harm than good by showing any form of active sympathy.

The Russians are holding their own in Poland & seem really to have given the Germans a smack. I still look to Austria–Hungary to be our war barometer and I watch it pretty closely. The Hungarian Independence Party is the bar of mercury. When the Russians are pressing they are regular enthusiasts for complete Independence; when the Russians are checked, they become the quiet tools of Tisza. Personally I think Tisza will win out with the Independent Party with him. After all, I imagine that he will go hard for predominance as against Independence. But all the Hungarian motives are complex as regards internal affairs but as a barometer Austria–Hungary are well worth studying.

I suppose you are still ding-donging at the trenches. I don't see what can be done without a vast amount of high explosives. The significance of the failure of the German attack with 3½ Corps 600 guns on a front of about ten miles has not I am sure escaped you. I wonder what Foch–Joffre think of it?

1. Sir Rufus Isaacs, Lord Chief Justice.
2. Sir S. T. Evans, Solicitor-General, 1908–10, President of the Divorce Court.
3. An unsuccessful attempt in August 1799 to employ the British Army on the Continent, Lord Chatham commanding. (See P. Mackesy, *The Strategy of Overthrow*, London, 1974.)
4. George Moore, who had made a fortune in American railways.
5. Churchill had visited French in early December 1914, to discuss the possibility of an offensive to recover Ostend and Zeebrugge. Such an operation was vetoed in Cabinet on 7 January, raised again by Churchill on 13 January, and finally dropped on 28 January 1915. (See A. J. Marder, *From the Dreadnought to Scapa Flow*, vol. ii, pp. 197–8.)
6. In his reply of 8 February Henry Wilson wrote '. . . being very human I do not propose to forget Squiff [Asquith], and his curious, and to me, quite unnecessary hatred & fear of me'. (HAG/35 no. 5, IWM.)

48
H. A. Gwynne to A. Bonar Law, 26 March 1915 (B. Law MSS 36/6/36)

There has been a good deal of talk about Coalition lately. I don't know how far the idea has gone but I thought I would like to dictate a few ideas on the subject which I send you herewith.

I hope to see you next week if you are not going away for Easter.

Memorandum on the question of a Coalition Government
For some little time past there has been talk both in responsible and in irresponsible quarters of the advantages of a Coalition Government, and I have reason to believe that the matter has been discussed in Government circles. It seems to me that before the Unionist party commits itself to any decision in the question, it should consider it from two points of view, (a) from the point of view of the nation's welfare, and (b) that of the party's welfare.

The National Aspect
Considering the question from the purely national point of view, the first thought that occurs is, the necessity for a Coalition must be expressed by the Government, for the Government alone is responsible for the carrying on of this war, and they alone have the knowledge of what is going on sufficiently to decide whether they themselves are able or unable to bring the conflict to a satisfactory

conclusion within a reasonable space of time. If the members of the Government think that it is quite essential for the welfare of the country that they should be helped at this grave crisis by the Opposition, then I would lay it down as a preliminary that they should openly and frankly say so. It may be argued that it would be unreasonable to expect that a Government, which after all is a party Government, should go to an Opposition and make a confession of weakness. My answer to that is that they are the sole judges of the needs of the present situation especially as regards the war, and if they think that the war can be brought to a successful conclusion only by the active help of the Opposition, it is their bounden duty to say so.

If such a request for our co-operation is not made, it seems to me that it does not lie with us to make any offer beyond that which has already been made, namely, loyal support of the efforts of the Government to carry on the war; and I would suggest that as a preliminary to any further talk on this subject that those members of the Government who seem anxious for a Coalition should put forward a definite request for help. It would in my opinion be impossible to refuse such a frank request, though I think we would be quite justified in making it a condition of acceptance that the Coalition should be merely an *ad hoc* Coalition, to be dissolved at the end of the war. Such a request being made, let us examine it in its details. The Departments chiefly concerned in carrying on this war are the Admiralty, the War Office, the Foreign Office, and the Treasury, and in a lesser degree the Colonial Office, the Board of Trade and the Home Office. I cannot imagine the present Government, when inviting the help of the Opposition, offering to the Opposition the position either of Chancellor of the Exchequer, Minister for War, or First Lord of the Admiralty. Therefore the influence of the Opposition would be limited to Departments which are of secondary importance only in the carrying on of the war, and the conduct of the war would remain in the same hands as at present. Indeed I would go farther and say that although the appointment of some members of the Opposition to these secondary offices might help the Government, yet it could not materially influence the conduct of the war.

There is another aspect of the question, too, which would have to be taken into consideration. I am now discussing the question of a Coalition Government purely from the point of view of the national interest. If a Coalition were formed it would result in the displacement of a number of members of the present Government from their offices to make way for members of the Opposition. This displacement would most likely result in the establishment of a cave which might in its turn develop into a 'Stop the war' party. It would be idle to shut one's eyes to the fact that there is a vast number of pro-Germans in the country, and an even greater number of people who think that our task will end when we have driven the Germans out of Belgium; and even a greater number still who are honestly frightened of the great strength of Russia and do not therefore wish Germany to be too much enfeebled. The people holding these three opinions could very well form a formidable 'Stop the war' party; and if the formation of an *ad hoc* Coalition Government should lead to the formation of an anti-war party, then it would not be in the national interests.

When one goes into the details of such a scheme, one is confronted more and more with practical difficulties. Up to the present the Cabinet do not seem to have been able to influence Lord Kitchener's policy and the Admiralty's policy, especially in regard to munitions of war and the utilisation of the business talent of the country. Indeed I would go farther and say that there are indications that the Cabinet have given up to Lord Kitchener all kinds of control which they ought to have kept in their own hands, and that precedent being established I do not see how a Coalition Government can be of any practical use. The truth is that for good or for ill Lord Kitchener is trusted absolutely by the people, and we must put up with any mistakes he may make, for no Cabinet, be it Coalition, Liberal, or Conservative, could afford to quarrel with him; and I do not see how the advent of three or four members of the Opposition could alter the situation in this particular respect.

The Party Aspect
Regarded from the party point of view, it seems to me that the disadvantages of a Coalition far outweigh the advantages. In the first place, we could not coalesce with the Government unless we set matters right in Ireland, unless we gave satisfaction to churchmen in the matter of the Welsh Church,[1] and unless we came to some definite agreement as regards a tariff. In all these matters it seems to me that the Government are too far committed to go back, and even if they did agree the Coalition Government which would follow would be feeble inasmuch as it would weaken the Conservative party and break up the Liberal party. In reply to this it might be urged that this is exactly what is wanted, namely, that the progress of the Conservative party will depend to a great extent on the defection of the moderate Liberal, and a Coalition such as is now being discussed would bring this about. This may be true; but there is no reason to expedite a state of things which although it might place us in power for a few years, would be disastrous to the country; for His Majesty's

Opposition would then consist of the Labour party, the Socialists, and the extreme Left of the Liberal party, and we should end up with a class division in politics of the 'Have-nots' versus the 'Haves'. Mr Lloyd George was the prophet of class warfare and it seems to me he is now reaping what he has sown, and he is therefore anxious to lean upon the more solid part of the population in order to save himself from the consequences of his past action. It is not for the Conservative party to get into power by any means. That is not the only aim and object of the party. Its aim is to carry out those principles to which it is pledged, and any coquetting with the Government in the hope of securing a few offices, would irretrievably destroy the party. I think that every day in this war we have increased our power by the admirable attitude we have adopted towards the Government and the ready aid we have given them; but to go beyond these bounds would seem to me to be unnecessary from a national point of view and disastrous from a party point of view.

1. A bill for the disestablishment of the Welsh Church was placed on the statute book on 15 September 1914, suspended for twelve months or for the duration of the war. It finally came into operation on 31 March 1920.

49
H. A. Gwynne to General Sir Henry Wilson, 12 April 1915 (HAG/35 no. 8, IWM)

As I told you in my last letter, I have been meditating against you for some time a really long letter, and I am sending it herewith. If you have time to read it, do. If not, throw it into the wastepaper basket. It will contain nothing but vain imaginings on my part, to which you can attach the value they deserve. I am going to speak to you quite openly and tell you one or two things that have happened since I saw you last, and perhaps some of the information I can give you may not be useless to you. In the first place, it is very unlikely that I shall receive any further invitations to Head Quarters. I think that our mutual friend[1] is under the impression that I am a Kitchener-ite and an anti-French, though why he should think so I do not know. I do know that in all my conversations with him, and in all my letters to him, I have urged upon him the necessity for working in cordial agreement and cooperation with the War Minister, whatever opinion he might hold as to his talents or his tendencies. Unfortunately, however, like the hero in the play, 'I have been thwarted by a villain', for I am afraid that J. F[rench]'s friend, Moore, who has seen that I have no opinion of him either financially or politically or socially, or in any other way, has, quite rightly from his point of view, told J. F. that I am against him and all for K[itchener]. This is mere gossip and may not interest you, but, at the same time, I do feel that the man in question is a dangerous friend in every sense of the word, and being a friend of our mutual friend, I cannot tell you how sorry I am that he has allowed himself to be so completely influenced by him. The man is a wrong 'un from beginning to end and will certainly land the Commander in Chief in trouble. I hear on every side talk and rumours and nasty tittle-tattle, nearly always connected with the name of Moore, which show to me that J.F. quite undeservedly, is losing reputation with people here; and the reason is quite simple: it is that he has allowed Moore to be a press agent, and people here with experience of people who try to make a reputation by employing press agents, are beginning to suspect J.F. of being unworthy of his great position, merely because they think he has employed a press agent, which I know to be quite untrue. I am really most concerned about this, because take it by & large, J.F. is the biggest soldier we have got, and if he would think nothing whatever about his reputation, but devote every moment of his day to thinking and scheming how best he can knock out the Germans in front of him, he would be the biggest man in England. However, it is not my business to tell him all this, so I calmly await, though not without misgivings, the imminent and certain downfall of our friend Moore. All I pray for is that he will not bring down J.F. with him.

Having cleared off the personal aspect, I now can talk to you about things in general, and I will in the first place give you as clear an outline as I can of what is taking place here. This British Government of ours, after eight months of the war, have suddenly tumbled to the fact that K., although he is quite a good organiser and is a great driving force, is not a superman, and his experience in the East, not having fitted him altogether for the conduct of the biggest war this country has seen, he has, to put it bluntly, made several mistakes which may have a seriously delaying effect upon the war. Rifles, S[mall] A[rms] ammunition, Shells, High Explosives, are all wanting, and the rate of progression in their manufacture has not been what it should have been. We should have had at least a 10% increase each month in geometrical progression so that we should now have something like 100% over what we were producing at the beginning of the war; instead of which our increase in rifles has been about 15%, which I think is ridiculous. The Ministers, who, from the moment that you drove von Kluck in front of you on the Marne, have looked upon this war very much as a second South African war, allowed all this to go on without protest, and indeed apparently without knowledge. Suddenly Lloyd George, under the influence of some sensible man whose name I do not know, sits down and writes to the Cabinet a most pessimistic report regarding the progress of the war and the ultimate result.[2] Being a creature of mere impulse and without much reasoning, he has run this horse for all it is worth, and at the Treasury I am told there exists at the present moment a feeling of intense pessimism which did not exist in the early stages of the war when the German Army were driving you back on to Paris. Pessimism is a most excellent driver, but like everything else, it must not be indulged in too heavily, for it leads to such exhibitions of nonsense as Lloyd George's when he said that we had three enemies, Germany, Austria and Drink, and of the three Drink was the worst. Of course, not believing a word these fellows say, I am beginning to think that the whole thing is a concocted plan to run a sort of temperance scheme in time of war, but I would not like to say this definitely at the present moment until I have seen a bit more behind the scenes.

The Dardanelles is the greatest horror of the lot. Antwerp was bad enough in all conscience, but the Dardanelles is worse, for we were all given to understand that with the dismissal of Louis of Battenberg the conduct of operations at the Admiralty was altogether changed; that here was a great, strong man, Fisher, coming in, who would stand no nonsense and would insist that the expert's point of view should prevail. Unfortunately, the exact opposite has happened. I believe the man who originated the idea of the Dardanelles scheme was Hall, who is now D[irector of] N[aval] I[ntelligence]. Perhaps you may recall him if I tell you that he goes by the name of 'Blinker' Hall. For some time he has been urging the forcing of the Dardanelles as a Naval operation quite feasible provided always that it was undertaken simultaneously with the landing of a large military force.[3] At last he persuaded the Admiralty to study the question seriously, and they did, and came to the conclusion that it was a feasible thing and not only feasible, but not very difficult, provided all the ships wore crinolines and, especially, that a military force should be landed at the same time. Winston gets to hear of this and having no military knowledge whatever, but being at the same time a man of dramatic instincts who looks upon every phase of this war as an opportunity for him to appear before the footlights, he rushes the thing through. Crinolines would take six weeks to make: then no crinolines. Floating mines could be stopped in some mysterious way of his own, which he never divulged. A large force would take two months: another delay in the dramatic coup. In vain Jackie [Fisher] and his Board protested against the supersession of the crinolines and the military force. He carried this precious War Committee of the Cabinet with him, and I am told on authority that I can absolutely trust, that he gave the Committee to understand that on this question the Board of Admiralty were with him. You know the rest of the story. Three ships lost, very little achieved, and the Germans and the Turks put on their guard for all time. Now Jonnie Hamilton[4] is cruising somewhere about there with a large force, with an awful job in front of him, for how he is going to land at Enos – I believe it is in that neighbourhood – even under the guns of a very powerful fleet, with the Germans waiting for him I do not quite know, and to tell you the truth I am looking daily for news of a disaster from that quarter. The *Queen Elizabeth* is at Devonport. Being a new ship she has developed some defects which want making good, and I do not suppose they will go forward with the operations again until she is back.[5] Altogether it is a most hopeless business and entirely due to the hotheadedness of a man who ought never to have been in charge of that Department.

We are expecting daily to hear the news of our French friends breaking through the line, and if that happens, we expect big developments, for taken in conjunction with the Russian activity on the East, the Germans are stereotyped as regards the amount of forces they can afford east and west. If anything indeed they would have to take from the west to the east rather than from the east to the west. From what I hear privately, the Austrian Army is beginning to show signs of the wear and tear of the campaign, and the Germans no longer hide from them or from themselves the fact that they can count upon it to very little extent. The Hungarians are fighting well and will I believe put up a good defence, but the Austrian Army is rotten because the best officers have gone, and the next lot are worse than anything in the field now.

We have been very much concerned about the German attitude towards Holland. It would seem that they went out of their way to irritate the Dutch into hostile action. I fail entirely to understand the reasons underlying this; but the nature of the note sent by Bernstorff, the German Ambassador in America, to the U.S. Government is beginning to give me cause to think that there may be some motive for all this. I have always said, and I remember telling you, that the weak spot of the German position was that they had not prepared their people for anything like a retreat. They have been able to explain away their failure to take Paris and Warsaw and Calais by saying that they have fixed their grip firmly on the territory which they now hold and nothing on earth could move them. That I am told is what the ordinary man in the street in Germany believes. Now if they are going to be moved, as in my opinion they think they are, it will be very difficult to explain away matters to their own people. Besides which, I am sure that they do not want any of their territory invaded, and they are looking round for a good reason to give their people why they should conclude peace now on as favourable terms as they can get. Wherefor [*sic*] I think it may be their policy to make enemies of Holland, Denmark perhaps, and of the United States so that the Dynasty in Germany can turn round to the people and say, 'There, you see we have got the whole world against us, and it would be sheer madness to fight against such a combination as that.' This may sound rather fantastic, but I wish you would turn it over in your mind and let me know what you think.

I enclose you a cartoon from today's *Express* which I think is one of the funniest I have ever seen. K. in the temperance pond inviting the Prime Minister to take the plunge. By the way, the latter gentleman has been letting himself go very much of late and his example has been followed by his wife, who was so drunk in a private house about ten days ago that she was sick in the drawing room and on the stairs going away. Really such things as these make one blush for England, because if the top is rotten, the rest must be pretty bad; and yet there is not a Liberal paper, though they all know these facts, who will get up and tell the truth. . . .

1. Sir John French.
2. 'Suggestions as to the Military Position', memorandum by Lloyd George, 1 January 1915. (See D. Lloyd George, *War Memoirs*, vol. i, pp. 219–22.)
3. Hall was a believer, together with Sir Edward Grey and Lord Kitchener, that the arrival of the British fleet at Constantinople would produce a revolution in Turkey. Hall was also engaged, in the first half of February, on a scheme to buy Turkey out of the war for the sum of £4 million. (See A. J. Marder, *From the Dreadnought to Scapa Flow*, vol. ii, p. 217, and *From the Dardanelles to Oran*, pp. 29–32.)
4. General Sir I. S. M. Hamilton, GO Commander in Chief Mediterranean and Inspector-General Overseas Forces, 1910–15.
5. HMS *Queen Elizabeth*, with eight 15-inch guns, took part in the bombardment of the Dardanelles forts on 19 February; she was to be involved in the Allied landings on the Gallipoli Peninsula on 25 April 1915.

50
H. A. Gwynne to Lady Bathurst, 15 April 1915

. . . Whatever French's faults are (and I know a good many of them) the accusation of having ladies out to the front is not one of them. He is most particular and has sent back in the most ruthless way any woman who attempts to break through to Headquarters. Several have tried to – one, a Duchess, actually got there but was sent back by French who was in a furious temper with her. As for Lady ——, she has not left England during the war so that is another false accusation. . . .

51

H. A. Gwynne to Lady Bathurst, 18 April 1915

What has happened out in the Near East (I do not think it was in the Dardanelles) is that a large landing party of marines got ashore but was badly mauled losing 25%. The rest were withdrawn at night.

I do not like the expedition at all. It is a mad Churchillian scheme. But I will state all my objections in a letter I am writing to Mr Asquith tomorrow and of which I will send you a copy.

The General commanding the 4th Corps is Rawlinson.[1] Davies,[2] commanding the 8th Division was at one time sent back but he is now restored since the blame does not lie with him.

The Prime Minister has not taken the pledge because if he did he would die. Wherefore he should be urged to take the pledge.

The King, on Friday, talking to Billy Lambton said 'I've been sold a pup over this drink question'.[3]

1. Lieutenant-General H. S. Rawlinson.
2. Major-General F. J. Davies.
3. This relates to Lloyd George's scheme for the purchase by the state of the liquor trade. The scheme fell through, but not before the King had taken a pledge of total abstention. No one joined His Majesty on this particular wagon. Lambton was an ADC to the King, and Military Secretary to Sir John French.

52

H. A. Gwynne to H. H. Asquith, 22 April 1915

In the course of the present war I have once or twice submitted to you letters on aspects of the war on which it was difficult or impossible to touch in a newspaper, but which were important enough in my eyes to merit being put before you. I think the position in the Dardanelles is such as to warrant my submitting to you again some observations which may be worthy of your attention.

THE DARDANELLES EXPEDITION
The expedition against the Dardanelles which culminated in the loss of three warships has never, I must confess, aroused my enthusiasm. The objections to it are numerous, but two are outstanding and I venture to put them before you.

THE OBJECTIONS — POLITICAL
It is always a bad plan to mix politics with strategy, but there are exceptions to this as to other rules. I will discuss at present the dash

81

on the Dardanelles from the point of view of its political effect upon the Balkan States. Frankly I cannot conceive anything more likely to cause dissatisfaction and nervousness among the Balkan States than this attempt to take the Dardanelles and occupy Constantinople. To Greece the capture of Constantinople can be nothing else but a matter of embarrassment, for the question of its ultimate ownership is bristling with difficulties for that country. Bulgaria can hardly be expected to get enthusiastic over a change which might cost her Adrianople, which she regards as the prize she is to get out of the war. In this connection it is well to bear in mind that military experts consider that in order to hold Constantinople it is essential to possess Adrianople, and it is difficult to believe that Russia would be satisfied with a frontier running along the Chatalja lines. Romania is deeply interested in the question of the Bosphorus and the Dardanelles and could hardly be expected to view with much cordiality a change in the ownership of this channel, which is so vital to her sea-borne commerce, without adequate guarantees of free passage. In fact it might without exaggeration be said that not a single Balkan State wishes to hasten the change of ownership of Constantinople such as is contemplated by our expedition.

Another political question has to be borne in mind. To the average Russian, the greatest prize which this war can give his country is Constantinople. Our Ally now holds a considerable portion of Galicia and if the dash for the Dardanelles had succeeded and the fall of Constantinople had followed it as seemed to be the desire of the British Government, we should have *froissé* the Balkan States and made a present to Russia of the chief prize of the war. I have nothing to say against a broad-minded and generous treatment of Russia in the matter of Constantinople, but considering how little we are doing in Europe, it does seem that we are making things too easy for one Ally at the expense of the other. A further point, which I am diffident of raising, though statesmen should take into account all probable contingencies, is the possibility of our Allies wanting to stop the war at a time when we are just getting into our stride. If Russia should capture Cracow and so complete the conquest of Galicia, and if we made her a present of Constantinople, and if also France succeeded in wresting from the Germans Alsace-Lorraine, and, with our help, drove the Germanic forces out of Belgium, it might well happen that our Allies, who have made prodigious sacrifices, would come to the conclusion that they had done enough for their honour and welfare and for the security of their dominions. Indeed with these results achieved, it would be difficult to blame our Allies for considering that they had gained the main object of the war. At any rate I think I have said enough to prove that from a political point of view the attempt to capture Constantinople by British and French warships was not at all a judicious proceeding.

The idea that a dramatic coup such as the capture of Constantinople would have been such a striking demonstration of our power as to force some, if not all, the Balkan States out of their neutrality is a mistake, born of a misconception regarding the sentiments of these States. That the dash for the Dardanelles and the plan for the capture of Constantinople are mistakes from a strategical point of view is a suggestion I will elaborate. To kill a man it is more effective to get at his heart than to hack at his feet, and the quickest, and only way to achieve great results is to concentrate the whole of our force upon the heart of Germany, which is open to attack along the lines of trenches in France and Flanders and on the Polish and Galician frontiers. At no place can force be so effectively used as at these. Such a proposition seems obvious and the attempt to depart from sound strategy is a mistake.

Apart from the larger strategical question, graver mistakes have been committed. To attempt to force the Dardanelles and get into the Sea of Marmara through the Narrows is a proceeding fraught with the very greatest difficulty and the gravest risks. Indeed the risks involved are so great as scarcely to justify the attempt. In the old days of less powerful armaments it was an axiom of naval tactics that as a rule the bombardment of a fortress by ships was not worth the risks run, but the forcing of what is practically a river, with enormous forts and heavy modern armaments on each side, with the added dangers of mines and torpedoes, is a proceeding which I cannot believe the Naval experts of the Government could have sanctioned. At any rate, if they did sanction it, they must have laid down the obvious condition that such an attempt must be accompanied by the landing of a large military force on one side or other of the Straits. In this connection it is to be remarked that in view of the fact that great disaffection does exist in Constantinople and that a large number of Turks would, if they had the opportunity, revolt and desert, we met this state of things by a purely naval operation which gives the disaffected no *point d'appui*. Everybody who knows anything of Orientals is aware that they will never desert except to an army. Desertion to a fleet is a physical impossibility.

In conclusion I consider that the Dardanelles expedition was undertaken without sufficient study of the conditions, was worth very little from a political point of view, and was a mistake strategically.

THE RESPONSIBILITY

When I had the honour of writing to you on October 16, 1914 regarding the Antwerp expedition, I pointed out to you that I did not consider the First Lord of the Admiralty a man who should be in charge of the Fleet during this war. I considered that the Antwerp expedition thoroughly justified this opinion, and the recurrence of the same lack of study, the same desire to rush in without due preparation, and the same ignorance of strategic and tactical principles in the Dardanelles expedition confirms this opinion. What I ventured to prophesy in October has come to pass in March, and it is for the Government over which you preside to consider whether the First Lord of the Admiralty should continue to hold that office. I would like to point out that I have no personal animus whatever against the First Lord of the Admiralty; indeed I have a great admiration for his political talents and his perseverance and energy.

SUGGESTIONS

It might well be asked of one who has so freely criticised whether he has any constructive suggestion to make, and to th's I would answer that there is only one thing to do unless we are willing to run greater risk than the enterprise merits, and that is to give up the Dardanelles expedition at once; tranship the troops to Marseilles and send them up to the Flanders or French front. Such a course would have a double advantage. In the first place it would obviate the difficulties and risks which must follow the landing of a large force on coasts where the enemy has had ample time to prepare for such an invasion. Indeed when the enemy possesses a large number of machine guns, as he undoubtedly does, it becomes a question whether the landing of troops in the face of such opposition is a feasible military operation or not. To imagine that the guns of ships are going to clear an area of the enemy is to put too great a faith in artillery, a much greater faith than is warranted by our experience in this war. If the troops do not land and the ships remain more or less in the neighbourhood, making feints every now and again, we would have the advantage of immobilising a large body of Turkish forces who will still believe in the possibility of a landing being attempted, and we shall have increased our striking force in France, which is the vital spot where all our energies should be directed. In all other parts of the world we should remain on the defensive, using every man and horse and gun we can to push the Germans back into their own country.

THE DANGER OF INCREASED COMMITMENTS

The Government would do well to remember that subsidiary expeditions such as that contemplated in the Dardanelles or the....

neighbourhood of Constantinople often have a tendency to develop into expeditions of primary importance. It is not generally realised that according to the list of casualties published last week the original Expeditionary Force in France has been used nearly three times over. If we land in the Near East, say, 800,000 men and have severe fighting – which is but a reasonable expectation – the amount of wastage may be such as to force us to provide in a few months in drafts and reinforcements a number equal to the original number sent out. At any rate it would be wrong to form an estimate of the troops required without making a very generous allowance for wastage. Even allowing 50% that would, on the basis of 200,000 men, ear-mark a force of 300,000. The value of such a force in France and Flanders it would be difficult to exaggerate. By countermanding the expedition, disembarking it at Marseilles and sending it to Northern France and Flanders, we should effect much more quickly our purpose in the Dardanelles than by using the troops in the Near East, for with the collapse of Germany on her western or eastern front, the Turkish power of resistance would automatically decrease. There is another argument which is worth considering. Our forces in France are now veterans. The new arrivals have been leavened by the old stock, and in consequence they constitute much more valuable fighting material than could be obtained, unless after a considerable lapse of time, by a new expedition with no leavening of veterans. Their right place is under our best General, Sir John French, who has shown a capacity for leadership and for meeting difficulties which will entitle him to rank among our greatest military leaders. To deprive him of such a large force as will be necessary for the operations in the Near East is unfair to him and diminishes our chances of smashing up the Germanic forces by exactly the measure of strength that we withdraw to the Near East.

COMPULSORY SERVICE

While I have been a consistent and ardent supporter of compulsory service, I have not advocated it during this war for the simple reason that I consider such a great change in our national life should be consummated at a time when the question can be discussed without other preoccupations and the will of the nation can be expressed in such a way as to leave no doubt as to its desire. At the same time, when I hear that the Government is contemplating stringent regulations regarding Drink, I cannot help thinking that the imposition of compulsory service would solve exactly those problems which the Chancellor of the Exchequer hopes to solve by other methods. But, apart from this aspect of the question, we shall have to come to a form of national service in order to take our place at the Peace Conference

85

on terms of equality with other nations. By this I do not mean that we should at once raise a conscript army, but I think that any representative of Great Britain at the Conference would sit at an unfair disadvantage unless the British nation had adopted the principle of national service to be applied to whatever extent the Government thought fit.

TERMS OF PEACE

As a result of this war greater territorial prizes will be available for distribution among the various nations than has ever been the case in the history of the world. Those who think that this is a war against war and who hope that with it all war will end, are living in false security. The Balkan States were allied in a most solemn bond against a hereditary and secular enemy, and at the time no one, not even those who knew the Balkans best, contemplated that so soon after their victory, Bulgaria, Serbia, and Greece would be at each other's throats. What happened once may happen again, and I would earnestly urge His Majesty's Government not to delay a single moment in arranging the details of the terms of peace between Great Britain, France, and Russia. I would suggest that two principles should guide them: In the first place the Allies should decide on the allocation of all territory belonging to our enemies which they consider they may claim as spoils of war. In the second place, the case of all other countries not involved in the war, such as the Balkans and the smaller States of North West Europe, should be decided by all the powers at the Conference. In this way Great Britain, Russia, and France will attend the conference with cut and dried proposals regarding the spoils of war and will thus avoid the danger of quarrelling among themselves. In the case of the smaller nations, it would afford opportunities for the enforcement of a policy the object of which no doubt will be to remove all causes, at any rate in the near future, of international quarrelling.

53
H. A. Gwynne to Lady Bathurst, 23 April 1915

. . . Churchill has really been able to persuade the *French politicians* to his views but Joffre remains unconvinced. In his (Joffre's) view the whole thing is a silly little diversion against all the canons of strategy. He has summed up Winston – 'C'est un bluff n'est ce pas?' he said to one of our English officers in his suite. Italy will only come in in order to secure a seat at the Peace Conference.[1] And she will wait till the very last moment. I hope she'll be too late. . . .

I'm delighted you don't like *The Times*. I think (but then I'm a very conceited Editor) that we beat it hollow.

1. By the Treaty of London of 26 April 1915 Italy agreed to intervene actively within one month.

54
H. A. Gwynne to Lady Bathurst, 29 April 1915

I'm not depressed – far from it. For the Germans to attack is to play our game. But the *very* best sign of all is the lying in the German communiqués. That means they are really at a loss and have to keep their people's courage up.

If I mentioned the *Audacious* I should be sent to the Tower. If they'd send me to the front even as a private, I'd mention it tomorrow. I do so hate not doing 'my bit'. Palmer, my Secretary, with a wife and two children dependent on him has gone or is going – I with no children and a wife independent of me, am here. I suppose it is all right but I want to offer a greater gift to my country than that of advice. To live for one's country is *so* easy.

. . . You are all service and no talk. I am all talk and no service. There are times – like the present – when I positively hate myself. . . .

55
H. A. Gwynne to Lord Milner, 11 May 1915
(HAG/21 no. 37, IWM)

Many thanks for your letter and enclosure,[1] which I will return to you as soon as I have taken some extracts which you have marked. I agree with you that L[loyd] G[eorge] is the only man who might carry conscription, and I am becoming more and more of opinion that conscription, so far from being distasteful to the people, at the present moment would be heartily welcomed. After all, we have, I suppose, some three million voters who are taking part in some capacity or other in war or preparation for war, and they are a pretty solid chunk of the electorate; and they are, I should imagine, to a man in favour of it. I have not been advocating National Service latterly because I hoped that the stars were fighting for us in their courses; and I am now only putting it forward as the only remedy for I feel sure that in this matter the Government is behind and not in front of the people. . . .

1. On 10 May Milner had sent an article by Georges Clemenceau, in his capacity as editor of *L'Homme Enchaîné*, and suggested that certain passages

flattering to Lloyd George but rubbing in the necessity for conscription might be reproduced with good effect. (HAG/21 no. 36, IWM.) Clemenceau had been Prime Minister of France in 1906–9, and was to be again towards the end of the war. In his book *The Nation and the Empire*, London, 1913, Milner had praised the German system of obligatory military service.

56
H. A. Gwynne to Lady Bathurst, 12 May 1915

. . . Now as regards confiscation of property belonging to Germans in England, it is curious that your letter should come just as I had returned from a luncheon which I gave to Bonar Law, Austen Chamberlain[1] and Sir Edward Holden, Chairman of the London City and Midland Bank. All three are more or less financial experts and I wanted them to thrash out this question of the confiscation of German property here, taking into consideration, of course, the probable retaliation in Germany by the Germans. The result is they do not think there is anything in it; at least if there is, it is so near as to be of little value. Of course, there is a point to be made on the question of confiscation although the balance might be against us: it would at one fell swoop destroy all English and German trade relations; but as long as there are neutral countries this would not altogether stop, not because of the will, but because of the physical impossibility. Transactions via neutral countries are so wrapt up that the most patriotic Englishman in the world might be engaged in any transaction with the enemy without his having the faintest idea of it. Our financiers here have not invested in Germany for as early as in 1906 the princes of finance gave the word that they would look with disfavour on investments in German securities. As a matter of fact, industrial securities of Germany have been so shaken that no Englishman would care to take them up. You put your finger on an undoubted grievance when you say that our industrial people allowed the Germans to dominate to such an extent that they are now feeling the loss. This is a point which we, I think, should freely make. I do think with you that patriotism and private interest might go together if only they took the trouble to do so.

1. Chancellor of the Exchequer, October 1903–December 1905; Secretary of State for India, May 1915–July 1917. Chamberlain had written to Lady Bathurst on 1 May, to the effect that he was making enquiries about the confiscation of German property as a reprisal. On 17 May he wrote to her again on the subject, adding: 'Only this I must say: it would not do for us to turn the Government out if we could, for whilst we give them wholehearted support they could not secure the same for us from their party if the positions were reversed.' (Glenesk–Bathurst MSS.)

57
Walter Long to H. A. Gwynne, 13 May 1915
(MS Gwynne 20)

Congratulations on your leading Article today.[1] Personal[ly] I believe the formation of a *National* Government, not a Coalition, would be the best thing. It should not exceed fourteen and would have to include all Parties. However I don't suppose that this is within the range of practical politics.

1. One of these was on the subject of the internment of aliens; the other stressed the necessity for the immediate adoption of universal military service.

58
H. A. Gwynne to Walter Long, 1ᵗ May 1915
(MS Gwynne 20)

As you know, I have not been in favour of a Coalition and I hate the idea; but, of course, once the Government ask for help, we are in a position where it is quite impossible to refuse it. . . .

59
Walter Long to H. A. Gwynne, 16 May 1915
(MS Gwynne 20)

. . . I quite agree that the time has come for the Opposition to do something definite. I think we are all of one mind, but the question is how is it to be done. Personally I feel very strongly, and I am quite willing to write a letter or an Article for publication if you think it of any use. I am quite sure we want Compulsion both for the Army and for Munitions: I could give you a dozen cases to prove this which have come under my own experience. I am writing to Bonar Law and will communicate with you again. . . .[1]

1. Long suggested to Law that a motion be put down on the war and munitions in order to force Asquith's hand. Long to Bonar Law, 16 May 1915 (Long MSS Add. MSS 62404).

60
H. A. Gwynne to L. J. Maxse, 17 May 1915
(Maxse MSS 470)

Give me a few more details if you have them, and I will set on the idea with my whole heart. The facts as I know are: that Lloyd George and Churchill have for the last four months been making suggestions and proposals which have been sedulously carried to our side by F. E. [Smith]. A. B[onar] L[aw] did not like the thing from the beginning and would have nothing to do with it; so I suppose that A. J. B[alfour] is their new move. I heartily agree with you that, once we had a Coalition Government, a strong Boche party would result. With all the Ministers' shortcomings, with a Unionist Opposition we can stir them up – and stir them up with some effect, but given a Coalition Government we should get hopelessly callous and careless. I wrote some two months ago very strongly to A. B[onar] L[aw] on this subject and he entirely agreed with me. I will try and see if I can get you a copy of my Memorandum.[1]

1. See letter 48.

61
H. A. Gwynne to Long, 17 May 1915
(MS Gwynne 20)

I do think that the Opposition ought to begin to move now. Remember that we cannot suddenly have compulsory service without a vast amount of disorganisation in the national life, which is the thing we are particularly anxious to avoid. What I think the Opposition might do is to ask the Government to appoint a committee to inquire into the best methods of organising the country on a National Service basis. It would take at least six weeks of very hard work before this Committee could devise a plan. You might object that this means the adoption of compulsory service without actually putting it into practice. This, I think, is perfectly true; but I am afraid that the Government may, on an impulse, rush into the whole thing without proper preparation, and the result would be a fiasco, and a very dangerous one in the present state of national affairs. By having a committee we should know exactly where we were when the time came to adopt national service – for that it is coming I am quite sure. You will have to face the fact that our casualties will soon be at least 60,000 a month, and I do not think it is by any means possible to get enough men on a voluntary system to make up the casualties. We want to increase and not to decrease our forces, for that is the only way in which we may hope to win. I can see no way out of national service.

62
H. A. Gwynne to Long, 17 May 1915
(MS Gwynne 20)

Of course, much as I dislike the Coalition idea, I do not see how it could be stopped once they came to us and asked us to help them. But we have to bear in mind that there is nothing behind this Government, and that if it fails, England fails; and I am sure that you, of all men, will help to make it a success.[1] One thing I hope you will impress upon your colleagues is that only the best men must be selected, and that it is not a question of awarding men for their services or giving them positions because they are good speakers. Good, sound, honest and faithful men are what we want now.

1. Long took office as President of the Local Government Board in the Coalition Government.

Editor's postscript: In the leader in the *Morning Post* the following morning (18 May) Gwynne did his best to represent the position that Long, from his retreat in Trowbridge, was maintaining in his correspondence with Bonar Law and others. Under the heading 'National Government' Gwynne wrote:

'. . . the need for certain great changes in national policy grows more urgent as the war proceeds. We might enumerate a few of them thus: Expert control in military and naval matters; universal service; expulsion or internment of enemy aliens, with sufficient precautions against the naturalised enemy; national tradewar against Germany, with absolute blockade now; stringent economy in all non-essentials, and the husbanding and organisation of all our resources. Such in our view are some of the principles upon which the Opposition should insist as a preliminary to any share in the responsibility. . . . If the Government finds that upon the present lines it can no longer prosecute the war and desires the active assistance of the other party, it would be incumbent upon it to ask the Opposition frankly for its cooperation not only in men but in methods and principles. In such a case the Opposition would be forced to respond to an appeal frankly and publicly made, and if representatives of the Labour and Irish Parties were added we should then have an approach to a true National Government. Whether such a scheme is workable or not we are in doubt. The main thing at present . . . is expert and business control and a vigorous war policy.'

63
H. A. Gwynne to Lady Bathurst, 18 May 1915

Thank heavens W. Churchill is going. That is the very best news I have heard for a very long day and I confess that I am very cook-a-whoop. With his dismissal comes a great change which I am going to describe.

Last Saturday[1] Fisher handed in his resignation. He complained that Churchill wanted to take everything away from the Grand Fleet for the Dardanelles. He described Winston as a 'danger to the Empire'. The Prime Minister accepted his resignation. But Bonar Law who heard of it on Sunday, immediately went to Lansdowne and between them they drafted a letter to the Prime Minister saying that they could not allow this. They also expressed their desire that the Government should be reconstructed, meaning, of course, that Winston should go. The result was that the Prime Minister confessed that they could not carry on as they were and asked for the cooperation of the Opposition. This was virtually agreed upon on condition that Haldane, Churchill, Simon (I think) and Harcourt left.[2] Asquith actually wanted to get rid of K[itchener].[3] But B[onar] L[aw] stopped that.

There the matter rests for the time being. Austen, Carson and the chief men are in favour of such cooperation provided that Asquith publicly says that he has asked for the cooperation of the Opposition.

I don't like Coalition but I cannot see how it is possible to refuse such a proposal. I don't care a hang for party if only this war can be successfully carried out. The only way to get this Government out is by a general election and that would be worse than letting the Germans get to Calais. So I see no other alternative but to help, always provided that the ministry is purged of the rotters.

This is a scrappy note written in a great hurry. Nobody but you and I outside the Front Benches knows anything.

1. 15 May 1915.

2. In the result, only Haldane left the Government. Churchill became Chancellor of the Duchy of Lancaster, Sir John Simon was moved from Attorney-General to Home Secretary, and Lewis Harcourt (a former director of the *Morning Post*) from Colonial Secretary to First Commissioner of Works.

3. See Sir Charles Petrie, *The Life and Letters of Austen Chamberlain*, London, 1940, vol. ii, pp. 22–3.

64
Walter Long to H. A. Gwynne, 18 May 1915
(MS Gwynne 20)

I don't quite agree.[1] In peace time no doubt all you say is true, but really I believe now the whole Country is so ready for Compulsion that the necessary machinery would shape itself in no time. Surely what we want is for the W[ar] O[ffice] to say how many men they require, that is to say, supposing they want two million men, in what numbers do they require them – all at once, or 500,000 now and 500,000 in three months? Having done that all that would be necessary is to take the population of each County, and each town over a certain size, and by a simple rule of three sum find the proportion of each district. Then you want a Local Committee, which we have practically already got, to go into all the local circumstances and make the necessary reports to the W.O., as to whether there are local industries etc. which require men and therefore would make recruiting undesirable. This roughly would cover the ground, but of course there is a good deal to be filled in.

I am a little afraid of a Committee: it would be difficult to get one that would satisfy all Parties, and I fear they would in all probability get into a prolonged inquiry and delay us.

The Government should declare their intention of passing a Bill making service for all purposes compulsory when required, and then, if necessary, you could appoint a Small Committee just to work the thing out; but to ask for a Committee now would, I am afraid, lead to considerable delay and admit difficulties which I, with some knowledge of local administration, believe is [*sic*] exaggerated. . . .

1. With Gwynne to Long, 17 May (letter 61).

65
H. A. Gwynne to Walter Long, 19 May 1915
(MS Gwynne 20)

. . . As regards National Service, I am sure – with you – that it is to come but I am afraid I did not make myself clear in regard to the kind of committee I would like to see at work. I did not mean anything in the nature of a Parliamentary Committee but a small working committee of experts – soldiers preferably – who would go into the question of the present organisation and future needs and see whether the one could be made to help the other. I am perfectly sure that the announcement that the Government are going in for compulsory service would make a great difference to recruiting, but that kind is not what we want.

I am sure the time has come for the Opposition in the House of Commons to put forward a plea for National Service. It is the only way in which we can organise the country, and in my opinion it would be most popular, but whether it is popular or not, it is the right thing today. The future of the Unionist party lies in being ahead of the Government and not in lagging behind it, and if they persuade the Government to take up this matter they will be doing good for themselves and good for the country.

I am so glad you approve of my attitude to Speyer. I do consider his relations both with the Prime Minister and Churchill to be a disgrace, and I am going to peg away at it.

66
Walter Long to H. A. Gwynne, 21 May 1915
(MS Gwynne 20)

Bravo. You saved us by your description of the Coalition Conference.[1]

The other papers fairly landed us. I believe the Radical wire-pullers are deliberately doing all they can to keep themselves on top and land us in a mess. You saved us once again. Surely if we are to join in order to save the Government we ought to insist upon our own terms?

1. In the *Morning Post*, 21 May, under the heading 'Re-making the Cabinet'. From Long's point of view the main virtue of the *Morning Post*'s coverage was that it implied that McKenna, one of the 'Radical wirepullers', would be displaced from the Home Office. Long wrote to Bonar Law the same day: 'This Coalition business is being very badly stage-managed. The *Morning Post* has just saved the situation, but only just. . . . I have seen some men here, heard from others, and am expressing their views when I say that if McKenna remains in the Government the great majority of our men will bitterly resent it and will be scandalised if any of our Leaders consent to serve with him.' (Sir Charles Petrie, *Walter Long and his Times*, London, 1936, pp. 193–4.)

67
H. A. Gwynne to Walter Long, 24 May 1915
(MS Gwynne 20)

As you know, I have never liked the idea of the Coalition; but I think from the time that the Government asked us to cooperate a refusal was impossible, as it would have put the Unionist Party altogether in the wrong. I am going to support the Coalition for all I am worth now, because there is nothing between that and destruction. I shall leave all my criticisms and only put forward suggestions.

PART II

May 1915–December 1916

The first Coalition Government of the Great War was a far cry from the *Morning Post*'s 'ideal Government' which, as described in a leader of 18 May, 'would be a War Board of soldiers and sailors, men mainly from the Active List and in the prime of life, assisted by strong expert administrators', but its constitution did increase Gwynne's access to the centres of power. After its formation he escalated his campaign for the adoption of compulsory service, trying in August to mobilize both Milner and Lloyd George to work on Kitchener in this direction. His communications with Lloyd George ranged from the suggestion of a permanent committee for the examination of inventions to the supplying of a report on the Trades Union Congress at Bristol in September. In October Gwynne was active in attempting to halt the withdrawal of troops from Salonika, the latter being an expedition which he regarded as a good excuse for the winding up of its ill-fated precursor, the Dardanelles Operation. The resignation of Carson, also in October, provided Gwynne with a possible focus for something more nearly in the nature of a National Government, given that there were still reservations in many quarters about the suitability of Lloyd George, all the more so as the latter's displacement of Asquith might involve a general election. Although at the beginning of November Asquith had reduced, as Gwynne had anticipated, the size of the War Cabinet, Gwynne still looked forward to a Committee of Public Safety, and tried on Boxing Day to get the King to ask for one. In the previous month Gwynne had forwarded to Carson and to Bonar Law a 'Note on a National Policy' by his chief leader writer. This 'National Policy' included the revival and coalescence of campaigns for Tariff Reform and Compulsory Service through appeals to patriotism. The suggested motto of the British or National Party – 'Britain for the British' – was echoed as part of a League suggested by Gwynne to Lloyd George a few days later. In the New Year the search for a leader for this League and this programme was extended, at Lady Bathurst's suggestion, to include Lord Derby, behind whom Gwynne offered to place his own resources, the *Morning Post*, and four million votes for five years in the shape of the British Army. Derby's rejection of this as 'utopian' inclined Gwynne, though not General Sir Douglas Haig, who even in March 1916 was urging on Derby 'the necessity of *you* taking on yourself the complete control of the Government as long as war lasts' (Haig to Derby, 21 March 1916 (920 Der 26/3)), to look elsewhere. As dissatisfaction with Asquith increased and as even Kitchener came to be regarded as 'a danger'; and whilst Gwynne's friend Maxse concentrated with Milner on the encouragement of the British Workers' National League, which amongst other things was designed to counter the influence of the Independent Labour Party, and whose manifesto was published in March 1916; and as calls for a 'National Government' were made by Milner, by Lloyd George's Private Secretary, Arthur Lee, and others, Gwynne swung his attention back to using Sir Edward Carson, now Chairman of the Unionist War Committee, to supplant the incumbent Prime Minister. This process was delayed by the state of Carson's health, and then interrupted by the Easter Rising in Dublin and a quarrel with Walter Long, one of the first to express a preference for a National Government. Lloyd George, moreover, was diverted by Asquith into an attempt to solve the Irish Question. The aftermath of this episode inclined Gwynne still more to the conclusion that 'a military dictatorship is the only thing for England'.

On 1 July 1916 the battle of the Somme opened. It was to last until 18 November, and in it many of those who volunteered for the armies which Kitchener had been determined not to use if he could possibly avoid it saw action for the first, and for the last, time. This offensive was insisted upon by the French, every single unit of whose armies passed through the 'mincing machine' of Verdun between February and December of that year. In the late summer Gwynne went out once more to France, as part of the High Command's public relations exercise to present the Somme as a success. He returned to resume the taking to task of Lloyd George for his ministerial interference in Army matters. In November, the last month before Lloyd George took over as Prime Minister, Gwynne was advising a change of personnel at the Admiralty to Balfour, and suggesting the extension of compulsion to Ireland: 'There is an ugly feeling abroad and it will take an ugly shape if Ireland is still permitted to go Scot-free.' At the same time, Gwynne was trying to inveigle General Sir William Robertson, the Chief of the Imperial General Staff, into attending meetings with an overlapping membership and purpose to those set up by Milner earlier in the year. In the smaller matter of Robertson's participation in these discussions Gwynne was no more successful than in his efforts of August 1915 to get Kitchener to attend what the latter dubbed 'cabals'. In the larger matter of the breaking up of the Coalition Government and the replacement of Asquith with Lloyd George, success was much less qualified.

68
H. A. Gwynne to Lady Bathurst, 26 May 1915

. . . You have no idea of the feeling of comfort I have, when I take a bold line, to know that you will back me up. If success is attending the *M.P.* 99% is due to you. If you only knew how few proprietors are real patriots and if you could see how much I really lean upon you, though I don't show it, you would feel that you could take most of the credit. I can face easily all the snarling and back-biting of contemporaries as long as I know you are with me. Without your support, I should be a miserable creature fearing my own shadow.

Lord K[itchener] said to me on Friday 'I really think we are getting to the bottom of these Germans'. That is the first time he has been really optimistic so I pass it on for your comfort.

69
H. A. Gwynne to Lady Bathurst, 26 May 1915

. . . Well, I am glad you liked our going for Northcliffe. There is more in it than meets the eye and when I see you I hope to tell you the story that underlies it; and your only complaint will be that we were too mild.

The Special Correspondent's story of the battle of Ypres was by Percival Phillips, who does not belong to us. The arrangement that exists now is that we have to share our correspondents with other papers. Sometimes it is our turn and in that case we share with other papers. In the present instance it was the *Daily Express*, and I agree with you that the account is splendid. I am seeing that 12 copies are sent to the Commandant of the Red Cross Hospital at Cirencester with the passage marked.

I am very much interested in your conversation with the officer. It is a novelty to find a soldier who thinks the Germans are decent people – I must say they have very little sense of decency, what with this infernal gas and the blowing up of the *Lusitania*.[1]

The Coalition Government has been formed and is going to start on its work. Like yourself, I dislike it very much, but it is the last thing that England can do – at any rate, in the way of politicians, and we have to stand by it until it proves a failure, which I hope to God it will not, for we cannot afford to have any more failures. Therefore I am sure you will agree that I am doing right in standing by it to help with suggestions without criticism so that it can have a clear run for its money and can do its best without casting its eyes round for votes. The weak spot is McKenna[2] being kept; but I am glad to say, from what I hear, that Simon of the Home Office is likely to be a Tartar. At any rate I am going to see him tomorrow, and I hope it will result in the 'jugging' of two or three people at once who are much better in captivity. As regards McKenna, I do not think he can do much harm at the Treasury, especially as he appears to be somewhat in the nature of a warming pan. But what I dislike particularly is Lloyd George going to be Minister of Munitions. I do not think he is capable of the job, for what we want there is not a demagogue, but a quiet, steady going, hard working, strong, silent, business man.

Lord Fisher is going, I am thankful to say, and his place will be taken by (I hope) Jackson.[3] He is a first-class man and, from what I hear, he is popular with every sailor. I am glad Fisher is going because he was too old and I have always considered him more or less of a danger.

I think that one of the first things the Government will have to do is to bring in compulsory service. The country is crying out for it and if the Government are not careful they will see processions going up and down the country demanding it; there is no doubt in my mind that the public are quite determined to have it, and with these infernal politicians this is the only argument.

I must confess that if I had to criticise the compilation of the Cabinet I could find a lot to complain of; but it is no use weakening the only bulwark between us and absolute chaos, so we are bound to prop it up and help it in every way we can. But you may depend on our not giving up our independence, for Press and Parliamentary suggestion is all that is left to us.

1. The Germans first used gas, as opposed to an eye and nose irritant which they used at La Bassée on 27 October 1914, on the Eastern Front near Warsaw on 3 January 1915; the British first employed gas at Loos on 25 September 1915. The *Lusitania*, which was carrying munitions, was sunk on 6 May 1915 by a German submarine, with the loss of 1198 lives, 128 of them American.

2. Reginald McKenna, Chancellor of the Exchequer, May 1915–December 1916.

3. Admiral Sir H. B. Jackson, who was appointed to succeed Fisher as First Sea Lord.

70
H. A. Gwynne to Lady Bathurst, 3 June 1915

. . . As regards national service, the position is that the new members of the Government who have just arrived are not yet in possession of the facts; and I believe that the few meetings of the Cabinet that have been held have been mostly with a view to giving them information as to what has taken place. The result, from what I hear from members, is not encouraging; but they are determined to get the full facts of the position, for without them it is impossible to do anything at all. It seems that the late Government were content with mere perfunctory questionings of their experts – indeed, they seem to have been altogether too careless in getting at the true state of affairs.

As regards the Dardanelles the position is, that one of three things is to be done: (1) Retire altogether; (2) Hold on to what we have got, sending out as few reinforcements as necessary in order to retain the positions we have secured; (3) Send out very large reinforcements of something like 100,000 men at least. Of these three courses, I do not know on which they have decided; but my advice has been to urge Bulgaria to come in as soon as possible and request her to move on to Adrianople, to establish financial relations with the discontented people in Constantinople, and to hold on to what we have secured. I know that yesterday they were to discuss these proposals of mine, but I do not know what is the result. I will let you know when I hear.

Referring again to national service, I think the new members are going about it in the right way. They want to know exactly what our commitments are and generally to get the whole facts of the case. . . .

71
Memo by H. A. Gwynne for Bonar Law, 29 June 1915 (Law MSS 63/13/2)

THE EFFECT OF THE GALICIAN CAMPAIGN ON THE WAR
The German successes in the East – although, no doubt, they have been purchased at a great cost in lives – can only be considered by a student of the war as a great disaster for the Allies. This I think is true whether we look upon it in regard to its direct effect upon ourselves, or in relation to its effect upon neutrals. It has also the added advantage from the enemy's point of view of placating Austria and Hungary inasmuch as it removes the threat to the Hungarian plains which has been the cause of so much anxiety to the Hungarian nation

as to encourage some of the Independence party to talk of a separate peace.

As regards the effect upon the Allies, it is no exaggeration to say that such thrusts at the Russian armies and such pursuits of the Russian forces must render a Russian offensive impossible for many months to come. It is equally true that with a wide stretch of territory to choose from, the Germans will form strong lines along the Dniester, part of the San and the upper-middle Vistula of such strength as to free a great proportion of their forces for action elsewhere – whether in the West or against Italy, we do not know as yet. Apparently the French and our own armies in France seem to be of opinion that the blow may come at any time against their lines.

We must give due importance also to another recent fact in the war. The French, it may fairly be said, have failed to break through the German line. Long prepared, though not too well concealed, attacks took place in the neighbourhood of Arras; but in spite of fine staff work, magnificent bravery and intense artillery fire, although they have succeeded in killing a great number of Germans, the French have not broken through the German line, though they have bent it to some small extent. But even the most optimistic of them would not say now that they are any nearer a complete breakthrough than when they were at the beginning of these operations. These two operations seem to me to be of vital importance in a consideration of the war. The Galician retreat is a staggering blow to the Allies. The failure of the French to break through the German lines is a staggering disappointment. On the brighter side there is the Italian intervention and an indication that the Turks are getting somewhat tired of the campaign. But the broad facts remain, that the Germans have been able to hold us on the West and at the same time deal a heavy blow at their enemy on the East. There is nothing that I can see which is likely to stop the Germans for at least the next six months from holding the Russians in the East and bringing their phalanx to attack us in the West.

Simultaneous Action by the Allies
For this reason it would be madness to deplete in any way our front in France. Indeed, on the contrary, it is necessary that we should put as many men and guns out there as we can spare; that we should prepare strong positions in our rear (I believe this is being done) and make every preparation to withstand the German onslaught. This German onslaught – unless it succeeds in breaking through our lines – in itself is not a bad thing, for it might be laid down as an axiom in this war, that the chief aim is to kill Germans. Opportunities for big

victories will occur very rarely, if at all; so at least for nine months we must settle down to a war of attrition.

The objection to a war of attrition is that it searches out all the weaknesses of the combatants, and it drives them into a state of mind where the only comforts are daily bulletins – which are unsatisfactory things at the best of times. France so far has shown that she can stand this. We have hardly been tried; and Russia seems alone to have satisfaction in what one may call 'fluid campaigning'. Whether the Allies can stand another nine months of this war of attrition is a question which no one can answer; but they might bear it with equanimity if it was known that within a certain time a blow would be struck which would end the war within a short time. Our losses compared with those of Russia and France are insignificant. We have no enemy on any part of our territory, and we are therefore suffering less both physically and mentally. It behoves us therefore to take a lead among the Allies to give proof of our determination to carry on this war to the bitter end. For this purpose I think we ought to create at once a sort of military commissioner who should be a man of tact and of first-rate military ability; a man whose duty it should be to travel between Russia, France and London consulting, advising, suggesting, and generally keeping in touch with the military opinion of all these countries. His chief duty, however, would be to prepare for a simultaneous blow by all the Allies at a given moment – and this moment should be March next. We have got to face the fact that, unless there is a sudden debacle on the German side – which we have no reason to expect – we are to have another winter campaign, and there is no hope of ending this war at least until this time next year. In one respect this is an unfortunate thing because the public in England, France, and possibly Russia might not be prepared for another winter campaign; and the disappointment might result in a weakness in carrying on the war. But this we shall have to risk, for if we make up our minds to have a concerted movement – and this concerted movement should include Italy, too – at a certain time, we shall have the enormous advantage of being able to give nine months to the preparation for it.

Now these nine months, in my opinion, are months in which our destiny will be decided. First of all, we must form our plans with the Allies for a fixed time for a general attack, leaving the details, of course, for each country. In the meantime we should simply hold the Germans as they have held us; but we shall use the time to make preparations of every kind so that the month of March will find us prepared in every single particular in a way in which we have never been found before. We have to confess that the German organisations and preparations have been so wonderful that in every case they have been prepared for all eventualities. But at the time fixed we shall put them to the supreme test of a simultaneous attack, and on that attack will depend the issue of a *status quo* peace or a peace dictated by the Allies.

Need for Compulsory Service

The chief point to consider is, how this is to affect us; and I put forward some suggestions which are based on a very close study of the war which I hope may be useful. In the first place, I think we ought to delay no longer in passing an Act permitting compulsory military service. I admit that, in the present state of our supply of rifles, it may result in our having more men than weapons; but I do not advocate this so much because we want the men as I do for the purpose of showing to our Allies that we are really in earnest and that we mean to carry this war through to the bitter end. There are other advantages, amongst which would be the fact that, with compulsory service, the organisation of the men of the country could be much more easily effected. I would not advocate the immediate putting into force of the Act; but I would give the Government power to call every man whenever they think it necessary.

Training of Officers

In the second place we should institute a corps of officers at least 25,000 to 30,000 strong, not to be attached to any present army but to be trained as officers in the same way as they are now being trained at Sandhurst. They may or may not be used; but the claim for such a corps is that in six months they would be more or less efficient in a shorter time than is possible under the present system which was, of course, forced upon us by the circumstances of the war. Again, I claim that we have nine months for preparation, and in those nine months we have a magnificent opportunity for preparing these officers – which is a weakness of new armies. The objection might be made that men who are suitable for officers are either in the ranks or are already serving as officers. This is partly true; but there are a number of young fellows of 18½ and 19 who should be of use, and also a number of men who are serving in the ranks of the new armies – some of which are still without arms – who could be taken out and turned into officers in a very short time owing to the fact that they have already had some military training. I should think there would be little difficulty in getting 25,000 or 35,000 men of this type in a very short time. Given a good number of fairly efficient officers the difficulty of training the men becomes ever so much easier. We could use for the training of these officers a number of wounded officers who are not fit for active service, and we could also draw from the front some of those who have been in the war from the beginning and who could do with a turn at home to increase their effectiveness.

Machine Guns

Another weakness of ours is that of machine guns. . . . In the case of Germany, although their machine gun detachments are attached to battalions, yet they have, as far as I can make out – at least during this war – a number of men who form a separate little body and are attached to any brigade where they may be useful. I strongly advocate the creation of a machine gun brigade here in England of at least 10,000 strong. . . . Given Maxims in sufficient quantity, we shall have available a draft for the front of skilled machine gun men who can be attached to a battalion, a brigade, or a division or wherever they are wanted. . . .

The Need for a Scientific Inventions Committee[1]

I think that we should not neglect in any way the scientific and inventive genius of the nation. In conversation with young officers who have spent most of their time in the trenches, one constantly hears of suggestions for improving their methods of warfare. These suggestions, of course, in many cases, do not come back in their entirety but only as they filter through their superior officers, with the result that a good deal of their suggestiveness is lost. Would it not be possible to institute a strong committee of the scientists, mechanical engineers, physicists, chemists and doctors of this country, who could examine all these ideas and forward to the War Office those that they think practicable.

Conclusion

In conclusion, if we get a concerted action by the Allies and can give a big blow in March, we shall take from the Germans the initiative, will force them to fight on two or three fronts at the same time, and with munitions in plenty and our armies up to full strength, we ought to be able to inflict a blow on the enemy which will be the first step towards the ending of the war.

1. This was a matter which Gwynne, who had already been instrumental in encouraging the invention of the trench mortar (see C. Addison *Politics from Inside*, London, 1924, vol. i, p. 126), had raised with Lloyd George on 17 June. On being told that the War Office preferred to keep such matters to themselves, Gwynne offered to mediate. (See Lloyd George MSS D16/19/1, /2, /3.)

72

H. A. Gwynne to Walter Long, 2 July 1915
(MS Gwynne 20)

. . . I am afraid we do differ, but I hope that will not make us any the less good friends. My feeling is that the only way in which we can keep the French in a good temper over this winter – for I do not think there will be any really big push until next year – is by having National Service. Our Allies expect it of us, and not to have it will disappoint them. I know the opposition there is to it, both inside and outside of the Cabinet; and I am sorry that the arguments for it do not appeal sufficiently to those members of the Cabinet who are not in its favour. At the same time I cannot be enthusiastic about a thing[1] which falls so short of my desires and expectations. You will see from what I said in this morning's paper that I am desirous that the thing should go through. Although I do look upon it as a very excellent thing and likely to aid in the national organisation, it falls short very much – in my estimation – of the real thing, that is National Service. If I do appear to crab it, it is only because it does not go far enough; otherwise it is an excellent thing and, done by you, it would be extremely well done.

1. The National Registration Bill, introduced into the House of Commons by Long.

73

H. A. Gwynne to A. Bonar Law, 7 July 1915
(Law MSS 51/1/11)

I am committing, I suppose, an indiscretion in sending you Callwell's letter but he is such a cautious man in everything he says and especially in everything he writes that I think it best to send it to you as it is.

I am ordered off on Friday morning for 6 days holiday. . . .

Enclosure in letter 73
General Sir C. E. Callwell to H. A. Gwynne, 7 July 1915

I am afraid that we shall before long be in serious difficulties as to men. The recruiting is now not going at all well and as far as I can gather – for it is not part of my work – it will become a serious problem as to how casualties are to be made good when the Army grows by three hundred thousand men, or more, at the front.

There is a fourth Army in a fairly forward state of organisation, but it is no use sending it to the front if it cannot be maintained. As you no doubt know, great trouble has arisen in connection with the Territorials who have gone to the front – that was only to be expected as there was no Territorial reserve when the war began and recruits were for the most part drafted into the new Armies or depots for the old regulars. . . .

The truth is that I am afraid that K[itchener] is not letting his colleagues know the state of things, and that he wants to be able to say at the end of the business that he produced an army of so many Divisions by the voluntary principle. The truth is that for each new Army, you want a reserve depot army for maintenance purposes. For a battalion of 1000 you want another of 1000 of whom 500 must be trained men when the first battalion goes to the front; those 500 will have been expended within four months and within that time another 500 men will have become trained men; so that you start good for eight months; the reserve battalion has to be kept continuously filled up with recruits, just as the one at the front has to be kept continuously filled up with trained drafts. Could you not give a hint to some of the Unionists in the Cabinet? They are quite entitled to ask what provision is being made for maintaining the growing Army. The wastage when we have three New Armies at the front in addition to what there is now will be at the rate of quite 70,000 a month – more in a bad month – and if the wastage cannot be made good the whole thing comes to the ground.

74
L. J. Maxse to H. A. Gwynne, 17 July 1915
(MS Gwynne 20)

I was greatly impressed by Carson, as always. . . . He entirely agreed about the Dardanelles, and feels the whole thing quite as keenly as we do. Moreover he understands it . . . and will I think do what he can. He realises the importance of getting Henry Wilson over here, and would like to see him installed as Chief of the Staff, but said it was preferable that Bonar Law should bring the matter forward because he, Carson, is suspect as an Ulsterman, and his recommendation of a fellow Ulsterman has less weight than that of others.

75
H. A. Gwynne to Lady Bathurst, 19 July 1915

... I am very glad that you disapprove cordially of Mr Bowles' suggestion.[1] The reason that people look to us is that we have not given way to the glamour of headlines and sensation generally. When you alter the headlines, you alter the characteristics of the paper. Tommy Bowles' interest in the *M.P.* is not only because he finds it interesting but also because he finds nearly all the writers for his *Candid Review* among the clever fellows who are writing for us. I must say I admit that shows he is no fool, but he is a crank; and I can never forget that, as late as 1910, he voted in favour of a small Army and Navy.

... Lord Northcliffe, having failed to get out Lord Kitchener through the Munitions question,[2] tried to make an unholy alliance with Lloyd George to get rid of Asquith, Grey and Kitchener. I do not care who else he gets rid of, but I am determined it shall not be Kitchener; and I think I have nipped the conspiracy in the bud. I am told it is dead.

I do not like the Dardanelles business for they are still sending more troops than they originally intended, and if they are not careful they will be bleeding the Army white. I am working hard to stop the extra reinforcements, merely sending enough men to keep the present troops up to strength and giving them a chance to get out of the trenches for a few days.

1. What this was is not known. Lady Bathurst was in the habit of tearing in half letters from Gibson Bowles, the former Liberal MP for King's Lynn. On 4 March 1915 he had written to congratulate her on 'the bold independent national course' taken by the *Morning Post*, which he heard everywhere described as 'now the only paper worth reading'. In his view, a bold and courageous policy was all the more necessary 'because almost all the Press is now either cowed or sold & incapable of doing the public service expected of it'. (Glenesk–Bathurst MSS.)

2. In April and again in May 1915 complaints against Kitchener for not ensuring a sufficient supply of the appropriate kind of ammunition had been a feature of *The Times* and the *Daily Mail*.

76
H. A. Gwynne to A. Bonar Law, 27 July 1915
(B. Law MSS 51/1/38)

I enclose you a letter that I posted last night to the Prime Minister; the reason why I did not send it to you at the same time is that I did not get certain alterations to your copy in time. But I am now sending it down to the House of Commons by messenger and hope you will be able to cast your eye over it.

The point I am anxious to make is this: whether we like it or not, compulsory service has got to come for the simple reason that the reserves necessary to keep men in the field that we have promised to keep there, will go far beyond what we can provide by the voluntary system. I have gone into the matter very carefully and I can come to no other conclusion. If you will take a pencil and a piece of paper and, taking as a basis the casualties that we have had up to the present – that is, 300,000 and work out that proportion to the number that have been in the field, you will find on computation that, to provide reserves for the men that we are going to put into the field, there is no other way open than an increase of recruiting which is quite impossible by voluntary service. I think that, being obliged – as I claim – to have compulsory service, the sooner we have it, the better; and it seems to me that some steps should be taken before Parliament rises which would, at least, give the Government permission to start a Committee at once to draw up regulations for compulsory service. In the ordinary course of events this Committee would not be able to effect much in less than a month, so that there would only be a fortnight lost; but if you decide to have such a Committee when the Session resumes in September, you risk to lose these four precious weeks.

I think that, on this question of numbers, K[itchener] is not quite sound, and I am sure that it would be worth your while to work the thing out for yourself. I believe the War Office computation is: 7% per month are casualties which are total losses, that is: killed, prisoners, or disabled beyond any hope of going back to the fighting line, and 20% being casualties that last for a period of from a fortnight to six months.

P.S.   I am sending a copy of this letter to Carson and to Austen.[1]

1. Austen Chamberlain.

Enclosure in letter 76
H. A. Gwynne to H. H. Asquith, 26 July 1915

I have from time to time ventured to address you on the subject of the war, especially on such aspects of it as could not be dealt with in the newspaper Press; and I should like at this very critical juncture in our affairs, again to set forth for your consideration some points which have impressed themselves upon me in regard to recent events.

We may take it as granted that the Russians are being very hard pressed in Poland and Courland. The result may – and is likely to be – the loss of Warsaw and a general retreat of the Russian armies north and east of the Vistula. In the West the Germans have so entrenched themselves and made their entrenchments so strong, that we cannot hope for any great success in that quarter, though we shall undoubtedly be able to press the German forces holding that line, but not, I think, to such an extent as to force them to bring reinforcements from the East to the West until such time as they have finished their Eastern business. Italy is gaining ground slowly against another fortress, but whatever success she is achieving or may achieve will be small in comparison to the whole operations of the war. Serbia, having driven out her greatest foe – typhus – is now open to attack by the Germanic forces. It must be admitted that such an attack is not outside the bounds of possibility or even of probability, for a successful attack by an overwhelming force in Serbia would affect the sentiment of Bulgaria and would have a reflex action upon the future policy of Romania.

The position is one of those which, history teaches, tries most the strength of an alliance. Allies when they are successful frequently quarrel over spoils; that also is a teaching of history. But another lesson we can learn from the past is, that allies are inclined to recriminate one against the other when things go badly. Things are going badly for Russia; things are not going well for France. What is in the mind of the Russian people and the Russian Government, we do not know; but I imagine that they must be profoundly resentful of the fact that we can help their operations in the East very little by an offensive in the West. The reasons are known to yourself and to the Government over which you preside.

Germany is now fighting for a *status quo* peace which would, in effect, be a defeat for the Allies, for a *status quo* peace would mean the postponement of all the efforts of civilisation and their conversion into warlike preparations which might result in a future victory of the very forces against which we are now making such a desperate effort.

We all – Liberals, Conservatives, Socialists – have underestimated the power of Germany. It is inconceivable that Germany at this moment – practically twelve months after the declaration of war – is able to undertake what her own soldiers before the war declared was an impossible task, that is, an offensive on both fronts. This offensive, be it noted, only took into consideration as possible enemies Russia and France, and did not contemplate the entry of Great Britain. It is, therefore, a fact that the Germanic forces are undertaking what practically amounts to an offensive not only in the East and in the West, but in the South and South-West. Of course, we do not know – not being in the secrets of the High Command in Germany – exactly how they regard this task, and whether they hope to accomplish it with success; but statesmen do not base their action on suppositions and do well to take facts alone as the guide of their conduct.

In such a case as the present, therefore, the Germanic powers can hope for one of two things: a *status quo* peace – which is nothing short of a disaster – or the detachment of one of the Allies. By this means she would, with the least amount of sacrifice of territory, say, in Alsace and Lorraine, be able to recoup herself, supposing it were possible to arrange matters with France, by territory won from a defeated Russia or a defeated Great Britain. As for Italy, it is necessary to bear in mind that Germany and Italy have not yet declared war against each other; that it is reasonable to suppose that Germany is all the time impressing upon Austria the necessity for giving up what the Irredentists require; and that it is not beyond the bounds of possibility to imagine that some satisfaction might be offered to Italian claims, and that Italy might be bought off.

The four Great Powers now in alliance against the Germanic forces have to contemplate another winter campaign, and to look forward to striking a great blow, which should decide the war, next spring. Russia will have all her work cut out to prepare for the great blow. She will require a vast importation of munitions and, above all, of rifles; she will have to make good enormous losses. In France the sacrifices made are already enormous and the number of men that she can put into the field is strictly limited. At any time Germany, holding interior lines, might – at a great expense of men, I will admit – inflict still greater losses upon France and may, indeed, bend the line to her advantage. Great Britain is helping her to the extent now of some 60 to 80 miles. All the time France is losing men, and young men too, and the flower of the nation is disappearing. They are too generous and too courageous to ask more than we are willing to give; but anyone who has studied the situation of France and the French way of regarding the war, will admit that they regard our efforts – though more than perhaps we promised – as being inadequate in this great struggle.

To speak quite plainly: whether we like it or not, if we are to win this war we must have compulsory service. It is the only answer to the capture of Warsaw;[1] it is the only means of satisfying France. Without it, we may make a breach among the Allies and may find ourselves fighting alone. France, as you know, has recently refused a tempting offer;[2] France would always refuse tempting offers; France is firm and determined; but all the time she is thinking that, in this great struggle between right and wrong, she is giving all that she

111

has – and England is only giving a part. But, as I said before, whether we like it or not, we are bound to have compulsory service for this very simple reason: in the spring we are going to make a desperate effort. Let us suppose for the sake of argument that we shall have at the front a million men: I hope there will be more. Our casualties up to date are somewhere about 300,000 men, and, with the exception of the operations that ended in the Battle of the Marne, we have been engaged in no very serious fighting. With the great offensive in the spring, and allowing for the casualties of the winter (which will not be small) it is a matter of arithmetic to calculate what reserves we shall require to fill up the battalions at the front. This reserve, I contend, will take more than we can reasonably hope for by voluntary service; indeed I go so far as to say that, even to fill up the forces now in the field – if the Germans turn their offensive on to the West – will strain the voluntary system to the utmost. I would beg you to examine very closely into the question of the reserve of men. Munitions are now our difficulty; but I think our great difficulty in the future is going to be men to fill up the gaps caused by the wastage at the front. In this case – and I think on examination you will agree with me – it will be essential at some date or other that we should increase our forces by some other means than the voluntary system which, according to all the experts with whom I have spoken, has reached its limits; and I contend that only two alternatives remain before us: the amalgamation of depleted battalions at the front, or the adoption of the principle of compulsory service.

If you will allow that these alternatives are the only alternatives – and I am convinced that they are – then it seems to me that the sooner we adopt compulsory service, the better. If we are going to make our great effort in the spring we have still in front of us seven or eight months in which to train an army and to fill up the wastage. It takes a long time to train men and to obtain equipment and rifles, and to send the men out to the front in a proper state both of training and equipment; and no advantage can be obtained by postponing the decision which I claim will have to be made by Great Britain unless she is to be content with a *status quo* peace.

One more argument in favour of national service is this: it will cement the alliance between the four Great Powers still fighting; it will be a most effective riposte to German success in Russia, and I believe it very probably will have the effect of showing to Germany that we mean to fight this war to a finish. I feel sure that, if you could spare the time from your many duties to read the German comments on the subject of compulsory service in England, you would be convinced that, on the principle of 'what your enemy hates is right' – that it is the reasonable and proper procedure to adopt at once.

Delay is not only dangerous, but would deprive us altogether of the advantages of compulsory service. It must be done now or not at all. If Ireland objects, Ireland could be left out. We do not want a divided Great Britain, but a united effort to defeat the Germans.

I hope you will excuse this very long letter, but I feel that His Majesty's Government may not have considered all the points that I have put before you.

1. Warsaw was entered by the Germans on 5 August.
2. Possibly a reference to information received by Asquith on Christmas Day 1914 to the effect that the Germans were prepared to evacuate Belgium and give full compensation and securities against future attack. In June and July 1915 German efforts for a separate peace were concentrated on *Russia*. (See M. and E. Brock (eds), *Letters of H. H. Asquith to Venetia Stanley*, p. 339; and F. Fischer, *Germany's Aims in the First World War*, London, 1967, p. 196.)

Editor's postscript: Gwynne sent a copy of this to Kitchener through Fitzgerald, with the note: 'I am coming round to the W[ar] O[ffice] tomorrow – if I can have only 5 minutes with Lord K. I know I can tell him things that he ought to know.' (Gwynne to Fitzgerald, 28 July 1915 (Kitchener MSS PRO 30/57/73).) On the previous day (25 July) General Sir Henry Wilson had written to Gwynne a long letter stressing the change in the situation as a result of the Russian retreat. (C. E. Callwell, *Field-Marshal Sir Henry Wilson*, vol. i, p. 241.)

77
Lord Milner to H. A. Gwynne, 15 August 1915 (HAG/21 no. 39, IWM)

Sorry about Wednesday, as I do want to see you rather urgently.

I think there is going to be a great push made this next week or two to finally compel the Government to take the plunge about National Service.[1] It is the 11th hour, indeed it is 11.50, & I am afraid, if they keep on pothering over the thing any longer, we shall be beaten. It does seem to me to be a choice between compulsion, & all that it implies, & defeat. At the same time I wish it could be brought about without an agitation. It is so unsuitable & humiliating, & altogether *infra dig* of a great nation to have a public wrangle, in the middle of a great war, as to whether or not our young men should be compelled to do their duty. Odious! Why can't the Government just take the bull by the horns & save us all this discord & discredit. If Kitchener were to ask for conscription *in a straightforward way*, & not try to get it in effect by all sorts of rather mean & wholly undignified shifts & dodges, he could carry it with *very little resistance*.

If he won't move, or if Asquith has blanketed him, as he seems to do everybody, & to reduce them to his own uselessness, I don't see what there is for it but for us all to put on the maximum of public & private pressure. Personally I have with great difficulty lain low, &, with the exception of a single letter to *The Times*, at the time of the Coalition[2] (which was framed with the sole intention of making it easier for the Government *then* to come round the corner, & so worded as to enable Liberals to be converted with the least appearance of inconsistency) I have kept absolutely quiet, feeling very miserable all the time but also feeling that if by relieving myself with open swear-words I was doing more harm than good, it was my duty as a good citizen to possess my soul in patience.

But if the Government really are quite absolutely determined to go on with the present slip-slop, then I really think it will be necessary to give them one hearty kick behind before it is *palpably too late*. Only the other day I declined to sign a letter to the Press clamouring for public meetings to advocate conscription, because I doubted the opportuneness of such a method of procedure. But if such a movement is started, & provokes, as I expect it will, a counter movement, & the battle is once joined in spite of me, I don't see how I, or you, *or any of us old believers in &* advocates of National Service can keep out of it. We cannot sit still, while the issue is being decided against us, when what is at stake is nothing less than independent national existence.

In that connection there is one thing I have wanted for a long time to say to you. I am a regular reader of the *Morning Post* & 99 times out of 100 I am in cordial agreement with it. I think on the whole it has ploughed a straighter furrow than any other paper, & God knows how difficult it is to keep a straight furrow in such times as these. But once or twice lately I have seemed to see a bad wobble, & always, as far as I can judge from the same reason, animosity to 'the Northcliffe Press'. Now, it is just as well to have it clearly understood that the *M.P.* is entirely unconnected with Northcliffe, who excites so much opposition by his often unsavoury methods & often does harm to the causes which he advocates. If, when N[orthcliffe] makes a fool of himself, as he did in the personal attack upon K[itchener], you dance on his prostrate form, I have no earthly objection. But I must say I deprecate, as a rule, polemics between papers which have, in the main, the same object in view, because it does so play the game of the common enemy. I fancy the opponents of National Service in the Government are counting upon the unpopularity in many quarters of 'the Northcliffe Press' to save their own position. As saving their game means ruining the country, I hope they are making a miscalculation. But that depends upon us, I mean upon the convinced supporters of National Service, who are not Northcliffites, but people like you & me. Are we going to let our dislike of Northcliffe & his methods *divide the patriotic forces* at a time like this? We can surely fight with him, when he happens to be in the right without identifying ourselves with him, as I certainly never will do.

There is a personal aspect of this, which affects me very nearly. What I am now going to say is perhaps more than I ought to say, but to a man, whom I trust as I do you, I can run the risk of saying rather too much. There are certain papers, which N. absolutely controls, but *The Times* is not one of them. He could of course dictate the policy of *The Times*, but he would have, first of all, to get rid of Robinson.[3] The latter is a very intimate friend of mine, & I think I fully appreciate his position. In matters of business management he may defer to N., but, when it comes to big public issues, he does not – & never will. He suffers unjustly from the fact, that people insist on treating 'the Northcliffe Press' as a unit & do not use their own eyes to see that, not only in taste & tone, but in substantial questions of policy, the line of *The Times* is often quite different from that of the *Daily Mail* & other papers, which are not only owned by N., but actually run by him. The fiction that *The Times* is simply N.'s mouth-piece, is a successful invention of the enemy. Of course nothing would suit them better than to set *The Times* & the *Morning Post* by the ears, these being the two most sound & consistent patriotic papers – though they both wobble occasionally, we being all human. But Robinson & you are really on all vital matters agreed. You are both patriots first & journalists only in the second place, & I can imagine nothing more tragic than that you should fail to cooperate cordially – on independent lines, of course – at a time like this.

Forgive my extreme frankness, & above all my prolixity.

1. On 29 July Milner's selection as Chairman of the General Council of the National Service League had been announced. At the Cabinet on 11 August, so Milner had been told by F. S. Oliver, there had been pressure for conscription from Curzon, Lloyd George and Churchill. Later in August a Cabinet Committee was set up to examine the matters of conscription, manpower and resources. (See A. M. Gollin, *Proconsul in Politics*, London, 1964, p. 277.) And on 15 August itself the National Register of men between the ages of fifteen and sixty-five, designed to arrive at a view of the total manpower resources of the country, was taken.

2. See *The Times*, 27 May 1915.

3. Geoffrey Robinson (né Dawson), editor of *The Times*, 1911–19.

78
Lord Milner to H. A. Gwynne, 18 August 1915
(MS Gwynne 31)

. . . To come to the more important thing – your 'sizing up' of the Cabinet agrees precisely with what I learn from other sources. K[itchener] is to my mind the real obstacle, because we want *his authority in the country* to carry the thing.[1] That would do it easily. But unfortunately he is such a slippery fish that he is quite capable of giving *you* the impression that he is coming round when he is all the time working against it. Why he should be opposed to it, God only knows. But that is one of the mysteries about him. He is liable to fall under the domination of *idées fixes* and to cling to them desperately, even against all his own interests.

Asquith I am less afraid of. Of course he hates it like the devil. Of course he will use all his diplomacy to defeat it. But if he sees that it is a question of yielding or breaking up his Government he will yield. He hated Coalition almost as much – yet he accepted that rather than the Unspeakable Unthinkable – Loss of Office.

And my! with what moving eloquence he will then commend it to the House of Commons! 'The deepest convictions of a life time sacrificed etc. etc. to save the country.' And how the whole Press will gush over him next morning – quite rightly too – & laud to the skies this supreme exhibition of Courage and Statesmanship.

Yes. Do come and see me Thursday. I, like you, am not thinking about much else now than this, our last chance. 6.30 would suit me rather better than 6. But if it doesn't suit you, come at 6, I shall be here.[2]

1. Compulsory Service. In his capacity as Chairman of the General Council of the National Service League, Milner published a manifesto on National Service on 20 August.
2. Milner's diary records a visit from Gwynne at 6.30 on 19 August 1915. MS Milner 86.

79
H. A. Gwynne to H. H. Asquith, 18 August 1915

I make no apology for again approaching you on the question of national service, for anyone who has followed the operations of this war with reasonable intelligence cannot fail to come to the conclusion that something has to be done, and done quickly, if we are to reap the benefits of victory. The alternatives that are before

us are, a complete and crushing victory over Germany, or a stalemate peace. You yourself, Sir, have put a stalemate peace out of
the question in all your public declarations, and as far as you are
concerned you are pledged up to the hilt to a decisive victory over
Germany.

It is therefore quite unnecessary to dilate upon the dangers of a
stalemate peace, since His Majesty's Government are bound by your
declaration to pursue this war until we triumph over our enemies;
and I venture to say that, in making this declaration, you have had
the support – and will continue to have the support – of 90% of your
fellow countrymen. Matters have come to a point where you and
your colleagues must be assailed by doubts as to whether the Allied
Powers can achieve that victory which you have declared to be
essential to the country's safety, and without which life would be a
misery and civilisation a farce. How, then, are we to accomplish this,
and what are the facts that can help us to a proper appreciation of the
situation?

Of course, the outstanding facts are: first, the disaster which has
happened to the Russian arms. That no Russian army has been
caught in the cleverly conceived operations of the German Head
Quarters Staff does not detract from the fact that they have suffered a
disaster. No army can retreat, and go on retreating, giving up
important towns and strong fortresses, without losing its morale to a
certain extent, and without losses which are difficult to replace.
Pessimists may say that it is impossible to count upon Russia for any
offensive movement for a year. Optimists may claim that she will
recover by the autumn. Between these two schools of thought it is not
unreasonable to argue that it is impossible to expect any great
offensive operations on the part of Russia until next spring. The
second fact of importance is, that the great effort in the Dardanelles
seems to be a failure – at least in the sense that we have not advanced
across the Peninsula and that we have been unable to drive the Turks
from the southern part of it. Unless we are very careful, the Dardanelles Expedition will bleed us white. I venture to say it was a
mistake from the beginning; and presumably in all our calculations
regarding the future, we must count on a continued drain in this
quarter.

Though no doubt German successes in the East have been costly
in men and material, there are no signs that I can see of exhaustion
either of the one or the other. There is, in addition, the moral aspect
of great and undeniable victories. The Germans have not secured a
second Sedan;[1] but they have driven the Russians out of nearly the
whole of Galicia and the whole of Poland; they still seem to be
impregnable on the West; and the faint-hearted among our Allies

117

must at times begin to consider whether the task of beating the Germanic powers is not too great. You, Sir, have never given way to any such doubts: in all your public utterances you have given proof of your faith in ultimate victory which has, I am sure, encouraged both our own people here and our Allies abroad. But it would be useless to shut our eyes to the fact that, whether we like it or not, we are settling down to a war of attrition; and in a war of attrition the first requisite is absolute unanimity among the Allies. Russia is firm; Italy seems determined at any rate to push the Austrian frontier back to the lines dreamed of by her Irredentists. England, I firmly believe, is willing to carry this war on until she wins or is defeated – however long that may be. France, who has bled and suffered terribly, has some of her richest departments in the occupation of the enemy; and, as you know, there are influences at work trying to detach her from her Allies. Nobody – and least of all would I – cast such a libel upon the gallant French nation as to hint or insinuate that they will weaken before the incessant blows of a victorious enemy; but facts are facts, and hardly a month passes but a wail goes up at the terrible cost in young lives; and hardly a month passes but minor – though in some ways powerful – groups of politicians whisper the words: Can we stay the pace? All these influences are at work, and the chief argument which supports them is the argument that England, standing secure in her island, is not pulling her full weight in the Allied boat. There is only one way to secure France to the bitter end, and that is: by the imposition of compulsory national service in Great Britain. Unless this is done, we run the terrible risk of finding France indifferent or unwilling to go on to the end.

But grave as is the situation regarding France, I venture to say that the situation as regards ourselves is still more grave. It perhaps will come as a surprise to you, Sir, to know that, as we are at present, instead of reaching the apogee of our military strength in spring next – when the Allies hope to be at the top of their strength, we shall be on the downward grade.

Let us suppose that we have now 2,400,000 men, and that we hope to keep up a force in the field by March next of 1,200,000, leaving a similar number of men in reserve. Our recruiting numbers are, roughly, 80,000 per month; our losses are 7% effective, that is: killed, missing or wounded beyond hope of going back. There is an additional 3% who are able to return to the firing line within a month or six weeks. These I have counted as permanent casualties for the purpose of these calculations, inasmuch as that amount of men are always absent. Taking for granted that we wish to make our maximum effort next spring, and including this month and next March, this will give us eight months. On the presumption that we have

800,000 men in the firing line now – both in the Dardanelles and in France – and presuming that the casualties will be at the rate of 10% per month, this will give the number of men absent from the front as 80,000 per month. On the supposition that there will be a constant stream of 80,000 recruits per month, recruiting and casualties will balance; but the moment the force is raised beyond the 800,000 casualties will outbalance recruits. Besides, the amount of recruits will tend to decrease, while casualties will increase. Even if you doubt my calculation, it is quite certain that recruiting on the voluntary basis cannot keep up with the losses; and certainly if you increase the forces in the field – as we should increase them in order to bring this war to a quicker victorious end – voluntary effort will not do it. It is not too much to ask England to aim at keeping 2,000,000 men in the field and 2,000,000 in reserve; and this is quite hopeless under the present system. To do less would be to prolong the war; to do more, of course, would bring the end nearer; but to do that, it is essential to have compulsory service.

I have been for many years a strong believer in compulsory service, and the *Morning Post* for many years has been a strong advocate of compulsory service; and I am sure that the present situation is one that renders compulsory service *ad hoc* necessary, irrespective of the question as to whether it should become a permanent portion of our institution or not. With it, I believe we can win; without it, I am firmly convinced that we run the terrible risk of losing. Now, Sir, you are the head of this Government, and on your shoulders lies the enormous responsibility of the most terrible war in England's history. No patriotic man wishes to embarrass you or your Government; but I put it plainly to you, that the vast majority in this country are in favour of compulsory service being enforced at once; and I go further, and say that 95% of your Cabinet are in favour of it, and that 85% of the members of the House of Commons wish to see it carried now. With the best desire in the world to put oneself in the position of those who oppose compulsory service, I can see no argument against its adoption that carries weight. That some few cranks dislike it and oppose it; that the Irish party may refuse to submit to it, is true; but cranks would have to submit, and rather than diminish the national effort we might be forced to allow the Irish Nationalists to contract themselves out of it. But next spring, when the great effort is to be made which will decide the fate of England and Europe – if there is a lack of pluck now – we shall find ourselves face to face with the possibility of a stalemate peace, and the country will blame the Government and will blame you, Sir. For you have only to ask now for permission to impose obligatory service, and I venture to say that the opposition that you would meet with –

both in your Cabinet, in Parliament, and in the country – would be negligible.

1. At Sedan on 1 September 1870 Napoleon III surrendered, with 84,000 men, 2700 officers and 39 generals, to Prussia.

80
H. A. Gwynne to Lady Bathurst, 20 August 1915

Everything goes wrong with the war and that is why, like Mark Tapley,[1] I am cheerful. I will not give way to any despondency. I know our shortcomings – nobody better – but we *shall* win because we must will to win. Henceforth we must all of us hold before the people the carrot of victory and keep telling them that it can be secured if we will do our duty. Perhaps my cheerfulness is due to the fact that I see victory can only be got by national service and national service is, I believe, on the eve of being adopted. It has been hard work but well worth the labour.

... After all, the *M.P.* is you. None of us could do anything without your firm backing and whatever the credit is, it is yours. What I feel is this: you are so far superior to these dirty little notoriety seekers that it gives you a most tremendous pull. You do not want and never ask for that kind of recognition. Your reward is in the thing done. You see it gives you such tremendous power over the seekers after advertisement. Just as I feel a contempt for mere money makers I sometimes say to myself when I am brought up against one of these gentry 'Well you may be proud of your beastly money making but *I* can make *you* squirm'. And indeed, I do sometimes out of pure mischief.

But that does not prevent your feeling a sense of injustice when others reap where you have sown. But do they reap? They claim the credit but I doubt whether they get it. Take National Service. When it is adopted, won't everybody say well this is a triumph for the *M.P.* which has been consistently for it, when others wouldn't touch it with a barge pole. ... I am now engaged in frightening Ld. K[itchener] into National Service and I think – in fact I may say I am sure – it is going all right.

1. A character in *Martin Chuzzlewit* by Charles Dickens.

120

81

H. A. Gwynne to D. Lloyd George, 21 August 1915 (Lloyd George MSS D16/19/4)

I wired to you early this morning to say that Lord Derby's[1] dinner was off. K[itchener] unfortunately has to give dinner to several officers and as it is a long-standing engagement he cannot very well get out of it.[2]

I think the situation is ever so much clearer. K., I feel convinced, is determined to have compulsory service. But I imagine that he is awaiting an opportunity of making what he can of the register. I cannot help feeling, too, that he would like to have the consciousness of the support of the best men in the country. Possibly, he fears that a declaration on his part in favour of compulsion might result in attacks upon himself . . . he would like to fe l that he won't stand alone.

It has occurred to me that it would not be a bad thing if you could make it quite clear that you consider a declaration on his part to be a patriotic step and one that is demanded by the conditions of the present struggle. Perhaps you might think it a good thing to write me a letter on the lines of satisfying K. on the points I have enumerated above so that I could show it to him. But you will understand that the suggestion is entirely mine and not his, for indeed I have not seen him since his return from France.

I hope you will derive the fullest benefit to your health at Folkestone. In these days good men are rare.

1. Lord Derby, Chairman of the West Lancashire Territorial Association. Gwynne had been pressing Derby about the introduction of Compulsory Service since midsummer. In a reply of 6 August Derby told him that the authorities were afraid of the effect of bringing in conscription: 'A lot of the Trades Union people are dead against it and it might, though I do not say it would, end in a big general strike.' (MS Gwynne 32.)
2. To Lord Percy on 27 August Gwynne gave another explanation as to why the arrangement fell through: 'K[itchener] backed out saying it would look too much like a "cabal".' (MS Gwynne 21.)

82

H. A. Gwynne to General Sir Henry Wilson, 24 August 1915 (HAG/35 no. 18, IWM)

All the points I agree with – but although some of them are unattainable, Compulsion is, I think, certain. Its been the devil's own job to make K[itchener] see that national safety and his safety lay upon the same lines. The following gives you an idea of the curious way his mind works:– K: 'I have to contemplate the possibilities of a bad peace.' I: 'A bad peace will mean the end of you. Then there will be hangings. You must have Compulsion to avoid a bad peace.'

However I now think it is really all right. Squiff[1] has been the obstacle, and K. But figures are nasty things when they are against you and the figures are against both. K. has wanted careful handling. He won't be pushed and asks not to be pushed but promises to deliver the goods. If he doesn't, there will be big resignations from the Cabinet, including Carson, B[onar] Law, Lloyd George, Curzon[2] and Austen Chamberlain.

I get all your news via Percy. K. was much impressed by something that Joffre said to him. I imagine it was H[enry] W[ilson] speaking through Père Joffre. Am I wrong?

I'm working night and morning for the good cause*s*. I shall crack up unless I succeed for the waste of effort would bring on a reaction. But I mean to carry it through.

P.S.   Give my kindest regards to Huguet.[3]

1. Asquith.
2. Lord Curzon, Viceroy of India, 1898–1905, Lord Privy Seal, May 1915–December 1916.
3. French Military Attaché in London, 1906–11, head of French mission attached to the British Expeditionary Force.

Editor's postscript: On 24 August Kitchener, at Asquith's insistence, had been questioned by Lord Crewe's War Policy Committee concerning the manpower requirements of the army. Kitchener said that voluntary means alone would not be enough to raise the seventy divisions at which he was aiming, and that he would demand a Conscription Bill by the end of the year. CAB 37/133/10.

83
H. A. Gwynne to Lady Bathurst, 24 August 1915

. . . I have devoted every spare moment and every spare energy to the all-important question of compulsion. Now I will tell you what I have done and shall tell nobody else. If compulsion comes as I am firmly convinced it will come, I can fairly say that the final stages are due to my effort and I venture to say too that nobody will ever give me the slightest credit. Further, I don't care a twopenny hang whether they do or not but I'd like you to know that for a month . . . I have not ceased for one single hour. I have so managed things that K[itchener] has never been a day without the 'subtle poison' being instilled into him. I am sure he has never suspected me. Even in France, Joffre repeated to him words which were mine. I have now to work with vain men and make them believe that their arguments were their own and they have gone swaggering away quite convinced that they have done the trick.

I hope you will burn this letter when you have read it because I should hate you to think that I am, what your boys would call a 'buckstuck'. But I want to tell you this because I know you would like to feel that the *M.P.* (for after all I am a mere nobody except as Editor of the *M.P.*) has done more for National Service than all the press of England put together.

. . . Joffre and K. got on wonderfully well. They always do. Joffre whispered into his ear his private opinion that England would have to come to compulsion and the sooner the better.

. . . Please don't take Carson's letter as a snub for I lunched with him on Friday and he told me how sorry he was he could not manage to come and stay with you. He explained how the doctor had insisted on his staying at the sea side as the sea air was essential to his health. He is not a humbug and he's genuinely sorry he could not come.

84
H. A. Gwynne to Lady Bathurst, 26 August 1915

I am afraid that the real and the ideal are as far apart as the two poles. Take K[itchener], for instance. Here is a man of courage and resolution. Yet he neither perceives his great power and his great duty. And yet he seems to me to be the biggest man we have got. Perhaps it is that great responsibilities induce hesitation. Yet I think, were I in his place I would risk the chances that he seems to fear. This national service, which is coming, is such an obvious necessity that one would think that any statesman would 'go blind' on it. And yet he doesn't seem to dare unless the way is prepared.

You and I and all who are of our way of thinking must absolutely sink ourselves if only in order to shame the advertisers. Whether we come to have the credit or not, doesn't matter one single toss of a button, as long as the thing is done. Take K. for example. Every time I talk to him I suggest new ideas to his mind so that he can use them as *his own*. Speeches, orders, discussions and decisions in the Cabinet are put down to him and he has all the credit. And a jolly good thing too. What does anything matter as long as we beat the Bosches [*sic*]. I am almost reconciled to an armchair in an office because I know I am doing good work.

A correspondent of *The Times* – John Buchan – came to me today and wanted something done. He said 'I come to the *M.P.* because it is the only really clean and patriotic paper in England'. There was my and your reward. We'll win out because we absolutely forget ourselves.

. . . As regards the Dardanelles, it is a very unhappy business. But we can at least hold on till the Turks are sick. We can't retire and I don't think we can do much more than we are at present. . . .

85
H. A. Gwynne to Lady Bathurst, 30 August 1915

. . . About the Dardanelles, the chief reason why I think that we must stay on is that if we throw up the sponge there, the Mohammedans of Egypt, Northern Africa and India would be in a ferment. The Moslem only respects one thing – success and if we actually acknowledge failure by withdrawing, they would break out. Besides I think that a withdrawal is a tactical impossibility and we cannot get out now without dreadful loss of men and a total loss of guns. But it is only fair to say that men who are much better acquainted with warfare and strategy still advise a total evacuation as the lesser of two evils.

As for treating with the Turks, I am afraid that is impossible. We are promised to Russia and any arrangement with Turkey would sow distrust in Russia.

We are beginning a big move in France in order to help the Russians. The only thing is to pray for success.

86
H. A. Gwynne to Lady Bathurst, 31 August 1915

I feel with you that this Dardanelles adventure is bleeding us white. At the same time, I cannot hope that we can get out of [it] without such loss of prestige and such material losses as would do us infinite harm both in Europe and in all Moslem countries. It is one of those wicked mad adventures whose consequences seem never to be foreseen and are in my opinion quite unforeseeable. We must hold on now or all is lost. But I would dearly like to hang a few people who are responsible.

My secret information is that as long as Romania refuses to pass munitions through, the Turks *may* retire. Personally, I would not count on anything of the kind.

I have heard today quite privately that the Czar proposes to send the Grand Duke Nicolas off to the Caucasus and take over the command of the Russian Armies himself, with General Russki as Chief of the Staff. I hope this is not true but I fear it may be. The Grand Duke seems to have shown great qualities as a commander and if the Czar fails, I am afraid his throne may be in danger.

. . . Nat. Service is all right, thank God.

87
Viscount Esher to H. A. Gwynne, 3 September 1915 (MS Gwynne 18)

. . . I think Douglas Haig[1] would like a visit from you. . . . Northcliffe is sympathetic but so Lloyd Georgian that the 'Press' will not help us much. You will have to put your back into the question.

Nothing short of a complete change of system i.e. taking the charge of the Army Votes, will do any good.

Henderson[2] is mandarinized to such a degree that even he will not help us much.

1. Commanding the 1st Army.
2. Arthur Henderson, Labour politician appointed to the Board of Education, 25 May 1915.

88
H. A. Gwynne to Lady Bathurst, 17 September 1915

. . . Hield[1] told me that you had talked with him about National Service, and that you took exception to a line in the Leader in which we accepted National Service *ad hoc* for the duration of the war on the present system as a means of ending the war. I am the culprit in this matter, for I have felt all along that if we are going to make military service compulsory such as we shall be bound to have for the present war, it would kill National Service after the war, and for this reason: this Government will not do what I should like to see them do and that is, treat the new lot whom they will have to compel to come in on a different basis. They are afraid of the cry of cheap soldiers and although there might be a slight difference in allowances, there is no doubt whatever that compulsory service for the purposes of this war will be such that it will be hopeless to expect the same sort to continue after the war. This, of course, does not prevent our being perfectly consistent in saying that, during the war just as before the war we have been advocates of National Service, and also that after the war we mean to try and do all we can to make National Service a permanent part of our institution; but I am quite convinced that it would be impossible to continue the compulsory service necessary for the war, after the war is over, simply because the expense would be too frightful. In fact, as you know, I have agreed with Lord Roberts[2] that compulsion during the war is rather inclined to do more harm than good to our advocacy of permanent National Service. Anything done in a hurry is sure to be done badly, and that is why I advised the Leader Writer to agree that compulsory service *ad hoc* should be for the duration of the war only, for if we urge it now in a moment of crisis as a permanent part of our national life, we shall ruin National Service altogether: and I feel more keenly about that than about anything else except, perhaps, Tariff Reform, which I think will come as a result of the war.

I am afraid there is some dirty work going on over this National Service, but my last interview with K[itchener] seems to have put it perfectly right. I am enclosing you a copy of a confidential letter I wrote during my holiday to K.'s secretary, who is a great friend of mine who passes on my letters to his chief. I heard to-day that the letter had a very notable effect. You saw the speech of Thomas[3] in the House yesterday. Everybody is shouting about it; it is a great disaster to the country as it is a direct incitement to strike. That, of course, is what Asquith is continually saying to K.

1. Journalist on the *Morning Post*.
2. Field-Marshal Lord Roberts of Kandahar.
3. J. H. Thomas, Labour MP for Derby.

Enclosure in letter 88
H. A. Gwynne to Colonel O. Fitzgerald, 12 September 1915

CONFIDENTIAL

I saw your chief on Tuesday last and found him very disturbed and unsettled. I don't altogether wonder at it, for the politicians are putting the whole burden on his shoulders.

Roughly speaking he seemed to regard compulsion as a great difficulty and one that, at any rate, cannot be solved until the results of the [National] Register are sorted. He seemed, too, to doubt the result of the mixing up [of] conscripts with volunteers at the front. Anyway he was worried because he has not made a decision.

Now I can talk to you quite openly. I am afraid there is some dirty work going on. Will you put this to K[itchener]. The *Daily Chronicle* and the *Daily News* are at the beck and call of certain Ministers I know. I also know that the active campaign which they have carried on against compulsion has been in a way suggested. I admit all the folly of the Harmsworth propaganda but I see evil in the Radical press propaganda. K. has to stand alone. But he has also to consider these points. If, after a reasonable but not too prolonged an interval, nothing is done, I believe that Lloyd George, Carson, Curzon, Churchill and probably Bonar Law and Chamberlain will come out. Carson already talks of being useless in the Cabinet. He hated going in and it was your humble servant who persuaded him to come in. If they come out, bang goes the Asquith, McKenna, Harcourt combination. Now don't let K. make a mistake. Asquith is the most unpopular man in the country. His wife goes about talking pro-Germanism and his own Ministers feel a contempt for him. They are politicians pure and simple and they know that as long as they have K. they can keep themselves afloat. But do remember that in the country Lloyd George is ever so much more powerful than Asquith. If these men come out, as I really believe they will, your chief will be immediately affected, for you have said that he would go if Asquith goes. That, if I may say so, is a most futile decision. The country trusts K., it doesn't trust Asquith a yard.

The country has made up its mind that compulsion is necessary. I wish to God K. could realise his power. If he would only say now that he is examining the question of figures as a result of the Register and that he will give a decision within say a fortnight, *and if at the same time he would ask the P.M. and McKenna to keep their press quiet, and ask our people to keep theirs*, you would have no discussion; and K.'s decision would be accepted by this country most loyally.

K. told me very confidentially of a letter from French. To-day I received a letter which told me all about it, so there is no secret about it. And why, in God's name, should K. put himself into co-operation with a general whom he may at any moment have to supersede.

Believe me, my dear Fitz, the situation is grave beyond words. Let K. do as I advise – the whole thing will blow over. Otherwise I can see a bust-up and K. dragged at the tail of Asquith – a real disaster for the country and for him.

89
H. A. Gwynne to D. Lloyd George, 17 September 1915 (Lloyd George MSS D16/19/5)

I enclose you the Memorandum I promised to let you have.[1]

1. A copy was also sent to Bonar Law.

Confidential Report by J. D. Irvine, 13 September 1915, on the
Trades Union Congress at Bristol

There was much wire-pulling before the Congress met and also
during the week to influence its decisions on the war. The local
labour leaders in Bristol belong to the extreme 'Pacifist' or pro-
German section. They captured the party machine before the war
broke out at a time when trade unionism in Bristol was apathetic and
badly-organised. There has been no popular election of leaders
since, and the respectable artizans generally are disgusted to find
themselves tied to men who, they declare, do not represent the real
mind of the workers. A protest against their methods was made
publicly by Mr Whitefield, of the Bristol Miners Union, at the last
day's sitting of the Congress. Councillor W. H. Ayles, one of the most
prominent of the pro-German members of the Reception Committee, has made anti-war speeches on Durdham Downs, and has had to
seek the protection of the police against a crowd of enraged citizens.
Men of his stamp together with the local branch of the Union of
Democratic Control[1] have done everything possible by fair means
and foul to undermine the loyalty of the Trade Union delegates to the
prosecution of the war, and have conspicuously failed.

The fact that a 'no conscription' resolution was passed unanimously is not to be taken as an indication that in no circumstances
will the Trade Unions accept the principle of compulsion. It represents rather an emphatic declaration against what a leading
delegate called 'the attempt to boss or bounce us' into conscription.
The feeling also was general among the delegates that the war can be
brought to a successful issue under the voluntary system. This view
is held with perfect honesty and is not dictated by any disinclination
to face whatever further calls on labour – either for more men or more
munition workers – may be necessary.

Several of the most influential of the delegates assured me in
private conversation that if the Cabinet solemnly declares with
united voice that the compulsory principle is essential they will not
oppose its introduction. They say: 'Let the Government frankly take
the representatives of the organised workers into their confidence,
tell us exactly what they want, and they will find that they will shrink
at nothing which is requisite to bring victory to us and our Allies.'
This is the attitude, for example, of Mr John Hodge, M.P. (the
present leader of the Labour Party in the House of Commons) who,
at a meeting on 8 September denounced any man who would even
mention peace at the present time as a traitor to his country. It is

necessary to present this other aspect of the question that the introduction of 'conscription' – even with the authority of the Government – would inevitably create a good deal of ferment in the Labour world. The pro-Germans, at present a negligible minority, would use it for all they are worth to stir up strife and I think that, while the responsible heads of the Labour party would loyally stand by the Government, the pro-Germans would add to their ranks a considerable number of those who decline to believe that any departure from the voluntary system is required. A great deal obviously would depend on how the matter was put before the country by the Government. A declaration that without compulsory service we could not end the war, and that there would be no 'conscription' when the war is over would, I believe, reduce the opposition to a minimum.

The Congress demonstrated in the clearest fashion that the great bulk of organised labour is whole-heartedly in favour of the war and means to see it through. Only seven out of 607 could be found to oppose the resolution justifying the war, and expressing a determination to give every assistance to the Government. There is scarcely a delegate who has not a son or brother or some other near relative fighting for the country, and this 'human' element is an important factor in the situation. Many of them have made substantial sacrifices. Mr Seddon, the President of the Congress, is in trouble with his Union (the Shopkeepers Assistants) because, when addressing a meeting at Tunbridge Wells in support of recruiting, he said that every able-bodied man behind the counter who could possibly be spared ought to be fighting for his country, and urged ladies to refuse to allow themselves to be served with goods by young men who were fit for service. A section of his Union appears to think that Mr Seddon 'cast a slur' on shop assistants, but he stands by what he said.

Mr Lloyd George's visit and address to the Congress was timely and useful. His 'straight talk' has aroused no resentment except on the part of the extreme section. The Parliamentary Committee is to investigate the specific charges made by the Minister of Munitions. Its object is not to white-wash slackers or wrongdoers, but to get at the facts of the case from the Trade Union point of view. Beyond all doubt the responsible men in every Union concerned in Munitions work are determined to keep faith with the Government. They declare that they cannot prevent occasional 'sectional trouble' but admit it is their bounden duty to check it to the utmost of their power. Mr Lloyd George's speech did a great deal to remove the suspicion of 'profit-mongering' on the part of individual firms. The pro-German section has been mainly responsible for raising the cry that the workers are being exploited by their employers for the purpose of increasing the masters' profits, and for the suggestion that the Government will not implement their bargain to restore trade union conditions when the war is over.

To sum up: I am convinced that the proceedings of the Congress have been very helpful to the future progress of the war so far as organised labour is concerned. The evil-geniuses of labour have been pulverised and the nakedness of their cause has been exposed. They will continue their pernicious propagandism, of course, but with a greatly weakened authority. Labour is sensitive of the matter of criticism and it is worthy of note that at this Congress the custom dropped some years ago of according a vote of thanks to the Press at the close of the week's proceedings was revived. This resolution of thanks was moved by Mr Will Thorne M.P., who recognised the fair-minded fashion in which the newspapers without exception had dealt with the Congress and its business.

P.S.   It is pertinent to inquire what might have been the effect of Mr Lloyd George's 'Manifesto' issued today had it been within the knowledge of the delegates to the Trade Unions Congress last week. This necessarily to a considerable extent is matter of conjecture. Personally, I do not believe it would have influenced to any appreciable degree the decisions arrived at by the Congress. The speech of the Minister of Munitions to the Congress was a call for more men purely for munition work, and conveyed the impression that this being a 'war of machinery' the speeding up of the production of munitions is the matter of immediate urgency rather than any large addition to the combatant military forces. Mr Lloyd George says he wants 80,000 more skilled artizans and 200,000 unskilled workers of both sexes. The Secretaries of the Unions engaged in munition work declare on their honour that it is difficult to find in the country at the present time 80,000 skilled craftsmen not engaged on war work. They can only be obtained by removing men from private employment, or bringing back skilled men from the front. They are prepared to do all they can to find these men. They also have pledged themselves to render every assistance to the Government in providing more recruits for active military operations on the voluntary basis. I do not think that their objection to 'conscription' could be removed by the declaration of a single Cabinet Minister, however eminent he may be. They ask for a united declaration of the Cabinet coupled with a presentation of facts to justify the demand for compulsion. They have great faith in Lord Kitchener, and they point out that he, as Minister of War, has never declared the failure of the voluntary system.

1. Founded between the outbreak of war and November 1914 by MPs C. P.

Trevelyan, E. D. Morel, A. Ponsonby and Ramsay MacDonald and the writer Norman Angell in an effort to produce more public and parliamentary accountability in the formation of British foreign policy.

90

H. A. Gwynne to D. Lloyd George, 1 October 1915
(Lloyd George MSS D16/19/6)

. . . You cannot altogether drive the working man. He wants, as well, a bit of humouring. Monsieur Thomas,[1] in France, decorates those workmen in the munitions factories who do good work with the *médaille militaire*. Why not have a decoration for *our* workmen? At present those who do really good work seem to get from their fellow workmen more kicks than halfpence. They would be immensely proud of a decoration given them by the authorities as a mark of appreciation of their efforts. Everybody is 'doing his bit' to win but everybody who is 'doing his bit' likes recognition.

1. Albert Thomas, French Minister of Munitions.

91

D. Lloyd George to H. A. Gwynne, 2 October 1915
(Lloyd George MSS D16/19/7)

The suggestion you make has already been considered and a promise has been given of a medal to the hard workers. I am not sure it will produce very much effect. M. Thomas is coming over on Monday for a conference and I shall certainly put the point to him.

92

H. A. Gwynne to D. Lloyd George, 5 October 1915
(Lloyd George MSS D16/19/8)

Things seem to me to go from bad to worse.[1] Could I come and lunch with you on Sunday at Walton?[2] I would drive down in time to have a talk before lunch if you have guests.

I am so sorry I was out this morning or I should have been delighted to lunch with you.

1. On this day Lord Derby was appointed Director-General of Recruiting. On 7 October he informed Gwynne that the Trades Union Congress had said

they could get the men required by voluntary means and that he meant to let it be understood that if the scheme which carried his name failed there was no alternative to compulsory service. (MS Gwynne 32.)

2. Walton Heath, Lloyd George's Sussex address.

93
H. A. Gwynne to Lady Bathurst, 7 October 1915

The war comes home to one when in the same week, one of our staff and a dear old boy friend like John Kipling[1] are killed off. I only heard of it the day before yesterday so yesterday I went down to poor old Kipling and spent the day with him. Such splendid pluck. When I arrived, he said 'What did you come down for?' I said 'to see what I can do'. 'You can do nothing' he said but I saw a quiver in his lips which showed how the thing had gone home.

. . . Today I've worked from 9 to 6 preventing the Cabinet from going wrong – and, by God, I've succeeded! It's been the worst day I've had since the war began. I've only succeeded in delaying but twenty-four hours delay will do the trick. It's all about Salonika. The Government actually wanted to come away![2] I've stopped it, I think, but it's taken all the energy out of me for today. . . .

1. Rudyard Kipling's son; he had one other child, a daughter.
2. Two days before, on 5 October, one British and one French division had landed at Salonika with a view to assisting Serbia.

94
H. A. Gwynne to H. H. Asquith, 8 October 1915

I have from time to time ventured to address to you letters on certain phases of the conduct of the war which, in my opinion, merit the designation of crises. You will remember that I wrote to you just before the Gallipoli Expedition was landed begging of you to recall it, for I felt it was a step of such great importance and so mistaken from the military point of view, that the landing of that force might have such an effect upon the war as to deprive us of victory. Without appearing to assume the attitude of infallibility, I think you will now agree that, if you had acted upon my suggestion, we should have avoided errors which I am afraid have had consequences which are now irreparable.

On the occasion of the German advance to Warsaw I took the opportunity of urging the Government to adopt National Service as a *riposte* to the German successes, and as an urgent necessity of the war.

I again venture to think that, if this advice had been followed, our position to-day would be immensely strengthened.

But now has arisen a crisis which seems to me to be graver than any that has occurred in the course of the war; but before putting forward my suggestions I should like to tell you the facts as I know them from my diplomatic friends.

In the first place, we have solemnly promised Serbia that we will give her assistance if she is attacked by Bulgaria. In pursuance of that promise we landed troops, at the invitation and with the consent of the Prime Minister of Greece and of the Greek King. We were warned that a protest would be made, but that it would be merely formal; and I understand that, as a matter of pure fact, no protest has yet been addressed to the British Government against the landing of British troops, though the French Government have received the formal protest which they were told to expect.

Ever since Turkey threw in her lot with Germany, it was obvious to any student of the war that sooner or later Germany would attempt to move south-east; and I confess that I have seen no sort of preparation on the part of the Cabinet for such a move. Now it has come, it seems to have caught us quite unprepared. The defection, or treachery (whichever you may like to call it) of Bulgaria was so obvious that students of the Balkans looked upon it as the chief danger against which the Entente Powers should guard. Our diplomatists presumably must have known the character of Ferdinand,[1] and even as late as six weeks ago they should have realised the effect of the resignation of the Minister of War. Monsieur Take Jonesco,[2] a warm friend of the Entente, telegraphed to me from Romania at that time and warned me of the importance of that event. This warning I sent on to the Foreign Office – apparently without any effect. From that moment all students of Bulgaria knew that there was a movement afoot the chief object of which was to range Bulgaria on the side of Germany.

But without going back on the mistakes of the past, we have quite enough to do to consider the difficulties of the present situation. The invasion of Serbia by a German–Austro-Hungarian army, coupled with the possibility of a flank attack by Bulgaria can have but one result. Serbia will put up one good fight and then collapse and be obliged to make peace. Now the great asset we have in the Balkans – and we have held it for many years – is, that the Balkan States believe in our word and trust us. We have given the most solemn undertaking that in her great necessity, Serbia can count upon the assistance of British and French troops. British and French troops have indeed landed at Salonika with the consent of the Greek Government, but the number of the men that have been sent out is an insult to Serbia and a disgrace to us. The future attitude of the two remaining Balkan States that are now neutral hangs in the balance, and will depend entirely upon our line of action. If we break our word to Serbia, these States will think it better to guard a neutrality benevolent to the Central Powers. Germany will secure a road to Constantinople and then, a month after Constantinople receives the supplies of munitions so necessary for her, we shall be driven out of Gallipoli.

Now, Sir, these are the facts as I see them; and we are all anxious to know what the Government are going to do. Criticism is always easy, but what I put forward is not criticism, but suggestion. First of all, we must keep our word to Serbia; if we do not, we shall lose the confidence that has been built up by years of straight dealing with all the Balkan States. We shall lose the support of Romania and Greece, and we shall then have to prepare for a most vigorous attack on Egypt. In order to counter this, I would suggest that we at once evacuate Gallipoli and send those troops into Serbia. There is an objection to this, and that is: that Greece may not altogether like the evacuation of Gallipoli inasmuch as it would free Turkish troops to attack her along the Aegean. But this objection we can overrule if we promise additional military aid to Greece, and inform Greece that all that she can take on her eastern borders along the coast up to Enos, she can keep.

We have in Gallipoli not more, I should imagine, than 150,000 troops. These thrown into the Vardar Valley would be an effective check to Bulgaria. Your military advisers will no doubt tell you that the Salonika–Nish line is not of sufficient capacity to push a vast number of troops with speed, and in answer to this I would suggest that we only use the railway for supplies and munitions, and let the men and their transport march. The distance is really not very great: from Salonika to Kostendil is not much more than 150 miles, and though the troops would have to march a bit to the east in order to keep to good roads, they could certainly do it in twenty days. And surely Serbia can delay the forces both in her rear and in her front long enough to enable help to reach her. I would counsel the Army authorities to purchase supplies in Greece to a great extent, and to pay generous prices for all they buy; so that the Greeks would have no reason for resenting the presence of British troops.

In addition to the Gallipoli troops we ought, between us and the French, to send up an additional 150,000. You might, Sir, with justice retort on me by telling me that I am now advocating a subsidiary expedition which might become a major one – which was the very reason I gave for objecting to the original Gallipoli Expedition. This is true, but the analogies are not on all-fours. We had made no promise to any of our Allies or even friendly neutrals regarding Gallipoli. We had no engagements and whether we went or did not go made no difference to anybody except ourselves. Besides, from the number of men sent out, it showed that the Cabinet looked upon it as a minor operation instead of a major operation, which it always appeared to me, and which it has turned out to be. In addition to this, our success there would not necessarily have turned any waverer, for, as I have already pointed out, neither Bulgaria, nor Greece, nor Romania is enamoured of the idea of the Dardanelles being in the hands of Russia. Besides, the direct and solemn promise to Serbia leaves us no alternative. But it must be a big undertaking and we must even be prepared to contemplate a real diversion in the Balkans. It is the last outlet of Germany, and once that is blocked Germany is besieged and Turkey dies of strangulation. None of these considerations held good of the Gallipoli Expedition.

The facts of the position differing as they do from the facts of the original Gallipoli Expedition are of tremendous importance in the present struggle. The issue is really whether, in the first place, we are to keep our word to our friends – a matter to which I attach very great importance – and secondly, whether we are to have a million soldiers of Romania and Greece on our side, or against us; or at any rate benevolently inclined towards the enemy. I assert that, if we rise to the occasion, we can secure the active aid of these large forces; and once we have secured them, I think that the end of the war is in sight.

Apart from our obligations to Serbia, we stand under obligations to Venizelos[3] and the Entente party in Greece. 90% of the people and 60% of the Chamber are now in favour of the Entente Powers. If we land any large force – paying our way generously – and if we succeed in pushing back the Bulgarians in their attack on the Serbian flank and rear, we shall rouse in our favour the whole of the Greek nation, and not even King Constantine can stand against it. We should most probably, by the fact of our successful advance to Serbia, bring about a revolution in Bulgaria; and we might, by the exercise of prodigious activity, get the Bulgarians entirely on our side. But if we hesitate or do anything that shows our resolution to be weak, I believe it would give such an advantage to Germany as might even give her hopes of going beyond the ideal of a 'stalemate peace' to that of obtaining a real victory.

The soldiers will tell you, Sir, that it is difficult to get troops, to get equipment, to get transport; and somebody in the Government has got to take upon himself the task of driving, pushing, and hustling generally the military machine. It is not too late if the first step is taken at once; but if it is done in a week's time, it is too late. Upon the Cabinet lies this appalling responsibility, and because a body like the Cabinet may find it difficult to translate into immediate action their decisions, it is all the more necessary that someone should take the matter in hand now. I know of the objections to these proposals – military, naval, and political. I will not bother you with a recapitulation of them because I have no doubt you know them better than I do; but I have not seen one objection which is strong enough to be compared for one moment, in importance, to the enormous prize that we can gain by overriding it.

In conclusion, I should like to tell you of an incident that happened the other day at a cloak room of one of the London stations. Four private soldiers arrived from the trenches on leave and went to deposit their rifles and packs and their trophies which they had brought with them. The man in charge of the cloak room wished to charge 2d. for each package, whereupon one of the men spoke up as follows. He said: 'We shall pay 2d. for each of us. We have just come from the trenches and it is men like us who are shielding the men like you in comfort. If you do not take the money we offer you, we shall bash your head in.' The cloak room attendant saw the futility of further remonstrance and immediately gave in to the soldiers. The significant thing, however, is, that the crowd which followed the soldiers from the cloak room cheered them heartily after this difference with the cloak room attendant, and continued to cheer them till the soldiers went outside the station. I cannot help regarding that incident as significant.

The country does not know and realise the danger of the present situation. You, Sir, are the head of the Government that never warned the people of the coming German danger. The people are bitter and sore about it, and feel that their leaders were not wise enough to see the danger or were not honest enough to tell them of it. There is a seething mass of discontent throughout the country about the conduct of the war, and I should not be surprised at an outbreak. If we lose the Balkans believe me, Sir, Sir Edward Grey will have to go. It is part of my duty, as editor of a newspaper, to feel the pulse of the public, and never during my career as editor have I been so clearly convinced of the existence of a spirit of anger as at the present time. The public – and by the public I do not mean hysterical old ladies, but sound, sober thinking men of every class – show by their letters to me that they have a feeling that there is some influence at the heart of the Government which appears as if it does not want us to win the war. You may disregard this or laugh at the belief, but it is there; and if you have a real disaster this feeling will show itself in action and you will have riots – riots not in favour of peace, but riots in favour of a more vigorous conduct of the war.

One thing more and I have done. Germany on the whole has been most successful on land; she has dismissed nearly 100 officers;

France has done well, and she has done the same; Russia has successes to her credit, and she has also made great changes among her generals; Italy has, I believe, dismissed four already. We, who have not been so extraordinarily successful in the conduct of the war, have not dismissed one – except perhaps some smaller man who has been made a scapegoat. Are you aware, Sir, of the existence in the British Army in Flanders and Gallipoli of a deep-seated strong discontent? Any statesman who ignores it is making one of the greatest mistakes it is possible to make.

1. King of Bulgaria.
2. Leader of the Romanian Conservative Democrat Party; entered the Romanian Cabinet, 12 December 1916.
3. E. Venizelos, Prime Minister of Greece, 1910–March 1915 and August–October 1915; formed a dissident government in Salonika, October 1916; returned to Athens as Prime Minister in June 1917 after the abdication of King Constantine.

95
H. A. Gwynne to Lady Bathurst, 12 October 1915

. . . Yes, if the Old Turk – who was a gentleman – had been in power, we could have done something with him but the Young Turk was a beast from the very beginning.[1] They sold themselves body and soul to Germany and nothing we could have done (short of following into Constantinople the *Goeben* and the *Breslau*)[2] would have altered things.

A very great secret. Edward Carson is resigning (indeed he has resigned).[3]

At the end of this week, I will send down to you for your historical collection a full account of the last week's doings. I have worked like fifty-thousand niggers and I will describe it all. You will be interested. I think this Government will break up.

1. Since July 1908 the Ottoman Empire had been ruled by the Young Turkish Committee of Union and Progress.
2. German battleships, which escaped into Turkish waters in August 1914.
3. The fact of Carson's resignation was made public on 20 October. The *Morning Post* article on this stressed the need for a national policy and a national leader and for the exclusion of German interests from the economy of the British Empire:
    Hitherto our politicians have never once made a robust national appeal to the interests and the racial instincts of this stout old nation. . . . What is most urgently required is that those who think with Sir Edward Carson range themselves upon his side and organise themselves into a possible

alternative Government strong enough in men and interests to take over the heavy responsibilities which are being shirked by the present holders of office.

96
H. A. Gwynne to Sir John Simon, 18 October 1915
(HAG/30 no. 1, IWM)

You wrote me a letter on October 11 in which the following phrase occurred: 'Where, however, the instructions to the Press are reminders of the provisions of Regulations under the Defence of the Realm Act, and it is possible to institute a prosecution with a fair prospect of securing a conviction, a prosecution is, so far as I am concerned, always instituted.' Your letter was in answer to a letter of mine in which I complained that those papers who, like the *Daily Telegraph* and myself and others, not only carried out the letter of the law, but the spirit of it, received no encouragement; and that no punishment was meted out to those who most flagrantly broke both the letter and the spirit of the law. I wish to draw your attention to an article in today's *Daily Chronicle*, of which I enclose you a cutting, and I would particularly ask you to consider the following extracts.

> Lord Kitchener, as in duty bound, looks ahead; and in order to maintain in the field for the whole of next year the 70 divisions which the War Secretary estimates to be necessary, the present rate at which recruits are coming in will need to be doubled. In the next four months Lord Kitchener will want in round numbers 500,000 new men. A weekly flow of 30,000 men for the infantry is needed, with 5,000 more for ancillary services, such as the A.S.C., the A.O.C., and the R.A.M.C. – branches of the Army into which men above the present military age can be drafted.
>
> The National Register has revealed the existence of 1,900,000 unstarred men of military age, meaning by 'unstarred' men who are not engaged on munitions, in productive industries, and on the railways – for the railway service, though not a productive employment, has already yielded all the men of military age that can be spared. This total of 1,900,000 includes a considerable percentage of men who have already been rejected for the Army on account of physical disabilities. The number of men really available for the Army does not exceed 1,250,000.

May I draw your attention to the Defence of the Realm Act, Part I., which is a preamble setting forth the purposes of the said Act. In Section A, this purpose is more clearly defined.

To prevent persons communicating with the enemy, or obtaining information for that purpose, or for any purpose calculated to jeopardise the success of the operations of any of His Majesty's forces, or to assist the enemy.

In Section 14 it lays down that no person shall publish information

With respect to any works or measures undertaken for or connected with the fortification of any place, if the information is such as would be directly or indirectly useful to the enemy.

The fact published in the *Daily Chronicle* that Lord Kitchener has fixed the total forces of this country at 70 divisions is a breach both of the spirit and of the letter of the Defence of the Realm Act. It gives information of enormous value to the enemy. Whether the enemy knows or not, is beside the question – possibly they do. But the fact remains that a matter which has always been a profound secret is published and will be read by the enemy tomorrow morning. The details of the National Register lay bare the whole of our resources, and I consider – if you will allow me to say so – that it is your duty as Home Secretary to institute proceedings at once against the *Daily Chronicle* for the divulgence of information which is of material benefit to the enemy.

I hope you will not misunderstand this letter and think that it is dictated by any newspaper rivalry, or by any other motive except that of a desire to see this disclosing of secrets to the enemy discontinued once and for all. I can assure you that, unless this is done, the enemy will continue to receive information of the most valuable kind.

I feel so strongly on the subject that when Lord Milner made his speech in the House of Lords the other day about the evacuation of Gallipoli, I cut out all references to this and also references to Lord Lansdowne's answer.[1] We are all doing our best, both inside and outside the Government to obtain victory. But if we allow newspapers to give away continually valuable information, we are jeopardising the interests of the country.[2]

1. See *Hansard* (House of Lords), 5th Series, vol. xix, cols 1053–58, 14 October 1915. Lansdowne was Minister without Portfolio in the Coalition Government.
2. Simon did not answer this letter, though in a subsequent conversation with Gwynne he did admit that the action of the *Daily Chronicle* was a gross breach of the Regulations. (Gwynne to Simon, 29 November 1915 (HAG/30 no. 3, IWM).)

H. A. Gwynne to Lady Bathurst, 19 October 1915

I have rung up the Carsons and they will be delighted to come and dine on the 27th. . . .

Ian Hamilton ought to have been brought back[1] six weeks ago – the incompetent ass. Munro is a very good man. He is one of the few generals I don't know but I met him this morning and was very favourably impressed.

We *did* take hill 70 [*sic*], as you say and we lost it.[2] French seems incapable of telling the truth.

My brother has just come back from France. He tells me that the best thing to do to get you a position in a hospital at Boulogne would be to ask Sloggett the P.M.O. of the Expedition. Sloggett is a great friend of mine and if you like I will write to him.[3]

I have always hated the Dardanelles but its evacuation, *unless we had a good excuse*, was dangerous to our prestige in India and Africa. Now that the Serbian mischief has arisen, we can evacuate for a very good excuse – a change of front. Russia would never agree to bribe Turkey. She wants Constantinople. The Turks would cease fighting tomorrow if we promised them Constantinople. But Russia would never agree.

1. From Gallipoli.
2. Hill *60* was finally taken by the Germans on 5 May 1915, in the course of the second battle of Ypres.
3. Sir Arthur Sloggett, Director-General of Medical Services in the British Expeditionary Force.

H. A. Gwynne to J. S. Sandars, 21 October 1915 (Sandars MSS c768)

I thank you very much for your very long, very interesting, very well expressed, and very logical letter, which I have read with immense interest.

I, too, have my doubts about Lloyd George. Indeed, who has not who knows him? But as sure as we are alive we shall come to some appalling disaster if we go on under the present man. It is not that he is not able, or that he lacks energy; but he has the most fatal of all defects in a war: he cannot come to a decision. Carson's case is perfectly overwhelming and was more than moderately expressed in his statement yesterday. Five months ago the present situation was foreseen by every man who thought about the Balkans at all; but neither the Foreign Office, nor the War Office, nor the Cabinet would consent to take measures. And all this, together with the P.M.'s indecision, has landed us in what I cannot help thinking to be a very serious and dangerous position. Carson went out ostensibly on the Balkan situation; but his real complaint is, that the Cabinet never came to any decision – and never will under the present head. The technical point, that he resigned owing to the indecision of the Committee of the Cabinet, is beside the mark; if a Committee of seven cannot come to a decision, how on earth can you expect a Committee of twenty-three? No. I am sure that Carson is better out. I will not say that I am not a little bit afraid of Lloyd George, but frankly I would rather see Lloyd George Prime Minister than the present one.

The obstacle, of course, to any change is the Parliamentary situation; and there Edmund Talbot[1] is able to speak with much greater authority than I can. It is a fact, however, that we have never taken the trouble to obtain the vote of those members (and I believe there are about 80) who are serving;[2] and the consequence is, that we are handicapped when it comes to voting. If you put it to me that Lloyd George would mean a General Election, then I would prefer: the present man minus a General Election, to Lloyd George with one. I think the idea of a General Election is the most ridiculous of all, for I consider this to be physically impossible in wartime.

More about this when we meet.

1. Unionist Chief Whip.
2. And see letter 87, Esher to Gwynne, 3 September 1915.

99
H. A. Gwynne to Sir John Simon, 1 November 1915 (HAG/30 no. 2, IWM)

Please forgive the delay in writing according to my promise to you the other day, but I have been so overwhelmed with work that I have been unable to find time for a considered letter.

The question of the censorship has been much misunderstood, and its difficulties have been considerably overstated, for the simple reason that England has not been under censorship, I believe, in the whole of its history except in the good old times when the suppression of a newspaper – which made itself uncomfortable to the Government – was a matter of ordinary procedure. Even then it was recognised that such suppressions were merely political acts, and in no way did the conditions then existing resemble those of today.

At the same time, in order to evolve anything of practical value, it is essential to set forth as correctly as possible the general complaints of the Press against the censorship. I think they may be comprised under two heads:– one (for the want of a better word) I call 'Political', and the other I should term 'Technical'.

Under the 'Political' head, I should say that the Press has made it a grievance that fuller information has not been given to the public of England by the Departments concerned; in other words, they say that the country is not told the truth. I fail to see that this is the fault of the censorship. Ministers have talked of our being separated in Gallipoli from one of the most glorious victories of the war (I do not quote the exact words) only by a few weeks; and the country still sees us struggling hard in Gallipoli against great odds. The Foreign Office having, in the opinion of most journalists, made rather a mess of the Balkans, has, not unnaturally, been quiet about the real situation. I do not affirm or deny that these complaints have any substance; I am only setting out the facts. But by constant reiteration the public is brought to the conclusion that the Government are not telling the whole truth where the whole truth is known to the enemy. There have been organs which, in order to impose on the Government a certain policy – a policy they have every right to advocate – have used the alleged lack of truth as an argument to further their policy. Others have complained of too great a reticence on the part of the Government about matters the details of which are not known to the enemy, and, therefore, should not be disclosed.

Coming to the 'Technical' complaints: these are numerous, and are bound to be numerous. I have suffered myself from incompetent handling of my copy, and I suppose that every other paper is in the same boat. You have quite ridiculous examples of unhandy censors; but these sins, though they have generated a feeling of irritation in the Press, are really of lesser importance. It is obviously impossible to expect that, with the large number of Press Censors necessary for the work, mistakes will not occur; but the irritating delays – very often unnecessary, lack of comprehension of a newspaper's needs, all these form legitimate grievances which newspaper men feel very keenly.

In order to carry on a war one realises that the Government should be subjected as little as possible to futile criticism; but it has to be borne in mind that criticism so far has produced results. I will give you a few cases in my own experience. The Government were allowing reservists to go from America to Germany; we protested, and the thing was stopped. The Declaration of London[1] was adopted as a working model of international usage; we protested again, and it was modified. Contraband of war and other matters connected with our naval blockade were matters of comment in my own paper and in other papers, with the result that these things were taken in hand. But the most notable example is that of having a small committee to carry on the war; and I am informed that this is in process of being done. You might answer to this by saying: 'Yes, this has been effected; but in the process you have helped to disintegrate one Government and have done much to make the public lose confidence in another.' This is true, and it has always been a matter of great concern to me; for in order to achieve things, you have to attack; and in attacking, you weaken. But an alternative I have not yet been able to find.

On the supposition that the present Government appoints a small committee to carry on the war,[2] and the establishment of such a committee finds general favour with the public, I take it that the Committee would like to have a stronger control of the Press than the Government have had heretofore; and I am not opposed to the idea. But it is so difficult to mark a line between honest, fairminded criticism for a definite object, and carping criticism for no object other than to attack persons disliked or mistrusted by a newspaper proprietor, that I am afraid that any suggestion I can make will be of little value, for the simple reason that I can think of no good solution of the problem. I might put forward the suggestion that, if you are going to have a more rigid surveillance of the Press, you must lay down very clearly what they can do and what they cannot do; so clearly indeed as not merely to create unsuspected opportunities for prosecution, but to be understood by every sub-editor in England. When such rules are laid down (newspapers should be invited to discuss them before they become the law of the land), then I think that any infraction might be punished, in the last resource, by very severe penalties.

Suppression of offending newspapers at once occurs to the mind, but it is necessary to remember that the suppression of a newspaper in England is not the same as it is in France. To suppress a newspaper in France does very little harm because French papers practically depend on subscriptions, not merely on their advertisements; so that when *L'Homme Enchaîné* is suppressed for a week it means that the proprietors really have the advantage inasmuch as they keep the subscriptions for the time the paper is suppressed and do not have to supply the goods. In England the whole thing is on a different basis, and the suppression of a newspaper even for a week might kill it altogether. You will, therefore, have the greatest difficulty in the world in persuading the Press that suppression can be applied.

Personally, I would not suppress a newspaper; for I take it that no Government wants to kill a paper altogether; and suppression for a period certainly might kill it. I would, instead, deprive it of all power of comment: no leading articles for, say, a week, ten days, or even a month; that it should only give news that has been passed by the Censor, and nothing else to which the Censor objects. In fact, in order to punish a paper, I would put a Censor into the office – with instructions, if you like, to make himself as disagreeable as possible.

But there is another aspect of the censorship which is worthy of careful consideration. In discussing just now the Technical difficulties under which the newspaper press have been suffering in regard to the Press Bureau, I pointed out that they were irritating rather than important; but irritation plays a large part in the conduct of affairs in this world, and it is just as well for anybody who would attempt to improve the Press Censorship to do all in his power to allay this feeling of irritation. In the present circumstances, if I have a grievance I happen to know both Sir E. T. Cook and Sir Frank Swettenham[3] personally, and I can generally get it put right by telephoning to them direct. And here I should like to pay a tribute to the extreme courtesy and the willingness to help that both these gentlemen have displayed towards us. But the rule is that, where a query is to be submitted, it has to go through the representatives of the newspaper at the Press Bureau – sent up on a slip of paper – and the answer is sent back to him in the course of half an hour, an hour, or sometimes even an hour and a half. Obviously the representative of a newspaper cannot, on a sheet of paper, give arguments with the same force or at the same length that he could in conversation; and the consequence is that the irritation is increased by this rule.

What I would propose is, the establishment at the Press Bureau of a pressman, whose duty it should be to place himself at the disposal of the representatives of the Press at all times, to be their advocate with the Directors, and, in short, to hold a brief and fight for them where he thinks it is necessary. A similar man should be appointed to represent the Foreign Press Correspondents whose grievances are, in a good many cases, well founded. This system would, I feel sure, create a better feeling towards the Press Bureau on the part of newspapers and would tend to dissipate the suspicion with which it is regarded in many quarters.

Continuing this question as to how far the Press Bureau could help the newspapers, a difficulty arises in not knowing to what extent the Departments concerned will give a hand. News emanates from the War Office, the Admiralty, and the Foreign Office chiefly, and these Departments up to the present have not shown any great desire to satisfy the natural curiosity of the public beyond the official communiqués.

I put forward a few suggestions. There should be a daily communiqué issued by the Commander in Chief of the British Army in France, telling of the doings of our forces there. The Admiralty should issue, for example, a full account of what our submarines are doing in the Baltic. The Foreign Office might tell us a lot more than it does; but I will not give precise examples here, lest I should draw upon my head their august wrath. Still, I think that, with a little goodwill and an honest desire to satisfy the legitimate desire of the people of this country for more news, a great deal could be done that is not done at present.

Of course, you have taken into consideration this point. The Government have asked for new powers of a drastic nature to deal with the Press. When these powers have been disclosed you will get an almost unanimous outbreak in the Press against them, and this campaign – carried on as it undoubtedly will be by all the newspapers with zest and force – might intimidate Parliament to such an extent as to prevent the measures from being passed through. I therefore would strongly advise that the Press should be taken into the confidence of the Government before the new Regulations are promulgated. They should be told the object of the new Regulations, and should be invited to make suggestions. In this way I think you will divide what I may call the *good* papers from the *bad* papers: and the *good* papers would carry the day.

I am afraid these are rather scattered notes, but I send them on to you for what they are worth.

1. The Declaration of London of 1909 distinguished between absolute contraband, such as munitions, and conditional contraband, such as food and clothing. Although it had not been ratified by Britain, on the outbreak of war the government announced that it would adhere to it in practice.

2. On the following day, 2 November, Asquith reconstituted the War Committee, reducing its number to five: the Prime Minister, Balfour, Lloyd George, McKenna and Kitchener. By the time this was announced, on 11 November, the name of Bonar Law had been added.

3. Joint Directors of the Press Bureau, 1915–18.

100
H. A. Gwynne to H. H. Asquith, 4 November 1915

It would now appear that the British and French Governments have decided upon the dispatch of an Expeditionary Force to the Near East with a view to helping Serbia, and I venture to address you in order to bring to your notice some dangers which may ensue unless means are taken to avoid them now.

From what I am told, the Franco-British Expeditionary Force cannot arrive much before the first week in December, and it cannot be counted upon as a mobile force in the field until at least a fortnight later. Meanwhile, it is not unreasonable to expect that Serbia, pressed on the north, north-west, and the east, may be practically wiped out, or its army driven into the mountains and, therefore, rendered ineffective before the Expeditionary Force can be of assistance. This will release the Bulgarian armies – perhaps the best soldiers in the world – and they will be able to direct their attention to that portion of the Franco-British force which may be in the field, and would in all probability succeed in driving them south on to the Greek frontier. It is imperative that we should *now* know what would be the attitude of King Constantine[1] and his Government in such a case. This would be the position: a victorious Bulgarian army would be pushing an inferior Franco-British force in front of it. It would give ocular demonstration to the Greeks of our inferiority – at least in that particular part of the world – and it would supply King Constantine with numerous arguments in favour of the neutrality which he appears to have adopted. There is only one course for a neutral nation to follow – and it is clearly indicated by international usage – and that is, disarmament. In the peculiar circumstances of the case, there might be another course open to King Constantine, which would be, to allow the retreat of the forces on to Salonika.

I would put it to you, Sir, that King Constantine is much more likely to take up the obligations of strict neutrality than to risk coming to blows with a victorious Bulgarian army. If he does not declare in our favour *now*, it is hardly likely that he would risk being drawn into a quarrel against Bulgaria at a time when the Bulgarian arms had achieved victory and were menacing Greece. It is improbable, I claim, that King Constantine will adopt any other course than that imposed upon him by the usages of international law, and we should have the sorry spectacle of our Expeditionary Force interned for the rest of the war. The loss of our military prestige, and the loss of prestige on the part of the British and French Governments, would be very great; and would certainly prevent any intervention on the part of Romania in our favour. It seems to me that it is necessary to take steps to safeguard us in this eventuality *now*; and I would urge a very instant decision.

As I understand it, the object of the Expeditionary Force is to save Serbia; but I cannot see – and I have personal knowledge of the country, and I have some experience of military matters – how this is possible within the time unless we can get Greece in *now*;

and the first question you would naturally ask is, how this is to be achieved.

It is difficult to go to Greece and force her to fight on our side merely because we want her help, for that would savour too much of the behaviour of Germany to Belgium. But we have very clear reasons for exercising pressure on other grounds. King Constantine has broken his pledged word to Serbia and to ourselves. It was distinctly understood, I believe, that, when the Prime Minister of Greece invited England and France to send 150,000 troops, Greece was to join us. Even if such a pledge was not distinctly given, it was implied inasmuch as we dislocated our military arrangements to please Greece; and we have every right to say that we cannot allow this dislocation – if nothing worse – or the breach of faith to our ally and friend, to persist.

I would, therefore, suggest that, as this war is being waged to a great extent on the question of the sacredness of treaties, before we send any more troops from Salonika to the front we should say to Greece quite plainly, that we want her to decide *now* whether she is going to keep her pledged word or not, and that we do not mean to send an expedition up to the interior based on a port in doubtful hands. This has never yet been done in military history with success, and is condemned by every military writer that has touched upon the subject. If the threat of our enmity were rightly used, we should be able to save Serbia by the intervention of the Greek army *now*. As a result the Bulgarian forces would be threatened on the flank and they would find themselves obliged to form front to a southern attack. This would give Serbia ample opportunity to defend herself and even push back the Austro-German invasion. With the arrival of the troops that we intend sending out, the position would be most favourable. It would not be unreasonable to expect also that, if this were done, Russia could put pressure on Romania with some solid chance of success.

To recapitulate, it is in the highest degree dangerous to base an expedition on a port in doubtful hands. We can only save Serbia now with the help of the Greek army; we cannot save her by the Franco-British Expeditionary Force, for it will arrive too late. In order to get the co-operation of the Greek army, we have to use vigorous measures and make Greece understand that she must either declare for us, or against us. In the latter case we shall use the full strength of our Navy.

1. Of Greece.

Editor's postscript: This letter, like some others to the Prime Minister, followed a meeting with General Sir Henry Wilson. On their way to see Lloyd George on 3

147

November, Gwynne told Wilson 'the amazing news that Kitchener and Johnnie French were both going to be degommed [i.e. dismissed]. He had been commissioned to ask Kitchener which he would like: 1. Commander in Chief at home 2. Commander in Chief France. 3. Viceroy India. (C. E. Callwell, *Field-Marshal Sir Henry Wilson*, vol. i, pp. 260–1.) It is possible that Lloyd George had asked Gwynne to put these alternatives to Kitchener, for discontent with the latter was so general that on 21 October, after he had left a meeting of the Cabinet, all the others agreed that he could not remain as Secretary of State for War. On 2 November Asquith reduced the War Committee to himself, Balfour, Lloyd George, McKenna and Kitchener, and sent the latter away to report on the situations in Gallipoli and Egypt. (See M. Gilbert, *Winston S. Churchill*, pp. 558–63; R. Blake, *The Unknown Prime Minister: the Life and Times of Andrew Bonar Law*, pp. 268–72; and S. Roskill, *Hankey: Man of Secrets*, pp. 230–2.)

101
H. A. Gwynne to A. Bonar Law, 5 November 1915
(B. Law MSS 51/5/9)

The enclosed Memorandum on 'A National Policy' is drawn up by Ian Colvin, and is worth reading.[1]

1. A copy of this was also sent to Carson.

Enclosure in letter 101

NOTE ON A NATIONAL POLICY

The two sides divide themselves naturally into:
  (1) The Free Trade, pro-German, and Voluntary Service party.
  (2) The British, Protection, and National Service party.
  These three issues are, in fact, one. The Free Trade party has depended for years largely on German money. They were forced into the war against their will, but still look to a future in which German finance and trade shall be strong in England. They do not desire to destroy the German power in the world but merely to defeat it in the field, and then restore the previous positions. Grey's reported conversation with Lichnowsky on the eve of war, in which he spoke of England helping Germany after defeating her, is symptomatic.[1]
  This attitude of mind led the Free Trade party into a policy which is exceedingly unpopular in the country.
  (1) Lord Reading's judgements putting the registered enemy and enemy company on a level with the British subject and the British company.
  (2) The Government Proclamations allowing trade with the enemy through branches in America, etc.

148

(3) The delay and equivocation in dealing with the enemy population in this country.

(4) The indulgent treatment of German officers, and of Germans generally.

(5) Mr. Asquith's friendship with Sir Edgar Speyer, the naturalisation of Schroeder,[2] and other incidents of the same sort.

(6) The refusal to blockade Germany for the first six months of the war, which was dictated, not by any fear of America, but by a desire to placate German interests.

(7) Licences to trade with the enemy and the giving of war contracts to German-Jewish individuals, the case of Merton and Co., metal brokers to the British Government, and at the same time a branch of the Metallgesellschaft, being a case in point out of many.

(8) The illusory nature of the Order in Council of March 11,[3] and the recent relaxation of the blockade.

All these symptoms have combined to make the public very sore, angry, and suspicious. They have created a state of mind which would respond to any strong patriotic appeal for an honest national policy. Such an appeal might found itself in the maxim: Britain for the British. The question of Tariff Reform is given new force and life by this appeal: it is no longer an economic but a national question.

Tariff Reform as a means of fighting Germany would arouse enthusiasm in many who remain unmoved by economic arguments.

The pro-German party will naturally seek to concentrate on the prejudice against Conscription, and upon that point might win. They would inflame the working man with the suspicion that Conscription is a device to shift the burden and to fight Trade Unionism.

The proper course for the British party is to press the attack on the other eight points and to take full advantage of the unpopularity of pro-Germanism in their opponents.

Conscription ought not to be shirked; but when dealt with should be put on the highest ground: security for our homes, our women, and children involves the need to fight for them; equality of sacrifice, pointing to families which have lost every son and others which have lost none; the refuge which the foreigner in this country finds in the voluntary system; the value of military training to the youth of the nation; all these arguments should be enforced. To put Conscription on the mere necessity of raising a certain number of men is to take a low ground, and merely to puzzle people's heads with statistics. It is to repeat the mistakes which the Unionists made in fighting Tariff Reform in terms of wealth instead of terms of strength, with appeals to figures instead of appeals to patriotism. It is not the value of the German monopoly in dye-stuffs on which we should lay stress, but the power that monopoly gives to Germany for the injury of British industries. And so in every branch of the argument, the end in view should always be security against Germany.

If this were done wholeheartedly the issue of Conscription would fall into its right place: as a means of defeating the German both in Germany and in England.

The whole weight of the fight should be put into the assault on the underground friendship between the Asquith party and the Germans in this country.

The failure of the blockade should be represented in its true light as a betrayal of the national cause.

To carry out such an assault on the Free Trade and pro-German position, the British or National Party should throw over relentlessly any German connections there may be. We must have no Sir Ernest Cassels[4] and such like hung round our necks.

In short, the British Party must be true-blue and staunch with no reservations and exceptions. If we lose thereby the support of a few rich men we gain the trust of the nation.

We ought to have a programme dealing rigorously with the importation of cheap foreign labour as well as cheap foreign goods. Protection for labour as well as protection for capital. There should be a pledge to reform the naturalisation laws, and legislation to forbid foreigners engaging in retail trade and in industries. Thus we appeal to the working man, and make him feel that he will be protected in the labour market. 'Englishmen first' should be the motto.

The 'Party Truce' was for the Unionist Party a misfortune, because the Unionist policy of Union and Tariff Reform was devised to meet this very emergency of conflict with Germany.

It derived new strength from the struggle, whereas all the Liberal cries were proved false or antiquated.

Our party policy must be treated as the urgent requirements of the country for protection against Germany.

Union with Ireland is necessary because two Governments within these islands would be a terrible danger in war.

A party organised on these lines, if it were whole-hearted, could place the other side in a hopeless position and sweep the country.

1. Prince Karl Max von Lichnowsky, German Ambassador in London, 1912–14. This statement by Colvin entirely misrepresents the position taken up by Sir Edward Grey in his exchanges with the Germans. See G. P. Gooch and H. W. V. Temperley, (eds), *British Documents on the Origins of the War, 1898–1914*, London, 1926–38, xi no. 303.

2. Baron and Baroness von Schroeder had become naturalized British citizens after the outbreak of war. Their allegiance was questioned in, for

instance, the House of Commons on 27 July 1915, because their sons were fighting in the German Armies.

3. Announcing to the House of Commons a change in the terms of the blockade of Germany as a result of the Order in Council of *1* March 1915, 'there is no form of economic pressure to which we do not consider ourselves entitled to resort'. (See S. Roskill, *Hankey, Man of Secrets*, p. 158.)

4. Sir Ernest Cassel, financier, naturalized British citizen 1878; frequently an intermediary between the British and German Governments before the war.

102
H. A. Gwynne to D. Lloyd George, 8 November 1915 (Lloyd George MSS D16/19/9)

Herewith a draft of my suggested League.

Enclosure in letter 102
4 November 1915

(*SUGGESTED TITLES*)

THE LEAGUE OF PATRIOTS
THE PATRIOTIC LEAGUE
THE NATIONAL LEAGUE
THE WAR LEAGUE

The objects of the League are as follows:—

(1) To do everything possible inside and outside of Parliament to support the most vigorous prosecution of the war, and to see that all our resources, naval, military, financial, and commercial, are fully used towards that end.

(2) To secure that no peace is made which is injurious to us, our overseas states, or our allies, or that is inconclusive. It must be a war to the finish.

(3) To oppose with the utmost vigour all proposals which may tend to weaken our sea power.

(4) To put into practice the cry of 'Britain for the British'.

(5) To do everything possible to cut off and utterly destroy the German connections in Trade and Finance, and resolutely to refuse to the German in the future all privileges of domicile, naturalisation, trade partnerships, etc., which have been so abused in the past.

(6) To see that every man who has been disabled in the war shall receive adequate compensation, and to secure in an adequate form,

for those who have suffered in other respects owing to their participation in the war, the substantial gratitude of the nation.

(7) To work for the national good and not for any party ends.

103
H. A. Gwynne to Lady Bathurst, 6 December 1915

. . . Miss Pankhurst[1] was too amusing for words. Never have I read
such a farrago of nonsense mixed with little bits of truth in all my life.
Eyre Crowe[2] did more to push us into this war than anybody. Grey is
weak and a fool but he has not a word to say as to military operations.
I entirely agree with her that it would be a good thing to get rid of the
Asquith–Grey combination but if she'll tell me how to do it, I shall
be most obliged. I keep awake of night trying to devise a method but
Miss Pankhurst gives no solution. She is a cheeky incompetent
woman.

. . . the Government seem to be still in the throes of indecision. If
that Miss Pankhurst really wanted to save her country let her go and
play Charlotte Corday to the Prime Minister. K[itchener] I think
may go to form with Joffre some sort of Allied War Council. Frankly,
I think he is a danger here. He seems to have lost all his initiative and
all his forethought. The soldiers simply *cannot* get him to look
ahead. . . .

1. Activist in the Women's Suffrage movement.
2. Sir E. A. Crowe, from 1906 a Senior Clerk, and from 1912 an Assistant
Under-Secretary, in the Foreign Office.

104
H. A. Gwynne to Lady Bathurst, 17 December 1915

Many thanks for your letter. . . .

About Lord Derby, what I fear about him most of all is this.
Although he is an extraordinarily active man – in fact I would call
him indefatigable – yet he is influenced by the last man to whom he
speaks. He has no definite policy and he would not be strong enough
for a fight. You have to remember that in his present position he is
carrying out a job where everybody is practically with him, the
Labour people and both parties. I shall postpone judgement on him
until he has fought this fight, and if he does it successfully I think
there will be a good deal to be said of him. He is honest, and straight,
and a patriot, but knowing him as I do very intimately, I think

honestly that it would be a mistake to place in his hands the destiny of the nation. He has not education or big enough outlook. But I will readily admit that he has come out of this thing much better than I ever thought possible.

105
H. A. Gwynne to General Sir Douglas Haig,
20 December 1915 (HAG/11 no. 1, IWM)

May I be allowed to offer you my sincerest congratulations on your new appointment?[1] Ever since I met you in those strenuous days around Colesberg,[2] I have followed your career with interest and admiration and, if I congratulate you, I also congratulate the Government on its choice.

Although I have not the pleasure of anything more than an acquaintance with you, I hope you will not think that this acquaintance is too slender for me to accompany my congratulations with a few remarks which I hope you will think worthy of perusal. If you do not, I shall not feel the slightest bit offended if you consign this letter to your wastepaper basket.

The one point of admiration on which I have always dwelt has been your utter disregard for the Press. I write as an Editor and a journalist and yet I confess that your invariable attitude of not caring an iota for the Press, has always pleased me. And believe me that the best among the journalists of England share my sentiments.

There is, however, another danger for a General Commanding in the field, almost as subtle and even more full of pitfalls than the Press. I refer to the politicians. More harm has been done to the Army and the nation by soldiers becoming the plaything of politicians than by anything else. I always regard a soldier in time of war – or indeed of peace – as being in the position of a physician. The patient – that is the politician – comes to him for advice. If he gives it without fear or favour, he may be right or he may be wrong, but at any rate he contracts no alliance with them. As long as he keeps aloof, giving his advice when requested, the politician will respect him. The moment he gets mixed up with them, they will use him – and down him.

The Government here has had some qualms with regard to your appointment, in as far as they seemed to fear lest you should not work in well with the French. They insist – and rightly so – that the entente between the Allies is the cornerstone of this war. Doubts were expressed that perhaps your feelings towards them were not of the warmest. In conversations on this point, I always took the line that nobody was more convinced of the necessity for a cordial cooperation with the French, and I feel sure that this is the case.

One more word and I have done. There is a feeling prevalent in Government circles that a regular officer is very little better than a man who has learnt his soldiering during the war. Trench warfare is such an extraordinary development of the present struggle, that the assumption may not appear unreasonable. The fact, however, remains that the moment warfare becomes fluid again, the trained soldier will come by his own.

I hope you won't think this an impertinent letter. In this war we are fighting for an existence and all depends upon the conduct of the war in France. It is there that the decision will come, and nowhere else. Wherefore the Commander in Chief of the Army in France is, obviously, the most important man in the Empire today. If these few words can be of any use to him, I shall be very proud. If they are superfluous, I shall be very glad.

1. As successor to Sir John French.
2. An action during the Boer War.

106
H. A. Gwynne to Lady Bathurst, 20 December 1915

I have been down to the Foreign Office and seen the Danish Agreement and it is not as bad as we thought. The copy of the Agreement that we received was not quite correct; but really the principle of a rigorous prosecution of our blockade is the main thing.[1] While I cannot say that all our criticisms of the Agreement were absolutely justified, what I do say is, that my visit to the Foreign Office shows that they do not realise that the blockade could be ever so much stricter if they only put their hearts into it. The evil of the matter is, that the Admiralty and the Foreign Office do not pull together, and there are Departmental quarrels. I have tried my best to get the F.O. to adopt this procedure. I have suggested that they should go to the Admiralty and say: 'Tell us your ideal in the way of a blockade, asking us for everything you would like, and we on our side will do our best to meet you, having regard to neutral rights.' The F.O. answer to this is, that the Admiralty will not do it. I cannot believe this, but I am going to have a go at the Admiralty and try and get them to do this; for then the Foreign Office could not complain that they did not know the wishes of the Admiralty, and the Admiralty could not complain that the Foreign Office had paid no attention to them. It is the old story, that the Civil Departments would dominate the Military Departments in wartime because they have dominated them in peace time.

As a matter of fact, your suggestion has been partly carried out and Lord Robert Cecil has spoken to 20 Members of Parliament, who are more or less satisfied. I will not say I am quite satisfied, but I think that the Agreement is not as bad as it at first appeared. But as I have just indicated, the real difficulty and danger lie in the lack of cohesive working between the two Offices. Of course, as you say, Denmark is frightened of Germany, and it is natural that she should be, for she could only put 50,000 men in the field, and the German naval supremacy round there is great, too, apart from her military supremacy.

I imagine that you are right about the dull sameness of hats and clothes, etc., under the German domination, and I should be very much obliged to you if you would give me a few points on this for a Leader. There is something lacking in me in this respect to inspire a good Leader, but if you would dictate a few points in addition to those you have already given me, I think we might produce quite a strong attack on the damnable German *Kultur*.

1. See J. McDermott, 'Total War and the Merchant State: Aspects of British Economic Warfare against Germany 1914–16', pp. 61–76.

107
H. A. Gwynne to Field-Marshal Sir John French, 22 December 1915 (HAG/37 no. 1, IWM)

I am very much obliged to you for your letter. I can assure you that I, perhaps more than many of your so-called friends, have remained faithful to you.

When you were being accused here in the early part of this year, I think I did much to prevent a catastrophe. Nor was I alone in this concern for your other friends here, equally unrecognised, did all they could for you.

I would like to quote to you a portion of a letter I wrote to the P.M. on April 22nd of this year. I was protesting against the Dardanelles Expedition and I said that these forces 'should be under the command of our best General, Sir John French, who has shown a capacity for leadership and for meeting difficulties which will entitle him to rank among our greatest military leaders. To deprive him of such a large force as will be necessary for operations in the Near East is unfair to him and diminishes our chances of smashing up the Germanic forces by exactly the measure of strength that we withdraw to the Near East'.

These are not the words of an enemy, I venture to think.

Further, I wrote to Brinsley Fitzgerald[1] on May 27th of this year a letter pointing out the great danger that threatened you. After giving details of what was going on here, I said: 'I only tell you this because I know you are devoted to Sir John as we all are. For his sake, and for the nation, let him go on with his work of killing the Germans and not try to kick up ructions with K[itchener]. I want to see him come out of the war with a tremendously increased reputation but, as sure as I am alive, he will be recalled if he fights K.'

These, too, I venture to say, were not the words of an enemy.

I feel I ought to put before you my point of view and to assure you that as far as I am concerned I am as I always have been.

I feel that there is a tremendous sphere of good work opened up to you by your new appointment.[2] We want training and coordination here almost as much as in France and I feel sure you are going to render the nation great and useful service in command of the troops at home. If, at any time, I can be of any use, do not hesitate to send for me. . . .

1. Private Secretary to Sir John French.
2. As Commander in Chief Home Forces.

108
H. A. Gwynne to Lord Stamfordham, 26 December 1915 (HAG/32 no. 1, IWM)

No doubt you have heard that during this week there is bound to be a Cabinet crisis of considerable importance. Mr Lloyd George, Lord Lansdowne and Mr Bonar Law, together with some others, are determined to bring the issue of compulsion to the test and it is not impossible that the result will be a secession of eight or nine Ministers. If the Prime Minister redeems his pledges to Lord Derby by plumping for compulsion, at least for the unmarried youths, the situation may be saved. If he does not, a general election seems to be the only way out – and that would be a calamity.

The solution really lies in the hand of His Majesty. There are two alternatives. Mr Asquith may resign and advise His Majesty to send for Lord Lansdowne or Mr Bonar Law or he may advise that Mr Lloyd George be asked to form an administration. In the first case I think both the Conservative leaders would advise His Majesty to send for Mr Lloyd George as in that case an election is inevitable – on the compulsion ticket. If on the other hand Mr Lloyd George is sent for an election is equally inevitable, for he would find it quite impossible to get the House of Commons to follow him on compulsion.

I start with the assumption that a general election will be a calamity, unless every other means can be exhausted of avoiding it. Somebody has to take his courage in both his hands at the present moment and I would suggest that perhaps it might be worth while for you to make discreet inquiries in the House as to the possibility of the following resolution being adopted:

> That this House deprecates the proposal of a general election in so far as it would not give the whole nation an opportunity of registering its views. It, therefore, in view of the present crisis, presents a humble petition to His Majesty asking him to appoint, without any regard for political partnership, a Committee of Public Safety to carry on the war. This Committee shall consist of not less than three, or more than five, members, and the House of Commons grants full liberty to such a Committee to do as it deems best for the country in all matters, even to the institution of compulsory military service.

I could elaborate this resolution, but it is sufficient, I think, to indicate my idea. Of course, the present Cabinet would remain as Heads of Departments and the real Cabinet would be the Committee.

I should like to have an opportunity of talking this over with you. I go on Wednesday afternoon to my house in the country, Mawbyns, Little Easton, Dunmow (Telephone Dunmow 25) and would come up to town any day to suit your convenience.

109
H. A. Gwynne to General Sir Henry Wilson, 16 January 1916 (HAG/35 no. 23, IWM)

I should have written to you before to answer your letter of the 10th. First of all, let me tell you how pleased and delighted I am that you like your new job.[1] I thought you would and I prophesy success and big things generally for you.

The profound saying that great evils generally produce their remedy is showing signs of becoming true in case of this Government. Gradually there is growing in the H[ouse] of C[ommons] (whence all along I have been convinced that salvation would come) a feeling of such dissatisfaction that both parties have started a National Party. A plank in each, as far as I can see is a determination to play hell with the Government if they don't get *success*. That is and should be the test of all governments, sailors & soldiers in time of war.

I have been lecturing about a National Party.[2] It has gone very well indeed so much so that I am going to do a little humble stumping in the country. My immediate task is to get the Tory National Party in the House and the Radical Ditto[3] to coalesce and to further this I am going to speak in the National Liberal Club of all places.

The politicians seem never to have wisdom. Now some of the wiseacres are starting the hare that the Western Line is impregnable and that we should transfer our operations to Salonika, Turkey, Mesopotamia & God knows where. The egregious A. J. B[alfour] is one of the leaders in this movement. My answer is that the Anglo-British [sic] line is at its furthest only 200 odd miles from Germany. There is no reply to that.

Then there is that bloody committee of retrenchment[4] – Squiff, Runciman,[5] McKenna and Austen Chamberlain. They are talking of reducing our divisions to 50. Their line of country is that it is better to keep the force you can afford than to make sudden reductions when the money fails. My answer is that there is plenty of money and that is confirmed by all my city men.

A delightful story of Robertson.[6] When at last K[itchener] signed what was practically his own abdication[7] Robertson going to his room with the paper, popped in on a pal in one of the rooms, saying 'The b——r's signed' popped out again with a grin. As far as I can make out K. is chiefly engaged in the arrangement of his gardens and plantations at Broome. . . .

[P.S.]   Callwell has gone to Russia. I miss him dreadfully.

1. Wilson had left GHQ to take command of IV Corps.

2. On the evening of 12 January Sir Edward Carson had introduced an address by Gwynne at the Constitutional Club. Gwynne's address, 'Suggestions for a National Policy', ended with his programme 'of some of the principles upon which it was possible for a National Party to exist' (*Morning Post*, 13 January 1916, p. 5). The programme was exactly the same as that sent to Lord Derby a few days later (see letter 110 and undated note 111).

3. By 'the Tory National Party' Gwynne meant the Unionist War Committee, founded on 7 January 1916 with Sir Edward Carson as Chairman, and consisting at this time of between 80 and 100 members. The 'Radical Ditto' was the Liberal War Committee, the foundation of which, under the chairmanship of Sir F. Cawley, MP for Prestwich and Chancellor of the Duchy of Lancaster from December 1916–February 1918, was announced in the *Morning Post* of 13 January. It started with just over 20 members.

4. Cabinet Committee on the Co-ordination of Military and Financial Effort.

158

5. Walter Runciman, President of the Board of Trade, May 1915–December 1916. He was not a member of the Cabinet Committee on the Co-ordination of Military and Financial Effort.

6. General Sir William Robertson, appointed CIGS in December 1915.

7. Early in December Robertson had responded to Kitchener's offer of the position of CIGS by insisting that the War Committee be the supreme authority, with no military operations to be discussed by it without first being considered by the General Staff. He had also said that a professional soldier as Secretary of State for War was impossible. (See S. Roskill, *Hankey, Man of Secrets*, p. 237.)

110
H. A. Gwynne to Lord Derby, 20 January 1916
(MS Gwynne 22)

I sent you yesterday the rough draft of a few suggestions for a National Policy. . . .[1] My conviction that something of the kind is needed comes from a very careful study of public opinion in this country both before the war and during it. The bankruptcy of the old parties, in my opinion, was made manifest by the fact that such an obvious danger as the German menace was ignored by every party in the State. Germany herself could not help giving most definite warnings, but every single one of them was disregarded.

We had allowed politicians and their party feeling to usurp the place of statesmen and statesmanship, and in consequence the British public, before the war, had grown profoundly to mistrust all leaders and looked round like frightened children to see whom they could trust.

I had hoped and believed that this war would have thrown up a man in whom the public would have faith and confidence, not only in regard to his honesty, but also in regard to his statesmanship. So far nobody but Carson and yourself have appeared. Carson is a great big strong man and perfectly honest. But sometimes I begin to incline to the belief that he is too old to throw himself into such a job as the creation of a new party.[2] There remains yourself. You have got more energy than any public man I know. You have the saving grace of immense common sense which, after all, is the rarest of gifts. But above all this, you have the faith and trust of the people. You have never told them a lie and I know you never will.

. . . I do not want you to commit yourself without adequate preparation. That is why I suggest that you should get up a meeting for me and preside at it. But I don't want you to tie yourself to my suggestions. You can say that you are merely affording me an opportunity of explaining myself and leave it at that. I can then see

159

how the thing will be received. If it finds no support, then leave it. But if it goes well, then you can consider carefully how far you can put yourself at the head of the movement and make it a success.

As for myself, I want nothing. I have no political ambitions but my job should be, both by the *M.P.* and by going around speaking, to create an atmosphere favourable for the construction of a National Party. When that is done I shall consider my task at an end. . . .

Do think the thing over. Of one thing I am quite convinced . . . and that is, that you can never become a rank-and-filer in any of the present political parties. You would start with N.E. England with you, with a very powerful paper behind you, and I think that the prospects of success are enormous. But today is the psychological moment. Tomorrow or after the war is too late. Have you ever realised that in votes alone – for at least five years – we shall be able to count on 90% of the Army? That will be about four million votes to go on with.

1. See undated note 111. On 15 January, in a speech at Liverpool, Lord Derby had said:

As to the future of parties, there is little that one can say. Many old political associations will be broken up by the events of the last eighteen months. For my own part, I shall only look forward to supporting, and supporting with all my power, that party, whether composed of those who have been up to now Unionists or those who have been Liberals or have represented the Labour Party – if they can fuse in one great national party – a party that, having secured victory on land over the enemy and peace for ourselves and succeeding generations, will also take care that the fruits of our labours are not lost, and that the influence of foreign nations and the hold that they have got on the commerce of this country shall be destroyed for all time; and, just as the death of those who have died for their country shall have secured for ourselves and our successors peace, so their efforts shall secure for our children and our children's children the prosperity that should always come with lasting peace.

(See *The Liberal Magazine*, 1916, vol. xxiv, no. cclxix, p. 4.)

2. Carson, having become Chairman of the new Unionist War Committee on 7 January, was currently involved in the case of Slingsby v. Attorney-General. At the end of the month he was ordered to rest, and cancelled all his engagements for February.

Undated note by H. A. Gwynne (MS Gwynne 26)

Some Suggestions for a National Policy

1) That the National Party pledges itself to use every means available and legitimate for the successful conduct of the war.

2) It will agree to no terms of peace which are not approved of by the sister States of the Empire and by our Allies.

3) It will do its utmost to bring about the Fiscal and Political Union of the Empire.

4) Based on this Economic Union, it will spare no effort to secure a further Economic Union with our Allies, directed to confirm our common Trade and Commerce against our common enemy.

5) This war having been conceived by Germany for the purpose of securing the hegemony of the world, having been carried on regardless of all international rights or of the dictates of ordinary humanity, the National Party pledges itself to do all in its power to prevent any German for twenty-five years becoming a partner in any British concern. It will do its utmost to enact that no German, except those already domiciled, shall be allowed to acquire domicile in the Empire for twenty-five years.

6) It will support, to the full extent of its power, all efforts for the coordination and cooperation of Labour and Capital.

7) It pledges itself, in order that the nation shall not again be found unprepared, to remove all questions of defence – naval and military – and of foreign policy from the arena of party politics.

8) Since a lie told to catch a vote is immoral and destructive of all national virtue, the National Party will do its best to pass an Act rendering an election won by lies null and void.

9) The National Party binds itself to see that full and adequate compensation is made for the dependent relatives of those who have died in this war and for those who have been disabled.

10) The National Party will only have regard for the National Good and will not give its support to sectional or partisan schemes. Its motto shall be:

'For the Good of the Nation'

112

H. A. Gwynne to Lady Bathurst, 21 January 1916

. . . The National Policy is a very healthy child indeed – so healthy that it is beginning to shout before its time.[1] But, the awful lack of patriotism among our politicians appals and frightens me. They have been brought up to think of themselves only and nothing will change them. I think we can count on about 150 M.P.s but beyond that each one is a difficulty. What we really want is a Charlotte Corday[2] to get rid of Asquith. He's ruining everything and, instead of putting ginger into the Ministry, he simply lulls them to sleep more and more.

Your letter about the Compulsion Bill inspired this morning's article. Can you understand the point of view of a Prime Minister who finds the country with him on Compulsion and allows the Bill to be whittled down?[3]

Salonika is all right. There, by sheer accident, we've done a good job. Hence the German anger. . . . There are some of our governors who are very very lukewarm in this war.

What you say about the Derbyshire incident[4] is but a confirmation of what I hear daily. The cause is the same – the Prime Minister.

The whole tribe of politicians depress me beyond words and I long for a talk with a soldier or a sailor.

1. The *Morning Post* had leading articles on this subject on 19, 21, and 29 January.

2. The assassin of Marat in the French Revolution.

3. The Military Service Bill had been introduced to Parliament on 5 January. All unmarried men and childless widowers between the ages of 18 and 41 were compelled to attest for service, but exempt from this were those engaged on important war work, sole supporters of dependants, the unfit, and approved conscientious objectors. This became law on 27 January. On 25 May a second Military Service Act extended liability for service to all men between the ages of 18 and 41.

4. This may have been a reference to an appeal by Kitchener to the men of the Great Central Railway. At one station in Derbyshire only eight out of a staff of thirty-eight responded.

113
H. A. Gwynne to Lord Derby, 21 January 1916
(Derby Papers 920 Der, 26/3)

Thank you for your letter. I am glad you have been able to glance through my programme and, of course, the first criticism that occurs to one is, that it is Utopian; but I think it is no more Utopian than what we are seeing every day, and that is, the spectacle of men willingly going forward to death for the sake of their country. If that is not Utopian, I do not know what is, and if politicians cannot give up some of their little prejudices when other men are giving up their lives – well, so much the worse for the politician. . . .

H. A. Gwynne to General Sir Henry Wilson, 17 February 1916 (H. Wilson MSS 73/1/20, IWM

... Fisher started a very pretty little intrigue in the Press, his sole object being to return to power for the purpose – as he himself was silly enough to say – of smashing up the present Board [of Admiralty]. I got wind of it and came to the conclusion that Jacky should be smashed for all time. I therefore laid into him with a bludgeon instead of with a stick, and I think I have succeeded in smashing him into such small pieces that even his most devoted friends on the Press cannot reconstruct him again. ....[1]

... I am coming more and more to the conclusion that we can never do anything with Squiff; and I have therefore devoted the whole of my energies towards securing in Parliament a majority, one of the results of whose efforts would be Squiff's resignation. The thing is going very well, but we are all waiting for Carson to get out of his bed. He is all right, there is nothing the matter with him except what the doctors call a 'tired heart', and his tired heart is being set right by keeping him closely confined to his bed.

I pin very little faith in our people in the Cabinet, from Bonar Law down. They all seem to have fallen under the glamour of the P.M. and I see no hope except in his disappearance. Last night in the House, for example, if Carson had been there they could have carried a division against the Government on this silly Air question.[2] But in the process they seem to have given away more secrets to our friends the Boches in one night than the whole newspapers of England have done since the war began. It only emphasises the fact – which you and I have long known – that these men have no conception of what war is. I have got a nice little surprise up my sleeve which I cannot give you by letter, but I am optimistic enough to believe that we shall really be able to do something effective within a couple of months. By then I should not be surprised if Squiff were out.

1. See A. J. Marder (ed.), *Fear God and Dread Nought*, pp. 288–333. In a speech on 7 March Churchill was to ask for the recall of Fisher as First Sea Lord; and on 8 March Fisher attended a meeting of the War Council.
2. During the Debate on the Address Sir William Joynson-Hicks MP had introduced a motion deploring the omission from the King's Speech of proposals for placing the Air Defences on a better basis. (*Hansard*, 5th Series, vol. lxxx, cols 81–156.)

H. A. Gwynne to Lady Bathurst, 28 February 1916

. . . With regard to the question of economy, you see one side of the shield. If you lived in London you would see the most appalling extravagance going on as if the war did not exist. I never – or very seldom – have a meal in a restaurant though now and again I go to talk business with somebody who invites me; and I can assure you that, if anything, the extravagance is greater: dresses are worse than ever in the shape of expensive material and cut, champagne seems to be the normal drink, and expensive cigars *de rigueur*. You see, the best people are either fighting or doing service for their country, like yourself, and the consequence is that the scum comes to the top – the rich scum who have made money over this war and who are making it hand over fist. They tell me that jewellers' and other shops which trade in luxuries in London are doing better than ever, that is to say, although they do not sell so many small things they sell an enormous number of big things at very high prices, and so do better in the long run with less expense and trouble. I am watching several people for this extravagance. I know of one case where a man's salary was raised to £50,000 a year in order to defraud the Government of half the profits of the company. The thing is monstrous and as soon as I get the real facts I mean to speak out. These are the kind of people I want to go for, and I am sure they are the people you would like to go for, too. . . .

The German advance at Verdun is part of their big scheme to force a decision as soon as possible. In Germany the bankers and commercial men generally have impressed upon the German Government the fact that, unless they win a decisive victory very quickly, they will not gain anything out of a later victory for they will be bankrupt; and I imagine that this is their Government's answer. Whether they will be satisfied with Verdun, or whether they will try an offensive on the whole line, or attempt an invasion of these islands, I do not know. I cannot say if all three are possible, even including a dash out by the German fleet.

As regards the *Moewe*, it is very difficult to catch her. But we are hunting all over the southern Atlantic and the Admiralty people think her career cannot be a very long one: but I remember the *Emden* and I know that to catch her will be as difficult as trying to find a needle in a bundle of hay.[1]

The German losses have been appalling. I was talking yesterday to an officer who has come from Verdun and he said that the Germans are losing three to every one of the French; he further said that up to yesterday the French have lost 120,000 while the Germans have lost 300,000. These figures, of course, are mere surmises, but they are pretty near the truth.

1. *Emden* and *Moewe*: German commerce raiders. *Emden* had been caught in November 1914.

116
H. A. Gwynne to Lady Carson, 12 March 1916 (Carson MSS D1507/1/2/4)

. . . I was delighted with your husband's first little incursion into politics.[1] It was quite in his old style and made me feel that he was getting back health and strength.

We had Bonar Law to lunch today with Dr Jameson[2] and Capt. Hall. Jameson roasted poor Bonar most unmercifully and he left very depressed, obviously so.

. . . Get E[dward] C[arson] fit and well soon – the whole country is simply calling out for him. He is the only man who can save it. If we go on as we are we shall be done. The country wants a man and the only man is your husband.

1. On the previous day the *Morning Post* had published a letter from Carson refuting a charge made by Sir John Simon of referring in Parliament to a confidential document. Carson claimed to have had the permission both of the Prime Minister and of the author of the document.
2. Sir L. S. Jameson, Prime Minister of Cape Colony, 1904–8; member of the South African Legislature, 1910–12.

117
H. A. Gwynne to Lady Bathurst, 17 March 1916

Please forgive a typewriter, but I have been rushed more than usual during the last few days.

I am now in the nervous state of having prepared everything and am now waiting for the curtain to go up; one spends one's time thinking and wondering whether one has forgotten something. However, I think that everything is in order and I hope that, within the next ten days, the curtain will be drawn up with some effect. I may be wrong, but at any rate I have worked hard for the result and I can console myself that, if the event does not come off as I want, it will be through no lack of hard work on my part.[1]

Now about the married men. I entirely agree with you that they are being disgracefully treated, but at the same time the need for men is so great, (here is Haig with 38,000 men short) and the Government have so bungled matters, that I do not see how we can carry on without calling on all those who have attested, whether they are single or married. The truth is, that the thing has been bungled for lack of courage. Had we been National Service all round there would have been no complaints, no agitation, and every man when he was called upon would have felt that he had to go; and there would have been an end of it. Under such an organisation we could have taken the married men in the order of their obligations to their families and to their relatives, instead of doing as we have just done: that is to say, use moral compulsion which has been unfair in its incidence and is the cause of all this trouble. I do agree with you that many married men feel that they owe a duty to their wives and children which is above that which they owe to their country. This Government has set us the job of making the best of a very bad matter and, while one sympathises with the married men, one has to keep an eye on the main object of this war, which is, to beat the Germans. . . .

1. As an example of this, Gwynne had written to Carson the previous day:

. . . a great many of us have put our shirts on you. . . . Will Carson come back fit enough to save the country? The Government is weakened and discredited because at the head of it is a man who will not face facts. The ability to face facts and to grapple with them is the one quality which this country wants in its leader, and it is *the* quality which you possess. My own opinion is that a mere push would send the whole Government organisation tottering to destruction. But it wants a man to do that, and you are the only man. . . . the public doesn't believe in the purity of motive or the strength of any other public man. . . . I am keeping for you all sorts of cases and dossiers, so that you can come out with full information.

(MS Gwynne 17.) The Unionist War Committee and the Liberal War Committee met together on 13 and 14 March to put further pressure on the Government in relation to Military Service.

118
H. A. Gwynne to General Sir Henry Wilson, 20 March 1916 (H. Wilson MSS 73/1/20, IWM)

. . . Glad you like what I have been saying in the *M.P.* I am rather in the position of a man who cries for rain and who then has his house washed away, for undoubtedly the result of all our attacks on the Government is, that the whole edifice is tottering and may fall at any moment; and I am not ready for it to fall yet for Carson is not well enough to come in. And to form a new Ministry out of the remnants of the present one would be a mistake. However, I can only hope that Carson may find himself better quicker than he expects. But we shall have to hurry up for I really do not think that this lot can last much more than three or four weeks. . . .

Editor's postscript: On receipt of this letter Wilson wrote to Bonar Law advocating that he pull out of the Coalition Government. Law's reply of 31 March dwelt on the consequences of such a step:

> . . . the immediate necessity of a general election; . . . fought, in spite of the war, with almost the usual amount of party bitterness; and if our Party succeeded in getting a majority we would be faced with an opposition of precisely the same nature as that at the time of the Boer War. This would really mean . . . that in a very short time we would have martial law all over the country. . . . [W]e should find that the first effect . . . , when it was obvious that instead of even the appearance of unity the nation was bitterly divided, would be to discourage our Allies and make our enemies feel certain that we could not stay the course. . . .

Both letters are printed in full in R. Blake, *The Unknown Prime Minister: The Life and Times of Andrew Bonar Law*, pp. 280–1.

119
H. A. Gwynne to Lady Bathurst, 20 March 1916

I am afraid that I have *not* explained to you my plot though I thought I had. I have quite made up my mind that as long as Asquith was prime minister, so long would we fail to get a decision in this war. So I set about seeing the best way to get him out. I came to the conclusion that only by getting a majority in Parliament could we turn this Government out. To get a majority it was necessary to get a leader and I looked to Carson as the man. I have been preparing for his advent for the last three months. Everything is prepared and I am only waiting for him to take his seat. I have over 160 M.P.s of both sides sworn to stand by him, I have arranged the debates, got the facts together, got him private secretaries, his whips, in fact everything. He is rapidly getting better but I hoped to have him in the House this week. I am afraid it will be the end of next week. Then – we shall see.

Why I uttered a complaint – the result of nerves and too much work – was that you seemed to think that Carson couldn't do the job. I feel sure he can – if he's well enough.

The French G.H.Q. are now, it seems, quite sure that Verdun is a failure. We shall wait a bit until it is confirmed and then we'll shout.

120
H. A. Gwynne to Lady Bathurst, 24 March 1916

...You will be glad to hear that Carson arrives on Sunday and hopes to start in next week. The Government are now in such a state of muddle over the recruiting that there will be a crisis next week. The shortage of men in June – when they should be at the strongest – will be 400,000; but this figure you must please keep very secret. The whole of the figures come up before the Cabinet next week and I do not see how it is possible to avoid a break-up. This, of course, will help the 'Plot' as I call it and I am looking forward confidently now to the break-up of the Government within the next month or so. When people ask me whom I would put in I answer, that any dozen men out of the street would do better than these people. For, after all, it is not difficult to run the thing in time of war: you have only to let the soldiers and sailors have their way and provide them with all they want. . . .

121
H. A. Gwynne to Lady Carson, 24 March 1916
(Carson MSS D1507/1/2/6)

... My hearty congratulations to the 'trainer' for bringing the 'horse' up to time. Everything is prepared and I think you will find that the god of chance is on our side, for on Monday or Tuesday the Government have to decide whether they will have conscription or not. The military people have sent to them figures which prove a shortage of 400,000 men in June. At that time, of course, we should not only not be short at all, but we ought to have a superabundance in order to strike our blow. There is great talk of Lloyd George and the Unionists coming out, and if your husband could only appear for one day and voice this sentiment he would collect at once around him a strong nucleus of support. Of course, we must not overwork him and everything should be done to see that he is kept free for the big things. No small thing of any kind should be allowed to worry him at all; and I am sure we will all cooperate in this.

Perhaps when you come up on Sunday you would not mind ringing me up on Sunday night and letting me know whether I could put something in the paper to stave off enquiries.

Remember your husband is the only man who can save us, and everybody is realising that more and more.

P.S. I hope to arrange for Hughes[2] to come and see your husband at 5 o'clock on Monday at 5 Eaton Place.

1. To London.
2. W. M. Hughes, Prime Minister of Australia.

122
H. A. Gwynne to General Sir Henry Wilson, 27 March 1916 (H. Wilson MSS 73/1/20, IWM)

. . . Things are in a real mess now and I do not see how Squiff can carry on. The Unionist members of the Cabinet, together with Lloyd George, threaten to resign over the question of men. They say that the obvious and logical way out of the married men's difficulty is, conscription all round up to 45. Of course, the pro-Germans in the Cabinet such as McKenna, Runciman and Squiff himself, think this is impossible; and I see no other way out but the resignation of Bonar Law and his Unionists and Lloyd George. I am told that if this happens Squiff will resign and the King would send for Lloyd George. The truth is, that Lloyd George is not very popular with his own party and the most that he would bring into the jackpot would be about 23 members. Now 23 members is hardly a sufficient number to justify his taking charge, and so Bonar Law sees difficulties all round. I think that Bonar Law would like to take on the job himself and then appeal to the country in a short time; but he is not big enough for this. Carson has come back and I am putting more hope on him, because both Bonar Law and Lloyd George would serve under him and he is a big man who would get the country on his side.[1]

1. The *Morning Post*'s leading article the following day was entitled 'The Need for a Man'.

123
H. A. Gwynne to Lady Bathurst, 3 April 1916

. . . In one of your letters you say: 'Why should Ireland be exempt?'[1] I re-echo that question and I think it is a monstrous shame that Ireland and the Irish, which are benefiting to such an enormous extent from British gold, can claim to be exempt; and it all comes back to one thing: we have no man and until we have, we shall do nothing. Squiff has gone off to Rome and he brings on the Budget in order to postpone the evil day. But the evil day will come and I firmly believe that within a short time we shall see a crisis, which I sincerely hope and believe will end with his disappearance. He has failed to do his duty on every single occasion and now, instead of being near the end of the war, he has let things slide to such an extent that I do not see how it can end under a year from now; though, of course, I will admit that the Germans are in a much worse plight than we are. . . .

1. From conscription.

124
H. A. Gwynne to General Sir Henry Wilson, 1 May 1916 (HAG/35 no. 28, IWM)

I did not answer your letter of the 22nd before, as, in spite of the turmoil, I was taking mine ease in my cottage. I knew that things would only be in a simmering stage last week and would come to a head this week.

I am very much obliged to you for your quotation,[1] which I will most certainly use. But nothing seems to move these people. Of course, the fact is, as you rightly say, that the P.M. has not got a war mind, and as long as he is at the head of affairs nothing can be achieved in the way of a more vigorous prosecution of the war. Unfortunately the House of Commons does not reflect the opinion of the people of this country and will insist on thinking that the man who can soothe their angry feelings and generally manage them, is the best man to manage the war, and therefore it all comes back to the House of Commons.

If they could be persuaded to forget every bit of party and to put any man who was strong and really meant victory at the head it would be for the better, but I admit that I see no signs of this feeling in the House of Commons. With some men, party is so much part of their blood, that not even a European war of this magnitude can shake them out of it.

At the same time, things are undoubtedly better with Carson leading the Opposition, for he keeps them up to the scratch, at any rate much better than they were ever kept up before. Meanwhile, of course, they are boggling over universal service, though we all know they will have to come to it.

1. The quotation supplied bore on the subject of lawyers of 'simple, sorry, weak and doubtful stomachs'. Wilson to Gwynne, 22 April 1916 (HAG/35 no. 27, IWM).

H. A. Gwynne to Lord Derby, 3 May 1916
(Derby Papers 920 Der 26/3)

I'll see that you have a good report on Saturday.[1] For Heaven's sake come out on Carson's side against Squiff. Don't mince matters but tell your hearers plainly that, Consule Asquith,[2] we can't hope to win the war. I am quite convinced that we are in a frightful state. I am sure that we can only win provided the *country* puts every ounce into the war. I confess that I am terribly depressed about it. France gets to the end of her reserves in June, Russia hasn't enough big guns for a big offensive and Italy plainly indicates that she can't go on with the war after this year. And, then, imagine what these bloody muddlers will do when peace is mentioned. Your duty as an honest English gentleman is to go 'all out' on the side of Carson. . . .[3]

As for Ireland, I don't think Redmond would stand a Jew and I am quite sure Dillon wouldn't.[4]

1. On Friday, 5 May Derby was to preside at a special meeting of the Lancashire Division of the National Unionist Association in the Constitutional Club, Manchester. The speech was printed in full in the *Morning Post* on 8 May, under the heading 'Lord Derby on Compulsory Service – Reply to Critics'.

2. Literally 'with Asquith as Consul'.

3. On Thursday, 4 May Carson presided over a lunch of the Unionist War Committee. He told the hundred people present that the Committee was the outcome of dissatisfaction; that one of its objects had been to get the Government to take more notice of the House of Commons; that it had been charged with imperilling unity and conspiring against the Government. He then went on to call for 'action not words' and to demonstrate the extent to which British life and commerce were under German influence. These themes were not taken up by Derby in his speech at Manchester. (See *The Times*, 5, 6 May 1916.) On 3 May Asquith had introduced the Compulsion Bill in the House of Commons.

4. Sir A. Birrell had resigned as Chief Secretary for Ireland on 3 May. Edwin Montagu was one name mentioned as a possible successor. The appointment went to Henry Edward Duke, MP for Exeter.

126
Lord Robert Cecil to H. A. Gwynne, 29 May 1916
(HAG/4 no. 15, IWM)

I notice a singularly unfair attack on two officials of the Country in the *Morning Post* of Saturday. It is difficult for me to believe that you are really responsible for such an effusion. But if you accept responsibility for the paragraph entitled 'A Deed without a Name'[1] I am afraid we can no longer continue our old terms of friendship & correspondence.

1. *Morning Post* leader of 27 May; Barrington Hurst and Admiral Slade were the officials, suspected in this case of trying to devise a new definition of contraband, not stringent enough for Gwynne.

127
H. A. Gwynne to Lord Robert Cecil, 30 May 1916 (HAG/4 no. 16, IWM)

I have to acknowledge your letter of yesterday's date, in which you tell me that you cannot continue on our old terms of friendship and correspondence, owing to the attack on two officials which appeared in the *Morning Post* of Saturday last.

I take full responsibility for the attack and must accept with much regret the loss of your friendship.

128
H. A. Gwynne to Walter Long, 7 June 1916 (MS Gwynne 20)

You and I have not seen eye to eye over the results of the Coalition Ministry, and no doubt you think that the course I have adopted is wrong. That, however, cannot be helped; we each have our own point of view and, for what it is worth, it is our duty to believe in it and proclaim it.

I am writing you, however, on another matter[1] about which I feel more strongly than anything else. You used to be my ideal champion of Unionism and of Unionist principles. Today you are helping to betray those same Unionists in the south and west of Ireland who have so blindly in the past given you their trust. The argument that the Unionist people accept the situation is, if I may say so, no answer at all, for the Ulster people are driven by the trickery of the P.M. and Mr Lloyd George into accepting a situation which they know to be wrong morally and wrong politically.

It is well worth while looking at the facts. What you prominently, and others less prominently, have so often pointed out, has happened. Nationalist politicians have been telling Ireland that the hour of England's danger was the hour of Ireland's opportunity. The preaching has not been without effect and the Sinn Fein rising was a direct result. Having verified your predictions, it was reasonable to suppose that you and the other Unionists in the Cabinet would have refused to do anything else but see that either by the establishment of martial law or by a strong temporary Government in Ireland, no further revolution and insurrection should be allowed to disturb our conduct of the war, leaving the question of Home Rule and the exclusion of Ulster to be decided after the war. That was all that the Unionists of England expected and it was what the Unionists of Ireland desired. But you and your colleagues in the Cabinet have acquiesced in the negotiations which, in the middle of the greatest war we have ever known, are going to establish in Ireland what you know in your heart of hearts to be a hostile power. Is that sound politics? Is it even sound from a military point of view?

I implore you with all the strength of which I am capable, to pause and consider before you go any further. You are going to establish in three-quarters of Ireland a Parliament supported by British money, which will be bitterly hostile to Britain throughout this war. You know perfectly well – for your information on the subject is better than that of anyone else – that Redmond, if he had an election tomorrow, would be wiped out of existence by the Sinn Feiners. You must know that Redmond cannot and dare not hold a Convention, and so the Ulster people will be compelled to yield while the Nationalists will gain an advantage without even an appeal to their own people. Do you know that there is a fear of another outburst on Whit-Monday? Do you know that, when the first bad news came through of the fight off Jutland and people thought that we had suffered defeat, the Sinn Feiners walked in exultant procession in Cork, and the police were powerless to stop them? Do you know that every Sinn Fein prisoner is being met on his return at North Wall by cheering crowds; and that the very children of Dublin are playing at erecting barbed wire entanglements and barricades of bricks and sniping from behind dust-heaps? Do you know that arms are hidden throughout the country; that in all shops picture-postcards of those 'killed in action' and those who 'died for Ireland' are being exhibited and are selling like wild-fire? Do you not see that Ireland is now in a most dangerous state, and that the only chance of preventing a second outbreak and securing tranquillity at least for the duration of the war is, by the continuance of martial law – strictly, sternly, but justly enforced? This is no time to talk of Home Rule or to obscure the issue with politics.

As for the question of public feeling in America, I do not believe it for one moment. We are suffering from a weak foreign policy, and although in the elections in America a good deal will be made of the Sinn Fein rebellion and our so-called brutal suppression of it, that harm – so far as America is concerned – has been done, and we shall not be one wit the better as regards the Irish-American vote in America if we gave full Home Rule tomorrow.

You, my dear Long, were the champion of Unionism in Ireland at a time when our future looked its blackest. Now, at a time when we have merely to stand firm, you appear to acquiesce in the disruption of the Empire – for this is what it means. I beg of you, for the sake of yourself and for the sake of our old friendship, to pause before you commit yourself to such a deed. The principles of Unionism are as right now as ever they were, and you must not go back on them now. In the past you have, as you know, been a shining example to every politician who wanted to shuffle off the Irish difficulty and would not face the facts. I think it is due to you as much as to anybody that Unionism has recovered so quickly in the last few years; and now it grieves my heart to think that you may be one of those who will deal its death-blow.

You will understand that I write this in no spirit of mere criticism or with any desire to hurt you at all. It is written because I think that we are about to commit a great wrong to England, Ireland, and the Empire; and I want to feel that I have done my duty in warning my friends who have the power to avert it.

1. The settlement of the Irish Question in the aftermath of the Easter Rebellion. Lloyd George had been charged by Asquith to enquire whether there was any possibility of agreement between the Irish Nationalists and the Ulstermen.

129
Walter Long to H. A. Gwynne, 11 June 1916
(MS Gwynne 20)

Private and Confidential

It is true that you and I have not seen eye to eye over the Coalition Ministry. So far as I have been able to judge you believe that the party line is the right one. I, on the other hand, from the day the War broke out, have buried the past, ignored party, and devoted myself to what I believe to be my first duty, viz., the vigorous prosecution of the War. As you say, we each have our own point of view, and no doubt there is a good deal to be said on both sides. I know it is no use now to dwell on this difference of opinion, however much I may regret it, but it is not your policy so much as your method to which I have taken such strong objection. You have on many occasions thought it right to impute the lowest and meanest motives to men, who, you know perfectly well, are just as honourable, just as high-minded as you are yourself, and your letter of the 7th June is clear evidence of this.

I take two statements from your letter:–

First, you, a Unionist, writing to a Unionist, and one who has enjoyed and valued your friendship, do not hesitate to make this statement – 'Today you are helping to betray those same Unionists in the South and West of Ireland who have so blindly in the past given you their trust'. Let me say quite plainly that this statement is absolutely false and it is wholly inexcusable. If you had taken the smallest trouble to make yourself acquainted with the facts of the case, if you had come to me and asked for my views, you would have known that there is no foundation for this charge which you coolly, deliberately, and in a carefully considered type-written letter, make against me.

I pass to the second charge – 'But you and your colleagues in the Cabinet have acquiesced in the negotiations which in the middle of the greatest war we have ever known are going to establish in Ireland what you know in your heart of hearts to be a hostile power.' Here again you have written in entire ignorance of the facts, and I think I am entitled to ask before you write to a friend both personal and political and make charges of this kind you should at least take the trouble to obtain some accurate information.

I don't propose now to go into all your historical references, as I do not find anything in them with which I disagree. You ask me certain questions as to my knowledge of the existing state of things in Ireland. I will simply reply by saying that I believe the situation there to be very serious. When the right time comes, and if I see reason to defend myself, I shall be prepared to show that your description of the conduct of my colleagues and myself is wholly without justification, but I will only now express my regret that on such inadequate information you choose to bring against one to whom you cynically refer as a friend charges so offensive, so grave, as those which you have thought right to make against me.

130
H. A. Gwynne to Walter Long, 15 June 1916
(MS Gwynne 20)

. . . In your letter[1] you indicate that the difference between yourself and myself is, that I believe in the party line as the right one, while you have buried the past, ignored party and have devoted yourself to the vigorous prosecution of the war. I am sure this is quite a wrong conception of my attitude. If I believed that the party line was the

175

right one I should not have attacked our party leaders as I have felt myself bound to do. I belong to no party at all. I venture to say that, in my humble way, I try to get as near to your conception of duty as I possibly can, which is, to let party go hang and do my best to bring this war to a successful end.

Further in your letter you say that I have thought it right to impute the lowest and meanest motives to men who are just as honourable and high-minded as myself, and you proceed to quote two statements in my letter as proof of this charge. I said in my first letter to you: 'Today you are helping to betray those same Unionists in the south and west of Ireland who have so blindly in the past given you their trust.' This, you say, is imputing the lowest and meanest motives to you; but I say again that in effect, though, I am sure, not in intention: Today you are helping to betray those same Unionists in the south and west of Ireland who have so blindly in the past given you their trust. As a second instance of my alleged wrongful imputation of mean motives to you, you quote my words which were to the effect that you and your colleagues are acquiescing in negotiations which are going on to establish in Ireland what you know in your heart of hearts to be a hostile power.

To both these accusations of mine you answer that I am unacquainted with the facts of the case, and that I ought to have come to you and have inquired into them first. But, my dear Long, I do not ask to know what is behind it all; I am only entitled to criticise from the facts which are published officially and semi-officially and about which there is no doubt. I repeat everything that I have said in my first letter, and I go further and beg of you to consider the situation now before it is too late.

My view of the situation is this. A revolt breaks out, very dangerous as it was, and extremely dangerous in its possibility of success. It was what those of us who had studied the Irish question – and nobody has studied it or has better knowledge of it than yourself – knew to be likely to happen. But there is the fact, a pretty nasty, ugly fact, especially in the middle of a great war. Now, what was the duty of a Coalition Government composed of Unionists, Liberals, and Labour? To my mind its duty was as clear as the sun at noon, and that was, to take immediate steps so that for the duration of the war, a revolt of a similar regrettable nature should not recur. There began and there ended, in my opinion, the duty of the Government. It was not the business of the Government to settle the Irish Home Rule question. It was *ultra vires* and dangerous in the extreme. Now what is going to happen is this. You are going to hand over to Redmond a large portion of Ireland and you know, as well as I know, that 75% of Redmond's supporters are Sinn Fein rebels who will certainly take advantage of the favourable situation to embarrass us in the conduct of the war as far as they possibly can. If you think that this is a healthy state of things, I can only say that your optimism will receive a rude shock.

To look upon the matter as a party business is as far from my mind as I am sure it is from yours. I regard it purely from the military point of view. You are betraying – as I said before, not with intention but in effect – those supporters of the British flag who live in the South and West of Ireland. You are handing over the government of Ireland to a man who, though he may be loyal in intention, cannot be in fact because his supporters are disloyal. You are discouraging supporters of the British flag in the North; and you are going to create further military trouble for this country in the immediate future.

I fail to see – and I know you will be angry at what I am going to say – what effect the presence of Unionists in the Cabinet has had on the Irish policy of the Government. They ought to have had a great effect but I can see no sign of it; and the result is that, in the middle of the war, you are going to try and settle the Irish question; when you must know that it is not the right moment to settle it.

1. Of 11 June.

131
H. A. Gwynne to General Sir Henry Wilson, 15 June 1916 (HAG/35 no. 31, IWM)

Quem deus vult perdere prius dementat, is the old tag we learnt at school and it seems to be particularly appropriate to the present Government. What has puzzled me beyond words is that Unionists have been preaching for years that the Nationalists are disloyal and would take advantage of England's difficulties; and they deduced from that the theory that it would be a mistake to give independence to a nation lying on our flank which is hostile to us. This idea was eminently sound, and in the result turned out to be absolutely true: that is to say, that at the crisis in our history Ireland played the role that was predicted of her by attempting a revolt. It was not successful but it might have been terribly embarrassing. These are the facts. Now come along the Irish and say, 'Because of this revolt you are to give us Home Rule and settle the question for all time.' I am a Welshman and, therefore, I can understand a little more of the peculiarities of the Irish perhaps than the solid Englishman can; but I cannot comprehend on what ground or for what reason the Irish can demand a settlement of the question now. My own theory is that it is a bit of Irish cunning. They stampeded the Press (myself always excepted) and the result is, that Lloyd George is negotiating. It is a monstrous state of affairs for it looks as if we are going to hand over at a time of great crisis the destinies of our Western flank to people who are anxious for our downfall. It beats me, and I can say no more except to tell you that I have protested – both publicly and privately – in every way possible; but so far it has been without result.

Do let me know when you come over so that we can foregather and have a talk over things.

132
H. A. Gwynne to J. S. Sandars, 15 June 1916
(Sandars MSS c769)

. . . About Milner, I knew all the time I was fighting a losing fight in regard to him, for the simple reason that the present Cabinet would not think of allowing a sturdy outsider to come in: they are too much afraid of an independent politician. Lloyd George will have it[1] and will try and run the Munitions at the same time.

1. The War Office. This had become vacant with Kitchener's loss on the *Hampshire* at the beginning of the month, and the *Morning Post* had pronounced Milner the most suitable candidate. On 6 July Lloyd George was appointed Secretary of State for War; the Ministry of Munitions was turned over to Edwin Montagu.

133
Walter Long to H. A. Gwynne, 17 June 1916
(MS Gwynne 20)

Thankyou for your letter. I am afraid I am not prepared to accept your disclaimer in regard to my attitude during the War. I adhere to my view and we had better agree to differ.

In regard to your repetition of your charge against me in regard to the proposed settlement in Ireland, I can only repeat what I have said before, viz. that you have failed, indeed so far as I know have made no effort to make yourself acquainted with the facts.

I am surprised that it is possible for the Editor of a great leading newspaper to be in such a state of ignorance as to the facts of the case, and I must again express my regret that you should have seen fit to bring against me charges of a personal and offensive character.

I must decline to say more than this – that there is no foundation for the statement that the Cabinet have agreed as to the particular Imperial necessity which demands a settlement. They rest upon the statement made by the Prime Minister in the House of Commons on 25th May.

Secondly there is no authority for the statement that the Cabinet unanimously approved the scheme suggested by Mr. Lloyd George, which has never even been before them.

134
Undated note by Gwynne: Walter Long's own statement of his case for the Cabinet (MS Gwynne 20)

1. The Cabinet authorised Mr Lloyd George to undertake negotiations with a view to seeing if a basis of settlement could be arrived at under which a measure of Home Rule could be brought in without bloodshed after the war. (Authority for this are the Prime Minister's memoranda.)

This, of course, entailed maintenance of the distinct understanding that there was to be no controversial legislation, and the pledge to Irish soldiers.

2. The Cabinet had no scheme before them, but the understanding was that Mr Lloyd George should report negotiations to them for approval, revision, or rejection.

3. My interview with Mr Lloyd George was on May 30th. I saw then for the first time the rough draft of a scheme. I told Mr Lloyd George that no Unionist, Irish or British, would accept Home Rule during the war. I had an interview with Lord Lansdowne the same day, who later in the day saw Mr Lloyd George, and indicated our objections.

4. Information was received a week later that a definite scheme had been put before Ulster who had accepted it on two grounds:
   (1) that the Cabinet had approved of the scheme, and
   (2) that the Cabinet had authorised Mr Lloyd George to say that the national emergency and especially the fear of complications with America rendered necessary an immediate grant of Home Rule? [*sic*]

These grounds are without foundation. The American suggestion was never before the Cabinet, and there is, in my opinion, no force in it. If there was this scheme would only make things worse, and this difficulty, if it exists, should be dealt with in a different fashion.

5. My information shows that the state of Ireland is now very serious and that the talk of Home Rule has made the position more

difficult. The country is unfit for Home Rule. The effect of the scheme is to encourage and reward the rebels.

6. Home Rule during the war would be unsafe. A Home Rule Parliament will press for the removal of martial law and for the control of the police, etc. This can hardly fail to embarrass the Imperial Government in the prosecution of the war.

135

Undated report by Major Somerset Saunderson (MS Gwynne 20). (Note by Gwynne: 'Long first desired us to publish this & then the request was withdrawn.')

You will remember that after the meeting of the Unionist Council in Belfast on June 12th, we left with feelings of dismay and a sense that we had been sold and betrayed by our leaders in the Coalition Government which we were told had unanimously approved of Mr Lloyd George's proposals; one of those proposals being that a Home Rule Parliament should forthwith be set up in Dublin.

We looked on this proposal as a gross breach of the pledge under which the men of the Ulster Division had gone to the Front.

One of those Leaders is a man who himself was once the Leader of the Ulster Unionists in the fight against Home Rule, a man whose good Faith we could never question and I could hardly credit that he was a party to the proposal.

The man to whom I refer is Mr Walter Long.

As soon as possible after my return to London I went to see him and to my astonishment learnt (what we have since learnt from Lord Lansdowne in H[ouse] o[f] L[or]ds) that Mr Lloyd George's proposals had never been before the Cabinet. Mr Long himself could see no reason connected with the conduct of the War for experimenting with a Home Rule Parliament in the present condition of Ireland, and Mr Lloyd George was not authorised by the Government to make proposals entailing such an experiment.

I immediately informed Sir Edward Carson by letter, of Mr Long's statement, being convinced that he would immediately discontinue negotiations on the basis of the setting up of a Home Rule Parliament during the War, but to my surprise he was unwilling to accept Mr Long's statement as accurate. *Why I cannot fathom.*[1] I then took the earliest opportunity of seeing Sir Edward and told him that I entirely accepted Mr Long's assurance and must take complete freedom to do all in my power to upset the proposal. That I felt in honour bound to do so as a duty to the men serving at the Front.

I may say that I have left no stone unturned to accomplish this object. Time was too short to ask for your authority but I am convinced that I have acted in strict accordance with your views and *of Lord Leitrim who is, unfortunately, ill in Hospital and*[2] of Lord Farnham who is with the Ulster Division at the Front.

The Irish Unionist Alliance were kind enough to invite me to join their Deputation in London and I gave them a complete account of our proceedings in Belfast and they are now aware of the reasons and pressure which made us take the course we did.

That course has had the unfortunate result of making it appear that the Ulster Unionists have accepted the principle of Home Rule and the Prime Minister himself in our interview with him and Mr Lloyd George used that as an argument to induce the Unionists of the S. and W. of Ireland to do the same.

Everything that Mr Long said to me has been borne out by the statements of Lord Selborne[3] and Lord Lansdowne in the House of Lords.

It seems quite clear to me that the grounds on which the Ulster Unionist Council came to its decision on June 12th, were based on misconception and that that decision cannot stand and I am strongly of the opinion that the Unionist Committees of the three Counties Cavan, Donegal, and Monaghan should meet at the earliest possible moment and pass a resolution to that effect and forward it to Sir Edward Carson for communication to Ulster Unionist Council.

1. Words italicised crossed out.
2. Words italicised crossed out.
3. President of the Board of Agriculture from 25 May 1915; he resigned from the Cabinet on 16 June 1916.

136
H. A. Gwynne to Lady Bathurst, 26 June 1916

I have been asked by the French Government to go over to Paris to see some members of the Government – I imagine about this Economic Conference.[1] I also hope to have an opportunity of seeing Joffre and possibly Verdun.

First of all let me set your mind at rest about Kipling. For the first time the Government have done a wise thing. They have subsidised his pen and we have had nothing to pay for his articles. Every paper, of course, had them, though I think we set them out better.

We have been very busy over this Irish affair and I am glad that you approve of what we have done. It is a madness and a folly which is beyond belief or conception. However low a view one has taken of politicians, I never dreamt for one moment that they were capable, in the middle of the greatest war that we have ever had, of yielding to a rebellion and creating – from the military point of view – greater difficulties than ever. I do not know what can be the mental attitude of men who can do such things as that. Here was a rebellion started by enemies of England, inspired by our arch-enemies, the Germans, arranged by them, financed by them; and yet we turn round and say to the Irish: 'Poor fellows, you are a misguided lot of people!' But mark this, if the arrangement would succeed in keeping Ireland quiet for the duration of the war it might be an argument in its favour; but as it will increase unrest and most seriously affect our military operations, I cannot for the life of me conceive what object the Government can have except the dirty little political success, which they are going to purchase at the cost of England's security. There are times when one feels that a military dictatorship is the only thing for England.

1. An Inter-Allied Conference held in Paris in mid-June had passed resolutions concerning the industrial and economic future of Europe. These were reported in the *Morning Post* of 3 August 1916.

137
H. A. Gwynne to Sir Edward Carson, 14 July 1916 (Carson MSS D1507/1/1916/45)

Here is an extract from a letter I have just received, between ourselves, from Callwell, who knows what he is talking about:–

> Brade[1] sent me the Dardanelles papers which Winston wants 'laid', and I was able to give him a bit of my mind for the benefit of Squiff. I said that if the papers were laid at all the truth would have to be told about there not being sufficient men available to keep Hamilton up to strength, as well as what went on after Munro[2] was sent out with full powers. The result is, that the papers are now not to be laid, after Squiff had promised them, and there will, I suppose, be the devil's delight over it.

Do you think that you could urge in the House that the papers should be laid as soon as possible? There is no excuse why they should not be. The operations have finished and there is nothing to be given away to the enemy, for I cannot conceive that even this Government could contemplate another landing there. And if you were persistent enough to get the papers, you would be able to prove how right you were in resigning.

1. Sir Reginald Brade, Secretary of the War Office and Army Council, 1914–20.
2. General C. C. Munro, Commander in Chief Eastern Mediterranean Forces, 1915–16, GOC 1st Army, 1916, Commander in Chief India, 1916–20.

138
H. A. Gwynne to General Sir Henry Wilson, 17 July 1916 (H. Wilson MSS 73/1/20, IWM)

. . . I imagine that the Home Rule question will not come to anything after all for the opposition on both sides is growing so steadily that I believe now that, if Bonar Law went to Asquith and suggested that the whole thing should be shelved, he would agree to it. They interfere with martial law in Ireland so that it is no law at all. Redmond feels that [Lloyd] George has not been straight with him; Ulster people feel the same; and I am not sure that the underlying idea on the part of Squiff was not to land Lloyd George in a hole, which he certainly has done with great effect.

As for Squiff himself, the main quality he seems to have is indifference. I do not think he is keen enough to be a traitor. I think that there are influences which deaden any effort he might make towards throwing all his strength into the war; but all his mistakes, I feel sure, are the result of idleness, laziness, and a mind incapable of understanding the first principles of war. His record, as you put it, is deplorable, and it will be worse; but I blame the House of Commons even more than I do him. I believe that with that smooth tongue of his he could persuade them to accept bad terms of peace; and that is my constant dread. We had the opportunity of our lives when the Coalition was formed if Bonar Law had been strong enough to fight; but he is a weakling and soft, and he seems to have fallen entirely under the influence of Squiff. . . .

139
H. A. Gwynne to H. H. Asquith, 19 July 1916

The simultaneous pressure which is now being exercised on Germany by all the Allies and the success which is attending it, together with the evident depression in Germany, make it clear that the Central Powers are very hard pressed. History teaches us that the

Germans are admirable fighters up to a certain point, but when fortune turns definitely against them their military power frequently collapses. I do not wish for a moment to impress upon you an unfounded optimism, but statesmen have to take into consideration all sorts of contingencies; and one of the contingencies which seems to demand careful preparation by those who are in charge of the destinies of the Empire seems to me to be that of a possible early collapse of Germany.

Personally, I do not believe that such a collapse is coming perhaps for six months or a year, but, on the other hand, I think the thing is quite possible. What preparations have been made by the British or Allied governments towards elaborating a formula of peace terms which will cover all the demands, wishes and aspirations of all the Allies? By a formula I mean a broad and general definition covering the principles rather than the details of the aspirations of the Allies. Three days after the war broke out I ventured to address to the Foreign Office a letter urging the necessity for the preparation of such a formula.[1] I pointed out in that letter that Bulgaria, Greece and Serbia, united in the Balkan League against a secular enemy, fought a successful war and overthrew the enemy, yet ended in fighting among themselves. The common sense of the Allies will, I believe, prevent such a catastrophe; but history tells us that allies are likely to quarrel in defeat and over the spoils of victory. We can see indications of this truth in the nervousness of Austria and Hungary; but I hope that we shall never see the truth of the second axiom vindicated by mutual recriminations between the Allies in case victory crowns their efforts. Yet it would be neglecting the almost universal experience of former wars to leave until peace is declared all preparations for it.

These preparations can be divided into two groups: (a) the formula of a broad outline of peace terms, and (b) the preparation for the great task of solving the problems of demobilisation and the return of the civil population to its ordinary peaceful avocations.

I will deal in the first place with (a). France and England have agreed, I believe, to give scope to the Russian ambition in regard to Constantinople; and so far, so good. But I can find no evidence that the Allies have come to any other arrangement for solving the enormous difficulties which must arise as a consequence of victory in many other parts of the world. To define precisely the wishes and desires of each of the Allies in regard to every quarter of the globe in which they happen to be interested would, of course, be impossible; but I do think it would not be difficult to elaborate a formula embodying the principles which should govern the terms of peace. What we have to guard against is a peace conference where the legitimate desires of the victorious powers might be whittled down by diplomatists. The matter divides itself into two heads: firstly, the territorial ambitions of the Allies in Europe and, secondly, the settlement of the smaller nationalities in Europe. Perhaps it would be wise to add a third category, and that would be, the question of the German colonies and of the German fleet. The territorial ambitions of the belligerents in Europe are, I imagine, quite clearly defined. France wants Alsace and Lorraine, and a portion of German territory which in 1814 belonged to France. This runs from the borders of the Duchy of Baden along the southern bank of the river Queich including the town of Landau. Italy wants the Trentino and certain expansions of territory in Carinthia and Carniola. She has claims of nationality, at any rate, along some portions of the eastern shores of the Adriatic. Russia wants Constantinople; and Serbia, no doubt, wants Bosnia and Herzegovina. If all these aspirations could be embodied in a formula acceptable to all the Allies, we should be a long way towards getting over the difficulties which must confront all statesmen when they come to deal with the spoils of war. The belligerent powers, too, must make up their minds, it seems to me, as to whether they are going to ask for an indemnity or not and also what they are going to do with regard to Belgium. All these questions, I claim, could be settled by a very brief formula to which the Allies can now agree. In fact, *now* is the time for agreement. Later on, when the strain of the struggle is taken off, divergencies of views might much more easily creep in; and with these divergencies of views might even come divergencies of policy; and that would be a disaster. With regard to the question of the smaller nationalities, I think it would be quite fair to allow a conference to decide them and allow representatives of enemy countries to vote at such a conference. But the whole matter is so pressing that I cannot urge you too insistently to start negotiations *now* in order that we may not be found without a plan in case a sudden collapse occurs.[2]

With regard to (b), the obvious duty of the British Government is to devise now, while we still have time, a full scheme for the demobilisation of the Army, and our settlement of the country on former peace lines. I am one of those who regard this as perhaps the most difficult and intricate task which may possibly ever fall to the lot of any statesman. There are factors to be taken into consideration which are of the utmost importance and gravity: and for this reason. At present prices are very high – an invariable concomitant of war because war is wasteful – and the drain on the supplies of the world has been greater than its resources. In consequence of this prices have soared. But with the advent of peace we shall have almost the same drain and, in addition, the entry into the market of two Great

Powers, the effect of which must be to send prices bounding up. Wages, which are abnormally high in England at the present time, will become normal; and we shall be faced with an increase in the price of foodstuffs and a decrease in wages. History teaches us that such a condition of affairs generally leads to rioting and sometimes to revolution.

There are certain remedial measures which must be settled *now* and not left until a few weeks before the war is over. I would suggest in the first place that the Government, and all parties in the Government, should at once pass a bill giving that protection to key industries which has already been promised. The demobilisation of the Army will have to be carried out very slowly and soldiers should be released from duty as and when the labour market could absorb them. It will need a vast organisation to do this without creating friction and giving cause for complaint, but it is essential – more in the interests of the men than of the employers – that this should be done. The present regulations prohibiting charters for freights from being accepted by British shippers, except by licence of the Government, should be continued far beyond the war; for in this way only can we reply to the German entry into the open market. They will not have – in spite of their building – a sufficient number of ships to carry their goods and it is only by the State organisation of the carrying trade that we shall be able to keep down the prices to their present level. In addition to this, I would advocate a total prohibition of enemy goods until such time as we shall have settled our fiscal policy.

These matters, it seems to me, are all of the most urgent importance and should be undertaken immediately. Otherwise we shall find ourselves as unprepared for peace as we were unprepared for war.

1. See letter 4.
2. Pressure steadily increased upon Asquith until, on 30 August, he called for studies of war aims from various Government Departments. (See V. Rothwell, *British War Aims and Peace Diplomacy 1914–18.*)

140
Lord Stamfordham to H. A. Gwynne, 27 July 1916 (HAG/32 no. 2, IWM)

Many thanks for your letter of yesterday re the Duke of Cumberland. The matter has been for some time under the consideration of the King.

I begin by stating frankly that His Majesty considers these

questions as rather petty, when our minds ought to be centred on this terrible war, and upon it alone.

Those of the public who have time to trouble themselves about such matters, ought to realise that all these difficulties, about foreign titles and honours, find their origin in the Royal Marriage Act.[1]

So long as the Royal Family have to go abroad for wives and husbands these complications are bound to arise in the event of a European War.

The Duke of Cumberland is a great grandson of George III, and he is a Prince of the blood, therefore I do not see how any Act of Parliament can declare him to be otherwise. He married Queen Alexandra's sister.

He is not fighting against us, but is residing at his home in Austria.

Since 1866, when he was driven from Hanover, he has lived in Austria. I believe he wears an Austrian uniform, and has always been a great personal friend of the Emperor of Austria.

I cannot imagine that he has much affection for Germany as his father and he were driven out of Hanover by the Prussians after the Battle of Langensalza.[2] He has never been in England since his father's death, nor has he taken his seat in the House of Lords.

As to the Duke of Albany, when he inherited the Duchy of Coburg he became a German Prince, and had he not taken up arms in defence of his country he certainly would have been a traitor. He is not an Englishman though he is also an English Prince and in the Succession.

Similarly Prince Albert of Schleswig-Holstein is a German, and therefore was bound to fight for his country.[3]

In my humble opinion the House of Commons seem to have lost all sense of proportion on this subject.[4] However before you receive this you will have learnt from an announcement made by the Prime Minister in Parliament, that steps will be taken to arrive at some definite settlement of these matters.[5]

1. Of 1772.
2. Of June 1866.
3. Both the Duke of Coburg and Prince Albert of Schleswig-Holstein were grandsons of Queen Victoria.
4. Swift MacNeil MP had raised the subject in the House of Commons on 12 April 1916. (See *Hansard*, 5th Series, vol. xxxi, cols 1780–1.)
5. Following a discussion at the Cabinet held on 27 July, Asquith gave a holding answer in the House of Commons. (See Asquith to the King, 27 July 1916 (CAB 37/152/22); and *Hansard*, 5th Series, vol. xxxiv, col. 1864.)

141
H. A. Gwynne to Lord Stamfordham, 28 July 1916
(HAG/32 no. 3, IWM)

I am much obliged to you for your letter. I quite see that there are more obvious difficulties in the way of a drastic procedure than is apparent to the man in the street or even to the ordinary student of politics. But the point I wished to make was that this war has become a war of nations and the people of each country are engaged in it. They feel very keenly anything which might have the appearance of favouring any particular enemy. The attitude taken up by the Government was regarded by a great many people as being due to the King's reluctance to move in the matter and in consequence one began to hear murmurings against His Majesty. That was why I wrote to you.

If you like, I could give publicity to the *facts* about the three persons. They are new to me and would, I think, be news to most people.

Editor's postscript on letters 140 and 141: On 2 August 1916 the *Morning Post* carried a letter from 'a well-informed Correspondent' on the position of the German–English Princes. This was in effect Stamfordham's letter to Gwynne of 27 July (letter 140), combined with another of 29 July (HAG/32 no. 4, IWM). The letter in the *Morning Post* ended: 'Of course, an Act of Parliament can strike the three Princes out of the Succession, but I would ask is it really worth while to occupy the time of Parliament in guarding against a contingency that we all know is certain never to arise?' In replying to Stamfordham's expression of satisfaction that the letter had been published, Gwynne wrote that he hoped it would have 'a staying effect on those who are inclined to make hysterical inferences about the "unseen hand" and other such offspring of a very excitable imagination' (RA Geo. V., Q685/103). At this very time Gwynne's chief leader writer, Ian Colvin, was writing a book which was to be published in 1917 under the title *The Unseen Hand in English History* (Colvin to Milner, 28 March 1916 (MS Milner 44/105).) This attempted to deal with German influences in Britain since the Middle Ages. Gwynne himself, as we shall see, was not disinclined to think in these terms.

A Bill to deprive Enemy Peers and Princes of British Titles and Dignities was presented to the House of Lords by the Lord Chancellor in March 1917. (See also the file of material in the Curzon Papers at the India Office Library (MSS Eur. F. 112/186).)

142
H. A. Gwynne to J. S. Sandars, 10 August 1916
(Sandars MSS c769)

. . . You will be glad to hear that the little scheme – or rather plot as I would prefer to call it – about which you spoke has resulted in an utter fiasco for the two conspirators.[1] The Cabinet have written out to Haig expressing their full confidence in the way in which he is carrying out operations.

I was glad to get your opinions on the Bonar Law meeting yesterday; Maxse entirely agrees with your account of it. About Registration, I am in agreement with you altogether. I do think that the Lords as *pis aller*, ought to do something.

1. Sir John French, who had been replaced as Commander in Chief British Expeditionary Force by Haig in December 1915, and Churchill. The latter had produced a memorandum for the Cabinet critical of the Somme offensive. Haig replied to this on 1 August. (See R. Blake (ed.), *The Private Papers of Douglas Haig 1914–19*, pp. 158–9.)

143
Viscount Esher to H. A. Gwynne, 30 September 1916
(HAG/8 no. 5, IWM)

Many congratulations. You have shown fine courage in telling the truth, or a great part of it, about L[loyd] G[eorge].[1]

I thought that we were all bought up, Leo [Maxse], you and all of us, by the Marconigang [*sic*].[2]

No one admires L.G.'s gifts, his eloquence and drive more than I do. But his surroundings, his companions, their methods and vulgarity, their swell-headedness resulting in their treatment of our generals and hard worked administrative soldiers, all these are deplorable. K[itchener] always said L.G. would come to grief. Like so many of his prophecies, it looks like being fulfilled.

If you get involved in a controversy with L.G. wire to me and I will send you some 'facts'.

But I daresay you possess all you require.[3]

1. Early in September, in the course of a visit to the Western Front, Lloyd George had questioned General Foch as to the relative merits of British generals and tactics. Foch told Haig. On 28 September the following appeared in a leader in the *Morning Post*: 'The Army is perfectly aware of what took place during the recent visit of the WAR MINISTER to France. That particular form of what the French call *gaffe* must not be repeated; and we may mention that in

case of its repetition we shall feel it our duty to publish the facts of the occurrence.'

2. Lloyd George was accompanied to the front by Lord Reading and Lord Murray of Elibank, the Liberal Chief Whip, with both of whom he had been involved in 1913 in illegal speculation in the shares of the Marconi Company. One paper that had been acquired by Lloyd George's friends was the *Westminster Gazette*. Elibank was made chairman of the board of directors. (See P. Fraser, *Lord Esher*, pp. 331–2.)

3. In a letter to the editor published in the *Morning Post* on 29 September Lloyd George praised both the British Army and its generals and denied that he had gone beyond his legitimate sphere whilst in France.

144
H. A. Gwynne to Lady Bathurst, 9 October 1916

I am so sorry that I could not come and see you on my way back[1] although I promised to do so. But the truth is, that I arrived via Dunkirk where I had the opportunity (quite against all regulations) of taking part for a day on a monitor in the bombardment of the Belgian coast, which pleased me enormously. I then returned to England in a torpedo boat, which was the only way to get back.

I was received by Sir Douglas Haig very cordially and he insisted on my seeing everything that I wanted to see, and placed the whole of his organisation in that respect at my service. The consequence is that I have been able to study the whole organisation of this great army from G.H.Q. down to Brigade organisation, and I have come away absolutely convinced that our soldiers have performed a great miracle, in that our army out there is superior in material, in organisation, in efficiency, to that of the Germans. We have learnt the lesson of the Somme quicker than the French have done and we are now superior to them in infantry, artillery, and aerial tactics; indeed, this was freely acknowledged by General Balfourier in a long talk I had with him.

I am going to write in the *Morning Post* some of my experiences and I hope you will read the articles, because I know a little bit about soldiering and I am not talking without knowledge.

1. Gwynne had arrived at Haig's headquarters in France on 30 September.

145
H. A. Gwynne to General Sir Henry Rawlinson,
11 October 1916 (HAG/24 no. 9, IWM)

Forgive a typewritten letter, but I am in the middle of the most damnable job I have ever tackled. Your news about J. F[rench][1] was known to me yesterday, and I have been running about wearing out shoe leather trying to make our politicians see what a grave and irregular thing it is. The plot seems to be as follows.

French, Winston, Smith[2] and Lloyd George are all working hand in hand though with different objects. Lloyd George is, I think, merely trying to get the Army in the hollow of his hand and be able to order it about as he did the Ministry of Munitions. The others want to get rid of D[ouglas] H[aig],[3] but do not have any anxiety about the outcome. I have got satisfactory assurances that the plot will fail entirely, and that it may recoil on the heads of those who planned it. Do go over to D.H. and tell him not to worry about the thing at all. I have taken care that the right people shall be prepared for all the ramifications of this dirty little trick; and when J.F. comes back I shall have something to say that will knock him on the head for some little time. I have made up my mind that the 'little bit' I can do in this crisis is to see that the admirable [sic] of yours out there is left alone; and I will stop at nothing towards this end. I am writing now to the Prime Minister on the subject and I hope to enclose to you a copy of my letter to him before the Bag goes out. If so, you are perfectly welcome to show it to D.H.

I have not seen Carson yet but I expect to see him in the course of the week and will let you know about his coming out.[4] Please let me thank you for your kind hospitality. I cannot tell you how thoroughly I enjoyed every moment of the time I was with you and how tremendously I have been impressed by all I have seen. I am writing three or four articles on the subject of my visit which will, I think, please all the soldiers, though perhaps the politicians may hate them.

1. Following a meeting with Lloyd George on 4 October, Viscount French of Ypres, the Commander in Chief Home Forces since January 1916, went to France to meet senior French generals. He reported back to Lloyd George, not to the CIGS, Robertson. (See R. Holmes, *The Little Field Marshal: the Life of Sir John French*, pp. 328–9.)
2. F. E. Smith, Attorney-General since November 1915.
3. Haig refused to meet French in person during the latter's visit.
4. To France.

146

H. A. Gwynne to General Sir Henry Rawlinson, 17 October 1916 (HAG/24 no. 11, IWM)

Many thanks for your letter of October 15. Since then things have travelled rather fast. Seeing that matters between L[loyd] G[eorge] and Robertson were inclined to get worse instead of better, I took my courage in both hands and tackled L.G. with the result that I have now received a letter from Robertson telling me that he is quite satisfied with the state of things. In addition to that, I breakfasted this morning with L.G. and I think he sees how essential it is to work in with the Army. I have always looked upon him as one of the few men in this Ministry absolutely determined to beat the Boche thoroughly; and for that reason I am not at all anxious to quarrel with him, for if he were replaced by any other member of the Ministry I am afraid that things would go from bad to worse. We must give L.G. the credit for his desire to beat the Germans and, as I pointed out to him today, he cannot beat the Germans if he is going to be at loggerheads with the Army. He is a strong, wilful man, but I think he realises now that his best chance is to work in with the fellows who are fighting the battle out there. Of course, he has ideas which he will try and impress upon the Army; but he assured me that if the Army did not agree with them, he would as loyally carry out their decisions as if they were his own. So I think that, if you could have a talk with D[ouglas] H[aig], it would be a good thing if you could suggest to him that, as long as L.G. remains of this opinion, it is the duty of all of us to do the best we can to help him. I shall watch and see if he carries out his promises and I will give good notice if I perceive any inclination to diverge from them.

As for the J[ohn] F[rench] fiasco, the less said about it the better. Nobody pays any attention to him and his visits to France, and he has fallen quite flat.[1]

1. Even so, the King summoned French to Buckingham Palace on 25 November to tell him to stop undermining the authority of Haig. (See R. Holmes, *The Little Field Marshal: The Life of Sir John French*, p. 328.)

147

H. A. Gwynne to Lady Bathurst, 18 October 1916

. . . Your letter was written in a vein almost of despair and I can quite understand it. You are seeing every day the most horrible and depressing part of the war.[1] But I have seen the machine at work and

192

I am cheered beyond words, for I realise that, *if the politicians will leave it alone*, it is so superior to the German that it will beat it. I cannot, for obvious reasons, give you the facts which lead me to this conclusion but when we meet I will explain.

I came back to find things rather in a mess at the W[ar] O[ffice]. I enclose you copies of a correspondence I have had with Asquith, Lloyd George and Robertson. Will you, I wonder, be able to piece these together and see the work I have done between the letters.[2]

1. This refers to Lady Bathurst's nursing activities, both in France and at Cirencester.

2. Lloyd George had wanted to send divisions from the French front to Salonika. He had been attacked in the *Morning Post* at the end of September for alleged aspersions upon the British High Command. He had then threatened to send Robertson on a mission to Russia. (See R. S. Churchill, *Lord Derby*, pp. 222–4; and Viscount Esher and M. V. Brett (eds), *Journals and Letters of Reginald Viscount Esher*, vol. iv, p. 58.)

Enclosures in letter 147

H. A. Gwynne to Field-Marshal Sir William Robertson, 11 October 1916

I have had a talk with Bonar Law this morning. I expressed my alarm at various rumours I had heard about disagreements between you and L[loyd] G[eorge] and hoped they would not come to an acute crisis. His answer was that if they did come to that point he would certainly resign unless you had your way; and he said he was quite sure that the great majority of the War Council would be of his way of thinking. He always presumed that you would choose a good *military* ground for fighting.

Field-Marshal Sir William Robertson to H. A. Gwynne, 12 October 1916

CONFIDENTIAL

Many thanks for your letter. L[loyd] G[eorge] told me this evening he had received your letter. I had the whole thing out with him, and he gave me his word of honour that he desired me and our chief to carry on. He repeated this with emphasis. Everything is now settled amicably. I hope it will proceed smoothly. What he needs is more knowledge and a better entourage. *I* have no object but one – the same as you have. We will beat the Boche yet. Many thanks for all your good help.

H. A. Gwynne to D. Lloyd George, 11 October 1916

You and I are not seeing eye to eye just now. It is a great pity because you are the only man in the Cabinet who sees clearly that we have to beat the Germans thoroughly or go under. The rest of your colleagues are already whispering the words 'armistice' and 'peace'. But why on earth can't you let the Army alone? With it enthusiastically on your side victory over Germany becomes easier while if you quarrel with its leaders you will jeopardise the issue and lose influence in the country. And all the time we want a man who is all out for beating the German. You put those who are anxious to help you in that task in an awkward dilemma for while they are determined to do their utmost to prevent tinkering with the Army to its detriment, they want to stop it without injuring your reputation.

Maxse and I have been having a talk this evening and it has occurred to me that it would be a good thing if you could see him tomorrow. Do ask him to see you. His address is: 33, Cromwell Road, and his telephone number is Kensington 5672.

H. A. Gwynne to H. H. Asquith, 11 October 1916

It is no doubt not without your knowledge that Viscount French left yesterday for France, but you may not be aware that it is his intention to pay a visit to General Joffre. I am also informed that the Field Marshal has proposed to visit General Foch, whose Headquarters are quite near to those of our armies. You are no doubt aware that the distinguished Field Marshal is not on friendly terms with our Commander in Chief in France; and, therefore, his visit to General Joffre and his proposed stay with General Foch will be – to say the least of it – very embarrassing.

It is, however, I am afraid, the only part of a sort of plot whose ramifications I am not altogether able to trace. There seems to be on the part of the War Minister, Mr. Winston Churchill, Sir F. E. Smith, and Lord French, a common agreement in regard to the capabilities of the Commander in Chief of the British armies in France; and I am almost justified in saying that I perceive indications that the form which this understanding is taking is that of exalting the French system of tactics and strategy at the expense of our own. I have seen some signs of it among my French friends for some time; but it would be a mistake and an act of disloyalty to our Allies if I gave any impression that the French army is mixed up in this. Never was their loyalty greater and more appreciated by our armies than at the present time.

You know, of course, of the visit of Mr. Lloyd George to General Foch, where, with the Lord Chief Justice as interpreter, he ventures on criticisms of the British Generals and the British armies in France. This has aroused considerable indignation among our officers of all ranks out there; but they all acknowledge the straight-forwardness and loyal *camaraderie* of General Foch in circumstances which can best be described as unfortunate.

It will need your personal intervention to put matters straight, and I sincerely hope that you will take steps to see that nothing is done to destroy the good feeling between the French and the British armies in France, or to give to the Commander in Chief of our forces in France the idea that there is a spirit of intrigue against him. I do not write at all as a personal friend of Sir Douglas Haig, for I scarcely know him; but having visited the front I have come back lost in admiration for the magnificent way in which he has organised his armies into a state of efficiency which, I venture to say – and I speak with some experience of war – is superior to that of any army in the field in any part of the globe at the present time, not excepting that of Germany.

H. H. Asquith to H. A. Gwynne, 11 October 1916

I am obliged to you for your letter of today.

I feel sure, from what I know of Lord French, that his journey to France has no such purpose or meaning as you are inclined to suggest. Lord French I have always found loyal and disinterested.

In regard to the rest of your letter, I think it is right to say that I certainly agree with what you say as to the magnificent way in which Sir Douglas Haig has organised his armies. I saw them only a month ago. And the Commander in Chief knows, from what I have myself written him, that he possesses the complete confidence of His Majesty's Government.

You will forgive me if I do not deal with the other points raised in your letter.

148
H. A. Gwynne to Sir Philip Sassoon, 19 October 1916 (HAG/29 no. 3, IWM)

I am very much obliged to you for your letter of October 12. I have delayed answering it because we have been going through one of our customary crises.

I came back from France convinced that the organisation both of the fighting forces and of the machine behind it was as near perfection as one had any reason to hope for; indeed, I frankly confess that it surpassed my greatest expectations. I returned to London to find that matters at the W[ar] O[ffice] were going very awkwardly and it looked as though an intense quarrel might have resulted. L[loyd] G[eorge], while outwardly professing his desire to keep quite clear of all questions referring to operations, did not keep to this; more perhaps by reason of his lack of knowledge than because he wished to put a finger into the pie. Matters got so far that resignations were in the air. However, by a good deal of spade work and constant running to and fro, things have been adjusted; and for the moment, at any rate, they look as if they will run smoothly.

When I came back I found that the strong opinions that I had expressed about L.G. and his changes had given pleasure to the men whom I was least inclined to please, namely, McKenna, Runciman, and those whom I call – for lack of a better name – the Pacifist Group of the Cabinet. Whatever L.G.'s faults are one must, at any rate, concede that he is out to beat the Boche; and with these ideas in my head I went and had breakfast with him on Tuesday. We had a hammer-and-tongs talk for about half an hour and then we settled into a less violent and very practical discussion. He said that D[ouglas] H[aig] was delighted with Geddes[1] and welcomed his aid with enthusiasm. My contention was that I had seen something of the machine and that it seemed to me to be a mistake to touch it when it was running so well. I pointed out that it was of no use trying to run Transport on commercial lines. A shipload of hay might come in which required immediate unloading, and it might even happen that when its cargo had been placed on the trucks, the Commander in Chief might suddenly require a trainload of heavy shells. If there was no train at hand, out would go the hay and in would go the shells. This would be a thoroughly uncommercial proceeding but, from a military point of view, it would be both expedient and good.

However, as a result of our talk he assured me solemnly that he was only too anxious to help the soldier, and that he would interfere in no way with the operation of the war. I suggested that it would be a good thing for him if he had a soldier as military secretary. He expressed himself very anxious to have one and named General Callwell. Of course, this would be impossible as Callwell's rank would make his position difficult and, indeed, I am quite convinced that L.G. would then come to put up Callwell's opinion against that of the C.I.G.S. I mentioned the matter to Callwell who is one of the loyalest and best of soldiers I have come across, and he absolutely refused to entertain the idea and he said if it was ever offered he would refuse it. I then suggested Percy, but the C.I.G.S. says that he is too valuable. So we are all looking round for a man who would have the respect of the soldiers and who would perhaps be able to keep L.G. from little lapses due to ignorance, but none the less annoying to the soldier.

Of course, L.G. is wrong in his strategic conceptions, for he still talks of the West as being over-done from a military point of view. I suppose by this he really means that there are other spheres of action where we could more profitably send our troops. I think, however, that these are mere vague opinions which he does not urge to any extent officially.

I am afraid there is no chance of our getting conscription in Ireland. The Cabinet will discuss and delay until next June, as usual; and if we do get Irish conscription we shall have lost the value of the men until the June following. I will let you know if there are any fresh developments, which I do not anticipate.

1. Sir E. Geddes, appointed by Lloyd George as Managing Director on the Board for Ordnance Factories. (See P. K. Cline, 'Eric Geddes and the "Experiment" with Businessmen in Government 1915–22', pp. 74–104.)

149
H. A. Gwynne to General Sir Henry Wilson, 25 October 1916 (H. Wilson MSS 73/1/20, IWM)

You are quite right about the Cabinet. I do not think that any of them realise what is at stake, with perhaps the exception of Lloyd George; the rest of them seem to be quite content to go jogging along regardless of the fact that we are engaged in the biggest war that we have ever experienced and are ever likely to experience. When we want fervour, and vigour, and energy, we have the same old contented happy go lucky methods of procedure which are enough to muddle one. Take the question of men. Combing out is being done, I suppose, but conscription in Ireland – which is the only thing which would give us a really thumping big force of able-bodied men – is a question which is being postponed every day. One would imagine that the experiences of the last two years would have made one thing clear, and that is, if we want to make a big offensive in the summer we must prepare the men in the winter. But nothing of that kind is being done and although the Cabinet have flirted with conscription in Ireland, they have not got one step nearer a decision than they were four months ago. Meanwhile I am told by people who know Ireland well that the Nationalists themselves want conscription as the only means of saving themselves from the Sinn Feiners, only that they dare not say so openly. But what an extraordinary race they are and how little we can ever hope to understand them!

My little turn with Lloyd George did no harm. I realise that he is about the only member of the Government who grasps the gravity of the situation, and he has the sense to see that his political career is bound up with victory. He does his best but not always with judgement, and very frequently with an ignorance that is appalling. But I am the last man who wants to quarrel with him though I will not let him make a mess of the Army. . . .

150
H. A. Gwynne to H. H. Asquith, 9 November 1916

Do you think we can win this war under present conditions? We have against us a centralised naval, military, and political force which is used solely for the purpose of securing victory. We are suffering under the disadvantage of an alliance in which, of necessity, each ally has a voice in the direction of the strategy of the campaign. The balance against us can never be set right altogether though it can be reduced by frequent or – better – permanent consultations between all the Allies. But this is such an obvious necessity that I will not touch upon it now.

There remains for consideration the attitude of each individual Government of the Alliance towards the military problem. Russia, France, and Italy are relieved of one of the great difficulties which confront the British Government. They have had an organised form of conscription for so many years that it has become part and parcel of the national life. With us it is an innovation. But we have to provide the men. I will go into the details of numbers later on but I am now dealing solely with the task of providing the men. You are faced with the alternative of forcing compulsion to its extreme limits or of easing the situation by getting Ireland to give its quota.

By combing out to the uttermost degree you must face the unpopularity of a drastic application of compulsion to England, Scotland and Wales while Ireland enjoys immunity. The more you comb out the more glaring in the eyes of the public is the Irish contrast. Sooner or later you will have to bring in Ireland. Why not do it now?

What are the difficulties? I am trying to put myself in your place. It is your duty as Prime Minister of England to see that this war is conducted to a successful issue. You are pledged to it. It can never be won without getting more recruits than the Military Service Act provides. You must tap Ireland if you mean to win. But you will say:

'Do you realise that this measure will meet with the determined opposition of the Nationalists in the House of Commons? Do you think that the spectacle of 80 Members of the House of Commons being carried out of the House by force is likely to enhance our prestige abroad, especially among neutrals?' My answer would be that the spectacle of a Government determined to provide the men even at the cost of Irish obstruction will fill neutrals with respect. As for the effect in America and the Colonies, the harm has been done, for the Presidential Election is now over and Mr. Hughes has already suffered the full effect of Irish opposition to his scheme.

The timely and ample provision of men *now* means a stalemate peace or victory postponed till 1918. I will give you my reasons for these statements. I think you will allow me the premiss that if the Russians can force the enemy back into his own territory, and if we and the French can force him on to the Antwerp–Namur–Meuse line, victory is well in sight. Do you think the Russians can do it? I do not nor does any soldier whom I know. The Russians can, and no doubt will, perform a most admirable part in the common task. They will certainly occupy the enemy fully but they are not in a position, owing to their lack of guns, to push the Germans back on to their own soil. There remains then the western front. The reason why this front is to be the scene of the final victory lies in the fact that it is here that the Germans are strongest. To best an enemy on his strongest front is like a great victory at sea – all other advantages follow.

But to break the German front in Belgium and France is not an easy task. We alone must be prepared next year for 750,000 casualties without reducing establishment or depleting the ranks. That means that we shall require 1,500,000 men. Can we do it? Yes, if Ireland is brought under compulsion, but not otherwise. Without this we shall not be able to comb out our own people to the fullest extent because people will not stand the extreme application of compulsion while Ireland stands by rejoicing. There is an ugly feeling abroad and it will take an ugly shape if Ireland is still permitted to go Scot-free.

There are those who doubt our ability to break through or force back the German line in the West. They are mistaken. Indeed I think the civilian mind has failed to grasp the full importance and *portée* of the Somme offensive. For us there have been three very important events in the war – La Bassée, Loos, and the Somme battles. They are all milestones, as it were, on the road to complete tactical superiority over the Germans. It is difficult to explain in the scope of a letter the nature of the lessons we have learned but I think I am not exaggerating when I say that a British division today is worth twice as much as a British division in the days before La Bassée. By this I

199

mean that, owing to the tactical lessons we have learned – sometimes somewhat expensively – a British division today can inflict twice as much loss on the enemy in given circumstances as it could a year and a half ago.

This has been achieved, thanks to our growing superiority in artillery material but even more so by the splendid use to which we have learned to put the arm. It would really be worth the while of the War Council to have before it an artillery expert from the Armies in France to explain what has been and is being done in the matter of the destruction of the enemy's batteries.

I have only touched on these subjects in order to lead up to the conclusion that this war, as far as we and the French are concerned, can only be won on the Western Front. We can force back the German line next year and after a German retreat on that front we can put a fairly accurate limit to the end of the war.

How is the German line to be forced back? This is a question the answer to which sums up the whole of the military situation. Soldiers have talked of breaking through the line in a way which has confused civilian students of the war. When they talk of 'breaking through' they do not mean a great rush and a push, a successful assault that in one or two days will smash up all enemy defences and will leave a gap wide enough for an army to deploy. This may, of course, happen but it is not, I think, the idea of most soldiers. What I feel sure we can do is, so to weaken the defences at *two* points that the enemy will have to retire simply because he will have used up the men necessary to hold the whole line, in defending one particular point of it. For example, suppose we had begun the Somme fighting early in April, having behind us a reserve of 750,000, or, in other words, able to stand casualties up to this amount, we could have placed 250,000 to strategic reserve anywhere between the Somme and Ypres. We should have pushed the enemy on the Somme until he had scraped thin the rest of his line to meet the offensive. This he has actually done this summer. Had we possessed 250,000 extra men with ample guns this year we could have broken through the German lines practically wherever we liked. It was positively painful to talk to Army Corps and Divisional Commanders stationed away from the Somme. They had in front of them skeletons of divisions – corps with nothing but divisional artillery. They could have broken down the opposition almost anywhere along the front with comparative ease, but there were no reserves behind them to do it. As the Germans had skimmed their line so we have been obliged, in order to feed the Somme offensive, to do very much the same though in a lesser degree. Many soldiers believed – and I feel that they were right – that the very knowledge of the existence of a big strategic reserve elsewhere than in the Somme would have induced the Germans to move back from several advanced positions without firing a shot.

I need not enlarge upon the fact that next year we must have this necessary strategic reserve if we are to have victory in 1917, and also on the fact that in order to have this reserve we must put the men into training *now*. I see no way out of it except compulsion for Ireland, and immediate compulsion. It is not merely necessary to train the men but it is essential that they should be put into the line before the great offensive next year so that they shall not be quite raw troops when they go into action. As we stand now it is getting on towards the middle of November, and in order that the new troops should be in the line by the end of February we have three months in hand. This is hardly sufficient time even in these strenuous days and I would again urge upon His Majesty's Government the imperative necessity for getting every man we can lay hold of *now*. Without them I feel sure we shall be obliged to postpone the date of our offensives next year and we may, in consequence of their postponement, be obliged to face another year of war.

It is really a question of the duration of the war and I put it in brief terms in this way. By scraping together every man in England and having compulsion in Ireland now, we can produce a strategical reserve sufficient in strength to force the Germans on to their Meuse line next year. If we do not, we can only have a partial victory which will not force the Germans back to this line, and we shall, therefore, be obliged to fight into 1918.

151
Field-Marshal Sir William Robertson to H. A. Gwynne, 18 November 1916 (HAG/26 no. 10, IWM)

On consideration I think it best to be absent on Thursday night. It is very kind of you to ask me. I feel that I ought to keep clear of any particular sect or movement. They are all bad. The only difference is that some are worse than others. In any case, I need to keep on a straight and unbiassed road.

Editor's postscript: On the night of Thursday 23 November there was a dinner at 23 Cambridge Square attended by Milner (who had returned on 19 November from a week's visit to the front in France), F. S. Oliver (businessman and author of *Federalism and Home Rule*), Lord Eustace Percy, Arthur Henderson (Paymaster General), Robert Brand (Secretary of the Inter-Colonial Council and Railway Committee), Lionel Hichens (Treasurer of the Transvaal, 1902–7) and Geoffrey Robinson (editor of *The Times* and, like Hichens and Brand, a disciple of Milner's since their time together in South Africa). Robinson had a talk with Robertson on his way to that gathering. (See MS Milner 87 (Diary for 1916) and MS Dawson (Diary for 1916).)

152
A. J. Balfour to H. A. Gwynne, 23 November 1916 (MS Gwynne 15)

CONFIDENTIAL
. . . I have to go to Edinburgh to meet Jellicoe and Beatty.

This is in consequence of changes already made two or three days ago at the Admiralty and the Grand Fleet, but not yet announced – changes *the character of which* you will not find it difficult to conjecture.[1]

I beg you to keep this an absolute secret for the present . . . I am sending this note to your home rather than to your office, lest it should get into indiscreet hands. You I know I can trust.

1. It was announced on 30 November that Beatty would take over command of the Grand Fleet from Jellicoe, who would become First Sea Lord. In a letter to Balfour of 8 November Gwynne had suggested this, amongst other changes of personnel at the Admiralty. (See Balfour MSS 49797.)

153
Lord Milner to H. A. Gwynne, 27 November 1916 (HAG/21 no. 44, IWM)

I am so sorry that I can't join your gathering of 'All the Talents' on Thursday. But I have an important engagement, which I can't throw over.

I am very anxious. It seems to me that any slight chance there is of retrieving the situation depends on getting the Government of the country into stronger hands. But every attempt to do this is regarded as an 'intrigue'. The majority of the Government, paralytics though they be, indeed perhaps just because they are paralytics, regard themselves as indispensables, in duty bound to stick to their posts. They have the power of staying there, if they choose, because no one is going to tear the nation in pieces at this moment by trying to oust them. They could only be ousted by *a bitter fight*, for they have the party machinery, &, if they were attacked, all the pacifist and disloyal elements would at once rally to them, as well as the large number of perfectly loyal but deluded people, who do not realise either the gravity of the situation, or the mismanagement which has caused it. And to plunge the nation into a bitter internal controversy at this moment would require more courage than any mortal man possesses.

The only chance seems to be a break up of the Government from within. If Lloyd George & Carson had come out *together* last year, they would probably have been in office long before this and they might have done something. Perhaps it is not yet too late for Lloyd George to come out, and take at least one or two others with him. That would, I think, shortly produce a collapse & the possibility of a reconstruction.

But it is desperately late.

Editor's postscript: On 27 November Milner dined at F. S. Oliver's. Present were Carson, General Sir Henry Wilson, Robinson of *The Times*, and Waldorf Astor, Conservative MP for Plymouth, 1910–19, and owner of the *Observer*. As Robinson recorded it, Carson was 'counselled to pull L[loyd] G[eorge] out rather than go on with the present indecision about everything'. (MS Dawson 22.) Milner's politicking on Thursday, 30 November took place over lunch with Arthur Lee, Lloyd George and Carson. (MS Milner 87.) His engagement of that evening was not a political one; and there was in fact no meeting that evening of those who had dined together the previous Thursday (see editor's postscript to letter 151). On Thursday, 7 December, however, there was another dinner at 23 Cambridge Square, consisting of Milner, Oliver, Brand, Hichens, Robinson, A. E. Zimmern (Intelligence Bureau of the Foreign Office) and Dougal Malcolm, a friend of many of Milner's disciples. (MS Milner 87.) This was one of several groups or clubs which met on a regular basis to dine and to debate. The membership tended to overlap. Throughout 1916 Lloyd George, Carson and Milner had frequently dined together on Mondays, for instance, the numbers being made up from amongst Robinson, Astor, Oliver, Henry Wilson and Philip Kerr, a co-founder of the journal *The Round Table* and Private Secretary to Lloyd George from December 1916. (See L. S. Amery, *My Political Life*, vol. ii, p. 82; and S. Roskill, *Hankey, Man of Secrets*, vol. i, pp. 422–4.)

PART III

December 1916–November 1918

In a letter of 8 May 1918 to Asquith (see letter 226) Gwynne was to claim to have had no hand in the 'vulgar intrigue' which resulted in Lloyd George's assumption of the premiership. The *Morning Post* had, however, praised Lloyd George in a leading article of 23 November. On 25 November, moreover, Gwynne had warned General Sir Henry Wilson that some members of the Cabinet were considering the question of an armistice. Wilson went to see Lloyd George that day. So did Gwynne. Also on 25 November Carson talked with Lloyd George's Secretary, Arthur Lee, about 'the scheme which is on foot to place L[loyd] G[eorge] more and more 'in command of the war' as a kind of Dictator, whilst retaining Asquith as nominal Prime Minister'. (A. Clark (ed.), *A Good Innings, the Private Papers of Viscount Lee of Fareham*, pp. 159–60.) Wilson saw Lloyd George again on the 26th, and on the 27th dined with Carson, Milner, Robinson of *The Times*, Waldorf Astor and F. S. Oliver. According to Wilson, all were agreed 'that Lloyd George should smash, that Bonar Law should come out, and that a real fighting Government should be formed round Lloyd George, Carson and Milner'. On Friday, 1 December one of the *Morning Post*'s leading articles was a sarcastic piece called 'The Survival of the Unfittest'. Refusing to believe there was no alternative to the Asquith administration, it maintained: 'It is time [Members of Parliament] began to think of loyalty to the nation.' This was followed on 2 December by another article, 'The Need for a New Government', praising Lloyd George for being one of no more than two members of the Government who possessed 'any of the elements of statesmanship', voicing the view that 'nothing is to be hoped for as long as Mr Asquith remains Prime Minister', and threatening to publish shortly 'an examination of Mr Asquith's policy previous to the war and his conduct of the war itself'. The latter, Gwynne maintained, was 'not a

205

record in which a great self-respecting country can find honest satisfaction'. On Sunday, 3 December Gwynne saw Carson, who had returned to London at Lloyd George's request. (I. Colvin, *The Life of Lord Carson*, vol. iii, pp. 207–8.) The next day, under the title 'Who Killed Cock Robin?', Gwynne began: 'We gather from the Prime Minister's *communiqué* that there is a political crisis going on, and we confess that we are not in the least surprised to hear that Mr Lloyd George . . . has threatened his resignation.' He went on to try to play down the influence of the press, and particularly the North-cliffe press, saying: 'We suppose there are some people who still believe that John Keats was killed by a *Quarterly Review* article. And so, no doubt, there are some who believe that twenty-three gentle-men can all be thrown upon their beam-ends by a puff of newspaper wind.' Lloyd George was praised, and the connection made with Carson: 'Both men want to win the war, and are prepared to sacrifice everything else to that purpose.' The question was, 'whether Sir Edward Carson and his friends will reach their objects better by reforming the present Administration or wrecking it in order to make way for another'. As Cock Robin still refused to lie down, the Lloyd George–Carson connection continued to be stressed, and Bonar Law urged to stand firm with it, for the next two days, until the new Government could be welcomed.

It is worth contrasting Gwynne's remarks of 4 December about 'newspaper wind' with the views of some of those who were buffeted by it. At a meeting on the evening of 7 December between Lloyd George, Curzon, Lord Robert Cecil, Austen Chamberlain and Walter Long it was recorded:

> The question was raised as to the desirability of taking further powers for the suppression of the kind of Press attacks which had done so much to discredit and finally to bring about the downfall of the late Adminis-tration – on the lines advocated in the earlier days of the Coalition Government. Mr Lloyd George thought it undesirable to announce any restriction of the Press in the earlier days of the new regime, but suggested that an enquiry should be made as to what is done in France.

(Memorandum of conversation between Mr Lloyd George and certain Unionist ex-Ministers, 7 December 1916 (Curzon MSS 11/12/12).)

In his memoirs *Down the Years* (p. 117), Austen Chamberlain quotes a letter to the Viceroy of India of 8 December: 'Lloyd George, towards the middle of last week, presented to Mr Asquith a proposal which was very much in the nature of an ultimatum; the whole Harmsworth press and the *Morning Post* were mobilised in support of him, and Asquith was bidden to stand and deliver. This was the situation on Saturday last (Dec. 2nd).' Gwynne's contribution amounted to more than a mere 'puff', and the force of the newspaper wind was, as we shall see, something that was never to be lost upon the Welsh dragon. The beneficiary of it on this occasion, Lloyd George lived to regret his parrying of the concern of the former Coalition ministers, when that part of it led by the *Morning Post* began to blow strongly against him less than a year later.

Despite Gwynne's involvement in Lloyd George's final push for the premiership, the new Prime Minister retained his popularity with Gwynne for less than six months. Lloyd George's appointment of Churchill as Minister of Munitions, in July 1917, was almost the last straw. Gwynne agreed with Lady Bathurst that 'whom the Gods wish to destroy they first make mad'. Gwynne seriously considered going into politics himself at this time, and entering what he called 'that abominable House of Commons', by opposing Churchill's re-election at Dundee. In August and September he helped to launch a new political party – the National Party. Throughout the year he watched, and commented upon, the progress of revolution in Russia; the passing through the House of Commons of the Representation of the People Bill, which was to increase the franchise dramatically, not least by giving the vote for the first time to women, albeit of a certain age (thirty); and a large number of serious industrial disputes.

The year 1918 was even more hectic. Gwynne and the *Morning Post* were heavily involved in warning Lloyd George not to interfere with the direction of the war and the command of the British Armies by Robertson and Haig; and then in actively opposing the plans of the Prime Minister to exert more control over strategy and the use of manpower. Accordingly the newspaper's military correspondent, Repington, was used by Gwynne and Robertson to denounce arrangements made at Versailles for control of the Allied Armies, and then to expose shortages in the strength of the British Army in France. This led, initially, to the removal of Robertson as CIGS and the prosecution of the *Morning Post* under regulation 18 of the Defence of the Realm Act. Its ramifications extended to the professional suicide of the Director of Military Operations, General Maurice, whose letter revealing the true state of affairs was published in the *Morning Post*; to the putting forward by Gwynne of, successively, Robertson, Sir George Cave, Asquith and Mr Speaker Lowther as alternative Prime Ministers; to attacks on Lords Milner and Derby and General Henry Wilson (who with Esher's blessing had taken Robertson's place); and to efforts by Lloyd George to close down the *Morning Post*, to discredit its military correspondent, and to bribe with offers of Privy Councillorships its editor.

The progress of the great German offensive launched on 21 March almost caused a crisis in Gwynne's faith in victory and in his relationship with his proprietor, for Lady Bathurst, herself in despair, momentarily believed that her editor had also given up the struggle. As the outcome of the German offensive did not become clear until the late summer Gwynne continued to wrestle with the problems of getting compulsory service applied to Ireland and retaining the loyalty and support of the owner. As the easing of the military situation coincided with a new wave of strikes and revolutionary rumblings there were the problems of anticipating the sort of peace that would be made and the adjustments that would be necessary to the immediate post-war world.

154
D. Lloyd George to H. A. Gwynne, 8 December 1916
(HAG/15 no. 8, IWM)

You need not worry about F. E. [Smith]. I have no idea of making him Colonial Secretary. About Balfour, I think you underestimate his courage. He has undoubtedly courage of a very high order, and although I like Grey very much, I think Balfour a much more courageous man. Moreover, if this reassures you, I propose to take a more direct interest in the more important concerns of the Foreign Office, because, as you very well point out in your letter, they are all essential to the winning of the War.

I also want you to bear in mind another point which as an old hand you will appreciate. There are many things to consider in the formation of a Government, and the placing of Balfour at the Foreign Office was of incalculable assistance to me throughout. After B[onar] L[aw] and Carson, he was the first man to come to my aid.

Of course Milner will be in if he accepts. I have not yet seen him.

Thousands of thanks for your congratulations and for the brilliant help which the *M.P.* is giving.

155
H. A. Gwynne to J. S. Sandars, 11 December 1916
(Sandars MSS c769)

I cannot let two letters go unanswered and I want to thank you for them. I have read them with very great interest and, of course, they have been extremely useful to me in this crisis.[1]

I am afraid that, as usual, the politician on our side has been too strong. They have all been demanding their rights instead of allowing themselves to be chosen for their qualities. I dislike Curzon on the War Committee because he is an obstructor, but Carson, no doubt, by virtue of his office, will be there.[2]

I am going away at the end of the week for a bit of a rest, but when I come back we must lunch together.

1. The emergence of the Lloyd George Government, the full constitution of which was published on 11 December.
2. The new War Cabinet consisted of Lloyd George, Curzon, Henderson, Milner and Bonar Law; Carson became First Lord of the Admiralty.

156
H. A. Gwynne to Lady Bathurst, 11 December 1916

Thankyou ever so much for your letter. It has done me a world of good and has bucked me up frightfully. Of course the Government is not perfection but I feel in my bones now that we are going to win. . . .

If you are up on Wednesday and if the Robertsons can come and dine with us, would you like to meet him. Perhaps you would ring me up at home (1690 Kensington) before 11 so that I may be able to try and fix it up. . . .

157
H. A. Gwynne to Lady Bathurst, 18 December 1916

. . . I agree with you about Balfour and the Foreign Office because, as you say, we do not want two strong men. I think that Carson's appointment was due to the fact that they had to find him a place on the Council without actually being of the Council for, as First Lord of the Admiralty, he would naturally have a word to say in the conduct of the war. But I think that everything will be different now because there is at the head of the Government a man who is anxious to win. As regards Kut and Mesopotamia, we have been waiting for two railways to be built, and as these are now nearing completion I am hoping that we shall soon be able to do something with the Turks, in fact, we have made a little advance already.

As regards Tino,[1] the truth is that there are dissensions between the four Allies. Italy is not altogether playing the game, as she wants Venizelos to be down in order that there may be a weak Greece instead of a strong Greece; it is her game, therefore, to preserve the divided counsels in Greece.

1. The Trentino.

158
H. A. Gwynne to Lady Bathurst, 26 December 1916

. . . These infernal Americans are really, in my opinion, jealous of Great Britain. Now that they see that we are getting the better of the Bosch [*sic*], it seems as though they are trying to put a spoke into our wheel. Of course, there are many explanations of Wilson's[1] conduct, but I should say that there are two very simple ones. The first is, vanity, and the second is – as I have said before – a desire to put a spoke into our wheel. However, I am glad to say that he is not altogether representative of American opinion, though he has certainly been able to make things awkward for us, and every dirty little nation like Switzerland is joining his outcry. If we made peace they would be the first to lose what they have got. What price could the Americans put on the Monroe doctrine[2] if we were out of the way? We told America pretty plainly the other day that we could have peace tomorrow on very favourable terms, provided that we allowed Germany to have a free hand in South America. That is the only thing, as far as I can see from the American press cuttings, which has really touched them. It is not that they love us, that they love civilisation, that they love right; it is because they are frightened and they are beginning to see that their only hope is victory on our part. . . .

I am going off the day after tomorrow for ten days in the cottage, and I am coming back on Monday week. The efforts one had to make in this change of Government has [*sic*], what the soldiers call, 'put the lid on'. However, as I recuperate in two days, I shall come back quite refreshed. . . .

1. Woodrow Wilson, President of the United States of America.
2. That North and South America was the sphere of influence solely of the United States.

159
H. A. Gwynne to Viscount Esher, 27 December 1916
(HAG/8 no. 7, IWM)

Many thanks for your letter of December 24th, and the enclosure which I have read with much interest.[1]

Surely your correspondent quite forgets the kind of beast we are fighting against. Treat him leniently and it is like treating a dervish leniently – he always thinks that leniency means fear. If we are going to have peace in Europe for the next fifty years, in my opinion it can only be achieved by punishing these attempts at world domination in a way that would make any attempts of the nature so dangerous as to be practically impossible.

There is another point to be borne in mind. We would make a great mistake if we asked as one of the terms of peace for any alteration in the dynasty of Germany, for that would tend to strengthen the Hohenzollen [*sic*] breed on their throne, but the indirect way of getting rid of them is by showing the German people that their ideas and aims are not only wrong, but have resulted in such a catastrophe to the nation that the nation will never again run the risk of a similar disaster, and so will probably come to the conclusion that the best way to avoid it will be by getting rid of their precious Hohenzollens. Now is the time I am sure for a stiff upper lip, and as you say a 'bloody victory'. Nothing else counts. You and I know that the Germans are more afraid of a second Somme than of anything else, and he knows that his line will have to go this year if he persists. Therefore we must shut down this peace talk, and look forward to the next offensive that will bring us all we want.

All kinds of good wishes for 1917.

1. On 24 December Esher had sent Gwynne some 'pestiferous stuff' protesting against an article of his in the *National Review*. (HAG/8 no. 6, IWM.) Esher, a regular contributor, had published in the December issue a paper entitled 'The Black Eagle's Feathers', which was a contribution to the debate on the terms to be imposed upon a defeated Germany.

160
H. A. Gwynne to Lady Bathurst, 24 January 1917

. . . But don't forget that we are now suffering from the mistakes of a bad old man – Asquith, who so little regarded the needs of the country and the necessity of organising it that he has nearly brought us to the verge of defeat. I do not mean to say that in a military sense but the nation's resources have been so frittered away, there has been such a lack of ordinary foresight that we are now faced with problems so ugly that, frankly, at times I try to turn my face away from them. It will only be by a supreme and most determined effort that we shall be able, now in the moment of our military apogee, to avoid a state of things which may force us to an inconclusive peace. We must give the new men time to turn round. We must suggest even more than criticise for there is one thing I have found and that is that, for the first time, the men in charge realise the danger.

As for Lloyd George and the King – the former seems to have a good inspiration – now and again – the latter never.

Milner is gone to Russia.[1] I am sorry for he could and did keep L. George straight. You know I have no illusions about the little Welshman. He's cunning and sharp and quite unscrupulous but has good courage and means to win the war. Still we must keep an eye on him. . . .

1. Milner had left on 21 January; he was back in London on 3 March.

161
H. A. Gwynne to Lady Bathurst, 30 January 1917

. . . I enclose you a copy of a letter I have written to *The New Europe*. The worst of these Suffragettes is that they will meddle with matters which do not concern them. They have been lately lashing at Sir Wm Robertson, who, to my certain knowledge has done more for England than any other man living at the present moment. They are now going for the *Morning Post* over our Hungary correspondent, whose copy is the best that any paper has had during the War. I am not foolish enough to think that the Independence Party in Hungary would allow one of their members to be a correspondent of the *Morning Post* unless they had an axe to grind, but I know exactly what the axe is they wish to grind, and I am content to help in the grinding of it. In a word they wish to have a leg in both camps, and I agree that it would not be a bad thing when peace comes. Personally, of course, I always thought it would be much better to have Hungary out of the War and Romania in, but that great genius – Sir Edward Grey – thought otherwise.

The present agitation against the Hungarian correspondent of the *Morning Post* is really not a fair one. It starts in newspaper jealousy. Wickham Steed – the Foreign Editor of *The Times* – when we first instituted our Buda-Pesth correspondent, tried to get a correspondent of his own, but as the Hungarians don't approve of Lord Northcliffe and his press, they refused to allow any of their people to correspond, whereupon he made a most violent attack upon the *Morning Post* complaining of inaccuracies on the part of our correspondent. Our correspondent has not been inaccurate. That would be the most foolish thing he could do, and I have gone into every complaint against him, and found that none of them were founded on fact. *The New Europe* which published this article, will, I hope, publish my refutation. The paper is supported by Czech money, and Seton-Watson,[1] who signed the article, is a man who receives a regular salary from the Jugo-Slavs.

I can assure you that I have gone into this matter very thoroughly, and all the complaints and charges against our Buda-Pesth correspondent are false. I have no objection at all to being criticised for having a Buda-Pesth correspondent; to that I can give a good answer, but to accuse him of forgery is a wicked thing. I am going to take this matter up in a more vigorous way, for at the bottom of it is newspaper jealousy. I may tell you for your own information that the Foreign Office – by this I don't mean Grey, who never had any imagination, and never would – but the people who know in the Foreign Office, strongly approve of our Buda-Pesth correspondent's work. The account of Austrian distress that he gives is perfectly true. It is confirmed every day by their own papers, and the Foreign Office official, whose duty it is to collect all the statistics regarding the enemy's economic state, absolutely confirms everything he says.

1. R. W. Seton-Watson, academic, expert on the Balkans. Together with H. W. Steed, R. Burrows (Principal of King's College, London) and F. Whyte, he founded *The New Europe*, the first issue of which appeared in October 1916. Gwynne's defence of his Budapest correspondent was a complete fabrication. The journalist in question, one Josef Szebenyei, was writing his articles in London, and was interned after questions were asked in the House of Commons. (See H. Hanak '*The New Europe*, 1916–20', *Slavonic and East European Review*, 1960–1, vol. 39, p. 381.)

162
H. A. Gwynne to Lady Bathurst, 9 March 1917

I am sorry to bother you about the question of the Fashion Column. . . . Whether we like it or no, the *Morning Post*, which has now become a political organ of no small importance, also has a reputation for being a fashionable paper. That dated from the days when we made a point of recording fashionable movements. . . . I cannot shut my eyes to the fact that the prosperity of the paper depends upon the prosperity and efficiency of the fashionable column, to an extent which I think it is impossible to exaggerate. The solid basis upon which we build up our revenue is the servants' advertisements, and these servants' advertisements depend, in my opinion, very largely upon the reputation for being a fashionable paper which we have enjoyed in the past. If the Fashion Column is interfered with in such a way as to make it less interesting in the sense of omitting the names of the more fashionable members of Society, we shall, I feel sure, experience a considerable drop in the domestic advertisements, and this would be nothing short of disastrous.

Personally, I hate the idea that the *Morning Post* should be regarded as a fashionable paper, but I am not so foolish as to shut my eyes to the practical benefits which result from that reputation. We are going to have, before the War is over, a pretty hard time, and I would not wish to see any experiments made with this vital and essential factor in our prosperity at this time. . . .

163
H. A. Gwynne to Lady Bathurst, 16 March 1917

Many thanks for your letter. I was much interested in what Sir William Haggard[1] says. I think he is absolutely right about Casement[2] and still more right about Morel.[3] Between ourselves I think in a short time we shall have Morel in gaol – he is giving himself away badly.

As regards the Foreign Office. I think he is wrong about Tyrrell, whom I know well. Tyrrell is a Whig and a thorough official to whom new methods and new ways are anathema, but he has always been conscious of the German danger, and, long before the war, when we used to meet, which we did pretty frequently, he was always insistent upon the fact that the war was inevitable. Tyrrell's only son was killed in the war, and this drove him to seek relief in drink. It was very sad. But he has pulled himself together and he is now a teetotaller. I never had a very exalted opinion of his talents, but it would be quite unfair to say that he was in any way inclined to condone or wink at the German danger.

As for Eyre Crowe. I have gone into his case pretty thoroughly. At the beginning of the war I was very much of the same opinion as Sir William Haggard, but I have seen Minutes of his, written a considerable time before the war, which prove to my satisfaction that he was the only man in the Foreign Office who had the pluck to stand up against the Germans. As you know, the dangerous time for us was between 1911 – the year of Agadir – and 1914, and that was the time when Eyre Crowe came out at his very best. I think it would be quite unfair to ascribe to him any pro-German proclivities, for the whole of his official life gives the lie to it. I may say that Maxse and I were much inclined to share the belief that Crowe would have been better out of the Foreign Office at the beginning of the war, but on enquiry we found such evidence of his antipathy to Germany and the consistence [sic] of his fight against Germany, that we felt that it would be a pity if the one strong man in the Foreign Office should be kicked out.[4]

I am now told that it will be all right if I go to France, and I expect to be off on Tuesday.

I think the Russian Revolution is going to turn in our favour.

1. Sir William Haggard, Minister-Plenipotentiary to Brazil, 1906–14, when he retired from the Diplomatic Service.

2. Sir Roger Casement, Irish Nationalist; tried for high treason and hanged 3 August 1916. On 5 June Gwynne forwarded to Basil Thomson, head of Special Branch, some letters of Casement's obtained by the Washington correspondent of the *Morning Post*. (MS Gwynne 22.)

3. E. D. Morel, radical MP, founder of the Union of Democratic Control in 1914, author of *Ten Years of Secret Diplomacy*, March 1915, and *Truth and the War*, July 1916.

4. It is clear that Gwynne had been allowed to see some departmental minutes which, in his time as Foreign Secretary, Grey jealously guarded from his Cabinet colleagues. He may even have seen Crowe's memorandum of 1 January 1907 on Anglo-German relations which, on 22 March 1917, Lord Robert Cecil refused to lay before the House of Commons on the grounds that publication would not be in the public interest. Whether there was any connection between Shaw MP, to whose Parliamentary Question Cecil was replying, and Sir William Haggard, is not known. (See K. M. Wilson, 'Sir Eyre Crowe on the Origin of the Crowe Memorandum of 1 January 1907', *Bulletin of the Institute of Historical Research*, 1983, vol. lvi, no. 134, (pp. 240–2.)

164
H. A. Gwynne to Lady Bathurst, 11 April 1917

. . . We have won a signal victory. The Vimy ridge is the pivot on which the whole Hindenburg line rests. We have pushed beyond that and the Germans will have, I think, to retire to the switch line Quéant–Drocourt. You will find it all in the map tomorrow. Our losses are not heavy – 16,000 all told up to this morning and as the wounded were mostly from machine-gun and rifle fire the percentage of deaths is very small. My own idea is that the Germans will not be able to stand our artillery. It is simply awful. Haig told me when I was out there that the morale of the German soldier was going and only discipline was left. I think the morale has nearly vanished after the last bombardment.

About the German system of Government I don't think it was quite what you describe.[1] It was a fraud even as a benevolent despotism – which we both agree is the best form of Government. The German system was not honest. It was Junker – Prussian in its worse [*sic*] form. It was corrupt for it was full of lies. If we condemn the bacchanalia of perverted democracy, so we must condemn the form of the Prussian system. They are both indefensible in my opinion. But when we handed over the pistol to our masters in 1832 we let ourselves in for all the evils that have pursued us. I am afraid it is hopeless to go back to the pre-Reform times but we can keep our flag flying. . . .

1. Gwynne here was taking issue with the views expressed by Lady Bathurst in her interview with *The Gentlewoman* in February 1917. (See Introduction, p. 6.)

165
H. A. Gwynne to Lady Bathurst, 19 April 1917

. . . To advocate that we should make peace with Turkey, on condition that Abdul Hamid[1] came back, is a course that I think would be wrong in itself, but, apart from that, I think that none of the belligerents – France least of all, and certainly not our own Government – would consent to it for one moment. We are tied by a Treaty to Russia, and, here again, I think that you and I do not see eye to eye about Russia. I cannot help thinking that the Moderates in Russia are playing a very skilful game, and I have no doubt in my own mind that in a very short time we shall see a Monarchy – deprived of some of its former autocratic powers – established in place of the Czar. At the present moment, the Extremists are having it all their own way with the consent and knowledge of the Moderates. They are weaving a very fine rope, with which they will hang themselves, for when it comes to the real struggle, the highly conservative agriculturists, who form the vast majority of the nation, will sweep out these Anarchists, who are now having the time of their lives. The chief argument, that they are using quietly, is the treaty, which gives them Constantinople. It is to our advantage to get the Russian in Constantinople, for the simple reason that this would form a barrier for many generations against the German 'pressure towards the East'. It would effectively destroy that dream, and, in the settlement, we have got to look to the future of Germany with some degree of nervousness. I know my England so well, that I am quite sure that when the German begins to whine, this magnanimous country of ours will begin to say: 'Poor fellow!' and, in twenty years, Germany will have recovered from the war, and will be a strong and powerful nation. I don't believe in all this talk about 'this war ending war.' It is the purest nonsense in the world. If Germany and Russia were to combine, we should be in a very awkward position, for Germany could threaten us on the sea in Europe, and Russia would be a menace to India. By bringing Russia down into the Bosphorus, we create an antagonism of interest between these two nations, which must last as long as Germany has any ambitions in the Near East. If we gave back Turkey to the Turks intact, the Germans would regain all their influence there, and we should have to fight another great war for our Eastern possessions. After all, they have chosen their bed, and don't you think that they should be made to lie upon it?

1. The former Sultan of Turkey, deposed in 1908.

166
H. A. Gwynne to Lady Bathurst, 24 May 1917

I was told yesterday, on fair authority, that A. Murray[1] had not been actually recalled, though his position was precarious. . . .

I was downhearted because with a country magnificently determined to win this war, we nearly had a general strike.[2] It was a case of sheer and stupid mismanagement. The voᴛ -catching politicians can never secure the confidence of working men. It can only be done by people whom they can trust. And who would trust a Dr Addison[3] or a Ulrich Wolff (the chief of the Labour Intelligence at the Munitions)?

1. Lieutenant-General Sir A. Murray, Commander in Chief Egyptian Expeditionary Force.
2. Since the end of April there had been widespread disturbances amongst the members of the Amalgamated Society of Engineers, affecting munitions production, relating to the abolition of the Trade Card Scheme and the introduction of the Munitions of War Amendment Bill. (See C. Addison, *Politics from Within*, vol. ii, pp. 130–44.) The Trade Card Scheme, devised by the Man-Power Board in November 1916, allowed Trade Union Executives to give cards of exemption from enlistment to certain categories of their own members.
3. Dr C. Addison, appointed Minister of Munitions, December 1916.

167
H. A. Gwynne to Lady Bathurst, 24 May 1917

. . . With regard to my letter yesterday, you will notice that I wrote most enthusiastically about your idea of bringing the wounded men in to take the place of those young enough to be spared, but I find that in this precious country that is one of the causes of the recent strike. I am considering what to do, for the proposal is so sensible and so obviously practical, that I cannot understand why it should not be adopted. The late strike was not a strike about grievances as appeared on the surface. It was simply due to the fact that the Government have not got a man that the people can trust, and it is becoming more and more clear to me that what they want is a decent honest man who has got nothing to get out of them, and who will not make them promises which he cannot keep for the sake of a few months' peace. I am afraid the settlement has been made on these lines and we shall have the whole trouble over again simply because the people who are in charge of labour in the Government will not trust them and will not govern them, and allow Shop Stewards and other traitors and pacifists to dictate their terms.

168
Viscount Esher to H. A. Gwynne, 1 June 1917
(HAG/8 no. 13, IWM)

I don't like the outlook. Henry Wilson who is not allowed by our idiotic government to pull his real weight may perhaps have written to you. If not, come over and have a talk.

What with strikers, socialists, *small* politicians, want of 'direction', and ingrained peace mentality, the Allies show signs of disintegration.

Your article on R. MacDonald & Co was excellent.[1]

It is a mere thread of suggestion, but keep your eye on government changes of personnel. There is a touch of something sinister in wanting to link up with the old gang.[2] No strong and self possessed ruler of our country would desire this. The mental currents of even our best men are unfathomable.

The rulers of France just now are *small* men, and we cannot get L[loyd] G[eorge] to 'take charge' which he could easily do.

Nothing could be more wholesome than the atmosphere at G.H.Q.

Nothing more mephitic than the atmosphere here.

Watch it.

1. Ramsay MacDonald was Leader of the Independent Labour Party; the article, claiming that he represented 'the anti-British and pro-German Party in this country', appeared under the heading 'The Stockholm Mousetrap' on 1 June.

2. Esher rightly suspected that Lloyd George wished to include Churchill in the Government. (See Viscount Esher and M. V. Brett, *Journals and Letters of Reginald, Viscount Esher*, vol. iv, p. 121; and J. M. McEwen (ed.), *The Riddell Diaries* p. 191, entry for 11 June 1917.) In a few days' time Esher was to be told by Lord Murray of Elibank that Lloyd George looked for 'a very moderate peace, and at an early date. A peace based upon the status quo, modified by concessions here and there, but "We must give the Germans one more good hammering first".' (See P. Fraser, *Lord Esher*, p. 366.)

169

H. A. Gwynne to Viscount Esher, 4 June 1917
(HAG/8 no. 14, IWM)

Many thanks for your letter which I am obliged to answer by typewriter as I am off tomorrow to France. I shall probably be staying at G.H.Q. one or two nights out of my visit, so perhaps we could arrange to meet. I should like to come on to Paris but I have to get back quickly.

I agree with nearly all you say about the outlook. It is bad only because people are afraid of shadows. I am quite certain that this country is solid for the war to the bitter end but they are frightened of the talkers. One of the remedies seems to me to be a League of Patriots, who would number I feel sure nine-tenths of the population. It is the small men who are losing the war.

170

H. A. Gwynne to Viscount Esher, 4 July 1917
(Esher Papers 5/52)

. . . I cannot understand Franklin Bouillon's statement[1] about D[ouglas] H[aig]. Of course D.H. is an awkward customer with politicians. It is no use discussing the fact, but as he is in nearly every case absolutely right and they absolutely wrong, they have got to put up with his manner. He is inclined, as we know, to lose his temper, but I don't wonder at it, because a man with that enormous responsibility really ought not to be bothered by silly suggestions which are not even considered before they are made.

I hope you will read the articles I have been publishing in the *Morning Post*. They will show you my opinion of what D.H. is doing and the progress we are making. In my opinion if we can go on hammering him a little more the Boche will break somewhere and have to go back. In this connection I wish you would do me a kindness. The French W[ar] O[ffice] have issued a handbook to their officers, which is a word-for-word translation of the handbook prepared by our artillerymen in France for the use of our officers. I would like to show it about to a few of the doubters. You will easily get hold of it and it would be a most valuable asset to me here. D. H. I think is absolutely the right man in the right place. It is a dogged fight which must be carried out by armies that are absolutely efficient, and he has made the British armies in France the most efficient instrument of war that the world has ever seen.

As for the rewards that should come to D.H. The politician is so absorbed in his own little tricks that I really don't think that it has ever occurred to him to do the right thing by the armies out there. Think what a tremendous buck-up it would be to the fellows fighting out there, as well as to their commanders, if Parliament passed a solemn vote of thanks to their armies in France. I will see what I can do towards this end,[2] though I don't think I shall have much success. I don't imagine the Government is very strong. They are getting mixed up in smaller politics and in Ireland, and the old gang is always standing by to step into their shoes.

I will see what I can do with your letter,[3] but it is so frank and open that it is difficult to summarise it in such a way as to make it effective and yet at the same time not to give away anything.

1. Henri Franklin Bouillon, President of the External Affairs Committee of the French Chamber. In a letter of 28 June Esher had told Gwynne of Bouillon's remark that Haig was being criticized in London for not 'breaking through' and for not 'making more use of his successes'. (See Viscount Esher and M. V. Brett, *Journals and Letters of Reginald, Viscount Esher*, vol. iv, p. 128.) Bouillon had been an advocate of the Salonika Expedition.

2. Note by Esher in margin: 'He has done this.'

3. Note by Esher in margin: 'He has done this very well in his articles.'

171
H. A. Gwynne to Viscount Esher, 19 July 1917
(Esher Papers 5/52)

Please allow me to thank you very much for the enclosure in your letter, which will be a powerful argument one of these days. Since you wrote and before I had time to answer, things have all gone wrong here. The old Latin tag, which says that those whom the gods wish to destroy they first make mad, seems to be extraordinarily true of Lloyd George. I have never, since the war began, seen such indignation against a Government or man as is raging now against Lloyd George for the appointment of Winston [Churchill].[1] I think the result will be that this feeling will find expression in a fight against him (Winston), and I think it is the best way out. One doesn't want the old gang in, and yet Lloyd George, like the fatted pig, is cutting his own throat, as it seems. He has not got an easy job, Heaven knows! but why on earth he should challenge public opinion on its tenderest point by such appointments as he has made, passes my intelligence, except on the assumption that he has really lost all sense of judgement.

H[is] M[ajesty] is all right, though I think the majority of people are of opinion that these changes in names and titles[2] are rather a foolish concession to a few anonymous letter-writers – most of the public really don't care a hang one way or the other.

The best thing I have heard for some time is the rioting in Petrograd, for it seems to me that at last the Provisional Government feels itself strong enough to challenge the extremists.

I have put your letter VERAX in[3] and thank you very much for it.

1. As Minister of Munitions. The announcement was made on 18 July.

2. On 18 July it was announced in the Press that the House of Saxe-Coburg-Gotha would henceforth be known as the House of Windsor. (See H. Nicolson, *King George V*, pp. 309–10; and letters 140 and 141.)

3. Entitled 'Mesopotamia and After', this was an attack on the handling of the Mesopotamia Enquiry; it appeared on 19 July.

172
H. A. Gwynne to Lady Bathurst, 20 July 1917

I hardly know what to think about the situation, for Lloyd George must I think have some ulterior motive for his extraordinary action.[1] It is always well to bear in mind that he is a politician, and his sole claim to fame lies in the fact that he has more sense than a good many of his fellows and realises that he is likely to be hanged unless we win this war. Therefore it puzzles me that he should have affronted public opinion in England to such an extent, unless he is really anxious to go and form an Opposition, otherwise I think what you say is true, that those whom the gods wish to destroy they first make mad. The question I have got to consider is how to stop it, and the only way I can think of is to fight Winston Churchill at Dundee. Time is horribly short, but I think something might be done and I am doing all I can to do it. If we can defeat him at Dundee then I think we shall avoid an enormous danger. If he stays, the Government is doomed, for as sure as I am writing he will commit some horrible error of judgement, which may delay munitions and guns and even allow him to push forward some pet and absurd scheme of his own. As you rightly say, he has committed every blunder possible, and yet he is entrusted again with great responsibility. It's sickening, and it takes the heart out of one, and increases what is still more dangerous – the unrest in the country. One of Winston's chief duties will be to deal with Labour, and if there is one man more unqualified, by his lack of tact, judgement and character, than Winston, I have yet to find him. It is an appalling disaster, greater I think than has fallen on us during the whole of the war. I am really quite upset about it. . . .

1. In appointing Churchill.

173
H. A. Gwynne to Lady Bathurst, 27 July 1917

. . . I have in addition to the *M.P.* work been wearing out my shoe leather in work which we pay several of our precious politicians £5000 a year to do.

I know you are anxious to learn all about my mysterious telegrams about standing. I felt so strongly about Churchill and Montagu[1] that I got enough money together to start a fight in Dundee and tried to do the same in East Cambridgeshire. Both my attempts have been failures but last Saturday, things looked more hopeful. The difficulty in both was the question of candidates. You see all the good men are away and only the scum of military age are left. I therefore as a last resort, thought that it was my duty to step into the breach. I hated it but I thought it incumbent on me to do it. At any rate I wanted your permission in case I might have to decide in a hurry. Luckily, the occasion did not arise. We were advised that in both cases there was little chance of success but especially in Cambridgeshire. In Dundee the people are on holiday and wouldn't come back to vote.

. . . Don't imagine for a moment that I have the very slightest desire to go into that abominable H[ouse] of Commons. It would only be at the most urgent call of duty that I would make the attempt and as soon as I could get a substitute I would. . . .

These awful examples of waste of effort and material that you tell me of make one writhe over the awful expense. I saw a man – a good sound businessman who is in the Government – who told me that he thought the expenses of the war could be reduced to £4,000,000 per day. We have achieved something. We've got a committee to examine expenditure and perhaps we may get something done. . . .

I quite agree with you about Russia and I am dying to speak out. But we are on the knife-edge of the war and if we did, we might do infinite harm. If we wrote what we all think, the Germans would take our article, reprint it in Russia and distribute it broadcast to the benighted soldiers. I can see the headline, 'What England thinks of you'. I am quite sure such an article would do harm to the common cause. But don't you think also that people are realising all you say? The revolutionary feeling here is dead. The Russian Revolution killed it. But there is still, thank heaven, a strong revolutionary feeling against the politicians.

1. Edwin Montagu, appointed Secretary of State for India, 17 July. Both Churchill in Dundee and Montagu in East Cambridgeshire had to seek re-election.

174
H. A. Gwynne to Lady Bathurst, 7 August 1917

Now as regards Russia. Our opinion of mildness and violence differs considerably. Here I have got a letter from a friend of mine, in which I am informed that the Russian Government Committee of India House, who have great weight with the Government, are trying to get a ban placed on our paper in Russia, because they say that we are damaging the alliance and attacking Kerensky.[1] I don't know what to do yet, but it seems evident that strings are being pulled to injure us. However I do agree with you entirely that if we are going to kow-tow to all these pro-German agitators, then Heaven help England and the *Morning Post*! Lady Buchanan puts the case quite rightly,[2] when she says 'It is German, all of it.' Remember that I have gone further than anybody in England, and we must bear in mind that to go beyond a certain point does do harm to the alliance. I only want to do what you want to do, and that is to tell Russia that we believe in the better and more moderate Russia, and not in these German paid scoundrels. But Kerensky, although he is an extreme Socialist, seems to be the only man who can save the situation and responsibility seems to have had a sobering effect upon him.

1. Head of the Provisional Government in Russia.
2. Georgina, Lady Buchanan, the wife of Sir George Buchanan, the British Ambassador in Petrograd, was Lady Bathurst's sister-in-law and wrote to her as circumstances allowed throughout the war. This particular letter was written on 22 July 1917, during the Bolshevik uprising against the Provisional Government. The disposition to hold the Germans entirely responsible for events in Russia was widespread. The conviction that both Lenin and Trotsky were not only Jews but German agents was to be found in the War Cabinet at this time, and was not easily dispelled. (See G. Katkov, 'German Foreign Office Documents on Financial Support to the Bolsheviks in 1917', *International Affairs*, 1956, vol. 32, pp. 181–9.)

175
H. A. Gwynne to Lady Bathurst, 13 August 1917

. . . As regards the Russian situation. Marsden is the man who wrote the Rasputin thing,[1] and, frankly, I think his judgement is not his strongest point. One is entirely dependent on one's correspondent for opinions regarding the country which he represents, and I must confess that I was somewhat disappointed. I saw Lord Duncannon[2] when he came back from Russia, and from what he told me I thought that a revolution was quite inevitable and told Marsden so, getting back from him a letter practically telling me I knew nothing about it. However I was right and he was wrong. I am not sure that he is right now. That is to say I am perfectly sure that he is right that the revolution, although it was not started by the Germans, was carried through by Germans, and I am quite sure that three-quarters of the Soldiers' and Workmen's Council are Germans. I have thought and I still think, that Russia will go back to a limited Monarchy, and every step that the Russian Provisional Government have taken confirms what I say. Petrograd no more represents Russia than the East End of London represents England. . . .

1. A thirty-page typescript report on Russian affairs, sent on by Gwynne to Lady Bathurst.
2. MP for Dover and ADC to General Sir Henry Wilson, who went on the mission to Russia at the beginning of the year.

176
H. A. Gwynne to Viscount Esher, 17 August 1917 (HAG/8 no. 17, IWM)

. . . There is one thing that nobody can do, and that is to put a new backbone into a man – not even the most skilful surgeon can manage that. Our governors for the last year have been afraid of Labour instead of cooperating with it. They have allowed the Pacifists to grow, indeed, they seem almost to have encouraged them – and now they are faced with the results, they come down with a clumsy foot, and do what they ought to have done a year ago.

I don't agree with you that the result will split England. It will split up the Labour Party. In fact every party in this country is split up – the Liberal Party between Asquith and Lloyd George; the Unionists between Bonar Law and the young bloods who think he is no good, and the Labour Party in every direction. But France I admit is much more critical. If Thomas[1] goes, there will be definite opposition on the part of the Socialists to everything the Government says or does. I agree with you that we ought to work the British Socialists through the French, but we rather trusted Lloyd George would do this, as he is supposed to be such a great manager of men. I think he has failed rather ignominiously.

1. Albert Thomas, French Minister of Munitions.

177
Viscount Esher to H. A. Gwynne, 23 August 1917 (HAG/8 no. 18, IWM)

I have just got back from the North. If you have seen Leo Maxse he will have told you that the spirit of strong confidence is fully maintained. I believe that D[ouglas] H[aig] is the only man in a high position in England or out of it, who believes in his heart of hearts that the Boche can be beaten.[1] This want of faith in others is the most serious element in the situation. I wish I agreed with you that the split is only in the Labour Party. People who come over here,[2] and who move in what is called society say that fatigue and discouragement and above all scepticism as to the attainment of a military success are prevalent in those circles as well as among the industrial population.

When in profound peace all men speak of war there is great risk that war is imminent. When in the throes of war, all men talk of peace, there is a probability that Peace is not far off. . . .

1. Esher had doubts even about Robertson. (See Viscount Esher and M. V. Brett, *Journals and Letters of Reginald, Viscount Esher*, vol. iv, pp. 121 and 131.)
2. i.e. France.

178
H. A. Gwynne to General Sir Henry Rawlinson, 23 August 1917 (HAG/24 no. 14, IWM)

I was delighted to hear your cheery voice over the telephone the other day, though I heard it with much searching of the heart because I promised to write to you and tell you about things. The truth is that my whole time is taken up doing the best I can to watch the politician, who has been up to his tricks, as you will see by the appointment of Winston [Churchill] and Montagu.

But apart from that things have not been going well here though they have been going very well with you. Lloyd George is making the fatal mistake of trying to carry on the war and at the same time to create a party. The main object of his appointment of Winston was to deprive the Asquithian lot of the advantages of a man of energy and authority. Personally I should have thought that even from the political point of view it would have been better to leave a man like Winston, who is hardly an asset to any party, to the Asquithians rather than take the burden on one's own shoulders. However evidently Lloyd George does not think so and we are burdened with

Winston. One of his first acts was to write a memorandum, which he circulated among the Cabinet, advocating a great naval offensive[1]. . . . Everybody has laughed at it, and it has been turned down, but it shows which way Winston's mind is turning. He is a man who never seems able to rest, and it is quite possible that he will follow up his naval offensive by some wild scheme of a military offensive. At the bottom of it all of course is his dislike for Douglas Haig and Robertson. But I think they are both too high in the public estimation to be got rid of.

As regards the general military situation. I think, without being too optimistic, we can say that we are pretty well off. The Russians have failed us, it is true, but at the same time the Germans, as far as I can make out, have not been able – owing to the uncertainty of the situation – to derive much benefit from their pusillanimity, and I think there is no chance from all I hear of their making a separate peace, though I think we cannot count on their doing anything very big in the way of an offensive until next year. Korniloff[2] privately says that he can get an army together in order to bring about an offensive this autumn, but I doubt it very much.

In Palestine, as you know, we are meditating a stroke which may come off. What is pleasing out there is undoubtedly that we are raising the Arabs very successfully. This, as you know, was K[itchener]'s last job, and they seem for the first time to be working in unison and with a definite purpose.

The Labour position looks really worse than it is, for up to the present the men who have been able to manoeuvre and jerrymander the leaders have made it look as though Labour was not very keen on winning the war, but, as a matter of fact, 95% of the working men are just as keen as we are, and one of these days the patriotic fellows will make their voice heard.

I hope to come out[3] about the 3rd or 4th of next month, and I am particularly anxious to have a talk with you, so I will suggest myself to you, when I have heard from D.H., with whom I am also anxious to have a talk.

1. The editor has been unable to trace anything matching this description amongst the extant Cabinet papers.
2. Russian General, later prominent in the counter-revolutionary movement.
3. To France.

179
H. A. Gwynne to Lady Bathurst, 27 August 1917

Many thanks for your long and interesting letter.

I feel very strongly that to legislate now, when all the best men are away, is very unfair to the men who are fighting for us, and that standpoint I have not abandoned in my general opposition to all these schemes of Liberal reform and such like, which seem to me to be initiated in order to diddle the men who are fighting for us.[1] Why cannot they wait? Is not a great war like this a sufficient task for anybody to carry it through? But the politician remains a politician in whatever circumstances he is placed, and cannot refrain from his little dodges any more I suppose than a dog can stop barking. . . .

Now about reconstruction. I am so glad to hear that your husband has joined.[2] As a matter of fact there was so much secrecy about the thing that I pledged myself to say nothing to anybody, but it seemed to me that the only way out of the present *impasse* was to try and create a new Party that would play a straight game with the people and would not always pander to them. You have put your finger exactly on the weak point of this new party. There are not enough big men leading. But really when you come to the big men, you find they are all tarred with the same brush, and are perfectly incapable of being what the Salvation Army calls 'born again'. To go back to the better days, when the leaders of the people told the truth to the people, is not possible with the old hands. We must have new men to do it. Between ourselves, I am not sure that the men we have got are the best, but Page Croft[3] is a hard-working man without very great brains, but he is honest, and I think willing to sacrifice himself for the good of the country. Duncannon has got brains and courage and enthusiasm, and I think he is the better man of the two. They are quite a small party but they want a leader and I don't see where the leader is to come from. Still as they are putting into practice what we have been preaching for the last two years, I think that we can do nothing else but support them. I have told them that the *Morning Post* belongs to no Party, not even to the new National Party, but as long as the National Party plays the game and carries out the programme it has laid down honestly and straightforwardly, so long will we support them, but they must not count on any blind support from the *Morning Post*. That I am sure is in agreement with your desires. We cannot tie ourselves to any party now, for our position of independence is also a position of enormous strength. People listen to us and are swayed by us. If we became the party hack, even of a new and better party, we should lose a good deal of our influence.

The programme of reconstruction is nothing new as far as you and I are concerned, for we have been preaching it for the last two years. Tariff reform is of course the great reform, and is more essential than ever it was. But it is not all. We have got to do something to prevent Labour and Capital quarrelling. Our policy is roughly that the question of wages is not a question for Parliament, for that way lies corruption, but rather a question of the best price a man can get for what he has to sell. We suggest that Labour and Capital should settle their own rate of wages, and not let the politician interfere, or interfere as little as possible. What is really happening now is that the country is undergoing a process of blackmail. Jones gets up and says that he is in favour of 5/- a week more, and Robinson gets up and suggests 7/6d. and so on. If this goes on no industry can live, and we suggest that an industry should settle between its employed and its employers the proper rate of wages. It is done in America, and I don't see why it should not be done here. The Radical has always played on the cupidity of the workman, always promising him better wages, when better wages were impossible. That does not matter as long as he gets the votes. Our plan I think is infinitely better. We say to Labour and Capital: Settle your own differences yourselves. Surely if a man wants to buy a thing and another man wants to sell, they can agree upon a price without going to the Government to settle it for them. That is a great reform and is second only to Tariff reform.

Then there is the question of a greater productivity. We shall have spent six thousand million pounds at the end of this war. Probably the payment of the debt alone will be three thousand million a year. We can never pay for this unless we produce more, and in order to produce more Trade Union rules cannot stand as they are, and we suggest that Trade Unionists should alter their rules so that a man is paid for what he does and not paid for what he does not. This at first sight looks an impossible proposition, but really it has worked so well in America that I don't see why it should not here.

My suggestion about making ourselves more self-supporting was not to make the British Isles absolutely self-supporting but to make them more self-supporting than they are, and the only way in which this can be done is to make farming a paying proposition so that there will be more production. That we can be absolutely self-supporting of course is impossible, but we can get more men on the land, and in order to do this I think what you say is right, we shall have to have recourse to bigger farms and the smallholder will have to go. If it results in more people settling on the land so much the better, for that is one of the essentials of any reform. But I don't see why the land should not be as much a business proposition as any other, and why people should not be paid a fair rent for their land as a manufacturer is paid a fair rent for the houses he owns.

As for the expropriation of land I don't believe it will come. For, after all, you have to bear in mind that robbery is robbery whether it is done by a State or whether it is done by an individual, and I can conceive of no party or system which can succeed on a basis of sheer robbery.

I put a great deal of faith in the soldiers who are coming home. I believe that they are better men for what they have gone through, and have a clearer conception of what a Government should be. After all, a system of government is not a religion, and what we have got to do is to try and govern this country so as to bring out the best elements and get the greatest production out of it.

There is nothing new in all this. We have preached it hundreds of times before, but I am glad to see that there are a certain number of people who are beginning to understand that we were right, and indeed think us so right that they are willing to stake their political existence on the success of the principles which we have advocated. . . .

1. On 15 August the House of Commons had begun to deal with the practicalities of soldiers' voting under clause 18 of the Representation of the People Bill.

2. The National Party.

3. Brigadier Henry Page Croft, MP for Christchurch. (See W. D. Rubinstein, 'Henry Page Croft and the National Party 1917–22', pp. 129–48.)

180
H. A. Gwynne to Lady Bathurst, 29 August 1917

The article, to which you took exception, was an attempt to show to the foolish British public that the war aims of the Socialist democrats, at any rate as far as they concern Germany, are impossible, that Germany has never wavered in her determination to keep her mode of government, and that it is hopeless to expect it. A sentence out of your letter will explain the difference between you and me. You say: 'You don't give privates in the Army equal power with the officers.' But that is exactly just what we have done with the people of England. We have given the ignorant and the unintelligent a vote, and you might just as well try to take a bone from the mouth of a savage dog as try to get that back. The arguments, with which I am in entire agreement, that you use, would have been excellent arguments to use before 1832, the time of the Reform Bill, but since then we have to recognise, whether we like it or not, that we have done exactly what you so much deprecate, we have given the privates in the Army equal power with their officers, and one has to recognise the fact that we have given it and that we cannot take it away. As Robert Lowe[1] says: 'All that is left to us is to educate our masters.'

The most that we can do, it seems to me, is to try and make the working man see that democracy has a large number of weak spots in it, but nobody can ever hope, in my opinion, to make him give up the vote. So far from that being possible, the present Government have increased the ignorant electorate by giving the vote to women,[2] so that in your house, whatever your opinion may be, you will count as one, while a number of servant girls, who probably don't know how to read and write, will have just as much power in the body politic as you have.

The *M.P.* has never joined that cry for the democratisation of Germany.[3] That is their own affair entirely. We have got to beat them, and when we have beaten them, I don't care what kind of rule they have. That is nothing to do with us it seems to me.

Between ourselves I think that Korniloff is going to try to create himself a Dictator. Whether he will succeed I don't know, but I would not be at all surprised to hear the news any day. . . .

Now about your question. You ask me how, with the higher wages and the necessary increase in the use of machinery, together with the increased size of farms, we are going to put an increased population on the land. My answer is that the moment we make the land pay decently there will spring up an ancillary population on the land to cater for the landed population. Your old market towns will revive, and the net result in my opinion will be a greater population, perhaps not strictly agricultural, but depending upon agriculture for its livelihood, throughout the country. There will be also an increase in the smaller agricultural industries such as market gardening, and so on, once the products of our own land are protected against foreign invasion.

As for the N[ational] P[arty] it is being launched to-day. I am afraid the names you mention would not serve on the Party. I do admire these young fellows for one thing at any rate, and that is that they are sacrificing their political careers entirely for the sake of what they consider right to the country. I doubt whether the Duke of Atholl would serve. I have just received the names, and they are much better than I thought. They are: Lord Ampthill; Lord Bathurst; Lord Leconfield; Lord Leith of Fyvie; Lord Stafford; and among M.P.s Burgoyne; Carnegie; Cooper; Page Croft; Duncannon.

It is a risk, but of this I am quite sure, it is the only way I can see of trying to instil wisdom into the people, and of getting rid of the money-making politician.

1. Robert Lowe, Chancellor of the Exchequer in Gladstone's first administration, December 1868–February 1874.
2. This had been debated in the House of Commons in May and June.
3. On this see my chapter 'Great War Prologue' in K. M. Wilson and N. Pronay (eds), *The Political Re-education of Germany and her Allies after World War II*, pp. 37–58.

Editor's postscript: The launch of the National Party was greeted by an extensive and positive coverage from the *Morning Post*. The leading article on 30 August likened the party system to 'dry rot in an old house: there was nothing into which a nail could be driven'. The hope was expressed that the new party would 'do its best to expose and prevent any divagation from or betrayal of the national principles'. Beyond that:

> What we should like to see would be an alliance between these gentlemen and what is best in the industrial forces of the country. There need not be union, but there might be cordial cooperation. The British Workers' League is also in its different way a possible nucleus of a national party, since it offers to our working men a policy at once democratic and patriotic. Between two sets of men of such different traditions and political principles there possibly never could be complete union; but they might meet on what is common to both – patriotism and the aspiration after a better and nobler system of government.

The National Party's manifesto and membership, and large extracts from a pamphlet containing a Statement of Policy, were also given on subsequent pages. On 31 August the *Morning Post*'s leader appealed to the 'fairness and honesty of our countrymen not to crab this new movement in British politics, but to give it a fair chance'. The founders of the National Party did not claim a monopoly of public virtue: 'They are willing if better men come along to share with them in the direction of the movement or to resign it to them; and they recognise that when the Army comes back this movement, which looks to the Army – the new nation, we might call it – will have so many and such stalwart recruits that the original promoters may be snowed under.' In 'Party and Perfection' on 1 September Bonar Law was taken to task for acquiescing in all the adventures against which Unionism stood, from Home Rule in Ireland to Home Rule in India. Even so, the new party was more than a defection from the Unionist Party: 'It is a new movement in British politics . . . a movement . . . of consolidation.' There was an article in the *Morning Post* every day in September, with leaders on the 4th, 13th and 17th.

Field-Marshal Sir William Robertson to H. A. Gwynne, 1 September 1917 (HAG/26 no. 14, IWM)

I am trying to get a week's rest from that 'hell' No. 10 and its visitors, but with mighty little success, having been once recalled and broken upon every other day. You see all you people (perhaps not *you*) overdid the L[loyd] G[eorge] thing and have banked on him, & therefore it only seems possible for me to make the best of him. But there *must* be a row one day I fear. Each day brings a fresh proposal more wild than its predecessor, regardless of time & space. There never was, and never is, any difficulty in knowing a brilliant way of quickly ending a war; but there is and always has been enormous difficulty in actually doing what one would like to do, especially if the enemy gets the first 6 tricks before one starts off. You have many times put the case so correctly that I shall not restate it. But what the hell is the use of people preaching patience and resolution when from hour to hour they display impatience and opportunist irresolution. And we have not *half* done yet what we must do before we win. So much for this aspect of the case. You can see how my mind is working, and what deceitful rot is sometimes spoken about more – interference with 'strategy'. *Interference is constant.*[1]

As to your letter regarding decorations etc, I am entirely with you in principle, and, as far as I can find the time, in practice too. I read your article, & I have written my thing to Derby, and the question will be reconsidered on Monday by the Army Council.[2] I think you may rely on a decoration being given at once to the men of the original Exped. Force, or if dead, to their relations. The other points you raise I will work for, and I think carry through. I will see you on return, & I am much obliged for the tip. I want you to realise that I have very little time for anything except keeping things on as correct lines as possible without having a real row.

1. For the view of Robertson taken by those in No. 10 at this time see S. Roskill, *Hankey, Man of Secrets*, vol. i, pp. 429–32.

2. The Secretary of State for War, Lord Derby, had on 24 August submitted a memorandum to the War Cabinet on the award of medals for the present war. (CAB 24/24, G.T. 1839.)

182
H. A. Gwynne to Lady Bathurst, 4 October 1917

. . . Of course this bombing business has been a nuisance, but it has really been more of a bore than anything else, because one has to be in the office and there is absolutely nothing to do until you get the ALL CLEAR signal. We have however managed to set off our papers in excellent time each night, and have not even missed the first edition, which most papers have done. As regards the behaviour of the men. It is not really panic or even fear so much as sullenness. Of course I only refer to the compositors, for the other men are all right, the stereotypers for instance not caring whether a raid is on or not, though they are equally, if not more exposed to danger than the others. I think you have to remember that what holds good in our office is true of all other offices, that is that the best men are fighting and the men who are left behind are the faint-hearted and the nervous. If I had had my old lot here we should have been working right through the raid, only stopping while bombs actually dropped, but it is much more difficult to get pluck and courage into the hearts of those who are left than it would be with the old lot. Please do not think of coming up even if they bomb us every night for I see a great improvement in the men, and I am perfectly sure that if they had continued to bomb us all this week it would have been all right by last night, for owing to the splendid example given them by other members of the staff who refused to go downstairs they came creeping up in quite a good number, apparently feeling somewhat ashamed of themselves. . . .

As regards the National Party's manifesto. It seems to me that the Party will have to be taken in hand. I have asked that I should be put on the Provisional Council as an honorary member, in order to see what is going on. They want an older brain, and – if I may say so – a calmer mind than they have got. The thing holds good of the Manifesto. You have put your finger exactly on the weak spot of it. Our job is to beat the German, then we can impose pretty well what we like upon them. But until we do, all threats are more or less idle. At the same time I think that by talking vaguely, and not definitely, about economic pressure and such like, it strengthens the hands of the commercial people in Germany who want to bring the war to an end at once, and, as a matter of tactics, it is not bad, but it is best done by newspapers not by a National Party.

I have just had a most interesting conversation with some Russians, and I will tell you about it when I come down. I really think it has given me a little hope. The position roughly is that if

Russia will keep in front of her the divisions that are now there we shall win the war in a comparatively short time, but if she makes a separate peace then Heaven help us. . . .

With regard to Percival Phillips. We do call the tune, and when I was out in France I had a long talk with him. He is not very expensive, and I told him there was too much Australians [*sic*] about his stuff and that he did not pay enough attention to what our own people are doing. He explained to me that that is not altogether his fault. I think it arises from the fact that Douglas Haig thinks that this war gives him an opportunity not merely of beating the Boche, but also of cementing the Empire, and he is inclined to think that the best way of doing so is to boom the Australians and Canadians. I had a long talk with him also on the subject, and I told him people were beginning to feel it very strongly. I see a great improvement now. On the occasion in question the Australians really did remarkably well and you must remember that the Censorship does not always leave a free hand to the correspondent. You will have noticed the improvement.

183
Earl Percy to H. A. Gwynne, 29 November 1917
(MS Gwynne 21)

Leo Maxse is very anxious that Lansdowne's effort in the *Daily Telegraph* this morning should be answered.

He says he thinks it has been done in collaboration with Bob Cecil who is a pacifist at heart. It is also aimed at Lloyd George whom Lansdowne has never forgiven for kicking him out. It is written on the same lines as that notorious memorandum which he wrote last year and which, I believe, was one of the main reasons for the fall of Squiff's Government.[1]

It will have a most unfortunate effect at this moment just as Russia is on the point of making a separate peace, and will be discouraging to all the Allies. The War Cabinet should issue a statement repudiating a peace on the lines laid down by Lansdowne which is nothing else than a proposal to make peace with the Boche before he is licked. Lloyd George might take up the matter if it was represented to him that this is really an attack on him. Do you think it would be worth while getting Carson to take it up with Lloyd George?

I see there is a section of the Press which hails it as a most statesmanlike utterance. The effect on Germany will be disastrous as we shall seem to be weakening at this critical moment.

1. Lansdowne's memorandum for the Cabinet, dated 13 November 1916, dealt with terms on which a peace might be considered (CAB 37/159/32); Lord Robert Cecil, then Under-Secretary of State at the Foreign Office, had produced a memorandum dated 27 November 1916 on the war situation and the need for industrial conscription (CAB 37/160/21); Lord Crewe, Lord President of the Council in the Coalition Government, also mentioned these two memoranda in the same breath, in the first paragraph of his account of the break-up of the Coalition, printed in H. H. Asquith, *Memories and Reflections*, vol. ii, pp. 128–38.

The letter which was published in the *Daily Telegraph* had been refused by the editor of *The Times* on the grounds that it was likely to discredit Lansdowne, who had just been put forward by H. W. Massingham, editor of *The Nation*, as an appropriate Prime Minister in place of Lloyd George, and because Lansdowne in conversation admitted that 'he had been headed off [presumably by Balfour since he seemed to have no other friend in the Government] from expressing similar views at this stage in the House of Lords' (memorandum by Robinson (MS Dawson 67); see letters 211 and 212, and the article by Lansdowne's son, 'The "Peace Letter" of 1917', pp. 370–84.

184
H. A. Gwynne to Lady Bathurst, 12 December 1917

. . . We are in the midst of a crisis. The Government will not face the question of man power and until they do we are in the very gravest danger. What worries me is that if we can produce the men (chiefly by conscripting Ireland) we have certain victory in front of us but if we leave the matter to the Greek Kalends we are done. The *M.P.* has forced the War Cabinet to consider seriously the question of Ireland. Up to the moment of our daily pressure, they refused even to discuss it.[1] At today's Cabinet meeting they had over the Chief of the Staff from Ireland and his evidence is to the effect that conscription can be arranged in Ireland with less than 100 casualties and without the help of a single extra man.

But it's weary weary work goading on a lifeless, backboneless Government but it has to be done.

1. The application of conscription to Ireland had been considered, and rejected, by the War Cabinet, on 26 November. (See D. G. Boyce, 'British Opinion, Ireland, and the War, 1916–1918', pp. 575–93; and A. J. Ward, 'Lloyd George and the 1918 Irish Conscription Crisis', pp. 107–29.

185
H. A. Gwynne to Lady Bathurst, 17 December 1917

. . . As regards the men, we must have men now. You are perfectly right in your supposition, but my contention all along is that you will not be able to get men now unless you promise to conscript the Irish. Here we are combing out various industries, sending men back to the front who have been wounded three or four times, really not fit to go, and all the time those Irish who live on us are racing and drinking and living a perfectly neutral life. Unless the Government make up their minds to conscript Ireland they will not get the men out of England. That is the whole of my contention. The Government are foolish enough not to see it – at least they do see it but have not the pluck to carry it out. . . .

186
H. A. Gwynne to Lady Bathurst, 25 December 1917

. . . I have received a letter from Sir Abs Bailey, a South African millionaire – a curious mixture of good and bad and not altogether without a soul. This is his letter: 'I would like to get the *M.P.* should it ever pass out of Lady B's hands, so be so kind as to ask her if she would care to dispose of her holding. I am not keen to buy it yet, as I am a believer in its policy.'

I therefore transmit you the message, as in duty bound. But I might permit myself the comment, that I don't think I would serve as Editor under anybody but you. Indeed, you must take the whole credit for the *M.P.* Without your guidance, I don't think it would achieve much. You remain the one disinterested Proprietor and because of that I strive to be the one disinterested Editor. . . .

The soldiers and the sailors (the brave honest inarticulate men who are *doing* things) rely on us almost entirely now. And when the war is over, we shall get our reward in their thanks and appreciation. . . .

187
H. A. Gwynne to Lady Bathurst, 30 December 1917

. . . I note what you say about the arguments against women suffrage. I am glad to have them in the concise form of your little article. I am afraid that the game is up.[1] The politicians have fooled us and the people as they have so often done before. History will, I think, form the verdict that they were guilty of incomparable treachery to the fighting men to alter the constitution of the country while they (the fighting men) were saving the country. It is the awful want of decent faith that depresses me. While the soldier and the sailor go on simply doing their duty, they are betrayed right and left by the politicians. What will happen when peace comes to be made? They are cowards too, and have not the robust faith in the country and its manifest destiny to uphold the flag. See how they are betraying the men in the trenches simply because they dare not apply conscription to Ireland, being afraid of scabby, unpatriotic, nationalist members. . . .

1. The Representation of the People Bill went to the House of Lords in December. For Lady Bathurst's views see Introduction, pp. 5–6.

188
H. A. Gwynne to General Sir Henry Rawlinson,
15 January 1918 (HAG/24 no. 17, IWM)

Just a line, a little belated, to wish you and all the good fellows out there a year of prosperity and victory.

I am afraid that things are not as rosy as they were this time last year, but I have great faith in our star, and in the pluck and resolution of our men out there.

Again the politician has let down the Army very badly. In May last year the Government were warned that the Russian Army was demoralised. The issue of the order about abolishing the death sentence in the Russian Army made it obvious of course to all soldiers that the discipline, and therefore effectiveness, of the Army, was at an end, but the Government instead of taking measures then to provide an adequate force to make up for the defection of the Russian Army preferred to wait for the Russian offensive in July, which as you know came to nothing. While allowing that that was quite reasonable, it can be no excuse for not making proper provision once that offensive had failed ignominiously, as the General Staff here prophesied that it would. It was then obvious even to the lay mind that the Germans would be able, sooner or later, to transfer to the West a vast number of troops. The obvious answer was the addition to our army of at least half a million men, but nothing was done, though every month from August until the beginning of this year the warnings of the General Staff became graver and graver, until it became obvious even to the politician that if he continued to neglect these warnings the country would find nothing but condemnation for him, and what was worse we might lose the war.

Unfortunately we are governed by men without faith in the country. Throughout this war from the beginning I have persisted that the country is as sound as a bell, and indeed it has never been sounder than at this time. Of course the Pacifist and the crank and the small man who wants to get some personal advantage out of the chaos of this great war are active, but they do not represent, and never have represented, more than a very small section of the population.

Now the Government apparently have put their foot down and they are going to comb out another half million men. But think what this means. These men will not be in a fit state to enter the lines – even if they are combed out this week – until May or June, while if the comb had been insisted on in September you would have had in the lines by February admirably trained troops and in great number to forestall the German offensive, and sufficiently trained to be effective in wresting the initiative from them. Now I am afraid the initiative will rest with them.

Affairs in Germany are very curious. I think the military party themselves are divided. Hindenburg[1] and Ludendorff[2] are in favour of a bold stroke on the West. There is a more cautious military influence which argues that if the offensive on the West fails – as our offensive failed on the Somme and in 1917 – that is to say as far as the breaking through of the lines is concerned – Germany will have played her last card and will be in a desperate position and at the mercy of the Allies in 1919 or even at the end of 1918. They therefore advocate peace manoeuvres, backed up always of course with the threat of a strong offensive on the West. The Kaiser I am told is of the moderate opinion and so is Hertling,[3] Von Kuhlmann[4] and Bernstorff. The Crown Prince has now become merely the puppet of Hindenburg and Ludendorff. Ludendorff is the brains and Hindenburg is the figurehead, and there has even been some talk of forcing the Emperor to accept a military dictatorship.

Meanwhile their potato crop, which was a very good one, has gone wrong. Our information is to the effect that they cut off the tops too early for fodder for the cattle, and this has resulted in the potatoes rotting. There is no doubt whatever that they are in very desperate straits, and if the big nitrate factory has gone, as I believe it has, it gives added reason why the moderate party should be strong. . . .

1. Field-Marshal von Hindenburg, Oberste Heeresleitung (OHL), appointed 29 August 1916.
2. General E. Ludendorff, Oberste Heeresleitung (OHL), appointed 29 August 1916.

3. Count G. von Hertling, Chancellor of Imperial Germany from October 1917.

4. R. von Kuhlmann, German Foreign Minister, August 1917–July 1918.

189
H. A. Gwynne to Lady Bathurst, 15 January 1918

. . . Believe me England is not rotten. It is a nation of lions led by asses and knaves. England is all right at heart. I have never lost faith in the people. But I have lost faith in *all* our leaders.

This is going to be a strenuous year and we must pray for strength and courage.

190
Field-Marshal Sir William Robertson to H. A. Gwynne, 22 January 1918 (HAG/26 no. 15, IWM)

I am 'going across' tomorrow for a few days – probably for a week or so. Will see you on return. Meanwhile let me thank you for your help. What a d——d disgraceful position for a Government to be in, to have to resort to such vile and unmanly tactics to get rid of those they don't like! But this time, & for the moment, they have overdone it.

191
H. A. Gwynne to Lady Bathurst, 25 January 1918

. . . As regards Turkey I can say nothing more at present except that I believe, especially now after the destruction of the *Goeben* and *Breslau*,[1] there is a chance of something definite happening. But it is too early to speak yet, though I will let you know all I hear.

What has been happening lately in the Press is that the Prime Minister instead of getting rid of Haig and Robertson, as he ought to have done if he thinks them inefficient, (although I think they are the only people who stand between us and destruction) gets Northcliffe and his reptile press to 'create an atmosphere' of hostility to these two men so that he can wreak his wicked will upon them. I stopped the conspiracy definitely and have made them curl up, but it's a desperate shame that these poor fellows who are fighting for us always have to have one eye looking behind to see if they are going to be stabbed in the back.

1. In operations on 20 January the *Breslau* hit a mine and sank; the *Goeben* grounded on a sandbank but escaped six days later.

192
H. A. Gwynne to General Sir Henry Rawlinson,
30 January 1918 (HAG/24 no. 19, IWM)

Many thanks for your letter which I need not say was very welcome.

Repington[1] was getting more and more dissatisfied with his position on *The Times*, because although Northcliffe for some months has been saying that *the* problem was the man-power question, yet when it came to forcing the Government to deal with it, his courage failed him, and he began to follow the Lloyd-Georgian tactics of abusing the soldier for having lost the men. There was never a more wicked cry, because as you know Pétain[2] firmly believes that it is thanks to our defensive that he has been able to pull round the French Army. But I am sorry to say that we have got to deal with people who will accuse anybody and anything rather than admit that they themselves have been wrong.

My disclosures about the man-power question have of course put the Government in a most frightfully difficult position, and now they are following the time-honoured advice of abusing the other side's attorney.

Hunter-Weston[3] made quite an excellent speech, and it went down in the House of Commons. But I am afraid the effect of it only lasted a few hours, for the House of Commons you must bear in mind is essentially corrupt, and the 670 members that compose it are not as patriotic as any 670 men you could take out of the street.

I am glad to say that Wully[4] has in part solved the question of man-power – at least for the present – in a way which I daresay you know, and if you don't know you will know in the course of a few days. He will save the reduction of the battalions per division from 12 to 9 – so will give you a fresh battalion to each brigade of another nationality speaking our own language – the rest you can guess.

I quite agree with you about the Cambrai inquiry.[5] But don't you see that Cambrai is merely being used as a stick with which to hit Haig and it is not really a serious argument? As you say it will be very hard on the Army if the Divisions are reduced. Thank heavens I think this can be avoided.

I have still a lot up my sleeve for the Government, and I will force them sooner or later to face this man-power question. My articles have had a great effect already, but of course I expect to get hit back.

Repington is coming over to France on Thursday or Friday. I hope you will get hold of him and have a talk. I myself hope to come out some time in February if things are quiet here.

1. Colonel Charles à Court Repington had resigned as military correspondent of *The Times* on 16 January. He moved to the *Morning Post*, which had been negotiating terms with him since early December 1917, with the intention, expressed to Gwynne on 19 January, of meeting the wishes of the General Staff that the 'man-power muddle' be exposed. Of his first article, published on 24 January, he wrote to Gwynne: 'I will get the General Staff to pass it through the Censorship if you like. I think that it will raise cain.' Gwynne wrote to General Maurice, the DMO, and the article was published without going to the Censor. Both editor and military correspondent expected to be imprisoned on this occasion. (See C. à C. Repington, *The First World War*, vol. ii, pp. 187–8 and 197; Repington to Corbett, 16 January 1918 (Northcliffe MSS Add. MSS 62253); Gwynne to Repington, 18 December 1917 (MS Gwynne 21); and Repington to Gwynne, 19, 20 January 1918 (MS Gwynne 32).

2. Marshal Philippe Pétain, appointed Commander in Chief of the French Armies, May 1917.

3. Lieutenant-General Sir A. G. Hunter-Weston, Conservative MP for Ayrshire North, 1916–18; the speech referred to was his maiden speech, delivered on 24 January. (See *Hansard*, 5th Series, vol. ci, cols 1234–40.)

4. Robertson.

5. An Inquiry was currently under way into the battle of Cambrai, when most of the ground gained by a British offensive spearheaded by tanks between 20 and 29 November 1917 was recovered by the Germans by 5 December.

193
H. A. Gwynne to Lady Bathurst, 30 January 1918

. . . I am not enthusiastic about the way in which the men behave. The Trade Unions, as you know, have stepped in and have issued an edict to the effect that nobody is to work from the time the 'Take Cover' signal is given until the 'All Clear' sounds. The consequence is that a raid is the most boring, monotonous thing you could imagine. There are bursts of fire which last about ten minutes or a quarter of an hour at the most, and for this brief period there is a certain amount of excitement, but the rest of the time one sits in one's office chair smoking a great deal too much because one has nothing else to do. The men congregate down below, and we in the Editorial department have to sit in our rooms and twiddle our thumbs.

The night before last we had bombs very near us, one fell certainly within a hundred yards, but no damage was done beyond shaking the building. Last night I did not come into the office at all having prepared the paper early. Instead I did a kind of amateur special constable's work at the Dover Street Station. The sights there sickened me. All the Englishmen were steady and amenable to discipline, but the Jew and the Belgian and the Russian aliens made one absolutely ashamed of one's manhood. One Russian Jew who thrust a little girl of 12 or 13 against the wall in his anxiety to get to safety, I had the pleasure of pulling out by the scruff of his neck and giving him a hearty kick into the street. That is the only way to deal with those people.

I am going to study Miss Pankhurst's programme very carefully, for whether we like it or not they have got the vote and they will have the power. But heavens help us if England is going to be governed by women, for though just now as you say she is patriotic, we never know when she will turn round on the other tack.

194

H. A. Gwynne to Lieutenant-General Sir H. de la P. Gough, 6 February 1918 (HAG/9 no. 5, IWM)

Many thanks for your letter and the two enclosures.

With regard to the paper on the state of Labour in England, I think your correspondent has taken a very exaggerated view. I don't for a moment mean to say that there are not great difficulties ahead, but I never have had, and I have now no sort of anxiety regarding the attitude of the working classes in this country towards the war. They have been so bothered about, and really very badly treated on the whole by the Government, in addition to which they feel very little confidence in the people who are governing us. And indeed I don't blame them for it. The truth is that we are governed by people who are not straight and honest, and as you know, as a soldier, more than anybody else straightness and honesty are the first qualities required in dealing with men.

But we can stand more blows yet, much worse than any we have received, and it will do us no harm, but will brace the nation. . . .

195

Field-Marshal Sir William Robertson to H. A. Gwynne, 7 February 1918 (HAG/26 no. 16, IWM)

I am just off for 2 or 3 days. The little man is all out for my blood, & is trying to isolate me from the other members of the Army Council. Keep your eye on things while I am away. My intention is, to see him out. If he wants me to go, he should *tell* me so. But he daren't. He is trying therefore to make my position impossible. And all the trouble is that I am trying to see that the fine British Army is not placed at the mercy of irresponsible people – & some of them foreigners at that. I see that the *Chronicle* today practically blames me because the Versailles people have had no pay. L[loyd] G[eorge] told Derby I was [to blame], this morning. Derby is supposed to have explained. But ½ hour afterwards L.G. said the same thing to another man, who told me. Of course, it has *nothing* to do with me. The general situation is – I have tried to insist upon right things being done. L.G. is *sick* of me because I would not give in and trim to his ideas. The country always claims that the soldier should 'stand up' to the politician. I have stood up. What will the country do?

[P.S.]   I go to Grand Hotel Eastbourne.

196
H. A. Gwynne to General Sir Henry Rawlinson, 11 February 1918 (HAG/24 no. 20, IWM)

Many thanks for your letter of the 6th.

I hear that there is a bit of a hitch with regard to the plan about which I wrote you, though I think it will be got over. The politicians in America really differ very little from the politicians here, for they want to throw the responsibility on the soldiers in France, and the soldiers in France are rather funking it. But I think it will come off all right because it is such a fine plan.

H[enry] W[ilson] is playing 'the dirty' again, and the Paris Conference, as you will see from today's *M.P.*, dissolved amid laughter – at least the laughter of the soldiers – for never was there a plan more calculated to create confusion and cripple the soldiers in the field than that which was adopted by the Paris Council. I hear however that all these decisions are subject to revision at the next meeting which takes place in six weeks, and I think that portion about the Reserves[1] will die a natural death.

1. A proposal that an inter-Allied reserve of some thirty divisions be created, under the control of the Supreme War Council.

197
H. A. Gwynne to H. H. Asquith, 11 February 1918

In case you intend to speak tomorrow[1] on the results of the Paris Supreme War Council,[2] I think you should know how things have developed. I gather that Sir William Robertson and the General Staff here were not opposed to the theory that there should be a strategic reserve and that this reserve should be in the hands of an authority superior to the two commanders-in-chief, Pétain and Haig. But Haig will not take orders from the Versailles Council as at present constituted. To meet this difficulty the P.M. has suggested that Robertson should go on to the Versailles Council Wilson taking his place here. To this Robertson answers that he will only go as C.I.G.S. They suggested to him an additional £1000 per year and a house in Paris as an inducement to him to accept the P.M.'s offer.

At the time of writing everything seems to be in confusion. The Army Council met this morning and seemed pretty decided to resign en bloc. Meanwhile the P.M. is in a great state of mind and is ready to accept almost any compromise rather than face Parliament.

The points which are of importance are:

a) the General Staff does not from what I gather object to the creation or the separate use of Reserves

b) the original decision to leave the disposal of the Reserve to the Versailles Council is already dead

c) the Army Council, up to the present, object to the arrangement and seem prepared to fight to the death to upset it.

1. For Asquith's contribution to the debate the following day see *Hansard*, 5th Series, vol. ciii, cols 14–21.
2. Held at Versailles, 31 January–2 February.

198
H. A. Gwynne to Lady Bathurst, 13 February 1918

. . . I have read the speech by Prothero, and I think that your reading of the situation is absolutely correct. Prothero, who should be a principal in all questions of food, is merely an underling, and Rhondda,[1] who is nothing else than a settler of prices, heads the scheme, and his idea of the settling of prices has resulted in a scarcity which is quite unnecessary. I have times out of number taken this matter up because we have been aware for some time of the state of things, and you will notice that the *Morning Post* has urged that we should have a Minister of Production, who should be an agriculturist and not merely a controller of prices. Rhondda really should go, for if he continues in his present wild career we shall have nothing left at all to eat.

I have just received a visit from two detectives, and as you will see from tomorrow's *Morning Post* Repington and I are to be prosecuted.[2] I have no fear whatever of the result.

1. Viscount Rhondda, Minister of Food Control, June 1917–July 1918.

2. On 9 February Repington and Gwynne had agreed to expose what the former called the 'absurd arrangement' made at Versailles. This article, having been submitted to the Press Bureau and been returned stamped 'Not to be Published', appeared on 11 February. Lloyd George wished to close down the *Morning Post*. According to Esher, writing from London to Haig: 'The War Cabinet spent a whole day (no exaggeration) discussing the seizure of the *Morning Post* machinery. This was decided upon, at 6.39 – at 8 p.m. a contrary decision was taken, Sir E. [*sic*] Cave having told Lloyd George that he would be beaten in the House of Commons.' (See C. à C. Repington, *The First World War*, vol. ii, pp. 228–30; Repington to Gwynne, 5 February 1918 (MS Gwynne 32); War Cabinet minutes 343; K. Middlemas (ed.) *Thomas Jones Whitehall Diary 1916–25*, pp. 52–3; and Esher to Haig, 13 February 1918 (Esher Papers 4/9).)

199

General Sir Henry Rawlinson to H. A. Gwynne, 14 February 1918 (HAG/24 no. 21, IWM)

Things are boiling up. I am not surprised that the Army Council are thinking of resigning – L[loyd] G[eorge] has not improved his position by his speech in the house and it is no use putting it down to his having a cold! It looks to me as if we were going to have a change of government before very long and if that change happened to coincide with a Boche attack which may meet with a limited amount of success like Cambrai, we shall get into a nasty mess. The opposing parties i.e. L.G., H[enry] W[ilson], Northcliffe and some members of the War Council versus Squiff, Wullie,[1] D[ouglas] H[aig] and the Army Council, will have a trial of strength and I am not at all sure that, with yours and Repington's support, the latter will not win. For the B[ritish] P[eople] are an eminently suspicious crowd and unless N[orthcliffe] succeeds in throwing dust in their eyes you have a very strong case. The position of Wullie and D.H. in the country is stronger than L.G. thinks and he will break himself on that rock if he is not careful. But it is most unfortunate that this crisis should supervene just at the opening of the Spring Campaign. It can't do any good & may do much harm. The solution is to put Wullie at Versailles with executive authority and move H.W. to London where he will not be able to do much mischief – especially if Squiff replaced L.G. as P.M. Let me know how the mess goes on? I am off to the S. of France for a few days leave next week.

1. Robertson.

200

H. A. Gwynne to General Sir Henry Rawlinson, 18 February 1918 (HAG/24 no. 22, IWM)

I have for many years been a friend and an admirer of yours. My dear chap, you are making the mistake of your life in accepting the Versailles job.[1] Don't let yourself be inveigled into a false position, now that you have accepted the job go there. But, if you'll take my advice, you'll report in a fortnight's time that the scheme[2] is unworkable, which it really is. Lloyd George is doomed. Asquith is only giving him rope. Don't, for heaven's sake, let yourself be drawn into this business. It's bad from top to bottom. You are to be used as an instrument and you will be left in the lurch. I am writing you from the point of view of an opponent of Lloyd George but as a friend of yours. Lloyd George will cast you for sure.

1. On the previous day Rawlinson had been appointed British Military Representative at Versailles.
2. Devised by the Supreme War Council at Versailles.

201

H. A. Gwynne to Lady Bathurst, 18 February 1918

. . . It is curious how both our minds have jumped together, and I enclose you the draft of a letter that I had prepared yesterday for publication. But on second thoughts I am postponing the thing until I have sounded people a bit more. You will see that I have exactly the same idea as you have.

We are now governed by a Junta of Press magnates with a bit of a scoundrel on top, and no man is safe in these days. As you rightly say: 'Anybody he may wish to remove will be secretly attacked long before until the public confidence in him is undermined and then he is kicked out.' If England is going to submit to this, well Heaven help England!

This is one of the things I have fought for in publishing that article. I knew the risks, and I was willing to take them. Robertson is to my mind the biggest, the straightest and the strongest man I have met. He has only one idea, and that is victory, and what is even far more important, he sees clearly how victory can be achieved. But he was one of those marked out for slaughter. It is a wicked dilemma that we should be in, that the only man who can really save him is Asquith, but he will only save him in order to get into power. With Asquith we should have a Pacifist Ministry.

I keep on hinting at some big man who should hold the reins of power, but I have definitely ascertained from Asquith that he will be Prime Minister or nothing at all. Then all that is left is to keep up the spirit of England and to urge our leaders and the country generally to look forward to victory.

I am sure that Henry Wilson will not last long. He is not the man to be Chief of the General Staff and he knows it himself.[1]

. . . I hear *The Times* has been sold.[2]

1. The announcement of Robertson's replacement by Wilson was made on 18 February.
2. This rumour was tried out on *The Times*, where it was denied. (See R. Pound and G. Harmsworth, *Northcliffe*, p. 618.)

Enclosure in letter 201
To the Editor of the *Morning Post*

The Way Out
Sir,

The removal of Sir William Robertson is a step which neither the Country nor Parliament can tolerate. His loss at this grave crisis in our military fortunes would be quite irreparable. His achievements, his character, his firmness and strength have raised him high not only in the estimation of his fellow-soldiers but of the Country generally.

Mr Lloyd George, in removing him, has run counter to the desires of the whole Country. The House of Commons on Tuesday last showed its feeling in this matter in a manner that was quite unmistakeable. It only refrained from translating its resentment into an actual vote of no confidence by the feeling, shared by all political parties in the House, that it is very difficult to find a successor for the Prime Minister. Although the House showed its warm approval of Mr. Asquith's defence of Sir William Robertson, it gave no indication of its willingness to entrust to him the guidance of the destinies of the nation.

The truth is that the Country is looking earnestly for someone who is not in politics at all in any capacity, who is an honest and true man, and one who sees only victory for us at the end of the war, and intends to ensure it. Such a man is ready to our hands. He is Sir William Robertson – a son of the people, a great military genius and an ideal leader of the nation in the great crises of this war. There is no political leader who possesses the confidence of his followers who would refuse to serve under him.

Yours etc.

247

H. A. Gwynne to Margot Asquith,[1] *18 February 1918*
(MS Gwynne 14)

I am much obliged to you for your letter received this morning. I waited for you at the Bath Club at one o'clock but no doubt you were engaged.[2]

I can see no way out of the awful tangle except the creation of a Government under a man who has no political past or future, gathering to him all the best men in politics. That, I understand, is a suggestion which does not appeal to Mr Asquith. Then I see nothing but chaos.

I know that Lloyd George and his band of journalistic braves are intensely unpopular both in the country and the House, and I am also aware that it would take very little to upset him. But I am equally sure that the alternative of a Government with your husband as P.M. would not meet the present needs or the desires of the nation. People are looking for a man with no political axe to grind and no wish but to bring the war to a victorious end. You don't like my suggestion of Robertson. But is there nobody else under whom he would serve?

What is wanted now is a man who will not palter with peace, except on our conditions. If we can find nobody in the ranks of our political leaders, we shall have to look elsewhere. I think Mr Asquith would rally the whole country to his side, if he did two things (a) declare himself in favour of war to the only end – victory, and (b) state his willingness to work under any non-political man of sufficient strength and integrity to deserve and hold the confidence of the people.

Personally, I have long ago forgotten to which party I belonged. I have praised and blamed without thinking of the party colour, and my only desire now is to see in power men of sufficient strength, knowledge and firmness to bring us victory.

1. Mrs Asquith was seeking support for an Asquith–Lansdowne coalition. (See S. E. Koss, *Asquith*, pp. 232–3; for Lansdowne's attitude see Viscount Esher and M. V. Brett, *Journals and Letters of Reginald, Viscount Esher*, vol. iv, p. 180.)

2. She had in fact tried to keep the appointment but had been unable to find the entrance to the Bath Club, not for the last time.

203
H. A. Gwynne to J. St Loe Strachey,[1] 18 February 1918
(Strachey MSS 5/18/5/4)

The True Issue

Dear Sir,

In spite of the efforts of the Prime Minister's supporters in the press to confuse the public mind, the real issue involved in the controversy over Sir William Robertson's dismissal is plain. The House of Commons, as the representative of the nation, has got to choose between two men, Mr Lloyd George and Sir William Robertson, and to choose between them in regard to a military question. That is the true issue. That is the question which must be decided. No one can be at one and the same time on the side of the Prime Minister and the Chief of the Imperial General Staff. Sir William Robertson has told us that he has not resigned. It is difficult to think that any sane man can believe that on a war issue it is safer to be on the side of Mr Lloyd George than on that of Sir William Robertson. For those, however, who ask for proof I would point to the Paris speech.[2] That speech, as we now see, was directed against Sir William Robertson, the advice which he tendered and the policy which he had advocated on the Western Front, the policy which Mr Lloyd George in effect represented as battering the army's head against a brick wall and incurring unnecessary casualties, when it would have been so much easier and better to have found another and better hole from which to attack the enemy. Will anyone now say that it would be a wise policy merely to hold the Germans on the Western Front and to send the so-called surplus troops elsewhere? The situation in the middle of February amply justifies the policy in regard to the Western Front advocated by Sir William Robertson.

Once more, is the nation going to endorse the opinion of one of the best and ablest military minds of our time, or the opinion of a politician who, when he imagines – of course wholly without warrant – that the combat is too stern a business for the nerves of the nation as a whole, casts round for some military substitute which will be equal to the best fighting? Happily the nation knows that no such substitute exists, and that in the last resort wars are won by high resolve and the willingness to endure heavy sacrifices.

May I in conclusion express my satisfaction at seeing your advocacy of the proposal to develop the present Ministry into a truly National Ministry under an impartial Prime Minister.[3] I still believe that the man most capable of holding such a position with the full confidence of the nation and the Empire is the present Speaker. In my opinion there is no man at this moment more worthy of the supreme trust than Mr Lowther. Mr Asquith has shown ever since he left office the highest qualities of patriotism and the most magnificent determination to win the war. We may feel sure then that he would raise no objection to serving under the Speaker.

I am,
Your obedient Servant,
The Editor,
The Morning Post.

1. Editor of the *Spectator*. Gwynne's letter was not printed in that journal.
2. On 12 November 1917.
3. In an editorial note to a letter from Sir Gilbert Parker, Conservative MP for Gravesend, 1900–18, in the *Spectator* of 9 February, the point of view expressed in an article entitled 'A Northcliffe Ministry' (26 January) that a National Ministry was preferable had been reinforced.

204
H. A. Gwynne to Lady Bathurst, 19 February 1918

The case[1] begins at 10.30 on Thursday.

Judging by what the lawyers tell me I don't think it will take very long and it ought to be over by lunchtime, though I am not quite sure.

We are calling the Director of Military Intelligence and the Director of Military Operations to give evidence. We are contesting on a point of law in the speech, and this will be followed by a speech in regard to the maliciousness of the prosecution, and as far as I can judge, even with the slow-going methods of the law, it ought to be over by one o'clock. But of course I cannot prophesy.

I am beginning to think that we shall win, and I look forward with some confidence to the dismissal of the case.

1. See letter 198.

205
H. A. Gwynne to Lady Bathurst, 20 February 1918

. . . I think you will be pleased with our defence.

Between ourselves, all I have done was with the warmest approval of Sir W[illiam] R[obertson] and the whole of the General Staff.

With regard to the first article from Repington, there was in my mind doubt as to the value it might give to the enemy, and also again between ourselves, before I published it I submitted it to the soldiers, who assured me that the enemy could get nothing of value out of it, except what it was known they were already possessed of. The same holds good of the article on which we were prosecuted.

There is one accusation which I will never have launched against the *Morning Post*, and that is that it gave information of value to the enemy, and I safeguarded myself in this respect by consulting the soldiers. So that really the prosecution is a political one and nothing else. And I think we shall be able to bring this out tomorrow.

Of course what is terrible to me is that we have not been able to save Robertson. I feel that the disappearance of Robertson is the greatest blow we have ever received during the war. Not even the Dardanelles disaster is comparable to it, and I will tell you why. Robertson had not only a very clear brain as regards strategy, but he was the only soldier I know, who was clever enough and strong enough to stand up against the politicians. If one-tenth of the expeditions that have been suggested by the politicians had been accepted by Robertson we should have been in a state of great danger, but he was firm and strong and always fought on his own military ground. You are mistaken in thinking that he has been sent out to the East – he has been given the Eastern command in England, which any ordinary General could do quite well. It is a dreadful blow, but I think that circumstances will force him back again, and not at a very distant date either.

. . . I am so glad you approve of all I have done. I am sure that it will not be long before the whole Press will thank me for the line I have taken up, for, as the regulations are at present interpreted, an official communiqué is a direct breach of them, and that is absurd. . . .

206
H. A. Gwynne to Lady Bathurst, 21 February 1918

You will read tomorrow morning the account of the case, and I hope you will see in it one outstanding fact, and that is that we have proved beyond all question of doubt that we have given no information of value to the enemy. It ought to be said in justice to the Crown that they did not charge us with that.

The points of the case are these. The Government, in order to carry the country through a state of war, devised a set of regulations, which have the force of law, called the Defence of the Realm Act. The sole object was to preserve the State from danger in time of war. Regulation 18 practically deals with the Press, and it was drafted undoubtedly to prevent information reaching the enemy. In order to make sure of their ground the draftsmen of the Government included every sort of possible offence, but they were all governed by the words, 'that they might be useful to the enemy.' This, as I have said before, was not even a contention of the Government, but the magistrate, who I hear is a brother of Dickinson the Pacifist,[1] and belongs to a Liberal and Radical family, would insist upon regarding the offence as one which included that grave offence of giving information of value to the enemy, and he has fined me the full amount he can fine me – £100 and 60 guineas costs, while Repington has received £100 and 40 guineas costs.

The question which I have to decide this evening is whether we will appeal or not. An appeal goes, according to the Defence of the Realm Act, to the Court of Sessions presided over by a Recorder, and the main portion of the Court consists of magistrates of the County of London who have a voice in the verdict.

As far as I personally am concerned, I don't care one hang about any Court decision, for I know I have done my duty as clearly as I have ever seen it, and I have absolutely no regrets whatever. But I think mostly and chiefly of the *Morning Post*, and I do not see that we can sit down under an aspersion that the *Morning Post* has afforded aid to the enemy. The thing is really monstrous.

The truth is that Lloyd George was determined that England should not know – though France knew, and Italy knew, and the Germans knew – all the decisions of the inter-Allied War Council, and Lloyd George brought out a rule, which was issued to the papers, that no accounts of this were to be published. This injunction was not issued by the War Office, but by Downing Street.

I think we can bring most of this out in the appeal, and we are having a consultation this evening at which the matter will have to be decided. I am strongly in favour of trying to reverse this aspersion on us.

About Repington. There is this matter and other matters about which I really must come down and see you, and I would suggest, that if you would let me, I should come down next Wednesday and sleep the night and talk things over.

I am distressed and alarmed about the state of affairs and I want to discuss them all with you.

I could never contemplate a peace under any circumstances whatever. That I think would be the worst thing that could happen to us, and I, frankly, would rather go tomorrow into the trenches and be blown to atoms trying to kill a Boche, than sit still and allow the enemy to triumph over us. . . .

1. G. Lowes Dickinson, Fellow of King's College, Cambridge, author of *The International Anarchy 1904–14*, London, 1926.

207
H. A. Gwynne to Lady Bathurst, 5 March 1918

... We are not agitating in the *Morning Post* for a change of Government, but we are trying – in fact this is the result of my conversation with you at Cirencester – to let the people from time to time get accustomed to the idea that the alternatives are not necessarily Lloyd George or Asquith. There might be somebody else. And I think this is working along the lines that we discussed.

But we cannot be accused of following the Northcliffe Press example. The Northcliffe Press have been attacking officers when they had no right of reply. Nobody has made any complaint against them for attacking Ministers.

I think you need not be anxious about Lord Lansdowne. But his letter has done infinite harm to the English cause – still, as you say, I think it is somewhat the result of senile decay rather than any lack of patriotism. But today he has written another beastly 'white flagger'.[1]

Alan's[2] account of the state of affairs in Palestine and the system of promotion does not encourage one to put much faith in the boasted improvements that the War Office made such a fuss about the other day. However I hope when Alan comes home he will be able to get work suited to his experience and his knowledge.

Sir William Robertson lunched with me on Sunday and was full of very interesting news. He gave me a very interesting account of the crisis. I am afraid that the man who comes out of it worst of all is our friend Lord Derby.[3] Nobody ever accused Lord Derby of being clever or able, but everybody thought he was a straight man. I am afraid we shall have to alter our opinion.

You might like to keep the enclosed narrative by you – it will be an historical document one of these days. I think you should mark it as The Narrative of the Dismissal of the C.I.G.S.

1. Published, like the letter of 29 November 1917, in the *Daily Telegraph*. Lansdowne drew attention to points of similarity between a speech by the German Chancellor, Hertling, on 25 February and the proposals of President Wilson; he developed these arguments more fully in a speech in the House of Lords' debate on the idea of a League of Nations on 19 March.

2. Lord Apsley, Lady Bathurst's eldest son.

3. Derby had been appointed to the War Office on 10 December 1916. (See R. S. Churchill, *Lord Derby*, pp. 295–334 for another account of Derby's role in this particular crisis. See also letter 217.)

Memorandum by H. A. Gwynne

1. The C.I.G.S. has always recognised that the principle of constituting a strategic reserve from the British and French armies, and of placing this reserve under the direction of some authority superior to the British and French Commanders in Chief, was a perfectly sound one. He reminded the War Cabinet last Thursday [14 February] that he had advised this course three weeks before the Versailles Conference took place. He had also discussed it with Generals Foch,[1] Haig and Pétain who were all agreed. Furthermore he had told the Prime Minister before the Versailles Conference that in his opinion the only person who could exercise this authority for the dispositions and employment of the strategic reserve was the C.I.G.S., because he was the only person directly responsible to the Army Council and the Government for the British Army. Any other principle would involve divided control; it would involve the handing over of executive power to a committee which would not be responsible for the consequences of its actions. Sir D. Haig, Sir W. Robertson, and the Army Council would remain responsible for the army and yet Sir H. Wilson would have power to move their troops about without their consent. He stands for the great principle that executive authority must be accompanied by responsibility. The command of the reserves should therefore be exercised jointly by General Foch and by Sir W. Robertson.

2. At the Versailles Conference all the soldiers present agreed to this principle of command, except Sir H. Wilson who was not present when the subject was discussed. While the question was still under consideration Sir H. Wilson produced a plan of his own whereby the Supreme War Council should be made the superior authority responsible for the employment of the reserves. The C.I.G.S. warned the Prime Minister privately in the most emphatic terms that this would lead to hopeless difficulties, confusion and perhaps disaster, for the reasons given above. The Prime Minister nevertheless insisted on it and the Conference accepted it without demur. The C.I.G.S. did not protest officially against it at the Conference as he was not a member of the Versailles Council and he had previously imparted his views to the Prime Minister. Sir D. Haig had previously expressed his agreement with these views.

3. On his return to London he informed the Army Council of the decisions which had been taken at Versailles and a meeting took place to consider them. At this meeting the Army Council were unanimously of opinion that the proposal would prove not only dangerous but wholly unworkable, since Sir H. Wilson was not a

member of the Army Council and would be wholly independent of them, of the C.I.G.S. and of the Commander in Chief in France. They struck at the root of every elementary principle of command. A memorandum to this effect was therefore sent to the War Cabinet.

4. On Monday February 10th [*sic*: Monday was the 11th], Lord Derby informed the C.I.G.S. that this decision having been considered by the War Cabinet, the latter had decided that Sir H. Wilson was to be C.I.G.S. and that he (Sir W. Robertson) should go to Versailles as Military Representative. In order to induce him to accept this post they informed him that he would remain a member of the Army Council and that he would be equal to General Foch and share with him the responsibility for the employment of the strategic reserve. To make this offer still more palatable they announced that they would increase his pay by £1000 a year and give him a house free of charge in Paris. Sir W. Robertson in reply pointed out that this proposal did not get over the difficulty. The fact that he would be an Army Councillor did not alter the situation. The old vicious principle of divided command remained. He would be in point of fact independent of the Army Council, the C.I.G.S. and the Commander in Chief. If he accepted it he would be accepting a principle which both he and the Army Council had condemned. This proposal was also considered by the Army Council and rejected by them unanimously (with the exception of the Q.M.G. who was not present). Sir W. Robertson therefore declined to accept the post offered him, *but he did not resign*. He was told that he was to be suspended as C.I.G.S. and asked when he was to go, but he never resigned.

5. On Wednesday [13 February] the War Cabinet asked him to reconsider their original decision i.e. that he should remain as C.I.G.S., the Versailles system to stand as originally stated. To this he replied by repeating all his old objections, and he put up a concrete proposal to help the Government out of their difficulty. This proposal was that the C.I.G.S. should be on the Executive Committee of the Versailles Council, and that in his absence in London he should have a deputy to represent him at Versailles. He has held all along that there was no difficulty in working such a system. Again there was no question of resignation. He was merely asked whether he would remain as C.I.G.S. (having been told two days before that he was dismissed) and he could only reply that whether he went or stayed the bad system remained.

6. On Thursday [14 February] he attended a meeting of the War Cabinet at which he reviewed the whole question. He pointed out the seriousness of the position, the probability that we should have to face in the near future a most critical situation in France, and in view of this he put it to the War Cabinet –

1. Whether he was the right man to remain as Supreme Military Adviser, seeing that his advice was not being accepted on the matter in question. If not the War Cabinet had better at once dismiss him.
2. If, however, they decided to retain him, he put it to them whether it was wise or fair to him to entrust him with carrying out a system which he regarded as dangerous and unworkable.

During the course of this meeting, the Prime Minister asked the C.I.G.S. whether, if they accepted his principles, he would consent to go to Versailles as deputy to Sir H. Wilson. He requested that they would not ask him to accept this position as he was senior to Sir H. Wilson. He did not think they ought to ask him to do so.

7. On Friday morning [15 February] he was informed that General Plumer[2] had been asked to accept the appointment of C.I.G.S. and, in the event of his accepting it, he (Sir W. Robertson) was offered the command in Italy. General Plumer refused to come home.[3] On Saturday evening [16 February] the Government announced that Sir W. Robertson had declined to remain as C.I.G.S. with reduced powers and had also refused to go to Versailles and the Government had accepted his resignation. This statement contains two falsehoods, one direct, the other implied. Sir W. Robertson had not refused to remain as C.I.G.S. with reduced powers. It is uncertain what this refers to. If it refers to the proposed abolition of the order in Council by which his original appointment was regulated, it is a matter of complete unimportance which does not affect him one way or the other. If it refers to the extension of the functions of the Versailles Council, it is true that he has declined to remain as C.I.G.S. and work this system. He has pointed out that it is unworkable and suggested that the Government should remove him from his post if they do not wish to entrust him with the running of a system he considers unworkable. He has also refused to go to Versailles because he considered this particular system unworkable. He has never resigned. By failing to mention the reasons for his actions the Government create a wholly false impression. There is an interesting point to be noticed in connection with the above. The position of the Government is that the Versailles Council is of such extreme importance that the C.I.G.S.'s objections to the extension of its functions cannot be allowed to upset the plans of the Government with respect to the Council – plans with which all the Allies have agreed. But it will be noted that the Government actually asked if Sir W. Robertson would go to Versailles as deputy to Sir H. Wilson if they accepted his principle. One of two things must have prompted this question. Either they did not consider the extension of the

functions of the Council to be of such supreme importance; or they were trying to put Sir W. Robertson in a false position by making out that his objections to the system were due to personal jealousy of Sir H. Wilson. It is an interesting consideration of the attitude of the War Cabinet towards the question.

Sir W.R. has been a full General for more than two years. Sir H. Wilson is only a Lieutenant-General with temporary rank of full General. The latter was given him when he went to Versailles in November.

1. Marshal Ferdinand Foch, appointed Chief of Staff of the French Armies, May 1917.

2. General H. C. O. Plumer, in command of 2nd Army, 1915–17; GOC Italian Expeditionary Force, 1917–18. The War Cabinet offered the position of CIGS to Plumer on 14 February.

3. Plumer's grounds for rejecting the appointment were precisely those being advanced by Robertson. This was the reason adduced by Lord Derby, who had suggested Plumer on 8 February, for his offer to resign from the War Cabinet, made on 16 February. (See Derby Papers 920 (Der) 27/7.)

Enclosure 2 in letter 207
Note by H. A. Gwynne

The following facts are also of importance.

Sir Douglas Haig was sent for by the War Cabinet and interviewed by Mr Lloyd George on February 8th or 9th.[1] He was asked whether he accepted the principle that Sir H. Wilson should command the reserves, and he said 'No'. He was then asked whether if Sir W. Robertson were to go to Versailles and command the reserves, he would accept that proposal. He said 'Yes'. He seems at that time to have been under the impression that the Government's intention was that Sir W. Robertson should remain C.I.G.S. and be Military Representative at Versailles also. In any case he did not fully understand the position. After his return to France he wrote to Lord Derby and told him that he considered any other proposal than that of Sir W. Robertson quite unworkable. Lord Derby had this information in his pocket but did not inform the Army Council. On Saturday the 16th, Sir Douglas Haig came over although the Government through Lord Derby had told him not to do so. He insisted however on coming over because he refused to allow Mr Lloyd George to represent him as having acquiesced in the decisions of the Versailles Council. On this point the Prime Minister (it will be remembered) told a falsehood, or at least implied it to the House of Commons. His words were (in answer to Mr Hogge's question as to whether Sir D. Haig and Sir W. Robertson had approved of the decisions) 'Certainly they were present, and all those representatives approved.'[2] What this means it is impossible to say. These two soldiers were not representatives of the Conference, so this statement is technically correct but implies a falsehood. It is vital that the House should ascertain the truth by asking whether the Secretary of State for War, the C.I.G.S. and the Commander in Chief were informed of the proposals for the extension of the functions of the Supreme War Council, and whether they agreed to this extension before it was decided upon.[3]

The real position with regard to the Supreme War Council is not fully understood. The War Cabinet has always said that the principle has been accepted by all the Allies who have made none of the objections which have been raised on this side of the Channel. The reason is not far to seek. The situation of the various countries concerned varies radically. France is of course delighted with the arrangement, because they have in fact the system for which the C.I.G.S. has always contended. That is to say Foch, the Chief of the General Staff, put in his deputy, General Weygand, on the Council to act as his mouthpiece. There is in the case of France no divided control. Italy and America both gain by the arrangement. They are represented on the Council and have a voice in allied strategy although they are carrying no corresponding share in the war. Moreover their strategical dispositions are not interfered with. Italy's troops can only be used in Italy. America's army has not yet taken the field. Nobody can therefore play about with Italian or American soldiers, and yet the Italian and American representatives have full power to play about with British soldiers, and can suggest how the war is to be carried on in theatres where only British troops are engaged.

The situation with regard to Great Britain is wholly different as already explained. The Council can move about British troops without any responsibility for the consequences, and the British representative will be wholly independent of all authority save that of the civilian War Cabinet. Neither he, however, nor the War Cabinet will bear any blame if the results of the order given end in disaster.

1. This was on 9 February. (See R. Blake, *The Private Papers of Douglas Haig*, pp. 283–4.)

2. See *Hansard*, 5th Series, vol. ciii, col. 29, 12 February 1918.

3. The Secretary of State for War, Lord Derby, drafted a note for the Prime Minister on 4 February. It began: 'I might as well have been a dummy for all the advice I have been asked for'; and ended: 'It is absolutely impossible for anybody in my position to accept such a situation.' (Note by Derby, 4 February 1918 (920 (Der) 27/7).)

208
Viscount Esher to H. A. Gwynne, 9 March 1918
(HAG/8 no. 21, IWM)

In this morning's *D[aily] Mail* there is a detailed statement of the German position 'should the war end with the enemy holding what they possess at the moment'. Then a position is drawn of the German control of all the routes from everywhere and to everywhere.

If this picture is accurate after 3½ years of war, the *D. Mail*, *Times*, Northcliffe, Rothermere[1] & Co are among all Englishmen and Newspapers the most responsible. The war has been fought *their* way by the agents of *their* choice.

The British people should recognise where both potential praise and blame should lie. I wish you would rub this in a bit. Northcliffe is in either for a Dukedom or a Halter.

But so shall be the Editors of the *D. Mail* in a minor degree.

Rothermere came up to me in the H[ouse] of L[ords] the other day and said 'Well, what do you think of things? We are in the most dangerous plight of our whole history. The Napoleonic menace was a joke to this'.

What do you think of that attitude of mind in a *Minister*!

The man is what the French call 'detragué'.

He cannot see things in proper perspective.

1. Harold Sidney Harmsworth, younger brother of Northcliffe, joint founder of the *Daily Mail* and the *Evening News*, proprietor of the *Daily Mirror* and the *Sunday Pictorial*, appointed Minister for Air, 26 November 1917.

209
H. A. Gwynne to Viscount Esher, 11 March 1918
(HAG/8 no. 22, IWM)

Thankyou very much for your letter and your observation on the *Daily Mail* with which I am in entire agreement. I see with you the defects of the present system – indeed perhaps I see the defects even more clearly than you do for I am living in the midst of them. But it is extremely difficult to know what to do. I suppose that with a certain amount of effort it would be possible to get Lloyd George and his myrmidons of the Press Gang out, but I cannot contemplate with any degree of complacency the re-entry of Asquith.

I think he is a last man and a last shilling man, but he is too easily influenced by men who are far from holding that view. I could see a way out for him if he would only adopt it, and that would be for him to make a public speech very soon, in which he would declare his firm belief that there was only one way out of this war, and that would be by victory. And if he further stated his intention, if ever he should have the reins of power in his hands, to install as Ministers only those who were of the same opinion, I am not sure that the country would not gladly accept the alternative. But with a wobbly entourage, such as he possesses, the House of Commons and the country generally do not seem inclined to entrust him with power.

Another consideration that affects him I believe – personally I would pay very little attention to it – is that if Lloyd George went out, the Press Gang would make such a formidable opposition that he does not think he could face it. It is curious how these men are affected by newspaper criticism. If I were in power I would not take the slightest notice of it except to counteract it by speeches in the country.

When you come up to London let me know, for there are a lot of things I want to talk to you about.

210
H. A. Gwynne to Lady Bathurst, 18 March 1918

. . . About Repington, I will tell you all I know. Repington ran away with a Lady Garstin at Cairo and married her afterwards. Wilson was his superior officer at the time and got him turned out of the Army. So, naturally, I think that there is no love lost between them. Wilson was acting on superior orders, so had no personal bias in the matter. I suppose (though, honestly, I don't know) that the ill-feeling between the two has not died down. But whatever the relations between the two are, they should never be allowed to enter into the *M.P.* and they don't.

Repington is the best military writer in Europe. He stands far and away above everybody else and the *M.P.* has secured the best man and in so doing, has gained a great deal of credit. If you ask me whether I like Repington personally I will answer you quite frankly 'no' but my personal likes or dislikes do not affect the question. There are men in the office – good hard workers – whom I dislike very much but I would never allow my personal inclinations to affect them in any way. . . . If Repington tried to use the *M.P.* to score off an old enemy, I would not allow it for a moment. But I am a great personal friend of Wilson and know him intimately. I have told him to his face that he has allowed his dirty little personal ambitions to interfere with the proper conduct of the war. I have said to him that he and he alone will be regarded as the man who initiated civilian control over military affairs and in so doing, has betrayed the army to which he belongs and has risked our success in the war.

Repington's ability as a writer on military matters is simply invaluable to the *M.P.* in this time of a great war. If you get rid of him now, you will lose a great and most valuable asset. In this time of terrible stress for all papers, my effort is to keep alive, in spite of the shortage of paper, all the chief characteristics of the *M.P.* so that when peace comes we shall have lost nothing of our personality and can build on firm foundations. One of our merits has always been that in the *M.P.* we were sound on military affairs. Now we are not merely sound but brilliant and to lose that would be a terrible blow. I don't worry you with all the cares and anxieties of the paper because I look upon myself as the man who is paid to ward off these incessant and, sometimes, almost intolerable little worries. I can see our way clear, with the eight columns struggling through to the end of the war but we must be careful to keep up our standards or we may lose all. Believe me, I had only the good of the paper in view in engaging Repington and to lose him would, in my opinion, be a very heavy blow to the paper.

I do agree with you about less criticism but it is not easy when this nation of lions is led by such a lot of asses – and, some of them, knaves. But I will give our readers something cheerier from time to time.

211
H. A. Gwynne to Lord Lansdowne, 21 March 1918 (HAG/14 no. 1, IWM)

You might perhaps like to see the *Neue Freie Presse* with its comments on your letter.[1]

You will not mind my saying, after a diligent reading of the German press, that I have come to the conclusion that you have undoubtedly given a great fillip to the War Party in Germany.

1. See letters 183, 207.

212
Lord Lansdowne to H. A. Gwynne, 24 March 1918 (HAG/14 no. 2, IWM)

I am obliged to you for your thought of sending me the *Neue Freie Presse* article, which does not in the least shock me.

You tell me that my letters have 'given a fillip to the War Party in

Germany'. If everything that has this effect is to be ruled out of order, must not half the ministerial statements, as to shipbuilding, loss of tonnage, impending scarcity and the like, be ruled out also? The writer of the article refers pointedly to these statements – it seems to me to show, not so much that the War party has derived encouragement from my letters, as that they have given a fillip to the Peace Party in that country: a party which to my mind deserves all the encouragement we can give it.

But pray do not imagine that I resent your observation. . . .

213
H. A. Gwynne to Lady Bathurst, 3 April 1918

. . . You state that in our leader yesterday we advocated military service for everybody. We did not. If you read the lead again, you will find that we advocated the extension of the Military Service Act to civilians up to fifty years of age. This did not run counter to your objections which I always understood to be against *universal* national service, including women. The article in question merely advocated the use of the whole *man* power of the country up to the age of fifty. What I was trying to explain was that there should be no exemptions. That is to say that men between the ages of 18 and 50 become *ipso facto* servants of the nation. The system of exemptions has been rotten from beginning to end. Men without a care for their country, men who have openly preached pacifism or have become shop-stewards, in fact the whole of conscientious objector, the sedition-preacher, the syndicalist class obtained exemption for their Trade Unions. I want (and I certainly thought that you would agree with me) everybody to be nominally called up, not because of their trades but because they were in the limits of the prescribed age. In France a man between 19 (or 20, I am not quite sure) and 45 belongs to the State the moment the mobilisation papers are out. Frenchmen who talk treason to the State are promptly sent to the trenches. They are all in the service of the State *which alone* grants exemption. Here we have tribunals, Trade Union officials, all sort of people who can and do grant exemption.

There has been nothing in our conversation which would lead me to think that you objected to this. Indeed during the first days of the offensive we boldly advocated the raising of the military age and I should have thought that you were in entire agreement. Indeed I felt sure you agreed.

The article to which you take exception did *not* advocate *universal* service. But that was recommended by you in the *Morning Post* of Jan.

14.[1] I was away at the time or I would have drawn your attention to it.

As for the way in which men are used, I thoroughly agree. But the remedy for that is to have a government of decent administrators and keep out a good deal of the present incompetents.

But above all, I do want to tell you that I have always scrupulously observed your desires as proprietor. I don't think you can show a single example of a case where I have run counter to you. In one case I went slower than you liked but I wanted to be assured about the military position.

As regards Foch, you will find that at the time of the Versailles Supreme Council dispute, I said more than once that a generalissimo was the ideal plan but that with national armies at war I did not see how it could be done. In the present instance, where British and French troops are sandwiched all along the line there is imperative need for a generalissimo. But have you considered the answers to the following questions:

1) Who is responsible now for the Operation in France?

2) Has the British Government not formally given up all control of its armies in France?

3) If a disaster occurs, who is to blame?

4) Is it in the interests of the Entente to put the British Army under a foreign general, for if anything went wrong the British soldier would blame the Frenchman and there would be bitter recrimination?

5) Suppose the question should arise where the Channel Ports (the gateway to England) had to be defended or Paris threatened or vice-versa, are we to leave the decision in the hands of a man naturally prejudiced in favour of his own capital?

6) We have deprived Haig of all voice in the conduct of the strategy of the war, is this right?

7) Do you think that a permanent generalissimo is a wise measure, however much we may approve of the present provisional appointment?

I am frankly nervous about the generalissimo question. If we had among the Allies a Napoleon or a Marlborough I would say 'yes' to the proposal. But I fear very much if things go wrong that the generalissimo idea may do a good deal towards destroying the splendid spirit of cooperation and mutual loyalty which now prevail.

1. See Introduction, pp. 5–6.

H. A. Gwynne to Viscount Esher, 9 April 1918
(HAG/8 no. 28, IWM)

Many thanks for your letter and enclosure which I hope to publish.

Don't you see that already they are throwing the blame on the soldiers? and poor Gough has been brought home. Of course you and I know what was said of Gough out in France. He has made mistakes, but there was no more gallant action than his retreat with his fourteen divisions in front of forty German divisions.

I entirely agree with you about Douglas Haig. It would be a disaster if he left, but I am told that he said to Gough, as he passed through on his way to England, that he would be following him in a week's time. If this is true, then we are really up against it, for as you rightly say Haig certainly won the confidence of the whole Army. He was a man who took the blame himself when blame was going and gave the credit to other people.

215
H. A. Gwynne to Lady Bathurst, 11 April 1918

. . . The great point that I wish to make about universal service is that in the first place we have to put ourselves at the disposal of the Government for we are in a great crisis. That I think nobody can deny. On the other hand I agree with you that there has been a wicked waste of material and a wanton dislocation of suitable men, which comes really from an inefficient Government. Nine-tenths of our troubles have been due to the fact that we granted exemptions, not according to the military requirements but in order to placate the Trade Union leaders.

I do not suppose that you have realised that up to the present moment the Trade Unions had real power of exemption, and knowing our Trade Unions, it has not surprised me in the slightest degree in the world to find that they have invariably exempted the agitator, the stirrer-up of strife, and such like men. Now a strike in the midst of this war has always appeared to me to be not merely insensate but one of the wickedest things that British workmen could do. I have had a certain amount of sympathy with them because of the inefficiency of the Government in dealing with them, but I do realise, and I always have realised, that more than half of the unrest has been due to the freedom and licence that have been granted to these agitators. Now things will be changed. The moment the Bill[1] passes, we shall all of that age belong to the Government. It does not for one moment mean that everybody is going to be taken out of his job, where perhaps he is doing great national work, and put on another job, like your friend the hairdresser and the plough. But it does mean that we shall have no more trouble with these agitators and Syndicalists and shop stewards, as they can be ordered off within the law to do their bit in the trenches.

I am perfectly sure you will see a difference in England owing to this. In France there have several times been very ugly movements, but they have always been crushed by this power which the Government possess of transferring anybody who makes himself objectionable into the trenches, or within reach of German shells, and this has been most effective.

That the Government will use the men who are thus put at their disposal rightly and properly, I doubt. There will be bad cases of the hairdresser and the steam plough again, but on the whole the advantages to be gained from no exemptions are so great that I think we ought at all hazards to press for them.

The position of things in France is not so bad as appears at first sight. Pétain, the French General, has done remarkably well, for he has not yet used his reserves. The position, roughly speaking, is this. He has kept back the German thrust west and south-west by using not more than 10 divisions of the ordinary type. These divisions have been brought from other parts of the line, and in this way he has been able to keep his reserves intact.

The whole of Foch's career shows that he does not believe in remaining on the defensive, and I think you will find that in this case he will make an attack, but he will not do so until the Germans have used up pretty well all their reserves. I hear that they still have thirty to forty divisions which they can use, and he will keep these in check without going back on his reserves. When the German reserves have been used up to such an extent that they cannot be replaced, I think we may expect a strong Franco-British offensive.

But the pity of the whole thing is that this was all foreseen by Robertson. He wanted to provide for it, and did his best to provide for it. But Lloyd George was blind. He would not see.

I wonder whether you remember a series of articles about man-power which appeared in the *Morning Post* before Christmas? In one of these we said, we feel perfectly sure that as things go (I am not quoting the exact words) the Government will be forced to conscript Ireland in a panic. Why not do it now, when it can be done without any trouble? I really think we deserve a pat on the back for that[2]. . . .

1. The Military Service Bill, introduced into the House of Commons 9 April; received the Royal Assent 18 April.

2. The Military Service Bill empowered the Government by Order in Council to extend conscription to Ireland.

216
H. A. Gwynne to Lady Bathurst, 16 April 1918

Have you been following Lloyd George's recent tactics. The man is impossible and will lose the war for us for certain. He has flaunted the warnings of the soldiers, he has lied to everybody, including the House of Commons and now, with the enemy battering at our gates, he still wants to play his dirty little political games. I don't believe he is sincere, even in his desire to conscript Ireland. He has played fast and loose with England and will bring her to the dust. I do think we ought [not] to restrain our opposition any longer. Whoever succeeds him must be better. He has surrounded himself with the rotters of finance and the newspaper world. There is neither good nor conscience nor any sense of right in him – only low political cunning.

I am quite convinced that if he remains at the head of affairs, we shall lose the war.

217
H. A. Gwynne to Lord Derby, 18 April 1918

. . . I cannot help regarding your transference to Paris[1] in any other light than that of a bribe.

You have told me times out of number personally, and you told the British public on one very notable occasion, that if anything happened to Robertson, you would resign your appointment as Secretary of State for War. Robertson fell, and you remained. Not all the excuses in the world could explain your action away.

May I, without in the slightest degree wishing to hurt your feelings, tell you why I regret that you should have fallen a victim to the bribery and corruption of modern politics? Believe me, it is not a personal matter but a national matter. I am a high old Tory, and I have never pretended to be anything else, and always believed that the aristocracy of this country were more patriotic, more unselfish, and more honourable in public affairs than the ordinary politician. I have seen, during this war, a decided rapprochement being attempted between the Socialist and the Tory, not because in policy there was much in common, but because the working man was groping round to find an honest man, and he was beginning to believe that he had found it in the representatives of our old families.

You and Curzon have destroyed this belief, and in destroying it you have done a great injury to the country.

When you told the Aldwych Club[2] that you would stand by Robertson through thick and thin, and then allowed him to go without a murmur, you not only did yourself a great injury, but you did a great injury to England, for you destroyed the belief of the Man in the Street in your promises and in your integrity. When Curzon declared in the House of Lords that a certain measure was catastrophic and most dangerous in every way, and yet would not vote against it, he did the same[3]. . . .

1. As Ambassador to France; Milner took over the War Office. Lloyd George had been contemplating these adjustments for some weeks. (See S. Roskill, *Hankey, Man of Secrets*, vol. i, p. 501.)
2. On 29 January 1918.
3. Curzon it was who wrote to Derby on 18 February to tell him that the War Cabinet was unanimously of the opinion that his resignation of 16 February should not be accepted. (Curzon to Derby, 18 February 1918 (920 (Der) 27/7).)

218
H. A. Gwynne to Lady Bathurst, 20 April 1918

Very Secret

. . . First of all let me set your mind at rest regarding Repington's articles. There is no fear of suspension for they are all submitted to the Censor and we only print them with his imprimature.

The situation is this. The Germans have altogether 240 divisions, of which now about 203 or 4 are on the Western Front. The rest are still stationed in the East, doing garrison duty and some are in Schleswig Holstein and at other strategic points within the Empire. We have on our side British 60 divisions, French 99, American 12 – giving a total of 171 divisions as against German 204. This gives the Boche an advantage of 33 divisions, actually at the front with a reserve of 20 say which he could at a push bring back from the East.

The French have 40 divisions in reserve of which not one single division has been used yet. The Germans have used (not used up) about 127 divisions. We have had a terrible hammering and except the Australians and the Canadian Corps, all our divisions have been in the fighting. Some have lost terribly, others very little. The French, without using their reserves, have taken up the line to the Somme. This they have done by taking divisions out of quiet sectors of the line, where the Germans have done the same. Foch is holding the line from Noyon to the Somme with 10 divisions only. Where his reserves are I cannot say, of course.

Now the position is this:–

British divisions	60 Total	French divisions	99 Total
Badly smashed	28	Badly smashed	12
Slightly smashed	24	Slightly smashed	5
Not at all touched	8	Untouched	42
		In reserve	40

American Divisions
   Total 12
All untouched

Now out of the whole total of the Allied Forces (leaving out the Belgians and Portuguese who don't count), this is how things stand:

Divisions badly smashed	40	Germans	
Slightly smashed	29	Divisions badly smashed	87
Untouched	62	Slightly smashed	40
In reserve	40	Untouched (holding	58
	171	the line)	
		Still in reserve	19
			204

Still available from Russia say 20

Now these extra 20 divisions can only come gradually and in the meantime, the Americans are coming ... at the rate of 25,000 a week. They will be available for the line in 3 weeks or a month. The Germans cannot bring their divisions any quicker from the East. This American reinforcement is *in addition* to the normal increase of about 25,000 a week. These latter come out as divisions with all their artillery, ammunition etc.

To make up losses the French have 700,000 good recruits, the Germans about 530,000 and we *nil*! That's where the situation is so awful and where Lloyd George and the Cabinet should be hung up on the lamp posts.

I think all that I have said gives a true account of our present situation. Although it does not look so bad on paper, remember that when a numerically inferior army is being constantly hammered by a superior force, each day makes things harder for the defenders. The attackers can pull out divisions and give them a rest while the defenders cannot always do this.

As regards artillery we are pretty equal. The Bailleul attack was a surprise.

I don't despair but I do despair if L.G. continues in office. The only way is to go for Cave[1] and a good honest *war* government.

If I see that the war is lost, I shall go off and try to kill one Boche before I die. That is the least a healthy man like myself can do.

The hopelessness of it all simply frightens me but I have not yet lost courage. We must do all we can here at home first and if that fails and there is no hope at least one can die. I really could not live with England on her knees to the Hun.

[P.S.] The French have not made a line but they have their reserves ready at the strategic point. The good thing is that *they have never been used yet*. Foch is waiting and I ought to tell you that he and the French G.H.Q. are very very confident. Too confident, I think.

1. Sir George Cave, Secretary of State for Home Affairs, December 1916– June 1919. Two days later, on 22 April, the *Morning Post* proposed Cave for Prime Minister.

219

H. A. Gwynne to Lieutenant-General Sir H. de la P. Gough, 22 April 1918 (HAG/9 no. 8, IWM)

Very many thanks for your letter of the 19th inst.

I know how difficult it is to do nothing but honestly I do not think you will get any satisfaction out of this Government. As long as Lloyd George is there you will never get justice. You see his plan is quite simple – he does nothing to prepare for a crisis and when the crisis comes he looks round for a victim. You were handy and he threw you to the lions, and I think that justice will only be done you when we get a new Government of honest men, if we ever see such a thing in England again. Meanwhile, I hope you are preparing your case and that you made a full note of your interview with Derby for that is very important. I know him to be a liar and utterly untrustworthy, and the public would rather believe you than him, so do get this down in black and white quickly. As for civil work somehow I hate the idea of your going in for it though I know and appreciate the spirit that prompts you to do so, but before you decide let us have a talk. You will surely be coming up to town, and if you will let me have two or three days' notice we can have lunch together and a good talk over matters. . . .

220
Lieutenant-General H. de la P. Gough to H. A. Gwynne, 25 April 1918 (HAG/9 no. 9, IWM)

My wife is seedy with a virulent cough, but if she is out of the wood next week I think I shall be in London on Wed. next, 1st May. I could lunch with you either that day, or the next, if it suits you. Will you let me know.

I have received no reply whatever from the W[ar] O[ffice] yet about my Enquiry,[1] though I have written twice! Very typical! From Bonar Law's answer to Mr Lambert, it seems as if they were weakening on the Enquiry & had merely called on the Chief for a report. What do you think?

Who is Mr Lambert?[2] I wish Archer-Shee[3] & others would not try to defend me on the plea of 'don't hit a man when he is down'! I am not down! My career is nothing & I know that all that was possible was done to deal with the ——[4] by the 5th Army. The only thing that has surprised me a little was to discover the amount of jealousy against the 5th Army that existed among other Armies! Not very big ideas I fear, but the cause was Sir D[ouglas] H[aig] unfortunately (& really between you & me unnecessarily) always moving the 5th Army into other Army's sectors whenever a fight was in prospect.

There is no question of my wanting 'justice' from L[loyd] G[eorge]. I don't want or expect it. But it is a question of the principles of sound Government, & can any Empire stand when it is run by men whose only means of government is the most unscrupulous use of intrigues however low, petty & far-fetched? In my position I think it would be very wrong to serve this Government again without exposing & protesting firmly against their methods.

1. The Inquiry into the performance of Gough's 5th Army before the German offensive of 21 March.
2. George Lambert, Liberal MP for South Molton, 1891–1924, Civil Lord of the Admiralty, 1905–15. Bonar Law's answer to his question was delivered on 23 April.
3. Lieutenant-Colonel M. Archer-Shee, Conservative MP for Finsbury Central, 1910–18.
4. Word indecipherable.

221

H. A. Gwynne to Lieutenant-General H. de la P. Gough, 26 April 1918 (HAG/9 no. 10, IWM)

. . . Thursday next would suit me admirably. Will you lunch at the Bath Club at 1.15? We can then have a good long talk.

What you say about the War Office does not surprise me, but I do think that they might at least answer your letters.

I think that the Government are frightened of disclosures about the 5th Army, and I think that very likely they are not a bit anxious to have anything published about it, in fact I should think they would be desirous of burking the whole affair, for it cannot redound to their credit. As for sound government, of which you talk, there is no sound government here. At every corner I meet instances of some kind of duplicity and want of principle and justice and everything else, and that is what I am fighting against now.

222

H. A. Gwynne to Lady Bathurst, 29 April 1918

. . . You are right, we *are* in a bad way. Tonight I hear that we have lost Mont Rouge and Scherfeuberg – two important points in the mountain range which we hold in the North. It is not nice and it is very depressing but I have, by no means, lost hope and faith. But I do not feel any better because I know that all this was foreseen by the soldier and ignored by the politician. Why is it that the H. of Commons has so miserably failed us. If I stood at the door of this office and chose the first 670 men that passed, I could produce a better, a more patriotic, a more unselfish lot of men than the elect of the people.

As for Lloyd George, I don't agree with you that he can survive the Irish business. Everybody tells me that he himself feels that he cannot carry on. Look at his crimes, the Eastern adventure, the failure to produce men and the mess in Ireland.[1] I have just received a letter from Chetwode[2] from Palestine (this between ourselves) in which he tells me a pretty tale. Smuts[3] and Amery M.P.[4] (a little pipsqueak who knows as much about strategy as I know about astronomy) was [*sic*] sent out to Palestine to report on the situation. They advised a big expedition to the Hedjaz railway. Allenby[5] and Chetwode (two great soldiers) reported against it but the War Cabinet decided that it was to be carried out. It was carried out and was a failure and a costly failure at that.

271

We have done our duty in putting forward a possible successor. We could not do otherwise. *L. George can never win the war for us.* At least we should try somebody else.

As for Derby, please do not think that I am always looking out for somebody to attack. Really and truly, I would much prefer to say nice things about people than to say nasty things. But Derby has been a worm. He was a man who, by his position and wealth and family . . . had the ball at his feet. His geniality was a great asset and, if only he had been straight, he could have been a great and valuable counterpoise against socialism and revolution. After all, what we have said of him was nothing compared to what our Sovereign said *to* him.

About Repington, his vanity did show itself rather nakedly. But all the same, his opinion on military matters is worth all the other experts put together. I tell you quite frankly and honestly that I do not like him personally but I do think the *M.P.* has scored by his writing. . . .

1. As soon as the Military Service Act became law there had been serious disturbances in Ireland, including a General Strike on 23 April.
2. General P. W. Chetwode, commanding 20th Army Corps.
3. J. C. Smuts, Minister without Portfolio and South African representative on the War Cabinet, June 1917–January 1919.
4. L. S. Amery, at this time one of the personnel of the Cabinet Office. He and Smuts went out to Egypt in February.
5. General E. H. H. Allenby, Commander in Chief Egyptian Expeditionary Force, 1917–19.

223
H. A. Gwynne to Lady Bathurst, 2 May 1918

. . . [T]his Government, as you say, are doing their best to lose the war. As for the waste of money, of course there is no other word to describe it, except monstrous. And remember too, it is only a few occasional instances that come to light. The Ministry of Munitions apparently insist upon paying firms money, when the firms themselves protest that they have been paid. Between ourselves, I am pretty convinced that there is a vast amount of corruption. Indeed, if one had the time, and some members of the House of Commons really anxious to do the right thing and find out the truth, we might make public some of the grosser scandals and so warn the rest of the evildoers. But we are up against very clever men, who hide their tracks with great skill.

I am assured by all the people who are supposed to know – though whether they know or not I cannot tell – that Lloyd George is bound 'to take a toss' over this Irish business. I have just received a letter from Esher, which rather frightens me. He says: 'You are killing Charles to make James king. You are heading straight for a Squiff government unless you can get a right and left.' This is not encouraging and I hope it isn't true.[1]

The only time to my knowledge that the King has really spoken has been in the matter of D[erby]. He told him that he had not been straight and had not kept his word, and said many things of the most severe type and left his Lordship very much taken aback. But he has got a thick hide and an unstable character. Frankly I think that he and Curzon have done more harm to England – as we shall see when this war is over – than any other individuals. The Lloyd Georges, after all, one can fight, for they are obvious enemies, but with people like these two, showing such absolute lack of common honesty, the case is almost hopeless.

. . . Now the papers are praising Lord Rhondda. But we should not be on such low meat rations if it had not been for the mistakes he made, dead against the advice of people who knew.

There is a talk of Balfour taking Lloyd George's place. But although he is a straight and honest man, he is terribly weak, and has not got any of the attributes of a man.

1. On 1 May Esher had written to Henry Wilson: 'Gwynne and Co are doing all they can to shake down L.G. . . . There is nothing to fear so long as Asquith shrinks from office. . . . If I were L.G. . . . I should at once adopt the 'Federalist' platform in the boldest fashion – on the lines of Chamberlain's old speeches. In this way he would obtain what he lacks, a Party as against a following. . . .' Wilson passed this on to Lloyd George. (Lloyd George MSS F/47/7/24. See also J. Kendle, 'Federalism and the Irish Problem in 1918', pp. 207–30.)

224
H. A. Gwynne to Viscount Esher, 2 May 1918
(Esher Papers 5/55)

You may be right about Squiff. But Squiff, bad as he is, would be an improvement on this man, though of course I shall fight hard against his re-appointment.

We have got to the stage now, that there is not a single man, even in Lloyd George's own Ministry, who believes a single word he says. A lie seems to come more easily to his lips than the truth, and sometimes even quite unnecessarily. . . .

H. A. Gwynne to Lieutenant-General H. de la P. Gough,
6 May 1918 (HAG/9 no. 11, IWM)

I am very much obliged to you for your two letters of 3rd and 4th May, enclosing Reinach's[1] article on the work of the 5th Army. I am so glad that the French have realised the work that you have done, and have not hesitated to say so.

As regards the enclosures from the War Office and your answer. Personally I think your answer is most admirable. The only criticism I have to make is that you have not, it seems to me, quite made enough of the formal promise given you by Derby, that you should have an inquiry, for surely in a department the new-comer is bound by the decisions of his predecessor, especially on matters of this kind.

Tomorrow morning you will see in the *Post* a letter from a distinguished soldier, who is risking the whole of his career in order to tell the truth. The effect of this letter I think will be to show up Lloyd George in his true light, which is that of a man who has no regard whatever for the truth. It may indeed result in his losing office. I sincerely hope so, for I am quite convinced that it is impossible to win this war with Lloyd George as Prime Minister. He is doing – unconsciously let us hope – all he can to make the Army lose confidence in its Government, and therefore in itself. The result is that the Army will be weakened much more by such subterfuges and intrigues than ever it can be by the attacks of the enemy. You are one of the victims of a system which is ruining England, and I am not sure that the time may not arrive very soon, when you may be obliged to come out into the open and tell the truth. The whole thing seems to be part of a fixed plan of the politicians to conduct the strategy of the war themselves, and when it fails to throw the blame on to the soldiers. No war is ever won in this way, and certainly not a war of this magnitude and this importance.

I was so glad to see you the other day and find you full of confidence and pluck. Things don't look very well just now, but I do feel that we are on the way to getting rid of the present system, at least I am going to make a very good try.

1. J. Reinach, editor of *La République Française*.

Editor's postscript: On 6 May General Maurice, the DMO, went to see Gwynne and Repington about the publication of a letter in which he took issue with the Government's statements of 9 and 23 April concerning the extension of the British front in France and the fighting strength of the British Army in France before the German offensive of 21 March. Gwynne sent the proof of this letter to Asquith, so that the latter might prepare himself to take action in the House of Commons: 'It is primarily an affair for the House of Commons, since there is ample evidence in the letter that the Ministers of the Crown have lied to the House of Commons.' The text of Maurice's letter, printed in the *Morning Post* on 7 May under the heading 'The Truth', ran:

Sir, – My attention has been called to answers given in the House of Commons on April 23rd by Mr Bonar Law to questions put by Mr G. Lambert, Colonel Burn, and Mr Pringle as to the extension of the British front in France (Hansard, vol 105, No 34, p. 815). These answers contain certain misstatements which in sum give a totally misleading impression of what occurred. This is not the place to enter into a discussion as to all the facts, but Hansard's report of the incident concludes:

> Mr Pringle – Was this matter entered into at the Versailles War Council at any time?
> Mr Bonar Law – This particular matter was not dealt with at all by the Versailles War Council.

I was at Versailles when the question was decided by the Supreme War Council, to whom it had been referred.

This is the latest of a series of misstatements which have been made recently in the House of Commons by the present Government.

On April 9th, the Prime Minister said:

> 'What was the position at the beginning of the battle? Notwithstanding the heavy casualties in 1917 the Army in France was considerably stronger on the 1st January 1918, than on the 1st January 1917.' (Hansard, vol 104, No 24, p. 1328)

That statement implies that Sir Douglas Haig's fighting strength on the eve of the great battle which began on March 21st had not been diminished. That is not correct.

Again in the same speech the Prime Minister said:

> 'In Mesopotamia there is only one white division at all, and in Egypt and in Palestine there are only three white divisions, the rest are either Indians or mixed with a very small proportion of British troops in those divisions – I am referring to the infantry divisions.' (Ibid, p. 1327.)

That is not correct.

Now, Sir, this letter is not the result of a military conspiracy. It has been seen by no soldier. I am by descent and conviction as sincere a democrat as the Prime Minister, and the last thing I desire is to see the government of our country in the hands of soldiers.

My reasons for taking the very grave step of writing this letter are that the statements quoted above are known by a large number of soldiers to be incorrect, and this knowledge is breeding such distrust of the Government as can only end in impairing the splendid *moral* [sic] of our troops at a time when everything possible should be done to raise it.

I have, therefore, decided, fully realising the consequences to myself, that my duty as a citizen must override my duty as a soldier, and I ask you to publish this letter in the hope that Parliament may see fit to order an investigation into the statements I have made.

I am, Sir,
Yours faithfully,
F. Maurice,
Major-General

226
H. A. Gwynne to H. H. Asquith, 8 May 1918
(MS Gwynne 14)

It seems to me that the almost immediate effect of General Maurice's letter and your motion[1] must be the dissolution of the present Government and the disappearance from it of Mr Lloyd George and Bonar Law. A consequent change will, in all likelihood, be your accession to power.

I have been a political opponent of yours of many years' standing and I was a steadfast advocate of your supersession by the present Prime Minister. I confess, too, that within the last few months when it became obvious that Lloyd George was rapidly losing the confidence of the House of Commons and of the country, I have not hailed with enthusiasm the alternative of your return to power. . . .

I had no hand in the vulgar intrigue which resulted in your being replaced by Lloyd George. . . . At the same time I do not hide for a moment the fact that I ardently desired to give the present Prime Minister a chance of showing his mettle. He has been a failure. What have been the chief causes of his failure? In the first place, he was trying to conduct a great war and form a party at the same time. He could not see that to play off one man against another, or one party against another, cleverly and cunningly as it was all done, was not in consonance with the grim and determined spirit of the country, which is one of the results of the war. Another cause for failure lay in his unwarranted and unwarrantable interference with military operations. He could never leave the soldiers alone to work out their problems and he has brought us in consequence to the edge of disaster. He was acclaimed by the people who gave him full rein on the assumption that he would leave all political questions severely alone and devote himself entirely to war problems. And above all, he intrigued and lied to such an extent that even his political friends and supporters confessed that they could not believe a word he said.

It is only natural that the accumulation of these faults and mistakes should bring about his fall. It may fall to you to succeed him and my object in writing . . . is to suggest some thoughts which may help you to guide the nation to victory. . . .

The nation stands on difficult ground. The House of Commons really does not represent the spirit of the nation which, as I read it, is absolutely determined to beat Germany or go under. I cannot altogether blame the House, for it has never had the case put before it in such a way as to arouse its enthusiasm. I believe that if you told the House you intended to devote yourself to one object – the winning of the war – and that you would allow nothing to interfere with that object, you would gain the ready and willing allegiance of Parliament.

The Irish question is a great and instant difficulty. But, here again, I feel sure that you would carry the House of Commons and the country with you, if you insisted on the carrying out of the law and postponed all discussions on Home Rule till after the war. I am not writing now as a convinced and steadfast Unionist but as a man whom the war has deprived of all political bias. Purely from the war point of view, to arouse discontent in Ulster, where the ship building, aeroplane manufacturing, ammunition making are an important part of our military strength, would be to risk a disaster as great as the late defeat on the Somme.

No Government can carry on the war without attempting to solve some of the great and urgent problems caused by the war. Reconstruction must be an essential part of the programme. To do this on party lines would be fatal. To avoid a revolutionary upheaval after the war, we must lay our plans now. I cannot see how we can avoid the drop in wages, work and in capital necessary for increased manufacture unless we embark on a policy of greater production, and to secure greater production, some form of protection seems necessary. If it were possible to divide the Kingdom into industries and let each industry, masters and men, put forward their proposals, this would be something tangible for the Government to work upon. At present you have nothing but the bleatings of poor Dr Addison.

You will have a hostile press. But no press can do the slightest injury to any statesman if he goes forward with the single aim of winning the war. . . . Once he devotes his energies to less important political ends, he is doomed.

We are in a very sad case. We have to look forward, to my mind, to at least 2 years of terrible fighting. But the nation is all right. It means to win or die, and if you can guide and lead this spirit of victory to its goal, then you will find an ample reward in duty done, and difficulties overcome, and the final end achieved. . . .

1. Asquith's motion, debated on 9 May, was heavily defeated. (See C. à C. Repington, *The First World War*, vol. ii, pp. 295 and 298; I. Colvin, *The Life of Lord Carson*, pp. 351–4; and N. Maurice (ed.), *The Maurice Case*.)

227
Viscount Esher to H. A. Gwynne, 10 May 1918
(HAG/8 no. 30, IWM)

I have only seen a telegraphic summary of the result of last night.[1] I told you how it would be. Asquith is not a winner. He is more unpopular all round than L[loyd] G[eorge] and the instinct of the country is perfectly sound. If Wully[2] and F. Maurice wish to make a protest and if they thought it was their duty to do so, their protest should have been made any time between October 1916 and April 1917. Either they should have got the *men* at that period that D[ouglas] H[aig] asked for or they should have forbidden the operations of 1917. That would have been real business. All this letting off of squibs after the event is mere futility. Now for the future.

What do you say of the revelations that Clemenceau[3] is permitting the French papers to make about the negotiations of Poincaré[4] and Ribot[5] with Austria?[6] What can an Army do that is not backed up by an efficient diplomacy? All its sacrifices are bound to be in vain. The lessons of history evidently go for nothing. We are in pursuit of a mirage – the destruction of German militarism – and Leagues of Peace are mere verbiage. The 'decisive moment' is a phrase that applies with equal force to diplomatic as well as to military strokes. Sir John French said in 1915 that it would take more than one campaign in which to defeat Germany. The little man had a better flair than these political geese in France and Italy. You cannot resist the evidence that there was a moment when Austria and Bulgaria were arrayed against the German Junkers. We failed to drive in the wedge. For this failure the Foreign Office ought to be swept out and regarnished. Here is a task you might help to accomplish, if you were to turn your mind to it. Pin pricks are no use, but the sword should be driven well home. Please think it over.

1. The 'Maurice Debate', in which Lloyd George secured a Government majority of 187.
2. Robertson.
3. Clemenceau had become Prime Minister of France on 15 November 1917.
4. Raymond Poincaré, President of the French Republic, 1913–20.
5. Paul Ribot, Prime Minister and Foreign Minister of France, March–September 1917.
6. These negotiations took place in the autumn of 1917.

228
H. A. Gwynne to Viscount Esher, 13 May 1918 (HAG/8 no. 31, IWM)

I am much obliged to you for your letter. I never regarded Asquith as a winner. But I did think he would put up a better fight.

I think the instinct of the country is for a continuance of Lloyd George in preference to Asquith. But at the same time I am quite convinced that a prolonged regime of Lloyd George is going to lose the war for us. You cannot project into a mind like Lloyd George's, the 'war mind', or anything approaching it. The difference between him and the soldier is that the soldier prepares for the worst and hopes for the best, while he invariably hopes for the best and will never prepare for the worst. That is why he is found wanting.

Today is the 13th May – that is getting on for eight weeks since the offensive started. I see by the secret official communiqué that we are losing at the rate of about 30,000 a week. It is purely a matter of calculation how much the strain is going to tell on us. And yet Lloyd George has done nothing whatever to meet the strain. He still puts his hopes on American help, but that is where he differs from the soldier, who wants to prepare for the worst whilst hoping for the best. He will not face the worst or make any preparation for it. It will be sheer luck and by diehardiness on the part of our troops if we hold out this year. The Germans are in no hurry for they have the whole summer in front of them having begun early, and Amiens will be their objective. It will want the most strenuous fighting and great reserves of men to stop it, and I don't see where these reserves of men are coming from. You cannot, in the middle of a war like this, with Germany at the height of her strength, go on the principle of hoping for the best and never preparing for anything else. Disaster is bound to follow.

As for the Foreign Office and the way in which they have handled policy, of course this is on a par with Lloyd George's military preparations.

I am watching the French papers carefully to see whether I can really do anything. As you say, it is no use pin-pricking, one must hit to kill.

229
H. A. Gwynne to Lady Bathurst, 15 May 1918

Please forgive me for not answering your letter of the 11th before but, as usual, I have been wasting shoe leather doing work for which members of the Government are paid £5000 a year to do.

The situation is serious. And for this reason. This war is one in which the *spirit* of the nation is engaged. Men are fighting and dying for their country not because they hope to get anything out of the war. This spiritual force is the only thing that can win the war and must be directed by men of a single and unselfish heart. The moment materialism shows its ugly head, we shall lose all our spiritual inspiration. Now when the Prime Minister deals in lies, he is not merely doing himself an injury but he is destroying the only force – the spiritual – which can win this war. As things are, at present, the soldiers and the sailors, the men who face death for the sake of their country, are the only men who are imbued with the real impulse – the true motive. L[loyd] G[eorge] looks upon this war as a supreme opportunity for himself. Now nobody who thinks of himself is worth a hang in these days. L.G. has corrupted Parliament. Walpole was much more honest because he was much more open. L.G. has betrayed England because England to him is merely a pawn in the game of his own political advancement. One great argument that is urged in his favour is that he is all out for war to the bitter end. Yesterday I had a Foreign Office man lunching with me and he disposed of that argument by telling me to beware of the Prime Minister because he is capable of making a disgraceful peace at any moment.[1]

We are going through dark days. I will never give up hope and now more than at any time we have need of all our courage. L.G. will pass because he is false. But just now he seems to have the upper hand.

Do trust me. This is not a case of personal animosity or partisan feeling. We have all the trumps in our hands but they must be used with skill and care. Today, most people are damning the *M.P.*, tomorrow they will say that it has been right. I don't care a tinker's curse for the opinion of the people. It is always wrong and ill-informed. But we, of the *M.P.*, have a big role to play. We are the only independent paper left and we have to bear the burden of this position as well as stand the racket of hate which independence always creates. Only last week, I was approached by a mutual friend of the P.M.'s with suggestions of rewards and dignities and even money. That shows what a bad way they are in. But if we stand

280

steady and steadfast we'll win out and, what is much more, will win the war.

All these violent attacks on us are just part of the great plot to enslave England. Repington is a pawn in our game but a salient in the enemy's position which he assails vigorously. But Repington is right and they are wrong. Repington is fighting for the fighting men and he has carried a bold lance. He is not allowed in the *M.P.* to air his personal animosities, and our enemies know this. . . .

The Censor plays the devil with our stuff. You are quite right. They delayed our telegrams and *The Times* and other papers scored.

[P.S.] *L.G. via Derby is intriguing with Thomas and the French socialists against Clemenceau.*

1. On 4 May Repington had commented on the harsh reception given by the Foreign Office to the former Dutch War Minister, [. Coleyn, who had been invited in connection with negotiations for the exchange of British and German prisoners of war, which the Cabinet Office anticipated would produce overtures from the Germans about peace terms. (See C. à C. Repington, *The First World War*, vol. ii, p. 295; S. Roskill, *Hankey, Man of Secrets*, vol. i, pp. 571–2; and V. Rothwell, *British War Arms and Peace Diplomacy 1914–18*, pp. 201–6.)

230
H. A. Gwynne to Lady Bathurst, 22 May 1918

. . . That I am right in this attitude we have taken up I am quite convinced but I have been through great strain and stress in order to create a public feeling which would support the *M.P.* without a murmur. If you think that we cannot succeed then we must sit quiet and do as you desire. Indeed you are and should be the final arbiter. Mind I am not sure you are right and because I am not sure, I accept your decision without a word. Because if I were quite sure I would urge you with all my power to allow me to continue. But how can I bring arguments to bear unless I myself am quite certain in my own mind? So I accept your decision and am almost grateful for it.

At the same time the dark days do not appal me because we have gone through so many – the sun has come out in the end because we have been right. But I have no right or wish to jeopardise *your* paper and I do not mean to.[1] Your confidence is and has been one of my chiefest supports; that and the determination to look for victory through everything have kept me going. We shall come out on top but will let other people prove that we are right and not ourselves.

About Repington, believe me the Army is with him to a man. I cannot tell you definitely that Sir D. Haig agrees with everything that Repington has written but what I can assure you is that I have been told by one of Haig's staff that if it had not been for the *M.P.*, he would have lost courage, owing to the attacks on him made by the politicians. But I will keep Repington severely alone to his military writing where he is certainly supreme. . . .

1. Gwynne had written to Percy on 13 May that he believed the Government would, if they had the slightest chance, do their best to suppress the *Morning Post*. (MS Gwynne 21.)

231
H. A. Gwynne to Lady Bathurst, 27 May 1918

I am back to work on Friday much refreshed and in good heart again. As you said in your letter this war does put a tremendous strain on one and at times one is inclined to see everything *en noir*.

I have been reading your letter again under the improved circumstances. I agree with you that our proper line now is to sit quiet and construct . . . as regards the *M.P.*, Peacock[1] tells me that never since the war began has the paper been so prosperous. He assures me that if we had paper enough we could add to our circulation by 20,000 without any difficulty. People are content to remain on a waiting list in order to get the paper and he tells me that there is a greater call for it than ever. This disposes, I think, of the assumption that the *M.P.* has suffered from our attitude.

You must bear in mind that we have no friends but a whole heap of enemies. We have arrayed against us the cleverest, the most unscrupulous scoundrels in England. There is [*sic*] no lengths to which they would not go. I will tell you in confidence one of their latest attempts. Beaverbrook[2] is now practically the sole adviser of L[loyd] G[eorge]. He it is who governs England. He is rich, very rich and ruthless as well as exceedingly clever. The other day a correspondent here of an American paper offered Colvin a fantastic sum to go to America and become a writer on an American paper. When we pushed the matter, Beaverbrook was the inspiring genius of the proposal.

Everywhere he goes, he drops poison against the *M.P.* He it was who organised a series of letters to me from people all over the country, damning me for the way the *M.P.* has been run. He has been saying that I have been knocked out by overwork and that I have become hysterical and so forth. No doubt you have received many of these letters. Now whatever I am, I am not hysterical. I simply will not bow to the corrupt powers which govern us. We have to walk very warily because they have the power and the means of exercising that power. Beaverbrook and L.G. have the whole press of England in his hands and the *M.P.* is the one paper that spoils his game. Naturally there is no limit to their annoyance and no limit to their unscrupulous cunning. But you need not be afraid. I shall not land the *M.P.* in any disaster. No more Bow Streets for me. But we must keep our flag of honest patriotism flying. Else, I believe, England would go to the dogs.

Offers have been made to me in roundabout ways which only amuse me. The last was a Privy Councillorship. But I am content to live and die plain Mr. as long as we can make the *M.P.* the one honest independent journal in a wickedly dishonest and corrupt press. These dark days when the forces of our enemies are strongest against us will pass and England will one day be grateful for our attitude. I know the Army is. There at least, we can be sure of unstinted praise and admiration. It's an uphill game but this is the time for courage and fortitude and calm resolve. Believe me we shall be amply justified in every way by all we have done.

1. Business Manager of the *Morning Post.*
2. Owner of the *Daily Express*, Chancellor of the Duchy of Lancaster and Minister of Information from February 1918.

232
H. A. Gwynne to Lady Bathurst, 28 May 1918

I hope to answer your letter tomorrow. In the meantime I send you this.

Enclosure in letter 232

Memorandum on the Conduct of the War by the present Prime Minister

It is impossible to give more than a brief sketch of the chief causes of complaint that we have against the Lloyd-Georgian conduct of the war, but I will give a few examples to show how justified we are, and have been, in everything that we have said.

With regard to unity of control. Last year – I believe about November – Sir William Robertson proposed the scheme by which General Foch would be Chairman of a War Council at Versailles, which would practically give him command of the armies in France. This memorandum was a very able one and forestalled the idea of a generalissimo, which was adopted in a panic. Sir William Robertson's scheme was to put Foch practically supreme, with a British and French Chief of the General Staff with him, the former of whom would be the channel by which Foch would transmit his orders to the British Army. He was against the principle of an absolute Generalissimo, because he said – and I think rightly – that it would be a mistake to put British troops under the unfettered control of a foreign general without check.

What he foretold has happened. The French are now wanting to interfere with our supplies, in fact they have made a proposal to pool them, and the consequence is that a great deal of confusion has arisen. Foch has split up armies – and to some extent corps – and has sandwiched the British Army between the French Army, so that local control comes into the hands of the commander of the French Armies. This was never the intention of Mr Lloyd George when he instituted the Generalissimo, and I hear that he and Sir Henry Wilson are very anxious about the inevitable confusion and the reaction which is bound to follow. Indeed, my latest information is to the effect that Sir Henry Wilson has put in a memorandum practically recommending the revision of the Generalissimo on the lines of Sir William Robertson's original memorandum.

Sir William Robertson was against a divided command such as the Versailles Conference. He has always been in favour of a unified command.

Lloyd George is putting all his trust in the advent of the American soldiers. The Americans will let us down. We are supposed to be pretty extravagant in the way of the number of men we have behind the lines in comparison with the number of men we have in the line. But the Americans are worse. They have half a million men at least in France now, but only 130,000 are fit to take the line. Of course a good many of the men behind the line are men in training.

The main difficulty has always been a matter to which the General Staff have been bringing the attention of the War Cabinet. They started in October and did not cease until Sir William Robertson was dismissed from the War Office. Late in December, Sir William Robertson as Chief of the General Staff sent in a personal paper asking for men. In December Sir Douglas Haig wrote to Mr Lloyd George and said that unless he got more men he would have to reduce his establishment. With this reduced establishment he stated that it would be quite impossible for him to take up as much line as he was then holding, and he asked Lloyd George to arrange that in consequence of the lack of men the French should take over more line. The reply to this was that Haig was forced to take over more line which he knew he could not hold, with a consequence that we were driven back over the Somme.

Sir William Robertson was dismissed because he would not agree to a divided command such as the Versailles War Council was. Yet after he was dismissed they had the unified command in the form of a Generalissimo, and now, after nearly two months of experience of a Generalissmo, they are going back to the original idea of Sir William Robertson.

The General Staff was altogether against the expedition to Aleppo, and recommended that after the taking of Jerusalem the British forces should remain on the defensive there.

They recommended that three divisions should be brought back from Palestine and put into Gough's army. If their recommendation had been accepted the three divisions would have been in France at the end of February. This was refused, but directly after the offensive broke out – and too late to be of any use – the three divisions were ordered back.

Smuts and Amery, a civilian – both civilians really – were sent out to Palestine, without consultation with the General Staff, to persuade Allenby to undertake operations which the Prime Minister wanted to carry out against the wish of the General Staff. These proposals were condemned by Allenby, by Chetwode, and by Bulfin[1] as being dangerous. But Allenby's rigid idea of a soldier's duty to obey, even when he thinks obedience is dangerous, was the reason why he undertook the offensive against his own better judgement and the better judgement of his Generals.

In December Sir William Robertson recommended the bringing back of these three divisions, and another division from Salonika, and the using of the ships thus released for bringing over American troops in battalion. His proposal was to bring over by the middle of February 150,000 of the best American trained troops to take their part in the British brigades. This was over-ruled by the War Cabinet and by Lloyd George, with a consequence that the poor British Army with diminished strength had to bear the brunt of the greatest offensive of this war.

I could go on enumerating a lot more of these cases, but I hope in a short time to send you an official document which will convince you, as it has convinced me, that if we go on as we are, with Lloyd George ordering expeditions against the wish and desire of his military advisers, we shall lose the war in spite of America. It is only the danger of the position which is any excuse for an active polemic just now. This polemic is being stayed. But that we are right, and that we shall be proved to be right in a short time, I have not the slightest doubt whatever.

1. Lieutenant-General Sir E. S. Bulfin.

H. A. Gwynne to Lady Bathurst, 29 May 1918

. . . Your letter to me reached me at my cottage when I was at my lowest ebb of vitality and courage. You were right in thinking that the strain had been great but you were wrong in thinking that the strain had warped my judgement. I am quite sure, I am absolutely positive that the *M.P.* could not have done anything different. What are the facts?

We defended Sir William Robertson because he has been right all through. I think you know me well enough to be quite sure that personal friendship would never be allowed to sway me one way or another. As a matter of fact Henry Wilson is a much greater friend of mine than Robertson. But that by the way. I judged Robertson by his prescience and his character. When Korniloff's offensive in Russia last July petered out, as he knew it would, Robertson kept rubbing into the War Cabinet the fact that a supreme effort was needed in order to meet the inevitable onslaught in the West by the Germans in increased numbers and with a greatly augmented artillery. Week after week he pegged away, until the Cabinet was sick of the sight of him. Then L[loyd] G[eorge] started the Versailles Council. Now what was that famous Council, which is now as dead as Queen Anne? It was a Council to be composed of Prime Ministers and soldiers. The soldiers were to have supreme authority under the direction of the politicians. That is to say that General X, a British General at Versailles, could give orders to General Haig who was also to receive orders from London. Here was a divided not a unified command. 'Now', said Robertson 'that's not the way to do it. What you really want, L.G., is a generalissimo though you don't know it. Now this is the way to do it. Have a military council at Versailles, make Foch the Chairman of it, and let him have a British Chief of the Staff, agreed upon by me and Haig, to transmit his orders to the British forces, an Italian to the Italians & so on.' 'No' said Lloyd George 'I don't want that I want my Council.' 'But your Council' replied Robertson 'is a *divided command* not a unified command and it is unworkable.' 'I don't care' said L.G. 'I'm going to have it' and he did and L.G. dismissed his best military adviser. What was the result. The Versailles Council is dead as mutton and the generalissimo was created in a panic without any safeguards. *Last week* the War Cabinet was forced by the Army Council to try and restore some of the safeguards which Robertson wanted to create.

But the question of men was not touched by the Versailles conference. That was urgent. Robertson who foresaw the possibilities of a debacle urged and urged the War Cabinet to face the problem. In vain. At last as a *pis aller*, he recommended the bringing back of divisions from Palestine and Salonika to France and proposed with the shipping this released to bring 150,000 Americans over by the end of February. L.G. refused. On March 25th, L.G. made the General Staff do the very thing Robertson wanted and 65 battalions were withdrawn from Palestine and Salonika *in a panic* and the Food Controller had to give up ships that should bring food in order to bring Americans over here. Surely Robertson was right all through. Ten weeks have elapsed and, excepting raw boys of 18½ years, not a single man of the new conscription can be fit to go to the front for 14 weeks from last Saturday.

As for the U.S.A. they have let us down badly. They have accepted the united command *but so did Robertson* only he wanted to do it properly.

Now we come to Maurice. Your son-in-law is right when he said that Maurice's defence of his position at the Versailles conference was feeble. Of course it was, for L.G. would not let him tell the truth. Look at the enclosed. *The words underlined* [in italics] *were taken out by L.G. himself.* They were just the words which justified Maurice.

Now about the *Observer*. They made a wicked and unfair attack on us.[1] We were bound to answer or suffer by default. They talked about a dinner when the Maurice affair was arranged. There is not a word of truth. I don't go out to dinners. I never knew of Maurice's intentions until the letter was handed to me for publication. As for Repington, he is, I am sure, the first military critic in any country. I don't like him. He's a snob and conceited but he knows his job. *My* mistake was to rope him in for my polemic against L.G. He's too nervy and unbalanced when it comes to fighting but on his own ground he is supreme. And I am keeping him to that ground.

Believe me, we shall be amply and fully justified. I agree with you that we must go slow, but do think how great and dreadful is the crisis and how bitterly we are paying for the mistakes of the War Cabinet. If only the soldiers could conduct the war, we need have no fear for they are bred to prepare for the worst while the politician hopes for the best always and will never prepare for the worst. I don't think that, even within the near future, you will regret that the *M.P.* fought a good fight in the best of causes – victory.

1. On Sunday 12 May the *Observer*, in an article called 'An Exposure "Naturalised News" and Military Scandal Chapter and Verse' assaulted the reputation of Repington. This was Milner's revenge, arranged on 29 April with Waldorf Astor, the owner of the *Observer*, for a personal attack made upon him by Repington on the leader page of the *Morning Post* on 26 April. (See A. M.

Gollin, *Proconsul in Politics*, pp. 514–17; and W. M. Ryan, 'From "Shells Scandal" to Bow Street: The Denigration of Lieutenant-Colonel Charles à Court Repington'.) Repington remained on the *Morning Post* until 1920.

Enclosure in letter 233

Note by Gwynne: The deletions by the Censor are underlined [in italics].[1]

I feel, however, that I owe my readers a word of explanation on two comments which the Prime Minister made on my conduct, and these I can answer without disclosing secrets. The first is as to my presence at Versailles at the session in which the question of the taking over the line was discussed. I accompanied the British representative to Versailles, and I was present at the first meeting of this session of the Supreme War Council. *I received the agenda, and, later, the complete verbatim reports of all the meetings passed through my hands.*

During the meetings held after the first, *including that at which the taking over the line was considered,* I was in a corridor outside the council chamber, and, in the intervals between the meetings, was engaged on work in connection with the questions under examination. I hold, therefore, that my statement that I was at Versailles at the time is justified.

1. Gwynne's enclosure is an extract from a letter sent by Maurice to the press and published on 15 May. The complete text of the letter as published is to be found in N. Maurice (ed.), *The Maurice Case*, pp. 111–13.

234
Viscount Esher to H. A. Gwynne, 3 June 1918 (HAG/8 no. 32, IWM)

What is going to be your policy now?

Is the public to be fed with more lies, and false estimates of the military and diplomatic results of the war? Or, is the truth to be told baldly?

Why cannot Repington take 3 periods 1916, 1917, 1918 and calmly sum up the military and political positions as they have changed *all over the world* in favour of one side or the other.

Then, point out (a) the misleading speeches of L[loyd] G[eorge] and Co with references (b) the hesitation, laches etc in *action* of the Government.

All this in a series of articles covering say a week.

Then the conclusion?

A parliamentary holiday for six months.

A committee of public safety.

The closing of the Foreign Office.

We have reached a point now when unless some very drastic step is taken, we shall be beat, my friend.

The downward slope is getting steeper every day.

And from all I hear the Government is getting weaker, and so nerveless that its various members are shirking responsibility.

Presently they will turn tail before the country understands what is up!

So you had better look out. . . .

235
H. A. Gwynne to Viscount Esher, 5 June 1918
(HAG/8 no. 33, IWM)

Many thanks for your letter.

Frankly, though I agree with most you say, I find it increasingly difficult to get up any enthusiasm about any further fighting. I am getting heartily sick of pulling chestnuts out of the fire alone, and of being blackguarded by everybody as being unpatriotic and helping the enemy. Men, who are actually in the Government, tell me, when I meet them privately, that they thoroughly agree with me, but that they would not lift a finger to put things right.

Lloyd George has achieved power, and he is using it in a way which the Czar of Russia never dreamed of using his autocratic privileges. I have not lost courage, but I have certainly lost all faith in the power of this Government to secure victory, and, like yourself, I have not too much faith that it will be able to resist the temptations of an opportunist peace. But I must have time to organise my forces. I am quite alone in the Press and even independent public men in whom I have faith and trust, seem to consider an attack upon the Government as a sort of blasphemy with which they will have no part or parcel.

236
Lady Bathurst to L. J. Maxse, 6 June 1918
(Maxse MSS 475)

. . . You . . . kindly congratulate me[1] on the stand made by the *M.P.* Sometimes I do help or even originate a campaign but this 'stand' I have nothing to do with & Mr Gwynne deserves the entire praise for it. Indeed I at first thought he had perhaps suggested that you should write to me, knowing that I value your opinion & that I know you to be disinterested & patriotic, because to tell you the truth I have been somewhat recalcitrant lately. I agreed with the policy of doing whatever we could to retain Gen. Robertson as Chief of the Staff but in that we failed & I verily believe that nothing now can save the Allies. It is too late. The Germans, if they reach Paris, & I don't see what's to stop them, will begin the burning of it quarter by quarter. Do you think the French can stand that, why should they. I would not, in their place, with no hope of victory. This country has elected to [be] governed by Lloyd George, the head of democracy. Democracy is idiotic & can't win a war or govern. Very well, then it will be beaten & we, one or two little papers, only read by sensible people who think sanely, cannot avert defeat. We can die with dignity & decorum – that's how I look at it. I want to give up fighting when it can do no good. What can we do. The Government won't conscript Irishmen, they've let the second chance go even after the Vatican's assertion that the Pope knew nothing about the line taken by the Irish Bishops & priests against conscription. All that can be & is being done, is to take middle-aged men from occupations where they are badly needed unless the whole business of the nation is to collapse, & to put these men into khaki and pay them to waste their time in military affairs. I wish I was born French. The English make me tired. Thank Goodness I'm Scotch.

1. Maxse had written to Lady Bathurst the previous day, 5 June 1918.

237
Lady Bathurst to L. J. Maxse, 12 June 1918
(Maxse MSS 475)

Thankyou for your two nice letters. It was horrid of me to suspect Mr Gwynne, my bad conscience I suppose. Anyway I apologise to him though he doesn't know I thought he had asked you to write to me. Yes, of course, I'm not funking & I'm not clamouring for peace, only I realise that we are beaten & that if the Archangel Michael [sic] rose up to command our armies or guide our politicians it would be too late. It's curious how events affect different people. You become more democratic. I become more in favour of autocracy. This war is a triumph for autocratic governments as represented by the Central Empires. The cause of all our trouble is not so much Lloyd George or the failure to conscript Ireland or any of these smaller things as the Russian betrayal. And why did the Russian betrayal take place.

Simply because the Czar was too weak or too ill-informed. If he had shot a few hundred socialists & governed firmly Russia would have been all right today. America talks much but we have yet to see those millions & I doubt whether they'll ever be in time but even if they were, one can hardly call America a democracy except that Americans are wanting in respect to their superiors, but surely President Wilson has all the power and prestige of a Kaiser & is quite as autocratic. As for France and England I look upon their Governments as the most stupendous failures that the world has ever seen & that the Armies have done well is merely because there was a large class of men of good blood to lead them in both cases.

Poor Clemenceau he puts up a good fight but as he says, five to 1 is big odds & sometimes it's worse than that. I quite disagree with you about the great qualities of the people of England. I know many say openly that they want the war to last because of the high wages they are getting & the higher wages they get the less work they do. I see little but apathy and selfishness except among the middle & educated & farmer classes.

238
H. A. Gwynne to Lady Bathurst, 16 June 1918

. . . I am truly sorry that you see everything *en noir*. I will admit that there is mighty little of the silver lining about the sky just now but I am still convinced that we can and shall win. This is the darkest hour of all. Freed from the nightmare of a fight on two flanks, the Germans are taking full advantage of their opportunities to seek a decisive victory on the Western Flank. For warning the Government of this and begging them to do something to meet the obvious danger we were fined and the *M.P.* was threatened with all sorts of pains and penalties. But, if contemporaneous opinion will not give us our due, at least history will say that we did our best to warn the country and the Government.

So much for the *M.P.* Now for the actual situation. It is at its very worst. Of the 240 divisions which the Germans have, they have thrown every single one . . . at us and the French. They have won ground, they have had indeed notable successes but they have achieved nothing of a decisive nature. And meanwhile, spurred by the common danger America is throwing in troops at a magnificent pace – 30,000 a week and instead of a steadily diminishing Allied force in France, we are actually increasing while the Boche is losing his effectives. We must hold out this summer and then I think you will see the advantage turn in our favour and for the rest of the war the initiative will lie in our hands. Austria is in a bad way – a very bad way and cannot stand the strain much longer. The elements of her weakness – the nationalities are proving themselves weaknesses. . . .

We must not talk of not winning. The alternative is too ghastly for words. For believe me, there is no half-way house between a complete German victory and a complete Allied victory. And if there were, it would be cowardly to admit it or consider it because we should be throwing a heavier burden on our children and their children. Let us in God's name go forward and win. That way lies our only safety. To falter or to lose faith now in the very darkest hour is part of the way to defeat. We must keep our courage in spite of everything. But I can quite imagine how difficult it is in face of the way we are governed. But it will be in spite of the Government that we shall win.

Allen and I can never see eye to eye on the strategy of this war. Let me put it to you in this way. The Germans want victory. They know that victory can only be achieved by defeating their strongest enemies – the French and the British. If they were of Allen's opinion they would have sent down twenty divisions to Palestine and captured Egypt. They did not do so (although they have plenty of men) because they know that *whether they are to keep Egypt* depends not on the defeat of the British forces in Palestine and Egypt but on the defeat of the French and English in France. That is why they have concentrated every man they can spare on the Western Front. *And that is the reason why we must do the same.* We can win Palestine in France but we can't win a decisive battle in Palestine. Wherefore we ought to have every single man possible in France to meet the Germans in their strength. Suppose we took Aleppo and the Germans took Paris. What would happen? France might make peace and we should lose the war *and Aleppo* with it. I never could understand there being any doubt about the strategy. . . .

It is a killing wearying war but don't let us lose courage. Let us keep our heads and hearts up and we shall win. *Mais du courage, toujours du courage.*

239
H. A. Gwynne to Lady Bathurst, 18 June 1918

Many thanks for your letter, which I think has crossed one of mine from Little Easton. I meant to have written to you then about the Billing case, which I regard as a very serious indication of a state of feeling in the country which may be quite dangerous, and certainly would have been dangerous if left in the hands of Billing.[1]

I cannot blame the public for being misled, because successive Governments have done their best to instil into the people an idea of distrust. There has been undoubted tenderness towards the Germans. Whether this tenderness is really a result of our stupid magnanimity, or comes from a deeper and more sinister motive, does not really matter very much, since the result is the same in making people think that there is a hidden hand which protects the enemy at the cost of ourselves. Mrs. Asquith's connection with Speyer, the undoubted alliance between the Free Traders and the cosmopolitan financial people, the stupid way in which we neglect our economic weapon against Germany, all have combined to create a state of feeling which is positively dangerous. A Billing, or a Bottomley,[2] has it now in his power to bring about almost a revolution, for it is well to remember that there is a feeling of profound distrust throughout the country of the politician. After all, Lloyd George can win Parliamentary triumphs by sheer lying, but he does not win triumphs in the country, for every soldier knows that he lied when he said that we were stronger in Jan. 1918 than we were in Jan. 1917, and every soldier writes home and does not forget to tell his people the truth. In consequence nobody trusts any politician. Indeed, the only one who has been straight and honest in this war is Carson, and against him there is a conspiracy in the Press – especially the Northcliffe Press – which makes it almost impossible for him to be able to do anything.

I am watching Billing very carefully, for, frankly, I am frightened of him. I am very glad that you liked our treatment of the case.

1. N. Pemberton Billing, Independent MP, 1916–21. Billing was being sued for libel by an actress appearing in a production of Oscar Wilde's *Salome*. He used the trial to claim that the Germans had compiled a list of 47,000 'perverts', many of whom were prominent in English public life. (See M. Kettle, *Salome's Last Veil: the Libel Case of the Century*, London, 1977.) I have encountered no evidence to support Kettle's suggestions that Pemberton Billing was in receipt of a subsidy from the *Morning Post*, the finances of which would not have allowed a payment of the scale mentioned (£5000); and that Gwynne and Repington, with Generals Robertson and Maurice, were parties to a conspiracy to embarrass the Government and to stop the negotiation of an early peace with Germany.

2. Horatio Bottomley, Liberal MP, editor of *John Bull*.

240
H. A. Gwynne to Lady Bathurst, 9 July 1918

. . . I am glad you liked our leader on India. A few years ago such proposals would never have been allowed.[1] But now I do not know what seems to have got into the heads of our Government, except the fact that the people in charge of this country, are trying to get out of the way all thorny questions, so that they can be left free for a coalition when the war is over. Indeed no other theory fits the circumstances. . . .

As regards the future. We are in this position. We have spent, to defend ourselves, an enormous amount of money – some of it I am sorry to say wastefully. But the fact remains that we shall have a debt of something like eight or nine thousand million pounds. This debt has got to be met, and there are one or two alternatives. One is that we should have a system of confiscation, by which everybody worth more than a few hundreds a year, would have to give half their income to the State. There remains the obvious and better alternative – that of producing or creating greater wealth, and out of this increased wealth paying off our burden of debt.

In order to do this latter a good many preliminary steps are needed. In the first place, industries have got to be placed on a basis which will allow them security from unfair competition. For, mark you, Germany is in exactly the same position as we are, and there is going to be a terrible fight for the raw material with which to increase production after the war. I want the raw material, the great mass of which is in British hands, to be allocated to British industries. There is a party here who are not so keen about it, who contemplate without anxiety the possibility of a resuscitation of German commercial and industrial activity, even if it is at the cost of ourselves.

It seems to me that the duty of a British statesman is, first of all, to look after his own people, next to extend what facilities he can to the Allies who have fought with us. But it seems to me to be no part of his duty to go out of his way to help our present enemies. That, very roughly speaking, is one of the planks of the policy which we are advocating in the *Morning Post*.

You have touched upon the weakness of the position. For although definite plans may be laid down for the organisation of British trade and industries, when you come to labour the difficulties increase. For here you have to deal with human beings, who are often very unreasonable, and who, in any case, are determined to obtain for themselves at whatever cost a higher wage. Indeed, I do not see how, since they will possess the vote and therefore the power of controlling government, they are going to accept any change in affairs which will result in their getting lower wages. Wages are inflated now, but of course so are prices, and although the balance in favour of wages still remains high, it is not so high as it looks.

Personally, I think that the working men are going to stick to their present wages, however much prices may fall, and the only way in which this determination can be deflected into reasonable channels

294

is by persuading them that their safety lies in the safety and the security of the industry to which they belong.

The whole subject however has this disadvantage, that you cannot sit down in a study and work out schemes for human beings, for however pretty a thing may look on paper, when it comes to its adoption in a practical form, one finds a good many almost insuperable objections. You yourself have given one, which requires a lot of thought. Indeed it amounts to this: is it possible, even for the sake of wages as a livelihood, to condemn men to a mechanical sort of existence, in which there is no excitement, no recreation, and in which a man becomes a mere automaton like his machine?

I agree with you entirely in the joys of creation. I know myself with my carpentering, what a delight I take in the making of an object that a skilled carpenter would throw into the fire. Still, it is my own, and I have made it. This joy will be lost to the majority of working men. And it is for that reason that I have always urged that political reforms should take into consideration not merely the questions of labour and the conditions under which the working man earns his living, but also should pay attention to his recreations.

As far as my own experience goes, the politician dismisses the working man from his mind the moment he has left the gates of the factory, unless it is to entice him into a political meeting. They do not seem to care what becomes of the wife or the children, and this lack of sympathy with the life of the working man outside his factory is bound to have its reaction on the men themselves.

Your ideal of a nation of craftsmen is magnificent, but I do think it is impracticable. But it is an ideal to which we should all aim as far as possible. . . .

1. In leaders of 6 and 8 July the *Morning Post* had denounced the Montagu–Chelmsford Report on Indian Constitutional Reform, the recommendations of which were designed to promote the eventual self-government of India, and on which the Government of India Act of 1921 was based.

241
H. A. Gwynne to Lady Bathurst, 17 July 1918

The war has been such a strain on everybody and on you and Lord Bathurst as much as anybody, that, like better men, I have been content to grin and bear it. But as the war goes on the strain becomes almost unbearable. I have not thought it fair to you or to the paper to obtrude personal matters when the greater struggle for the very existence of the paper has been going on. But now, I think, we can say that we have won out and that we are well on the way to complete success. Such being the case, I have the less hesitation in writing to you and laying before you a few facts and figures which I hope you will consider.

It is fourteen years since I have been an Editor and, curiously enough, it is seven years to a day since I became Editor of the *M.P.* During these 14 years my salary has increased by £100. Now, please do not think that I have forgotten that it was not my intention or desire to refer again to money matters. The reference is forced on me by circumstances over which I really have no control. In 1914 my salary was £2600 and my income tax £60 to £75 while prices were moderate. Today prices have gone up 50% all round and my income tax is £750 and next year will be £850. Compared with 1914 my net income is £1850 to £2525. Allowing for increases in prices I calculate that my income works out at about £1400. I ought to tell you that upon me falls responsibility for three members of my family so that I have only about £1050 in real income, compared to pre-war days. That this is inadequate is borne in on me each year. This year I have had to sell out £600 of securities to pay income tax and what money I have been able to scrape together to buy war loans is now held by my bankers against advances.

I have made enquiries in various directions and I find that it has become a general custom since the war that Editors should receive, as a war bonus, the amount of the difference in income tax between now and pre-war days and I would ask you to do the same for me.

Believe me, I hate asking for increases. I am so happy in my work and see such a great future for the *M.P.*, that I ask no better than to be able to devote the rest of my life to making it the greatest paper in England. At the same time, I am sure you will agree with me that a man cannot give his best to his work, if he is continually worried by money matters. Even now, I would not have troubled you but I am forced to do it and I can do it with less hesitation because I am sure that the *M.P.* has definitely turned the corner. I may add that my wife's income is reduced by one quarter owing to the fact that several concerns, in which she has had money invested, have paid no dividends during the war.

242
Lady Bathurst to H. A. Gwynne, 18 July 1918

Your letter did not surprise me – because I knew that when we lately raised Mr Peacock's salary, it would be the signal for higher salaries throughout the staff. Formerly the Editor and Manager received the same – now Mr Peacock has 2000gs – & you have £2600. I will make this up to £3000. More, I cannot possibly do. Both you & Mr Peacock talk much of the wonderful things the paper will do in the future. I prefer facts. My father had an income of £40,000 a year. I have never had more than £20,000, not a very large profit for the owner of a business which brings in £200,000 a year. During the first years of the war I received nothing, & though a few thousands of what has been owing to me for these years have been paid in, lately, it all goes to pay for the house which is now a hospital, therefore it is of no benefit to me. This, however, is not the point. The point is this, that I cannot believe that *you*, like the Government, think that the only class to suffer by the war & to pay for it should be proprietors & landowners. If you lose half your income, so do we & with the most rigid economy, we can hardly meet our present liabilities and I do not like to think of next year. Moreover we have the worry of struggling to keep a large house and priceless heirlooms from deterioration and decay, not to speak of a large estate & farm in decent cultivation and repair, while man after man, even the old and decrepit is taken from us, & we have fresh demands to meet and fresh difficulties to face at every moment. I imagine that you see that if we are to suffer loss to the very great extent that we have done, it is only right that you should have your share of the war burden also. At all events, as I have already explained before, I do not intend to sell the *Morning Post*, but neither do I intend to bear all the worry & anxiety and trouble it gives me & the countless letters it entails in order to run it entirely for the benefit of the Staff. If after the war, I receive an income of at least £20,000 a year from the paper, we will see – but in the meantime I can do no more – I think you forget also, that while you have to pay income tax on money which you are free to spend, Lord Bathurst & I have to pay income tax on money which goes almost entirely to other people. . . .

243
H. A. Gwynne to Lady Bathurst, 25 July 1918

I have written to you officially about the Fashion Column and I have tried to show you that we are risking our position by making the drastic changes you desire. Please do not think that I am an obstructionist. I accept, with very great regret, your instructions because I honestly think they will ruin the column and do infinite harm to the paper. May I put forward for your consideration my suggestions? I have given much thought to that beastly column (which, all the same, is one of the chief sinews of the paper) and I have come to certain conclusions which at least are worthy of your consideration. In the first place, let us get down to first principles. The whole column, with the exception of the Court Circular, is a tribute we have paid to British snobbism. It is nothing else. You are not a snob, neither am I, and the column offends us both, because we are not. If you abandon the idea of being snobbish, well and good, but remember that we abandon at the same time a large revenue and, what is even more important, our position as a woman's as well as a man's paper. I think that the time may come, perhaps six or seven years hence, when we can do without any of these aids but, at present, we simply must have this column.

Now what is the attraction of the column? Let us be brutally frank. It is that people like to see their names in the same column with several Dukes, Earls and Lords. To you and to me this is a ridiculous and silly ambition but to Mrs Jones of Kensington it is worth a guinea, which she pays without a murmur, if not with joy. If we are to eliminate the Dukes, Earls and Lords, then Mrs Jones is not going to pay her guinea and the paper, at the present moment, will suffer. For, with the disappearance of Mrs Jones will go the announcements of engagements and the reputation of the *M.P.* as a purveyor of fashionable news. The question I would like to put to you is this. Do you wish the *M.P.* to cease to be the purveyor of fashionable news? If you do, well and good, I'm quite content though it will throw on us all a most terrible burden to make good without it. I am not sure we can. But if you say we ought to try, we will try and do our very best. But I should be doing my duty very ill towards you and the paper unless I warned you that we shall be taking an enormous risk.

This is my suggestion. We should follow out your latest instructions in the spirit but we should leave to Ferguson, who is in charge of the column, a large discretion. We *must* have Dukes, Earls and Lords if we are to keep our end up; he is the only man in whose discretion we should have full faith. He is steeped in the *M.P.* traditions and I have the most perfect confidence in his careful handling of all these things. You cannot make rules for a newspaper. If I give instructions, which I do fairly frequently, I always put in a clause giving whoever is in charge a large degree of discretion. My rules are broken every day and night but I judge the breaches of my regulations always on their individual merits. There are times when a man goes bang against an explicit rule and he is right. On other occasions he follows the rule and is wrong. I will admit, however, that the Fashion Column is more amenable to rules than the rest of the paper, but even here you must allow a wide margin of discretion.

I do wish you would try to see my point of view. Believe me it is not obstructive, but it is based on my knowledge and experience of the *M.P.* You will always have mistakes in the Fashion Column as you will have in other parts of the paper. But may I suggest that you should regard these mistakes as mistakes and not as breaches of regulations. I read six papers every morning and the mistakes I see in them are sometimes appalling. Barons are described as Viscounts, Viscounts as Earls with great frequency. Such mistakes seldom or never occur in the *M.P.* Fashion Column, which is far and away the most correct of all columns of this nature.

244
H. A. Gwynne to Lady Bathurst, 26 July 1918

I have purposely delayed answering – except officially – your letters to me. I wanted to try and see your point of view. First of all, with regard to salary, will you allow me to keep to my resolution? I formed a careful estimate of what I thought necessary to save me extra worry, over and above the office worry which is constant and heavy. I came to you, for to whom else should I go? You refused, so let us say no more about it.

But I have been hurt to the quick, much more than by your refusal to grant my request – by a sentence in your other letter regarding the Fashion Column. In it you say, 'I should be very much obliged if you would edit the paper more carefully and devote less of your time to seeing politicians and to all sorts of cabals and intrigues' etc., etc.

Many of my colleagues inside and outside the office have told me that the great mistake I make is to devote nearly all my time to office work. I am told by those who know my methods that I ought to see more of the outside world. I confess that their criticism always appeared to me to be worthy of consideration. But your criticism is unfair and unjust. I have never caballed or intrigued. I don't know how to. Everything I have done has been done from a sense of duty to the *M.P.* and the nation and there is nothing I have ever planned which I have not published more or less fully in the *M.P.* As for editing the paper carefully let me give you the number of hours which I spend at the office compared to other editors. I have been at pains to get them.

I spend in the *M.P.* office an average of 43 hours a week.
The Editor of *The Times* an average of 25 hours a week.
The Editor of the *Express* an average of 27 hours a week.
The Editor of the *Chronicle* an average of 20 hours a week.
The Editor of the *D. Mail* an average of 20 hours a week.
The Editor of the *D. News* an average of 18 hours a week.
Now I do not deduce from these figures that I work harder than they do. But I do pay more attention to the routine of the office than

they. But that is beside the question really. I have made up my mind to give the rest of my life work to the *M.P.* It is not work for me. It supplies an ideal which absolutely satisfies me. I go to bed thinking of the paper and rise with the same thoughts. So I feel hurt terribly hurt, that you should think I neglect my duties. I have not had a real holiday since the war began. I have never been away for more than 10 days and then only to my cottage where I have been in close and constant touch with the office.

As for 'colloguing' with politicians, have you not realised that they won't speak to me? For we have been frank about their absolute failure and have forfeited their friendship.

245
H. A. Gwynne to General Sir Henry Wilson, 20 August 1918 (HAG/35 no. 33, IWM)

There have been many points of difference between us, about which it serves no good purpose to talk or write. But I know the politician much better than you do, and I believe he'll try and have your blood unless you obey him. Now you are a soldier of long experience, and on all great questions of strategy your answer to the enquiring politician must be exactly the same as all other soldiers with your experience and training. I see in various forms and in various quarters the beginning of an agitation for some more side-shows. To these, I know your whole general staff study and knowledge will put you in to resolute opposition. I only want to tell you that when the moment comes to defend the sane and sound strategy of experienced soldiers, I am at the disposal of the C.I.G.S. whether he be Robertson or Wilson.

Always bear in mind that the War Cabinet does not possess the War mind, that they are bitten and thoroughly inoculated by the bacillus strategicus and are suffering from the consequences, military dementia.

246
General Sir Henry Wilson to H. A. Gwynne, 23 August 1918 (HAG/35 no. 34, IWM)

Read your *MP* of January: February: March & April on the dire consequences which were to flow from the removal of Robertson and his replacement by a poor tool and amateur strategist like Wilson, then take your maps whether of France or Italy, N. Russia or Persia, Albania or Palestine and after doing both these things write and tell me you were not absolutely correct in all your gloomy anticipations.

And having done all these things, then come and breakfast one morning.

The politician is welcome to my blood – he must be a thirsty creature – but my position is absolutely unassailable. I have three times resigned appointments during this war and three times gone on half-pay. I shall resign again whenever I think it is in the public interest to do so and I shall do it without hesitation and without regret, but until I do so I shall write, say and advise exactly what *I* think it right to say and advise and this may frequently not agree with some strategists, some writers, some advisers.

Now come and breakfast.

247
H. A. Gwynne to General Sir Henry Wilson, 5 September 1918 (HAG/35 no. 5, IWM)

I have just come back from France to find your letter. I did not want to go back on ancient history. I don't now. All I want you to know is that I am always for the soldier against the politician, for I am quite sure that the war can only be won by soldiers and never by politicians. Things are rosy now and the silly War Cabinet is yelling 'Victory', but you know and I know that there's a long, long and weary road in front of us.

Of course I'll come to breakfast any morning next week after Tuesday.

P.S.   Many congratulations on your promotion.[1]

1. Wilson had been gazetted a full general on 4 September.

248
H. A. Gwynne to Lady Bathurst, 5 September 1918

. . . It is not Hughes, the man, that we are supporting, but Hughes's policy, which is to make us secure in our homes, and so prevent a revolution. Make no mistake about it, the police strike[1] is the ugliest indication of worse things to come than we have yet experienced during the war.

I am not, as you know, an alarmist, and I have a very strong faith in the commonsense of the people. I don't believe in their wisdom, but I don't think they are easily rushed into dangerous stupidities, and worse, such as the police strike. Here you have one of the finest disciplined forces in England suddenly striking and leaving London utterly unprotected. But not only that. The Special Constables, who tried to the best of their ability to do the work of the police were, in many cases, set upon and hustled, and indeed in one or two particular cases were knocked about by the Regular police. In one instance some American soldiers came to the rescue and laid out the policemen.

I have heard something of the inside history of this. It appears that Sir Edward Henry[2] was quite aware of the undoubted grievances under which the police were suffering, and he has been doing his best to get the Home Office to grant the concessions which he thought they were justified in having. The advantage of this course would have been that he would have forestalled a good many grievances and would have removed the sense of injustice. But the Home Office delayed and delayed and kept putting matters off until the strike came. Then the Government, as usual, dismissed the man who did right, in order to cover the tracks of the politician. The man to blame is Cave. But he goes on his way rejoicing, while poor Henry is kicked out, more or less in disgrace, although he is given a baronetcy. Now this strike was worked up by the Bolshevik section of the Trade Unions. Today they are trying the same thing with the firemen of London – tomorrow they may try it with the railway people. I think there must be German money behind them, and if there is not, they are playing the German game most effectively. I have taken some trouble to look into their programme. Roughly speaking, their theory is that the social order, that has grown up for centuries, is all wrong, that it started wrong and therefore cannot be right. They believe that the only way out of what they consider the present impossible position is by overturning all the institutions of this country, political, industrial, social, and out of the chaos creating a new and a better world. They are therefore anxious, in order to effect their revolution, to suborn and weaken all the pillars of society, such as the police, soldiers, and the workers in such essential enterprises as railways. They are not numerous. But they are enthusiastic. And, as history teaches us, a great war like this breeds revolutionary ideas. There is a distinct danger that they may effect their object, to a certain degree at any rate.

Now the only cure for this is that luckily men of the Clynes[3] stamp, of the Roberts,[4] Thorne,[5] Havelock Wilson,[6] and even the Henderson[7] type, are dead against this sort of propaganda, and are fighting it with all their might, and with success, I am glad to say.

Therefore it seems to me that we can always join forces with those who wish to retain, against those who wish to break up, the present social system.

It is no use arguing now. The mistake we made was in 1832 when we gave the people the vote, and in 1917 when we gave everybody the vote. As Robert Lowe used to say, we have now got to educate our masters.

Unfortunately the Press of this country is all tied to one Party or another, or to one personality or another, and we really stand alone in protesting against dishonesty and stupidity, whether it comes from those with whom we have worked in the past, or from those who have been opposed to us. Really the only salvation I can see is in a National party. But a truly National party, composed of every political opinion. Page Croft is not a big enough man to lead it unfortunately, and we shall have to prop him up with strong and better men. But salvation does seem to me only to lie in the direction of a National party, which will not stoop to catch votes, but which will rally round it the best in every class. If I were fifteen years younger, there is nothing better I should like than to devote the rest of my life to such a task as the creation and consolidation of such a party. But it must be left to younger men. I think perhaps when the soldiers come home, we shall find ample material. In the meanwhile, however, time is pressing, and we may find ourselves engaged in a fight before we are ready.

Now about my visit to France.

I had the busiest time I have ever had in my life, covering on an average 120 miles a day in a motor car. I went down and saw the French and went up the line and saw our British fellows. . . .

Foch and I had a very interesting conversation. He shook his finger at me, and called me 'Méchant,' and told me I was against a generalissimo. I told him that was a mistake. I was against Versailles. Whereupon he told me that Versailles was the most ridiculous thing ever invented. He then asked me what was my difficulty in not wholly advocating a generalissimo in December last. I told him I was not quite sure who would be generalissimo – whether it would be Pétain or him, and I thought that the choice of either might be disastrous in the way of creating two schools in the French Army. But I added that I was delighted that he was chosen, and I was glad to think that Pétain took it so well. He replied that Pétain and he worked admirably together, and this I know to be true.

But then he told me a still more astonishing thing, which I confirmed afterwards in a talk with Douglas Haig. He said: 'Do you know who proposed a generalissimo? and who proposed *me* as generalissimo?' I said: 'Henry Wilson.' He said: 'No, Douglas Haig.'

Talking this over with Haig, he said it was quite true, he had all along been in favour of a generalissimo, but that Lloyd George had been opposed to it, and would insist upon the Versailles Council, which Haig with Pétain described as the biggest mistake that had ever been made.

I don't think Foch has any admiration for Lloyd George. He told me that he did not believe much in the political direction of armed forces, and he recounted to me a characteristic anecdote of Clemenceau. When he [Foch] had made all his plans for a counter-offensive, he went to Clemenceau, and said: 'Monsieur le Président du Conseil, these are my plans, and I would like you to give me some time in order that I should explain them to you.' Clemenceau answered: 'I don't want to see your plans, I only want you to beat the Boche. And you can only beat him in your way, not in mine.' I told this story to Douglas Haig, who sighed, and said he wished he had the same sort of master.

Foch of course is a generalissimo in the sense that he has to approve of all projects of attacks or offensives. But he does not himself always suggest them, and Haig should have the full credit for all the attacks we have made in the Somme region and north of the Somme, in fact Foch paid a most handsome compliment to Haig over this.

Pershing,[8] the American, however is a difficulty. When Haig started this offensive he had ten American divisions of fifteen thousand bayonets each, and felt quite competent to undertake an offensive which would last perhaps six weeks or two months. Suddenly Pershing determined to form an American national army and make an attack, and for this purpose he withdrew eight of the ten divisions and ordered them down to where he was forming his new army. Douglas Haig told me how hard this was on him, in fact it might have put out the whole of the offensive, and that he spoke to Pershing as he had never spoken to one of his own Generals, telling him it was nothing less and nothing short of a shame to withdraw these divisions. But he appealed in vain for Pershing was determined. He then appealed to Foch and Foch went over and saw Pershing and begged him not to take his divisions away. He also was unable to change Pershing's plans. Foch, in describing the incident to me, said that Pershing was absolutely determined to form his national army and to make a national attack. 'And,' he added, in his inimitable French, 'there will also be, I am afraid, a little American national disaster.' For Foch realises, as indeed does Douglas Haig, that the Americans are not yet fit in their higher commands, such as brigadier-generals, divisional-generals and corps commanders, to work out a big offensive.

Altogether I had a most strenuous time, but a most delightful one, for all the soldiers were so grateful for all the *Morning Post* had done, and I came away thinking the Englishman, when properly led, to be the finest soldier in the world.

I came back to find the police strike just over, and on reading the account I could not help comparing the police with those gallant fellows out there who go into action with cheeriness and pluck and the embodiment of the right spirit. . . .

1. This broke out on 30 August. (See G. W. Reynolds and A. Judge, *The Night the Police went on Strike*, London, 1968.)
2. Commissioner of the Metropolitan Police.
3. J. R. Clynes, Parliamentary Secretary to the Ministry of Food, July 1917–July 1918.
4. G. Roberts, Minister of Labour, August 1917–January 1919.
5. W. Thorne, Labour MP.
6. Leader, National Union of Seamen.
7. A. Henderson, member of the War Cabinet, December 1916–August 1917.
8. General J. J. Pershing, Commander in Chief American Expeditionary Forces in Europe, June 1917–September 1919.

249
H. A. Gwynne to Viscount Esher, 11 September 1918 (Esher Papers 5/55)

Many thanks for your letter of the 9th.

You guess right. The article about the W[ar] O[ffice][1] was written with an intention.

I have heard of course of the scheme,[2] and I am quite sure that your explanation is the right one, for at the bottom of it all is a desire to get Winston back at the Admiralty. I cannot imagine what flea has bitten Lloyd George, for although I have very little faith in public opinion these days, yet I cannot believe that it would stand the appointment of Winston. But there are wheels within wheels, which I don't pretend to understand. At the back of it all is some mysterious design – possibly against the Throne – and certainly for the perpetuation of the present régime – to stay in office with the present lot, to spare no effort and to stick at nothing. I don't like the situation at all.

1. Leader of 11 September in the *Morning Post*, entitled 'Beginning of the End' – a panegyric on Haig, deploring the failure of the Government to recognize his achievement.
2. To transfer Sir E. Geddes, First Lord of the Admiralty July 1917–January 1919, to the War Office.

H. A. Gwynne to Lady Bathurst, 11 September 1918

. . . I am sorry that you do not like the maps because our Circulation man tells us that whenever we publish a good map there is always a great demand for the paper, and we find ourselves in competition with *The Times*, which has remarkably good maps with very much detail. Of course I think everybody has got a personal predilection in the way of maps, and the simple one, that you like, is not, I think, one that is altogether popular. Of course we have to cater for all tastes. What I find is that there is an increasing number of people who take a meticulous interest in all operations, and they are not content with being told that a village is ten or eleven miles east of Amiens, but they want to see the name of the village and the contours round it, so that they themselves may form a judgement as to the difficulties of the operations. But I do agree with you that a general map, now and then, of which we have given several lately of the position as far as the Hindenburg line[1] is concerned, is very useful.

As regards Repington. I did speak to Haig about him, and Haig has always had a very high opinion of him. You must remember that the *Morning Post* has always taken as its policy to stand up for the soldier and the sailor in carrying out military and naval operations, just the same as we would stand up for cobblers, if it were a test of shoe-making between us and Germany; they are the only people who have been invariably right, and, indeed, they are the only people capable of bringing us victory.

If you read, as I do, all the other papers, you will find that there is a conspiracy among the Lloyd-Georgites and his myrmidon Press to give no credit whatever to the soldier, the idea being of course that the man who brings us the victory will be the popular hero hereafter, as indeed he should be.

I daresay you saw an article the other day in the *Morning Post* about the War Office. It was suggested by the fact that I was told that the latest scheme of Lloyd George is to put Geddes in at the War Office, under Milner, as a sort of civilian director of staff of administration, leaving only General Cowans in charge of the Supply and Transport. The idea is, or was, to put Winston Churchill back into the Admiralty. Of course as Lord Esher says, we cannot help beating the Boche except for our own folly. But if this scheme is persisted in, I really do think there is a possibility, even at this moment when victory seems within our grasp, of it eluding us.

It is a constant struggle to stand up for the soldier against the civilian, and in this respect Repington undoubtedly has the confidence of the soldier.

I agree with you that one of the advantages of Foch is that Lloyd George cannot get rid of him, and that is why Lloyd George, I take it, has always been against a generalissimo.

In this matter I think you are hardly fair to the *Morning Post*. For while we fought with all the strength that we could put into the fight against the Versailles Conference, which was called 'unity of command,' we never objected to a generalissimo, in fact, we pointed out more than once, I remember quite well, that what Lloyd George had in his mind, though he did not know it, was a generalissimo, and to this we never made any objection. I did see, however, at the time, that owing to Pétain's great ability, and his outstanding service in dealing with the French Army last year, the appointment of Foch might create dissension in the French Army. I think Haig himself would have preferred Pétain, but it was not for us to suggest whom the French should nominate as their generalissimo, and I think they have undoubtedly nominated the right man. But what we fought against was the Versailles Conference, which Foch himself described as the most ridiculous farce ever invented. Haig, when Foch's appointment was made at Doullens, on driving back with Milner, said to him the moment they were alone: 'Thank God I have got to deal with a man, and not with a Committee.'

We have been amply justified in our position [*sic*] to the Versailles Conference, by the fact that it is now condemned by everybody.

As regards Cave. I think you will find that we are hardly to blame about that.

In our first leader on the strike, we examined the cause of the trouble, and showed that Churchill's grant of a 12½% bonus[2] was the cause of nearly all our social troubles, and we went on to say that it was no time to compromise with such defiance as the police showed, and that if Sir Edward Henry could not restore discipline, he must give way to somebody who could. All the criticism made was in these terms: 'It is unpardonable that official obduracy and neglect should have allowed such a dangerous situation to develop, but since it has developed there is only one course possible.' etc., etc.

In the second article on the subject we pointed out that it looked as though Sir Edward Henry were being made a scapegoat, but, at the same time, we justly, I think, asked who was responsible – if not Sir Edward Henry, then Sir George Cave. After all, I think we were justified in asking whose was the responsibility for a state of affairs which, to my mind, was the worst sign that we have had since the war broke out.

Now, on top of that, came a circular from Cave, which I send you and which please return, in which he gave his explanation.

Almost immediately after that we received a notice from the Press Bureau saying that we were not to publish it. I send you both documents.

Apparently the Prime Minister forbade him to defend himself. And so the matter rests.

I have had a letter from Lady Cave, written without her husband's knowledge, in which she says that he had resigned but that the Prime Minister would not hear of his resignation. He is now in the position, according to her, of having to wait four weeks till Parliament sits before he can put forward his version. My answer to that will be that he can always resign.

I think Cave is an honest, straightforward man, and certainly he is not unpopular with the House of Commons. His name was suggested to me by Carson as being a man who might make an alternative to Lloyd George, and I still think that if the Unionist Party had any sort of pluck, they would have deposed Bonar Law, who is now a Lloyd-Georgite, pure and simple, in favour of a man of independent thought, who was at any rate a Unionist.

1. The line of prepared defences to which the Germans retired after 8 August.
2. The 12½% solution was a War Cabinet compromise of 13 October 1917 on proposals from Churchill for wage increases of 10–15% for engineering workers. The 12½% increase applied to moulders, tool-room, supervising and maintenance workers.

251
J. T. Davies to H. A. Gwynne, 16 September 1918
(MS Gwynne 20)

The First Lord of the Admiralty has passed on to me your Acting Editor's letter regarding the omission to invite you to attend a meeting of London Editors at 10 Downing Street yesterday, and as I was responsible for summoning the conference I hasten to offer you the following explanation:

The P.M. instructed me by telegraph from Manchester yesterday afternoon to call together as many Newspaper Editors as I could possibly find in the time to meet Sir Eric Geddes to hear from him certain information which the P.M. wished to give to the Press regarding the proposals of the Austrian Government. I very much regret that in my great hurry, and owing to the difficulty of getting replies from newspaper offices on a Sunday afternoon, I overlooked the *Morning Post* and I can only ask you to accept my very sincere apologies, together with an assurance that there was no intention to exclude such an important paper as the *Morning Post* from the Conference . . .

252
H. A. Gwynne to J. T. Davies, 17 September 1918
(MS Gwynne 20)

I am much obliged to you for your letter and must accept your explanation that in the short time at your disposal you overlooked the *Morning Post*. But you also overlooked the *Daily Chronicle* and the *Daily News*, and it was these omissions, in addition to the omission of the *Morning Post*, which led me to think that possibly there was a definite policy in the treatment of these three papers.

253
H. A. Gwynne to Lady Bathurst, 25 September 1918

. . . I will first answer your letter about the police. . . . I have seen several high officials of the police force, and they have expressed to me their conviction that the only paper that understands the situation is the *Morning Post*. The truth is that the police business was nothing more than a Bolshevik conspiracy. As indeed is the present railway strike. There are in this country about fifty thousand people – no more I think – counting everybody, who are determined in the turmoil of this war to destroy the present social fabric, and to erect, out of the ruins, some sort of an edifice after their own hearts. They are numerically very weak, as I have said. In activity they are very strong. Personally, in spite both of what the Intelligence people and the police tell me, I believe that there is German money behind them. The Government have ignored the warnings about these people with wicked persistence – with a persistence indeed which at one time led me to believe that they were not sorry to see the Bolsheviks working as they have done. I have now come to the conclusion that it was sheer stupidity. And, between ourselves, we have exceptional means of knowing what is going on in these Bolshevik circles. I cannot tell you more in a letter. But when I see you I will explain how and why this is. But we happen to be in a position, by good luck and a little management, to know exactly the plans of these people. Up to the present we have been able to warn various Government departments when these things were coming off. The police strike was the one

309

thing of which we had only a slight inkling. We however knew of the Coventry strike,[1] the Clyde strikes[2] and the railway strike.[3] We know the people who are working them – most of them of military age – and the Government takes no heed of our warnings or of the warnings of their agents.

It is no good reasoning with these people, because they are not reasonable. They are out for pillage. And I am sorry to say they have succeeded in seducing the police – at any rate for a time – and also the Guards, at least the Guards in England. All this is very serious. But their numbers are so few, and their activities so well known, that the Government have only got to make a stand, and I think that they would disappear.

Personally I would take away the exemption from every one of them, and send all those who are of age into the trenches.

The situation is really not dangerous provided the Government are firm.

But Lloyd George is a man who has given so many pledges in the shape of corruption to so many people, that I doubt whether he can afford to be strong. For example, I have no doubt in my own mind that Ramsay MacDonald, who is in a way – and in a very clever and subtle way – the leader of these Bolsheviks, has a hold over Lloyd George in regard to the Marconi case, which he dare not repudiate. That is the worst of having a Prime Minister whose past binds his hands for the present.

As regards the military situation. Of course, I, with you, rejoice with all my heart at the brilliant victory we have had in Palestine. But I still think that I have never been more justified in my own mind than I am today that our duty was to defend Egypt, and not to make an offensive in Palestine. Take the present situation. We have won a great victory. We have captured or killed probably thirty or forty thousand Turks, but only about five or six hundred Germans. We have lost probably four or five thousand men, and we have to send four or five thousand men out of England to make good these losses. We have inflicted a great blow on Turkey. But we have not, in my opinion, shortened the war by a single day. Germany is very glad to withdraw her commitments abroad, and I go further and say that if Turkey came out of the war now, it would not shorten the war by a single week. The whole of German activities are now turned towards Russia and in defending herself in the West. And I really think she would be glad to get out of her commitments both in Bulgaria and in Turkey. We could take Jerusalem on the Western Front, like we could take everything else. And it is on the Western Front that I still think we ought to concentrate. Now of course we have ventured so far we have got to hold what we have taken, and I do not grudge the men for that, though I still think that it was a military mistake.

As for Turkey coming out, you must remember I did my very best a year ago in this way, though not in the paper. We did enter into negotiations with the Turks, and I gave you a resumé of these negotiations. But, later on, we found that they were not intended to be serious, but only intended to persuade us to stay our hand in Macedonia and Palestine. Of course in this kind of procrastination the Turk is a past master. Whether he will come out or not I do not know. But we must bear in mind that Enver[4] and Talaat[5] are absolutely in the hands of the Germans, and they will only do what Germany dictates. I think that the more disasters we inflict on the Turks the more they will cling to their master, the Kaiser. And for obvious reasons. For they can expect nothing from their own countrymen, if they fail, and very little from us, and their only hope is that in case of disaster to their arms, the German Empire will be able to throw over them the cloak of their protection. . . .

1. 23 July 1918.
2. There had been a series of labour disputes in this region from March 1916 to August 1917.
3. This began in South Wales on 23 September.
4. Enver Pasha, Turkish Minister of War.
5. Talaat Pasha, Grand Vizier of Turkey, 1917–18.

254
H. A. Gwynne to Lady Bathurst, 1 October 1918

. . . As regards the Bolsheviks. I am determined to show up all I know of their ramifications, and I am working hard at it now. It is pure German – at any rate in the strategy of the thing. How the money gets into the country I don't know. But that there is money, and large sums of money coming, is very evident. The Quakers are strong supporters of all Pacifist ideals, and as Pacifism and Bolshevism are rather mixed up, it may be that some of the money that is subscribed for the Pacifist cause goes into the Bolshevik money chests. But even this assumption does not account for the large sums of money that are being spent.

I met last night at dinner the General who was in charge of the troops sent to South Wales. He said his boys, as he called them – he had a brigade of soldiers – were dying to get at the strikers, and although the Bolsheviks made some attempts to get at them in the public houses, they all reported the conversations to their officers, and asked whether it would not be possible, under the law, to seize them and bring them before a court-martial, which is all very good hearing. . . .

255
H. A. Gwynne to Viscount Esher, 7 October 1918
(Esher Papers 5/55)

Thank you so much for your most excellent letter, which I shall be proud to publish, and would not send back for anything in the world.[1]

The Germans have been quite clever in their latest move.[2] The appeal to Wilson is of course intended to divide the Allies, and I would not go so far as to despise the possibility of danger in this direction, for it must be borne in mind that victory is as fissiparous in its tendencies as defeat, and sometimes even more so. The whole thing depends upon Wilson. If he is going to take up the attitude of a world Dictator, then we shall have undoubted trouble, but if he keeps by his last declaration more or less, I think we shall be able to get the German to put his hands up, shut his eyes and open his mouth and see what we will give him. That is really the only way out.

1. Published over Esher's name in the *Morning Post* on 9 October, entitled 'The Meaning of Patriotism'.
2. Late on 3 October the German Government telegraphed the President of the United States, accepting his Fourteen Points and requesting 'an armistice on land and sea and in the air'.

256
H. A. Gwynne to Lady Bathurst, 16 October 1918

. . . Things have been fairly humming lately and it has taken me all my time to study the epistles of the learned and verbose President Wilson to see whether he means what he says or says what he means. Now if Clemenceau spoke, we could follow him blind for he knows his own mind, and the mind of his nation, but I am hanged if he [*sic*] can quite see what Wilson is up to.

Now about Repington. Will you let me put before you my considered opinion as to his value to the paper. That is the only way which both of us should look upon any of the staff. Is he worth while? That is the main question and I should say he is. Although as you rightly say, we have most excellent reports from our correspondents of the fighting at the front, yet even the soldier who is out there and is seeing the actual fighting, as well as the people at home, want to have a survey of the whole field and this, I am convinced, Repington does better than any living military writer. We are up against severe competition and a military correspondent is essential, especially for a newspaper like the *M.P.* I think I have secured the best.

You say that he is inconsistent in admitting that the regiments are up to strength and that last spring he bitterly complained about the lack of reserves. But in that he was right. Last spring there were no reserves and last winter Haig had to reduce his battalions in a brigade from 4 to 3. But when the disaster came which we always predicted would come and it found our reserves lacking, Lloyd George in a panic conscripted England Scotland and Wales up to 51 years of age, combed out the miners, and so produced reserves but too late to prevent the disaster of March. As for his praising Churchill for his provision of munitions, he only stated what was true. I loathe and distrust Churchill but after the great loss in guns and ammunition of March last, he made a prodigious effort and within 6 weeks all the losses were made good and a bit over. I really thought that I was obeying your instructions in giving praise where praise was due even in a case of a man who has blundered in other things. I feel sure that our readers will not think that our judgement is bad if we praise Churchill for meeting the munition crisis of March and blame him for his wicked senseless blunders in regard to Labour. Of course, the matter lies in your hands but I do assure you that in my opinion we should lose a valuable asset in Repington. The publishing people tell me that when he joined us, the circulation gave a bump upwards. Indeed it was the start of our good and increasing sales.

We had two leaders the day you mention because I was anxious to press two ideas upon our readers on such an important topic as peace terms. In the first I was anxious to make the point of the necessity for breaking Germany in the field and led up to Kitchener's remark to me.[1] In the second, I wished to emphasise the meaning of Wilson's speeches on the lines of absolute surrender.[2] In ordinary times, I would never have two leaders about such similar subjects but in this momentous crisis precedents and ordinary rules can be broken. . . .

1. On 14 October, in the *Morning Post*'s first leading article, Gwynne had quoted Kitchener as saying: 'Germany must be made to surrender *in the field*. In the field she has won all her triumphs. In the field she must be made to experience failure.'

2. The second leading article ended: 'To make terms with the Germans now would not only be to cheat our Armies of victory but our children of security.'

H. A. Gwynne to Lord Bathurst, 2 November 1918

Lady Bathurst has agreed to my request for an increase in my salary of £400 a year to date from Oct. 1917 but she wants to know a little more of the nature of the entertainment and outside charges, incurred only on behalf of the *M.P.* I am afraid she thinks I want to run in the office for large dinners *à la* Northcliffe and Lord Burnham.[1] There is nothing of this kind under the heading of 'entertainment allowances' as I understand them. You must bear in mind that for the outside world I am the only representative of the *M.P.* in London. You and Lady Bathurst, the proprietors, live in the country – and quite right too, if I may say so. But I do not think you have any idea what representation of the *M.P.* means. Not a week passes without my receiving one or two letters of introduction from influential people abroad, asking me to do what I can for Mr So and So, who is coming to England. From nearly all of these I obtain valuable information. Their introducers are our own correspondents, Prime Ministers of Dominions, Ambassadors and Ministers. To all of them I have to show courtesy and hospitality not, of course, as H. A. Gwynne but as Editor of the *M.P.* Then again, I have to keep myself *au courant* with all that is going on behind the scenes and I cannot ask a General or an Admiral to come and see me at the office. Indeed they would not come. So I have to invite them to lunch or dinner, because it is the only time they and I are free. I am afraid that Lady Bathurst thinks that I give dinners in order to persuade people to see things from our point of view. That is quite erroneous. I do all the propaganda I can on my own and I should never think of asking the *M.P.* to pay the expenses of an entertainment of that nature. That I would do with enthusiasm but never at the expense of the *M.P.*

I think I could best give you an idea of what I mean by entertaining which should fairly be charged to the *M.P.* by telling you what I have done in this way during the last fortnight – which is within my recollection. Last Monday week I gave Admiral Lambert, late 4th Sea Lord and Commander in Chief of the Aegean fleet, dinner. He came back from the Mediterranean and very kindly said he would like to have a talk with me. I could not ask him to come and see me, I could not find time to go and see him at his hotel, so I asked him to dinner and from him got news and views which were extremely valuable to the *M.P.* On the Tuesday I gave lunch to an American Senator who came with a letter of introduction to me from Washington. On Thursday of the same week I asked the Duke of Northumberland to lunch with me in order that I should know what is going on in Turkey, Austria and Germany. On Friday I gave dinner to a Romanian Deputy introduced to me by M. Take Ionescu. On Sunday I had M. de Fleuriau of the French Embassy to lunch to hear what the French had to say about the negotiations. On Monday I had M. de Brysson to the same meal. He is here to try and get machinery for the French to replace what has been destroyed by the Germans. On Wed. I had to dinner one of Sir D. Haig's staff and from him I got all his chief's views – most valuable. On Thursday night I gave dinner to Mr Baldston, who came to me with a letter of introduction from Washington. He is Pres. Wilson's private representative in England and he told me he was telegraphing the gist of my conversation to the President. Yesterday I had to lunch Donald,[2] who has left *The Chronicle*. I wanted to get from him some tips for the *M.P.* Now, none of these was a political meal. They were simply the only means by which I could talk to men to whom it was my business as Editor of the *M.P.* to talk. And this must go on if the *M.P.* is to remain a first-class paper.

These occasions bore a great hole in my pocket but I assure you that they are a very essential part of an Editor's business. The question you have to consider is whether they are of value to the paper. If you think they are not, then I will drop them but I think that no Editor in these days of fierce competition can do his work by only seeing people who will come to his office.

This is a part, though the most expensive part, of my extra-editorial work. Apart from those functions, I live a life of the very closest economy. Twice within the last ten days I have walked home after a terribly long day because my work has kept me beyond the hour of the last tube. I simply could not afford a taxi and a four mile walk at the end of a hard day's work is not the best way of expending my energy for the *M.P.* I have given up long ago all my clubs except the Bath but I keep on the Carlton simply because I think it my duty as Editor of the *M.P.* for there I get a great deal of news. Every morning I read six papers for which I pay out of my own pocket, for without knowing what other papers are doing I cannot do my work. But, of course, were I not Editor, I would not read more than one.

I wish I could persuade you to realise that I don't care a hang for money. My sole ambition in that way is to live decently and not extravagantly, to do my work for the *M.P.* efficiently and to be able to put on one side £500 a year for old age. But that I have never been able to do.

I only want you to look upon this thing from a business point of view. It would pay you, as proprietor of the *M.P.*, to relieve me, within reason, of every worry except the worry of the *M.P.* Then the

paper would get the whole of my energy, brain and devotion. . . .
Please excuse this long letter . . . but only a long explanation can
give you a fair idea of the nature and scope and complexity of my
work.

1. Proprietor of the *Daily Telegraph*.
2. Robert Donald, editor of the *Daily Chronicle*, 1902–18; Director of Propaganda in neutral countries, February–June 1918. The *Daily Chronicle* had a circulation of about 800,000 at this time. Donald had acquired General Maurice as military correspondent in May 1918, following the latter's dismissal as DMO. Both Maurice and Donald were dismissed from the paper when it was acquired by the Prime Minister in October. The purchase of this paper was something that Lloyd George had been interested in since early 1917. (See J. M. McEwen, 'Lloyd George's Acquisition of the *Daily Chronicle* in 1918', pp. 127–44.)

258
H. A. Gwynne to Lady Bathurst, 9 November 1918

. . . I owe you a full apology for a direct contravention not only of
your instructions but of my own ideas. The phrase 'our beloved
Prime Minister' ought not to have appeared.[1]

. . . I believe that there are not two people in England more in
agreement on the great principles of domestic and external policy
than you and I. . . . My conception of an editor's duty is that he
should carry out faithfully the policy of his proprietor. But he cannot
carry out *faithfully* such a policy unless he is in general agreement
with his proprietor. Otherwise he cannot put his soul into his work. I
think you know me well enough to realise that if I found myself
opposed to you in a matter of our essential policy, I simply could not
advocate it and would at once ask to be relieved. For no man can say
'yea' and 'nay' to the same thing. And the chief pleasure and delight
I have had in my work lie in the fact that I have always considered
that you and I are, more than any two people I can think of, in entire
agreement on the main points. Lesser things don't count. With you
to stand by me in this great national crisis, I feel that I can do great
things. But take away your confidence and I am worth nothing on
the *M.P.*

1. Some idea of how Lady Bathurst felt on the subject of the Prime Minister
may be obtained from the following lines, penned in one of her notebooks:

> Lloyd George when he goes to his ultimate end
> Will descend in a fiery chariot
> And sit in state on a red hot plate
> Quite close to Judas Iscariot.

Ananias will say to the Devil that day
My claim for precedency fails
So move me up higher, away from the fire
And make room for this liar from Wales.

259
H. A. Gwynne to Viscount Esher, 11 November 1918
(Esher Papers 5/55)

. . . [Northcliffe's] inordinate vanity, and the fact that he has a hold of some kind over Lloyd George, makes him doubly dangerous.

I have recently been reading some Bolshevik literature and surreptitious secret documents that are propagated throughout England, and, curiously enough, I find myself in general agreement with them, though not with the arguments deduced. The whole of the burden of their song is that England is corrupt, that the Government is corrupt, that Northcliffe is the real Prime Minister, and so on and so forth. They are just going along the right lines to create a revolution. The last man to stop a revolutionary feeling in this country is Lloyd George, for the simple reason that the Bolsheviks look upon him as the most corrupt man in the country, and corruption is what they are fighting against more than anything else.

I am just waiting for the rejoicings to pass over before I speak out, which I must.

260
H. A. Gwynne to Lord Stamfordham, 30 December 1918
(RA Geo V., Q859/2)

I was greatly surprised in reading the list of guests invited to Buckingham Palace to meet Mr Wilson, to notice that journalism was recognised in the persons of Lord Northcliffe, Lord Burnham and Mr J. A. Spender.[1] I do not understand on what principle the invitations were issued. If it was intended simply to pay a compliment to journalism, I could understand an invitation being issued to a member of the profession, a proprietor or editor who would be acknowledged to represent journalism officially throughout the Kingdom. But this plan was not adopted and the three gentlemen I have named were, by their appearance at the banquet, made to appear to represent London journalism. Lord Northcliffe is the proprietor of many newspapers of large circulation. He also aspires

317

to high political office, and, in his game of politics, the King would always be merely a pawn to be set up or knocked down exactly as it suited his purpose. Lord Burnham is an amiable and charming man, but, apart from the fact that he is Chairman of the Newspaper Proprietors Association, which deals entirely with the business aspect of newspapers, he cannot be said to represent journalism. Mr Spender is a journalist of repute, the editor of a London evening paper with the smallest circulation. He is, I gladly admit, a popular and highly respected man in his profession. But as long as the principle of selecting one official representative of journalism was departed from, I think I am entitled to ask why Lord and Lady Bathurst, the proprietors of the *Morning Post*, were altogether ignored. Surely the *Morning Post*'s record as a staunch and firm upholder of monarchy deserved some recognition. You will remember, perhaps, on the day of the Armistice that I telephoned to you and suggested that the King should drive out among his subjects, and I think I am not presumptuous in thinking that the suggestion bore good fruit. In this paper we have, when people listened to the silly talk of Bolshevism and began to talk of a Republic, spoken boldly and strongly for our Monarchy. We have kept His Majesty's name before his subjects throughout the war and Lord and Lady Bathurst deserve some credit for the loyalty and steadfast adherence of the paper to the Monarchy. When I see a man like Lord Northcliffe honoured by His Majesty on an occasion like that of the recent banquet, I feel I must sit down and write privately to you and tell you that I think the record of the *Morning Post*, the oldest daily newspaper in London, deserved better treatment.

1. Editor of the *Westminster Gazette*.

318

CONCLUSION:

The Rasp of War

The die-hard *Morning Post*, pre-war champion of Unionism, of Compulsory National Service, of Tariff Reform, of an unreformed House of Lords and of the British Empire, went to war under Gwynne's leadership in a healthy financial position. Its circulation, in the week in which war was declared, stood at a daily average of 86,550. It went into a war which its editor quickly perceived would be of substantial duration with every expectation of displacing *The Times* as the daily newspaper that mattered to 'the people who matter', and with every confidence that the course of the war would advance those causes of which its vision of politics consisted, and determined to play an active not a passive role.

Kipling had described Gwynne as 'a good fighter'. The war years provided more scope for his combativeness than the years of peace had done. He was not a man to keep out of harm's, or Harmsworth's, way. So far as were concerned the campaigns for the introduction of Compulsory Service, for the elimination of Lord Haldane from any Ministry, for the replacement of Asquith with a Prime Minister more obviously committed to winning the war, for a reduction in Free Trading and in laissez-faire, Gwynne and the *Morning Post* were on the winning side. So far as were concerned the campaigns for the extension of the example of Lord Kitchener into the principle that the ministerial heads of the Service Departments should be serving soldiers or sailors, for the application of Compulsory Service to Ireland, for a 'National Government', for the drawing up of and adherence to a programme of aims to be achieved by victory and maintained following the defeat of the enemy, and for the replacement of Lloyd George as Prime Minister, they were not. They were equally unsuccessful in arguing against a Unionist coalition with the Liberals, against the return of Churchill to political office, against any alteration to the terms of the Union with Ireland, against any

319

meddling with the franchise, against any deviation from the Western Front as a theatre of operations, and against any civilian interference with the autonomy of the High Command in its direction of strategy and resources.

Writing to Lady Bathurst at the end of July 1918, Lord Esher remarked that the *Morning Post* possessed 'the infinite merit of moral courage'. He went on:

> Although the country has played up so wonderfully during the past four years, it has in spite of, and not in consequence of the Leadership that has been so wanting. I believe that every one, from the King downwards, is frightened of the shadow of 'Dora' [Defence of the Realm Act].
>
> In the Napoleonic wars, men *said* what they liked. You remember Fox and Sheridan and all the Holland House gang. Well, from our point of view they were utterly unpatriotic. But Mr Pitt did not shut them down or up, and England was all the stronger because of the freedom everybody enjoyed.

Esher concluded:

> I think Gwynne a brave man, and Colvin a *most* brilliant writer. . . . But I should like them to go even further than they do in support of the principles of freedom and outspokenness and justice, whether to our friends or foes. What is wanted is the temperament of K[ing] Edward, and the insight of Disraeli.[1]

Whether Gwynne had or had not 'moral courage' depended, so far as his contemporaries were concerned, on whether or not they were in agreement with the line the *Morning Post* was taking at any given time. Others put it less kindly than Esher. Asquith, for instance, having just received from Gwynne a diatribe against Churchill's conduct of the Antwerp expedition, described him to Venetia Stanley as 'the lunatic who edits the *Morning Post*. . .'.[2] (The term 'lunatic' was frequently applied by Asquith to individuals who were not at one with him.) Similarly, Lloyd George described Gwynne as 'an ill-conditioned mind in search of mischief'.[3] This, however, was at a time when Lloyd George was being savaged by the *Morning Post* — and not only by the *Morning Post* — for disparaging the qualities of British generalship in the presence of their French opposite numbers. As for Esher, he had written in January 1918 from Paris to King George's Private Secretary:

> We seem to be approaching the brink of a crisis in the fortunes of our country. From weakness those who possess powers of resistance have

allowed the press to usurp authority that can only be compared to that of the Inquisition in the sixteenth century. The influence exercised by the press combine is unconstitutional and fatal to liberty. But no one so far has attempted to resist. In the French newspapers you can read accounts of the rise and fall of Lord K[itchener]; followed by the rise of Sir William Robertson, to be now followed by his fall compassed by the same agencies. The question is how much further rope will the nation permit to this power outside the control of the King, the Parliament and the law of the land . . . the symptoms are those of the autumn of 1870 . . . when an uncontrolled press destroyed one reputation after another and left France in the throes of a deadly conflict with a foreign enemy . . . we shall be ruined by the refusal to back our leaders when once we have chosen them. . . .[4]

The arguments used and principles deployed in this effort to get the King to intervene in the crisis over the High Command on the side of the existing CIGS, Robertson, contrasted mightily with those in the letter of July 1918 encouraging Lady Bathurst to allow Gwynne and Colvin to expand their assaults on the direction of the British war effort. There were, after all, leaders and leaders. If some newspapers could attack the political leadership, others could attack the military leadership, which was appointed by the politicians, and what was given could also be taken away, though more easily from the military by the politicians than from the latter by the former. At the level of backing military as opposed to civilian direction of the war, Esher and Gwynne were quite consistent. Esher's real complaint was not against the freedom or licence of the press as a whole, but that a particular combination of newspapers was being directed by Lloyd George against the High Command. All depended on how the war that particular individuals were waging against other individuals was going. In this war there was no such thing as objectivity, and arguments could be redirected and principles bent according to the state of play.

What Gwynne did not have was 'the temperament of King Edward and the insight of Disraeli'. Kipling had seen Gwynne 'serene and adequate' under fire (literally) in the Boer War. The Great War was a different story. In the larger conflict, Gwynne found it much more difficult 'to edit and be shot at' (metaphorically) – and to shoot (also metaphorically) – at the same time. He found it impossible to be both serene and adequate.

So far as temperament was concerned, Gwynne was never far from paranoia. Hence near the beginning of the war his professed inability to understand certain actions, 'except on the assumption that there is some treason'. Hence towards the end of the war his speculation that what he called 'undoubted tenderness towards the Germans' had some 'sinister motive'. He was himself one of those people who thought there was 'a hidden hand which protects the enemy at the cost of themselves'. For him, it was but a short step from this to accepting as genuine the *Protocols of the Elders of Zion* (that turn-of-the-century production of the Tsarist secret police, ascribing to the Jewish race a plot to take over the world), which came into his hands in 1919, and to using the journalistic resources at his disposal in an effort to persuade the public that the cause of the unrest in the world which so disturbed him had been found.[5] The remark of the essayist E. T. Raymond that the *corpus sanum* did not lodge a spirit quite in keeping with the valuable qualities of the *Morning Post* was entirely accurate, and well exemplified by that particular episode.[6]

So far as insight, or judgement, was concerned, a start may be made with Gwynne's confident prediction of the likely outcome of the contest between the *Morning Post* and *The Times*. A straight fight between the loss-making *Times* and the profitable *Morning Post* was one thing. The actual situation, in which the *Morning Post* took on the whole Northcliffe newspaper empire which was well able to go on subsidizing *The Times*, was quite another. Gwynne concealed this from himself or, at least, kept it out of his letters to Lady Bathurst. At the end of the war *The Times* had retained its pre-war circulation. The daily average of the *Morning Post* was down to 60,595. Still Gwynne remained optimistic, not appreciating for one thing the inroads that the massive casualty figures amongst British officers were to make on the future and potential readership of the *Morning Post*.[7]

This start may be followed up by the journalistic judgement that led Gwynne to dispense with the services of his military correspondent at the end of 1914 on the grounds that he 'can only write about the war or foreign affairs', all the more so as his work on the Balkan Wars in 1912 and 1913 had been enthusiastically received. The military correspondent in question happened to be Professor of Military History at the University of Oxford, and H. Spenser Wilkinson continued his distinguished career with newspapers with the *Daily Mail*.

On politics and politicians Gwynne had, as we have seen, made a bad start, falling foul of Lady Bathurst by supporting Balfour. He compounded this by adopting Austen Chamberlain as his candidate to take over the leadership of the Conservative Party from Balfour in the autumn of 1911. Bonar Law got the job. Gwynne compounded things still further by claiming to be a very great private friend of Bonar Law, whom he described as 'the acutest and most practical brain of any politician I have met, not excepting Balfour. Above all these qualities he has the one great one – conviction . . . , is scrupulously honest, fearless and a most excellent judge of men. . . .

Efficiency is his great motto.' When Lady Bathurst in her reply dubbed Bonar Law 'a cringer', Gwynne persisted: 'The man is a great big man, a born leader of men. . . .'[8] In September 1917, when the National Party was launched, the *Morning Post* was denouncing Bonar Law in the following terms:

> This defection (from the Unionist Party), of course, is a good deal the fault of Mr Bonar Law. There was not a single adventure against which Unionism stood, from Home Rule in Ireland to Home Rule in India, in which he has not acquiesced. And we do not see what he has gained for the country thereby save fresh reasons for anxiety. More-over, while this war has shown that if one reform is necessary it is a reform of our fiscal system, he has let that cause go by default, apparently in the belief that Protection would come by itself.[9]

This was not the only example of Lady Bathurst's judgement being better than that of her editor. To the latter the invalid Carson was yet another 'great big strong man', who in the next sentence was 'too old' for the job Gwynne had in mind. (This example is not entirely countered by the fact that Gwynne's judgement of Lord Derby, as a possible substitute for Carson in this regard, was better than that of his proprietor, for Gwynne proceeded to defer to her and allow himself to try to make what he regarded as a mistake – 'to place in [Derby's] hands the destiny of the nation'.) Again, in 1911 Gwynne had described Walter Long as 'a good honest fellow without a great superabundance of brains and weak as water – also not too strong on Tariff Reform'.[10] This, however, did not prevent Gwynne expecting great things from Long during the war, once the latter was in the Government. As Long was writing, on the subject of conscrip-tion, in April 1915: 'If Riots, Revolution, are inevitable then we must say so and abandon the effort . . .', and in August 1915: 'The situation is a very difficult one; during ten years the late Government had taught the proletariat that they could do as they liked and were masters of the situation, the result is that we have had to deal very tenderly with a people so unfortunately educated in the wrong policy',[11] it is not surprising that Gwynne's enthusiasm for Long did not last. What *is* surprising is that it lasted as long as it did.

Gwynne spent the whole war searching for the 'great big strong man', for the patriot above politics. He was successively a Carson man, a Derby man, a Lloyd George man, a Robertson man, a Mr Speaker Lowther man, and a Cave man. At one point, *faute de* Robertson (the 'man on horseback') and before and after coming out for Cave (perhaps as a way of rewarding him for the part he had played in obstructing Lloyd George's wish to close down the *Morning Post*), he seems seriously to have considered the return as Prime

Minister of Asquith, of whom it had been written in the *Morning Post* thirteen months previously: 'A man who has so discrowned himself, who in set terms assented to his own unfitness, and yet proposed to remain in office, will never again, we trust, be Prime Minister of England.'[12] Gwynne was not easily satisfied, and all his favourites let him down. Lloyd George, about whom there were always reservations, but who at one point was flattered as that 'rare' thing, a 'good man', remained in favour for less than six months. Milner, who was supposed to keep an eye on Lloyd George, and whom the *Morning Post* had backed for the War Office, developed pacifist and defeatist tendencies after his visit to Russia,[13] and was condemned for that reason and for interfering with the generals. Kitchener, who proved too ready to defer to Asquith,[14] came to be considered a danger to the nation.

Gwynne's search for leadership, and his choice of objectives, revealed his lack of political acumen. He proved unable to assess accurately the qualities of those with whom he was dealing. He never fully grasped the reluctance of the Conservative hierarchy to take responsibility, its willingness to submit itself to Lloyd George's dictatorship,[15] its fear of facing unrest of any kind. This last was something used successfully by both Asquith and Lloyd George. The former told the Conservatives in April 1916 after seeing Henderson that they 'may take it as certain that any proposal to extend compulsion beyond the limits of the present Act, by *whomsoever* put forward, will meet with the united and determined opposition of the whole Labour party, in and out of Parliament'.[16] The latter was reported early in 1918 as 'parading the needs of shipping etc. etc. [and] finally declaring that further inroads on our man power would lead to a social revolution'.[17] In April 1918 Bonar Law's reaction to the prospect of the application of conscription in Ireland was that it 'might involve a Home Rule Bill simultaneously and a double explosion – the Nationalists and Ulster'.[18]

Though increasingly disenchanted with the British political system and with most of the elements that composed it, Gwynne found himself, when helping to launch the National Party in 1917 as the vehicle for a National Government for which others besides himself had called,[19] resorting – as Milner in 1916 had found it 'rather ironical' to do – not only to elements from within that system but to an extension and prolongation of that same system.[20] The idea that the hold of Party could be broken by the formation of a new party was on a par with Gwynne's expectations as to whence that party would derive its electoral support. The unprofessional soldiery of the New Armies did not transform itself into the power base of a National Party pursuing Gwynne's version of a national policy, and the old soldiers simply faded away. Within four months of the appearance of the new party, Gwynne was reverting to his disposition to go outside the system altogether: the Chief of the Imperial General Staff as Prime Minister was the logical result of this. He was not quite alone in this. Leo Maxse was with him.[21] To consider a general as a political panacea was to confuse civilian with Army life. To believe that Field-Marshal Sir William Robertson or General Sir Frederick Maurice could, singly or in combination, bring down Lloyd George in the House of Commons was essentially romantic. To expect higher standards of honesty or probity from men in public life than from others was to fly in the face of human nature.

All these things betrayed a lack of insight into both the nature of politics and the nature of those who held, or those who wanted to hold, power and office. They all showed that Gwynne did not understand power in the way that Asquith, or Balfour, or Lloyd George, or even Curzon, understood it. In the end, as Gwynne found, for the professional politician *nothing* transcended politics; no power was greater than the power that Guest, Lloyd George's Chief Whip, encapsulated in the phrase 'The Power of the Man in the Saddle'.[22] And why should politicians, or generals for that matter, be more honest and open in their spheres than Gwynne was in his? He abased himself before Lady Bathurst as someone who was honest as the day is long, whose only concern was for the welfare of her property. And yet he was throughout the war a party to an arrangement for the illegal importation of paper for newsprint. He thoroughly disconcerted her when he proposed to run for Parliament against Churchill and Montagu. He only just resisted the temptation to write anonymous letters to himself for publication in the *Morning Post*. His protest to Lady Bathurst that 'I have never caballed or intrigued' was an outright lie: E. T. Raymond's speculation of 1919 that his 'capacity for manoeuvre' would 'secure his name some prominence when the secret history of the last fifteen years is laid open'[23] is proved entirely correct by the letters printed in this volume. Having persuaded Buckmaster that he could be trusted, he almost immediately proved that he could not be trusted. He was deliberately unfair and not even-handed in his treatment of, for instance, Churchill in 1914, whatever amends he may have tried to make in 1918.[24] To this extent Gwynne's search was as self-deceiving as his claims to be apolitical. His crusading spirit was flawed, as was the nature of those against whom he crusaded.

In July 1917, on the occasion of Lloyd George's appointment of Churchill and Montagu, Lord Charles Beresford wrote to Gwynne: 'Why your outspoken criticism has alienated the sympathies of your acquaintances and lost you the friendship of your former political friends, I cannot understand.'[25] What Beresford professed not to be able to understand was all too understandable by anyone inhabiting the real world. Even Gwynne, a year later, recognized that his frankness about what he called their absolute failure had forfeited the friendship of the politicians. In fact, having once been able to move freely in political and service circles, Gwynne had become relatively isolated. He had quarrelled with Henry Wilson. He had quarrelled with Lord Derby. He had quarrelled with Lloyd George and Bonar Law. He had quarrelled with Lord Robert Cecil. He had quarrelled with Lord Milner, whose retaliation lost Gwynne the friendship of John Buchan and of the editor of the *Observer*, Garvin, who had once written to Lady Bathurst: 'It has long been my intention . . . to back up the *Morning Post* whenever I could. For years I have maintained that if boldly yet steadily handled it might be one of the most powerful and wholesome political agencies in the world and a saving influence in the Empire.'[26] At the end of the year he quarrelled with Buckingham Palace. Not all these friendships and contacts were irretrievably lost. Gwynne responded positively, for instance, to Henry Wilson's overture of August 1918. Relations with Lord Derby were resumed in 1920.[27] Even Churchill, though never any friend of Gwynne's, was eventually to be given his due – in 1944.[28]

Gwynne's volatile temperament and general lack of insight had fed each other. Impatience and high patriotism, disenchantment and frustration, created a vicious circle which expanded the area of damage. Even Gwynne's relationship with Lady Bathurst became rather strained. Matters were not helped by the fact that, although capable of such a sentence as 'There is an ugly feeling abroad and it will take an ugly shape if Ireland is allowed to go Scot-free', Gwynne had no sense of humour. This was something that Esher, another seeker after 'big strong men', despite their proven record, remarked upon when, in all seriousness, the *Morning Post* suggested Sir George Cave as Prime Minister.[29]

The Great War did not do all that Gwynne had hoped that it would do for the *Morning Post*. The *Morning Post* did not do all that Gwynne had hoped that it would do in the Great War. It did, however, have its moments.

Many of the European countries involved in the war experienced internal contests for power between the civilian and the military authorities, between the service chiefs and the politicians. In Germany the contest was won by Hindenburg and Ludendorff.[30] In France it was won by Clemenceau.[31] In Great Britain it was Lloyd George who emerged victorious.[32] His determination to do so was put most succinctly of all to Esher: 'either Wully [Robertson] is Prime Minister or I am'.[33] The King's Private Secretary was told: 'If His Majesty insisted upon Robertson's remaining in office . . . the King would have to find other Ministers.'[34] Amongst the champions of Robertson, and of the generals in general, Unionists predominated. One of them, Lord Robert Cecil, wrote in February 1918 that 'it would seem to require an overwhelming case to justify civilians in overruling their military advisers'.[35] Over the dismissal of Robertson Cecil resigned, only to think better of it. So did Walter Long and Lord Derby. Gwynne, with his propensity to feel 'that a military dictatorship is the only thing for England' and his credo of the soldier as physician, was naturally on the side of the services.

If it is, perhaps, just as well that Lloyd George won that particular battle, it is, perhaps, equally as well that Gwynne did as well as he did do in another internal contest. This concerned that civil liberty, the freedom of the press. The critical role of the Fourth Estate expanded in wartime. If ministries were to command popular, as opposed to parliamentary, support they had to have a good press. This was more important to Lloyd George, who had no party base and no access to Liberal Party machinery, than to his predecessor. When in the negotiations leading to the formation of the Lloyd George coalition the Unionists pointed out the dangerous uses to which the press could be put, this was as much as anything a hit at Lloyd George. When in his reply Lloyd George indicated that he was not absolutely indisposed to curbing the press, this was of a piece with the cavalier attitude he was to display towards Parliament: in appointing ministers without regard to parliamentary need or credentials and in one extreme case, that of Smuts, the South African Minister of Defence, appointing someone who had no connection whatever with either House of Parliament, and this for eighteen months; in making no appearance at Question Time in the course of the years 1917 and 1918; and in making major announcements of war aims outside of Parliament.[36]

Lloyd George's friends and supporters in the world of newspapers included Sir George Riddell, owner of the *News of the World*; Sir Henry Dalziel, owner of *Reynolds' News*; Lord Beaverbrook, owner of the *Daily Express*; Lord Burnham, owner of the *Daily Telegraph*; Lord Rothermere, owner of the *Daily Mirror* and *Sunday Pictorial*; C. P. Scott, editor of the *Manchester Guardian*; and, until spring 1918, R. Donald, editor of the *Daily Chronicle*. As Prime Minister, Lloyd George increased his hold over the press by ennobling some proprietors, and further ennobling others, giving for instance a Viscountcy to Northcliffe. He increased it still further by making some of them ministers: Northcliffe's brother Rothermere was made Minister for

Air from November 1917 to April 1918; Beaverbrook was made Chancellor of the Duchy of Lancaster and Minister of Propaganda in February 1918. Robert Donald had been asked to report on propaganda arrangements at the beginning of 1917. Northcliffe was nobbled in May 1917 by being sent on a War Mission to the United States of America – this Lloyd George explained on the ground that 'it was essential to get rid of him . . . he had become so "jumpy" as to be really a public danger and it was necessary to "harness" him in order to find occupation for his superfluous energies'; another attempt to nobble Northcliffe was made in February 1918 when he was created Director of Propaganda in Enemy Countries.[37] Lloyd George looked to increase his hold still further. Early in 1917 he tried to gain control of the *Westminster Gazette*.[38] In October 1917 he paid the role of the *Morning Post* in resisting civilian interference with the Army the backhanded compliment of a complaint about the difficulty of removing Robertson when the latter 'had got so much of the Press'.[39] Having in January 1918 remarked on the importance of evening papers as compared with daily papers of limited circulation, Lloyd George went on to try to nobble Dudley Docker's independent evening paper *The Globe*, then being edited by Leo Maxse.[40] In September 1918 Lloyd George did gain control of the *Daily Chronicle*.[41] It was entirely in keeping with all this that, on Northcliffe's death in June 1921, the Prime Minister should attempt to acquire, and to become editor of, *The Times*.[42]

At the *Morning Post* Gwynne could not be shut up, bought off, diverted or subverted. He was not intimidated or deterred by the threats and treatment levelled at other newspapers in opposition to the Government of the day, such as the *Nation*, whose overseas sales were proscribed, the *Herald*, which the Cabinet considered suppressing in January 1918, and the *Daily News*.[43] He did not succumb to the blandishments of Asquith in the shape of invitations to write memoranda for the Cabinet or bribes of Privy Councillorships delivered by Beaverbrook on Lloyd George's behalf. He hung on to his post, to his chief leader writer, and to the recently acquired Repington. His voice remained, even if it was, increasingly, a voice in the wilderness. This was a real, and necessary, contribution to the preservation of civil liberties, even though success, in this particular instance, interfered with and delayed civilian control over the military.

It is a little surprising that the anti-libertarian Gwynne should put out any flag at all in favour of the values of a system that he clearly despised. Nor did he, in effect. Even though he was the editor of a major newspaper the freedom of the press mattered less to him than the opportunity, or as he saw it the necessity, to support the generals against the politicians. If Gwynne gave up the much-vaunted independence of the *Morning Post* to anyone, he gave it up to Field-Marshal Sir William Robertson and to General Sir Douglas Haig. Gwynne wrote to Lady Bathurst at one point in 1917: '. . . as Sir William Robertson said to me last night the *M.P.* has done more for England than the whole press put together. There are rewards which can only satisfy the right spirit within one. Not all the advertisements in the world would compensate you or me for the loss of that praise.'[44] Haig said, of the man whom he used to help cover up the Somme and Passchendaele fiascos: 'He is anxious to do the right thing, but, like most newspaper men, is very self-satisfied and talks as if he rules the universe. He has a commendable dislike of the politicians'; 'his only redeeming quality is that he is "out to help" '.[45] Robertson did not mention him at all in his own memoirs, *Soldiers and Statesmen 1914–1918*, and *From Private to Field-Marshal*. Both Robertson and Haig were mean operators.[46] In being used in this way, however, Gwynne was more than a volunteer; ie was Regular Army, and this was his way of doing his bit. It was ali part of life's, and the Great War's, and Gwynne's, and the *Morning Post*'s, rich pageant.

NOTES

1. Esher to Lady Bathurst, 29 July 1918 (Glenesk–Bathurst MSS).
2. M. and E. Brock (eds), *H. H. Asquith, Letters to Venetia Stanley*, p. 285.
3. T. Wilson (ed.), *The Political Diaries of C. P. Scott 1911–27*, p. 226.
4. Viscount Esher and M. E. Brett, *Journals and Letters of Reginald, Viscount Esher*, vol. iv, pp. 175–6, Esher to Stamfordham, 22 January 1918.
5. See K. M. Wilson, 'The Protocols of Zion and the Morning Post 1919–20', pp. 5–14.
6. E. T. Raymond, 'The *Morning Post* and Mr H. A. Gwynne', p. 177.
7. See J. M. Winter, 'Britain's "Lost Generation" of the First World War', pp. 449–66.
8. Gwynne to Lady Bathurst, 11, 12 November 1911 (Glenesk–Bathurst MSS).
9. *Morning Post*, 1 September 1917, p. 4.
10. Gwynne to Lady Bathurst, 11 November 1911 (Glenesk–Bathurst MSS).
11. Long to Balfour, 5 April 1915 (Balfour MSS 49777); memorandum by Long, 20 August 1915 (Long MSS 62420).
12. *Morning Post*, 7 December 1916, p. 6.
13. A. M. Gollin, *Proconsul in Politics*, Ch. xx.
14. R. Jenkins *Asquith*, London, 1964, pp. 423–4.
15. Law to Long, 27 December 1916: 'I agree with all you say about a Dictatorship. This is essentially George's Government and my own intention like yours is to back him to the fullest extent I can. There is I think no alternative.' (Long MSS 62404).
16. Asquith to Long, 8 April 1916 (Long MSS 62404).
17. Repington to Gwynne, 5 February 1918 (MS Gwynne 32).
18. Law to Long, 5 April 1918 (Long MSS 62404).
19. See P. A. Lockwood, 'Milner's Entry into the War Cabinet, December 1916' pp. 120–34; J. O. Stubbs, 'Lord Milner and Patriotic Labour, 1914–18', pp. 717–54; A. Clark (ed.), *A Good Innings, the Private Papers of Viscount Lee of Fareham*,

pp. 147–51; and R. J. Scally *The Origins of the Lloyd George Coalition: the Politics of Social-Imperialism, 1900–18*, pp. 280–336.

20. J. O. Stubbs, 'Lord Milner and Patriotic Labour, 1914–18', p. 728.
21. P. Fraser, *Lord Esher*, p. 392.
22. K. O. Morgan, 'Lloyd George's Premiership: A Study in "Prime Ministerial Government"', p. 130.
23. E. T. Raymond, 'The *Morning Post* and Mr H. A. Gwynne', p. 176.
24. In October 1914 Gwynne refused to print some letters he had received in extenuation of Churchill's action: see M. Gilbert *Winston S. Churchill*, pp. 125–30; and see letter 256.
25. Beresford to Gwynne, 20 July 1917 (MS Gwynne 32).
26. Garvin to Lady Bathurst, 18 July 1911 (Glenesk–Bathurst MSS).
27. Gwynne to Derby, 5 August 1920 (MS Gwynne 32).
28. Gwynne to Lady Bathurst, 20 January 1944 (Glenesk–Bathurst MSS). Having agreed with Lady Bathurst that Churchill 'has amply paid full toll for his sins of commission and omission for which we used to attack him', Gwynne went on to reveal more of his own incorrigibility:

> I remember once, during the time when we were criticising him I happened to sit next him at luncheon. We had hot arguments and to prevent it getting hotter I said this to him 'I disagree with nearly everything you have done since you have been in office but I would like to tell you this. If ever England was in mortal danger I would follow you blind'. He turned round to me and said 'Do you know that you have paid me a greater compliment than I have ever received in my life'.

29. R. S. Churchill, *Lord Derby*, p. 359; Stamfordham to Esher, 22 April 1918 (Esher MSS 5/55).
30. M. Kitchen, *The Silent Dictatorship*, London, 1976.
31. J. C. King, *Generals and Politicians: Conflict between France's High Command, Parliament and Government 1914–18*, Berkeley, 1951.
32. D. Woodward, *Lloyd George and the Generals*.
33. Viscount Esher and M. V. Brett, *Journals and Letters of Reginald, Viscount Esher*, vol. iv, p. 181, 16 February 1918.
34. Memorandum by Stamfordham, 16 February 1918, in Lord Beaverbrook, *Men and Power*, p. 412; War Cabinet minutes 347a, 16 February 1918.
35. Cecil to Long, 18 February 1918 (Long MSS 62423).
36. See A. J. P. Taylor, 'Lloyd George – Rise and Fall' in his *Politics in Wartime and Other Essays*, p. 141; and K. O. Morgan, 'Lloyd George's Premiership: A Study in "Prime Ministerial Government"', pp. 149–50.
37. T. Wilson (ed.) *The Political Diaries of C. P. Scott 1911–27*, pp. 296 and 336; S. Roskill, *Hankey, Man of Secrets*, pp. 390–1. And see J. M. McEwen, 'Northcliffe and Lloyd George at War 1914–18', pp. 651–72.
38. K. O. Morgan, 'Lloyd George's Premiership: A Study in "Prime Ministerial Government"', p. 136.
39. Henry Wilson Diary, 5 October 1917.
40. K. Middlemas (ed.), *Thomas Jones Whitehall Diary 1916–25*, vol. i, p. 44, entry for 11 January 1918; Maxse to Lady Bathurst, 5 June 1918 (Glenesk–Bathurst MSS).
41. See J. M. McEwen 'Lloyd George's Acquisition of the *Daily Chronicle* in 1918', pp. 127–44.
42. K. O. Morgan, 'Lloyd George's Premiership: A Study in "Prime Ministerial Government"', p. 153; *History of The Times*, vol. iv, p. 683 ff.

43. K. Middlemas (ed.), *Thomas Jones Whitehall Diary 1916–25*, p. 44; and S. E. Koss *Fleet Street Radical: A. G. Gardiner and the Daily News*, London, 1973, p. 231.
44. Gwynne to Lady Bathurst, n.d. but 1917 (Glenesk–Bathurst MSS).
45. R. Blake, *The Private Papers of Douglas Haig 1914–19*, pp. 168 and 254.
46. See J. M. McEwen, ' "Brass Hats" and the British Press during the First World War', pp. 43–68.

Select Bibliography

ADAMS, R. J. Q., *Arms and the Wizard: Lloyd George and the Ministry of Munitions 1915–16*, London, 1978.

ADDISON, C., *Politics from Within*, London, 1924.

AMERY, L. S., *My Political Life*, London, 1953.

ASQUITH, H. H. (Lord Oxford and Asquith), *Memories and Reflections*, London, 1928.

BARNES, J. and NICHOLSON, D. (eds), *The Leo Amery Diaries, vol. i, 1896–1929*, London, 1980.

BEAVERBROOK, Lord, *Men and Power*, London 1956.

BEAVERBROOK, Lord, *Politicians and the War*, London, 1960.

BLAKE, R., *The Private Papers of Douglas Haig, 1914–19*, London, 1952.

BLAKE, R., *The Unknown Prime Minister: the Life and Times of Andrew Bonar Law*, London, 1955.

BOYCE, D. G., 'How to Settle the Irish Question: Lloyd George and Ireland 1916–21', in A. J. P. Taylor (ed.), *Lloyd George: Twelve Essays*, London, 1971.

BOYCE, D. G., 'British Opinion, Ireland and the War 1916–18', *Historical Journal*, vol. xvii, 1974.

BOYCE, D. G. (ed.), *The Crisis of British Unionism: the Domestic Political Papers of the Second Earl of Selborne 1885–1922*, London, 1987.

BROCK, M. and E. (eds), *H. H. Asquith, Letters to Venetia Stanley*, Oxford, 1982.

BROWN, K. D., 'The Anti-Socialist Union 1908–49', in K. D. Brown (ed.), *Essays in Anti-Labour History*, London, 1974.

CALLWELL, Sir C. E., *Field Marshal Sir Henry Wilson*, London, 1927.

CHAMBERLAIN, Sir A., *Down the Years*, London, 1935.

CHURCHILL, R. S., *Lord Derby*, London, 1959.

CLARK, A. (ed.), *A Good Innings: the Private Papers of Viscount Lee of Fareham*, London, 1974.

CLARKE, P., *Liberals and Social Democrats*, Cambridge, 1978.

CLARKE, P., 'Asquith and Lloyd George Revisited', in J. M. W. Bean (ed.), *The Political Culture of Modern Britain: Studies in Memory of Koss*, London, 1987.

CLINE, P. K., 'Eric Geddes and the "Experiment" with Businessmen in Government 1915–22', in K. D. Brown (ed.), *Essays in Anti-Labour History*, London, 1974.

COLVIN, I., *The Life of Lord Carson*, vol. iii, London, 1936.

COOK, E., *The Press in War-Time*, London, 1920.

DOUGLAS, R., 'The Background to the "Coupon" Election Arrangements', *English Historical Review*, vol. lcccvi, 1971.

DOUGLAS, R., 'Voluntary Enlistment in the First World War and the Work of the Parliamentary Recruiting Committee', *Journal of Modern History*, vol. xlii, 1970.

DUTTON, D., 'The "Robertson Dictatorship" and the Balkan Campaign in 1916', *Journal of Strategic Studies*, vol. ix, 1986.

ESHER, Viscount and BRETT, M. V., *Journals and Letters of Reginald, Viscount Esher*, London, 1934–8.

FAY, S., *The War Office at War*, London, 1937.

FRASER, P., *Lord Esher*, London, 1973.

FRASER, P., 'British War Policy and the Crisis of Liberalism in May 1915', *Journal of Modern History*, vol. liv, 1982.

FRASER, P., 'The Impact of the War of 1914–18 on the British Political System', in M. R. D. Foot (ed.), *War and Society: Essays for J. R. Western*, London, 1973.

FRASER, P., 'Cabinet Secrecy and War Memoirs', *History*, vol. lxx, 1985.

FRENCH, D., *British Economic and Strategic Planning 1905–15*, London, 1982.

FRENCH, D., 'The Origins of the Dardanelles Campaign Reconsidered', *History*, vol. lxviii, 1983.

FRENCH, D., *British Strategy and War Aims 1914–16*, London, 1986.

GILBERT, M., *Winston S. Churchill*, vol. iii, London, 1971.

GOLLIN, A. M., *Proconsul in Politics*, London, 1964.

GOOCH, J., 'The Maurice Debate 1918', *Journal of Contemporary History*, vol. iii, 1968.

GOUGH, General Sir H., *Soldiering On*, London 1954.

HOLMES, R., *The Little Field Marshal: the Life of Sir John French*, London, 1981.

JEFFREY, K. (ed.), *The Military Correspondence of Field Marshal Sir Henry Wilson 1918–22*, London, 1985.

KENDLE, J., 'Federalism and the Irish Problem in 1918', *History*, vol. lvi, 1971.

KENNEDY, T. C., 'Public Opinion and the Conscientious Objector', *Journal of British Studies*, vol. xii, 1973.

KOSS, S. E., *Asquith*, London, 1976.

KOSS, S. E., 'Asquith versus Lloyd George: the Last Phase and Beyond', in A. Sked and C. Cook (eds), *Crisis and Controversy: Essays in Honour of A. J. P. Taylor*, London, 1976.

KOSS, S. E., *The Rise and Fall of the Political Press in Britain*, vol. ii, London, 1984.

LANSDOWNE, Lord, 'The "Peace Letter" of 1917', *The Nineteenth Century and After*, vol. cxv, 1934.

LLOYD GEORGE, D., *War Memoirs*, London, 1933–7.

LOCKWOOD, P. A., 'Milner's Entry into the War Cabinet, December 1916', *Historical Journal*, vol. vii, 1964.

LOWE, C. J., 'Britain and Italian Intervention 1914–15', *Historical Journal*, vol. xii, 1969.

LOWE, C. J., 'The Failure of British Diplomacy in the Balkans 1914–16', *Canadian Journal of History*, vol. v, 1969.

LOWE, P., 'The Rise to the Premiership 1914–16', in A. J. P. Taylor (ed.), *Lloyd George: Twelve Essays*, London, 1971.

LYTTON, N., *The Press and the General Staff*, London, 1921.

McDERMOTT, J., 'Total War and the Merchant State: Aspects of British Economic Warfare against Germany 1914–16', *Canadian Journal of History*, vol. xxi, 1986.

McEWEN, J. M., 'Northcliffe and Lloyd George at War 1914–18', *Historical Journal*, vol. xxiv, 1981.

McEWEN, J. M., 'The Press and the Fall of Asquith', *Historical Journal*, vol. xxi, 1978.

McEWEN, J. M., 'The National Press during the First World War: ownership and circulation', *Journal of Contemporary History*, vol. xvii, 1982.

McEWEN, J. M., '"Brass-Hats" and the British Press during the First World War', *Canadian Journal of History*, vol. xviii, 1983.

McEWEN, J. M. (ed.), 'Lloyd George's Acquisition of the *Daily Chronicle* in 1918', *Journal of British Studies*, vol. xxii, 1982.

McEWEN, J. M., *The Riddell Diaries*, London, 1986.

McGILL, B., 'Asquith's Predicament 1914–18', *Journal of Modern History*, vol. xxxix, 1967.

MACKAY, R. F., *Fisher of Kilverstone*, Oxford, 1973.

MARDER, A. J., *From the Dreadnought to Scapa Flow*, vol. i, Oxford, 1961, vol. ii, London, 1965.

MARDER, A. J. (ed.), *Fear God and Dread Nought*, vol. iii, London, 1959.

MARDER, A. J., *From the Dardanelles to Oran*, London, 1974.

MAURICE, Sir F., *The Life of General Lord Rawlinson of Trent*, London, 1928.

MAURICE, N. (ed.), *The Maurice Case*, London, 1972.

MIDDLEMAS, K. (ed.), *Thomas Jones Whitehall Diary 1916–25*, Oxford, 1969.

MORGAN, K. O., 'Lloyd George's Premiership: A Study in "Prime Ministerial Government"', *Historical Journal*, vol. xiii, 1970.

MORGAN, K. O., '1902–24', in D. Butler (ed.), *Coalitions in British Politics*, London, 1978.

NEILSON, K., 'Kitchener: a Reputation Refurbished?', *Canadian Journal of History*, vol. xv, 1980.

NICOLSON, H., *King George V*, London, 1952.

PETRIE, Sir C., *The Life and Letters of Austen Chamberlain*, London, 1940.

PETRIE, Sir C., *Walter Long and His Times*, London, 1936.

PONSONBY, A., *Falsehood in War-Time*, London, 1928.

POUND, R. and HARMSWORTH, G., *Northcliffe*, London, 1959.

PUGH, M. D., 'Asquith, Bonar Law and the First Coalition', *Historical Journal*, vol. xvii, 1974.

PUGH, M. D., *Electoral Reform in War and Peace 1906–18*, London, 1978.

RAE, J., *Conscience and Politics*, Oxford, 1970.

RAYMOND, E. T., *Uncensored Celebrities*, London, 1919.

REPINGTON, C. à C., *The First World War*, London, 1920.

ROBBINS, K., 'British Diplomacy and Bulgaria 1914–15', *Slavonic Review*, vol. xlix, 1971.

ROBERTSON, Field-Marshal Sir W., *Soldiers and Statesmen 1914–1918*, London 1926.

ROBERTSON, Field-Marshal Sir W., *From Private to Field-Marshal*, London 1921.

ROSKILL, S., *Hankey, Man of Secrets*, vol. i, London, 1970.

ROTHWELL, V., *British War Aims and Peace Diplomacy 1914–18*, Oxford, 1971.

RUBINSTEIN, W. D., 'Henry Page Croft and the National Party 1917–22', *Journal of Contemporary History*, vol. ix, 1974.

RYAN, W. M., 'From "Shells Scandal" to Bow Street: the Denigration of Lieutenant Colonel Charles à Court Repington', *Journal of Modern History*, vol. L, 1978.

SCALLY, R. J., *The Origins of the Lloyd George Coalition: the Politics of Social-Imperialism 1900–18*, Princeton, 1975.

SEARLE, G., 'The "Revolt from the Right" in Edwardian Britain', in P. M. Kennedy and A. J. Nicholls (eds), *Nationalist and Racialist Movements in Britain and Germany before 1914*, London, 1981.

SIMPKINS, P., 'Kitchener and the Expansion of the Army', in I. F. W. Beckett and J. Gooch (eds), *Politicians and Defence*, Manchester, 1981.

STUBBS, J. O., 'Lord Milner and Patriotic Labour 1914–18', *English Historical Review*, vol. lxxxvii, 1972.

SUMMERS, A., 'Militarism in Britain before the Great War', *History Workshop*, vol. ii, 1976.

SUMMERS, A., 'The Character of Edwardian Nationalism: Three Popular Leagues', in P. M. Kennedy and A. J. Nicholls (eds), *Nationalist and Racialist Movements in Britain and Germany before 1914*, London, 1981.

TAYLOR, A. J. P., *Beaverbrook*, London, 1972.

TAYLOR, A. J. P., *Politics in Wartime and Other Essays*, London, 1964.

TERRAINE, J., *The Western Front*, London, 1964.

TERRAINE, J., *To Win a War*, London, 1978.

WARD, A. J., 'Lloyd George and the 1918 Irish Conscription Crisis', *Historical Journal*, vol. xvii, 1974.

WEINROTH, H., 'Peace by Negotiation and the British Anti-War Movement 1914–18', *Canadian Journal of History*, vol. x, 1975.

WILLIAMS, R., 'Arthur James Balfour, Sir John Fisher and the Politics of Naval Reform, 1904–10', *Bulletin of the Institute of Historical Research*, vol. lx, 1987.

WILSON, K. M., *The Policy of the Entente 1904–14*, Cambridge, 1985.

WILSON, K. M., *Empire and Continent*, London, 1987.

WILSON, K. M., 'Great War Prologue', in K. M. Wilson and N. Pronay (eds), *The Political Re-education of Germany and Her Allies after World War II*, London, 1985.

WILSON, K. M., 'Sir John French's Resignation over the Curragh Affair: the Role of the Editor of the *Morning Post*', *English Historical Review*, vol. xcix, 1984.

WILSON, K. M., 'Spenser Wilkinson at Bay: Calling the Tune at the *Morning Post* 1908–9', *Publishing History*, vol. xix, 1986.

WILSON, K. M., 'The Protocols of Zion and the Morning Post 1919–20', *Patterns of Prejudice*, vol. xix, 1985.

WILSON, T. (ed.), *The Political Diaries of C. P. Scott 1911–27*, London, 1971.

WINTER, J. M., 'Britain's "Lost Generation" of the First World War', *Population Studies*, vol. xxxi, 1977.

WOODWARD, D., *Lloyd George and the Generals*, London, 1983.

WOODWARD, D., 'Did Lloyd George Starve the British Army of Men Prior to the German Offensive of 21 March 1918?', *Historical Journal*, vol. xxvii, 1984.

WRIGLEY, C. J., *David Lloyd George and the British Labour Movement*, Brighton, 1976.

Index

Abdul Hamid, Sultan of Turkey, 216, 217n.
Adams, 60–1
Addison, Dr C., 217 and n., 277
Admiralty, 40, 42, 44, 45, 74, 78–9, 98, 144–5, 154–5, 163, 202, 305, 306
Adrianople, 82, 101
Africa, 140
Albert, Prince of Schleswig-Holstein, 187–8 and n.
Aldwych Club, 267
Aleppo, 285
Alexandra, Queen, 187
Allen, 292
Allenby, General E. H. H., 271, 272n., 285
Alsace-Lorraine, 82, 111, 185
Amalgamated Society of Engineers, 217n.
Amery, L. S., 19n., 271, 272n., 285
Ampthill, Lord, 230
Ancient Order of Hibernians, 60
Angell, Norman, 131n.
Anglo-Russian Entente, 15
Antwerp expedition, 17, 38, 39, 41–2, 56, 78, 84
Apsley, Lord, 253 and n.
Arabs, 226
Archer-Shee, Lt-Colonel M., 270 and n.
Army Council, 242, 244, 245, 254–5, 286
Arras, 70, 102
Asia Minor, 55, 71
Asquith, H. H., 3, 5, 40, 73n., 126; on Gwynne, 11, 17, 320; Irish Question, 16, 172, 174n., 181; and the Antwerp expedition, 40n., 42–3n.; Gwynne's memoranda to, 66–71, 328; and the temperance movement, 80, 81;

Gwynne's letters to, 81–6, 109–13, 116–20, 132–7, 145–7, 183–6, 194–5, 198–201, 243–4, 276–7; and Coalition government, 92; War Committee, 97, 145n., 148n.; dissatisfaction with, 98, 99, 108, 127, 140–1, 152, 162, 163, 167, 169–71, 211; and conscription, 113, 116, 122, 156, 169; and Speyer, 149; retrenchment proposals, 158; and the Dardanelles, 182; Irish Question, 183, 277; letter to Gwynne, 195; loses premiership, 205–6, 234; Liberal Party split, 224; as replacement for Lloyd George, 246–7, 248, 259–60, 273, 278, 279, 324; and General Maurice's letter, 275n., 276, 278
Asquith, Margot, 80, 127, 293; Gwynne's letters to, 248
Astor, Waldorf, 203n., 205, 287n.
Atholl, Duke of, 230
Audacious, HMS, 48, 49n., 63n., 87
Australia, 234, 267
Austria, 15–16, 27, 71, 72, 79, 118, 184, 187, 213, 278, 292
Ayles, W. H., 128

Bailey, Sir Abs, 236
Baldston, Mr, 315
Balfour, A. J., 3, 10, 71n., 158; and proposed Coalition, 90; in War Committee, 145n., 148n.; letter to Gwynne, 202; in Lloyd George's government, 208, 209; Gwynne's opinion of, 273
Balfourier, General, 190
Balkan League, 184
Balkan States, 82–3, 86, 133–6, 141
Balkan Wars, 15, 20, 322
La Bassée, 199

Bath Club, 315
Bathurst, Lady: and the *Morning Post*,
  1–2; political views, 2–6; and the
  future of the *Evening Standard*, 63–4;
  letters to L. J. Maxse, 289–91; letter
  to Gwynne, 296–7; and Gwynne's
  salary, 296–7, 299, 314; *et passim*
Bathurst, Lancelot, 51, 52n.
Bathurst, Seymour Henry, 7th Earl, 1,
  7–8, 318; recruits, 25; and the future
  of the *Evening Standard*, 63; joins the
  National Party, 227, 230; Gwynne's
  letters to, 314–16
Beatty, Admiral, 202 and n.
Beaverbrook, Lord, 282–3 and n., 327,
  328
Belfast News, 60
Belgian Relief Commission, 64
Belgium, 21, 24, 25, 66, 75, 82, 113n.,
  185, 190, 199, 268
Beresford, Admiral Lord Charles, 25,
  26n., 47n., 325–6
Bernstorff, 79, 238
Billing, N. Pemberton, 292–3 and n.
Birrell, Sir A., 171n.
Blumenfeld, R. D., 7
Board of Trade, 74
Boer War, 56n., 154n., 321
Bolshevism, 309–10, 311–12, 317, 318
Borthwick, Oliver, 1–2
Borthwick, Peter, 1
Bosphorus, 82, 216
Bottomley, Horatio, 293 and n.
Bouillon, Henri Franklin, 219, 220n.
Bowles, Gibson, 108 and n.
Brade, Sir Reginald, 182, 183n.
Brand, Robert, 201–2n., 203n.
Breslau, 137 and n., 239 and n.
Bristol, 128
Bristol Miners Union, 128
British Empire Union, 4–5
British Workers' National League, 98,
  231
Brysson, M. de, 315
Buchan, John, 123–4, 326
Buchanan, Sir George, 223n.
Buchanan, Lady, 223 and n.
Buckmaster, Sir Stanley, 28n., 325;
  Gwynne's letters to, 35–6, 41–2;
  letter to Gwynne, 36–7
Bulfin, Lt-General Sir E. S., 285 and n.
Bulgaria, 21, 71–2, 82, 86, 101, 110,
  133, 134–5, 146, 184, 278, 310

Burgoyne, 230
Burn, Colonel, 275n.
Burnham, Lord, 314, 317–18, 327
Burrows, R., 213

Cabinet: Gwynne's memoranda to,
  58–62, 66–71, 328; Kitchener's
  independence of, 75; and
  conscription, 115n., 122; Gallipoli
  expedition, 135; and the Balkan
  States, 141
Cabinet Committee on the
  Coordination of Military and
  Financial Effort, 158n.
Callwell, General Sir Charles, 11, 35,
  106–7, 158, 182, 196–7
Cambrai, 240, 241n., 245
Canada, 234, 267
Candid Review, 108
Carlton Club, 315
Carnegie, 230
Carson, Sir Edward, 3, 10, 92, 109, 122,
  165n., 191, 203 and n., 234, 293, 308;
  resignation, 97, 127, 137 and n.,
  140–1; as possible Prime Minister,
  98, 159; ill-health, 123, 160n., 163;
  Gwynne's admiration for, 107, 165,
  166–7 and n., 168, 169–71, 323; and
  Gwynne's National Policy, 158n.;
  and the Irish Question, 180–1;
  Gwynne's letter to, 182–3; Lloyd
  George becomes Prime Minister,
  205, 206; in Lloyd George's
  government, 208, 209 and n.
Carson, Lady, Gwynne's letters to, 165,
  168–9
Casement, Sir Roger, 214, 215n.
Cassel, Sir Ernest, 150, 151n.
Castelnau, 38
Cave, Sir George, 207, 245n., 268,
  269n., 302, 307–8, 323, 326
Cave, Lady, 308
Cawley, Sir F., 158n.
Cecil, Lord Robert, 155, 206, 215n.,
  234, 235n., 326, 327; Gwynne's letter
  to, 172; letter to Gwynne, 171–2
censorship, 26, 35–8, 141–5, 234,
  245n., 281, 308
Chamberlain, Austen, 3, 88, 92, 109,
  122, 127, 158, 206, 322
Chamberlain, Joseph, 3, 7
Chatham, Lord, 73n.

340

recruitment, 25, 31–5, 49;
memoranda to Cabinet, 58–62,
66–71, 328; proposes going to front,
64–5, 66, 87; on proposed Coalition
government, 73–6; visits France, 98,
181, 190, 214, 219, 303–5; stands for
Parliament, 207, 221–2, 325;
prosecution, 244, 245n., 250, 252;
asks for increase in salary, 296–7,
299, 314; entertainment expenses,
314–16; temperament, 321–2, 326;
lack of political acumen, 324–6

Haggard, Sir William, 214, 215n.
Haig, General Sir Douglas, 125, 192
and n., 196, 207, 226, 234, 270, 306,
315; sees Derby as possible Prime
Minister, 98; Gwynne's letter to,
153–4; shortage of men, 166, 278,
284, 313; replaces French, 189 and
n.; Gwynne's visit to France, 190;
plots against, 191; Gwynne's
admiration for, 195, 219–20, 225,
239, 264; on German morale, 215;
High Command crisis, 244, 245, 254,
257–8, 263, 281–2, 286; and General
Maurice's letter, 275n.; and Foch,
303–4; on Gwynne, 329
Haldane, Lord, 49 and n., 64, 71, 92,
319
Hall, Admiral Reginald, 57, 78, 80n.
Halsbury, Lord, 3
Hamilton, Hubert, 42
Hamilton, General Sir I. S. M., 79,
80n., 140, 182
Hampshire, 11, 178n.
Harcourt, Lewis, 92 and n., 127
Harmsworth press, 63, 127, 206
Hawke, 42, 43
Henderson, Sir Alexander, 63 and n.,
64n., 209n., 324
Henderson, Arthur, 125 and n., 201n.,
302, 305n.
Henry, Sir Edward, 302, 307
Herald, 328
Hertling, Count G. von, 238, 239n.,
253n.
Hichens, Lionel, 201–2n., 203n.
Hield, 125
Hindenburg, Field-Marshal von, 238
and n., 326
Hodge, John, 128
Hogge, Mr, 257

Holden, Sir Edward, 88
Holland, 79–80
Home Office, 37, 74, 94n., 302
L'Homme Enchaîné, 87n., 143
House of Commons, 3, 60, 116, 119,
151n., 157, 163, 170, 183, 187, 199,
207, 215n., 222, 240, 247, 249, 271,
272, 277
House of Lords, 3, 139, 181, 187, 267
Hughes, 199, 301
Hughes, W. M., 169 and n.
Huguet, 122
Hungarian Independence Party, 71,
72, 102, 212
Hungary, 66, 70, 71, 79, 101–2, 184,
212–13
Hunter-Weston, Lt-General Sir A. G.,
240, 241n.
Hurst, Barrington, 172n.

Independent Labour Party, 98
India, 124, 140, 293, 295n.
Inter-Allied Conference, Paris (1916),
182n.
Ionescu, Take, 133, 315
Ireland: Easter Rising, 3–4, 98, 172–3;
Home Rule issue, 15–16, 28, 60,
172–82, 183, 277, 319; recruitment,
58–60; Tullamore by-election, 60–1;
German spies, 61–2; and
conscription, 113, 119, 169, 197–9,
201, 208, 235–6, 237, 265, 266n.,
319, 324; appointment of Chief
Secretary, 171 and n.; General
Strike, 272n., 273
Irish Daily Independent, 58
Irish National Volunteers, 59
Irish Nationalists, 58–60, 119, 197–8,
199
Irish Unionist Alliance, 181
Irvine, J. D., 58–63, 128–30
Isaacs, Sir Rufus, 71, 73n.
Italy, 21, 24, 86, 87n., 102, 103, 110,
111, 118, 185, 198, 209, 258

Jackson, Admiral Sir H. B., 100 and n.
Jameson, Sir L. S., 165 and n.
Jellicoe, Sir John, 43, 44n., 49n., 202
and n.
Jerusalem, 285, 310
Jews, 43, 223n., 241–2, 322

341

Joffre, General J. J. C., 30, 31n., 37–8, 46, 86, 122, 123, 152, 181, 194
Joynson-Hicks, Sir William, 163n.

Kerensky, Alexander, 223
Kerr, Philip, 203n.
Kiel, 70–1
Kipling, John, 132 and n.
Kipling, Rudyard, 7, 10, 132, 181, 319, 321
Kitchener, Lord, 11, 17, 30, 44, 47, 65n., 92, 98, 156, 158, 319; Gwynne's admiration for, 7, 123; Gwynne's letter to, 31–4; and the Antwerp expedition, 40n., 42–3n.; disposition of Army, 48–9; rivalry with Sir John French, 72, 77; independence of Cabinet, 75; and Constantinople, 80n.; and conscription, 97, 107, 109, 113–14, 116, 120, 121–2 and n., 126–7, 130; optimism, 99; complaints against, 108; Gwynne sends memoranda to, 113n.; Northcliffe attacks, 114; size of army revealed, 138–9; in War Committee, 145n., 148n.; dissatisfaction with, 148n., 152; on Lloyd George, 189; and Palestine, 226; on German surrender, 313 and n.; Gwynne's opinion of, 324; death, 178n.
Kluck, General Alexander von, 44 and n., 77
Korniloff, L. G., 226 and n., 230, 286
Kuhlmann, R. von, 238, 239n.

Labour Party, 128–9, 130, 221, 224, 225, 226, 324
Lambert, Admiral, 314
Lambert, George, 270 and n., 275n.
Lambton, Billy, 81
Lansdowne, Lord, 3, 19n., 92, 139 and n., 156, 179, 180, 234, 235n., 253 and n.; Gwynne's letter to, 261; letter to Gwynne, 261–2
Larkin, James, 61, 62–3n.
Law, Andrew Bonar, 40, 72, 88, 107, 163, 165, 193, 270, 308; Gwynne's letters to, 28, 58–63, 73–6, 106, 108–9, 148; and the future of the Evening Standard, 10, 63; and Coalition government, 17, 89, 90, 92, 94n.; Gwynne's memoranda to, 101–5; and conscription, 122, 127,

156, 169; in War Committee, 145n.; Wilson advocates withdrawal from Coalition, 167n.; and the Irish Question, 183; in Lloyd George's government, 208, 209n.; Unionist Party split, 224; and General Maurice's letter, 275n., 276; Gwynne on, 322–3; and Irish conscription, 324
League of Nations, 253n.
Leconfield, Lord, 230
Lee, Arthur, 98, 203n., 205
Leith, Lord, 230
Leitrim, Lord, 181
Lenin, 223n.
Liberal War Committee, 158n., 166n.
Liberal Party, 15–16, 75–6, 114, 224, 319, 327
Lichnowsky, Prince Karl Max von, 148, 150n.
Lloyd George, David, 71, 108, 203, 218, 232, 234, 243; and conscription, 10, 87, 88n., 97, 115n., 122, 127, 156–7, 169, 313; press censorship, 38n.; and the Antwerp expedition, 42n.; and Coalition government, 76, 97–8; military memorandum, 77–8, 80n.; and state control of liquor trade, 81n.; Irish Question, 98, 172, 174n., 178, 179–80, 181, 183; as Minister of Munitions, 100; Gwynne's letters to, 121, 127, 151–2, 194; speech to TUC, 129; 'Manifesto', 130; letters to Gwynne, 131, 208; as possible Prime Minister, 140, 141, 156–7, 169; in War Committee, 145n., 148n.; dissatisfaction with Kitchener, 148n.; as Secretary of State for War, 178n., 191, 192, 193n.; accused of disloyalty, 189–90 and n., 194–5; meeting with Gwynne, 196–7, 198; becomes Prime Minister, 205–7; tries to close Morning Post, 207, 245n., 282–3, 323; Gwynne's opinion of, 211–12, 225–6, 252, 266, 269, 271–2, 274, 276–7, 279–80, 317; Liberal Party split, 224; dismisses Robertson, 247, 249, 265, 286–7, 321; Cabinet alterations, 267n.; Irish General Strike, 271, 273; General Maurice's letter, 275–6n., 278; Gwynne's memo on conduct of war, 283–5; wants Geddes in the War

345

trade unions, 128–30, 262, 264–5, 302
Trades Union Congress, 97, 121n.,
    128–30, 131–2n.
Treasury, 74, 78, 100
Trentino, 209
Trevelyan, C. P., 130–1n.
Trotsky, Leon, 223n.
Tullamore by-election, 60–1
Turkey, 16, 55, 82–5, 102, 124, 133,
    137n., 140, 216–17, 239, 310–11
Tyrrell, Sir William, 11, 214; Gwynne's
    letters to, 18–19, 20–1

Ulster, 277
Ulster Unionists, 60, 180, 181
Ulster Volunteers, 59
Union of Democratic Control, 128
Unionist Central Office, 10
Unionist War Committee, 98, 158n.,
    160n., 166n., 171
United States of America, 80, 142,
    173–4, 179, 199, 210, 228, 243, 258,
    268, 284, 285, 287, 291, 304, 312

Vatican, 290
Venizelos, E., 135, 137n., 209
Verdun, 98, 164, 167, 181
Versailles Conference, 207, 243, 244,
    254–7, 263, 275n., 285–8, 303, 307
Victoria, Queen, 187n.
Vimy, 215

Wales, 311–12
Wallingford, Mr, 39–40
War Cabinet, 97, 145n., 148n., 159n.,
    163n., 193, 200, 209 and n., 234, 235,
    254, 255–8, 267n., 271, 284, 286–7,
    300, 301
War Office, 11, 17, 29, 69, 74, 93, 105,
    109, 141, 144–5, 178n., 193, 196,
    253, 270, 271, 274, 305, 306
War Policy Committee, 122n.
Ware, Fabian, 2, 7
Warsaw, 110, 111, 113n., 132–3
Welsh Church, 75, 76n.
Westminster Gazette, 64, 190n., 328
Weygand, General, 258
Whitefield, Mr, 128
Whyte, F., 213n.
Wilde, Oscar, 293n.
Wilhelm II, Kaiser, 57, 238
Wilkinson, H. Spenser, 2, 53 and n.,
    322
Wilson, Havelock, 302
Wilson, General Sir Henry, 11, 65n.,
    107, 113n., 147–8n., 203n., 207, 218,
    224n., 245, 303, 326; Gwynne's
    letters to, 71–3, 76–80, 121–2,
    157–9, 163, 166–7, 169, 170, 177–8,
    183, 197–8, 300, 301; relations with
    Asquith, 73n.; and possible
    armistice, 205; at Paris Conference,
    243; Gwynne's criticisms of, 260–1;
    High Command crisis, 244, 247,
    254–7, 284, 286, 300; letter to
    Gwynne, 300–1
Wilson, Lady Sarah, 56 and n.
Wilson, Woodrow, 210 and n., 253n.,
    291, 312, 313, 315, 317
Wolff, Ulrich, 217
Women's Suffrage Movement, 5–6
Wyman's, 9

Young Turks, 137n.
Ypres, battle of, 70, 99, 140n., 200

Zimmern, A. E., 203n.